EVERY PARENT'S GUIDE TO THE LAW

D1531324

EVERY PARENT'S
══ GUIDE ══
TO THE LAW

Deborah L. Forman

A Harvest Original
Harcourt Brace & Company
San Diego   New York   London

Requests for permission to make copies of any part of the work should be mailed to:
Permissions Department,
Harcourt Brace & Company,
6277 Sea Harbor Drive,
Orlando, Florida 32887-6777.

This book is designed to educate you about the law so that you can deal more effectively with the legal situations that concern you. It is sold with the understanding that the publisher is not engaged in rendering legal services. Federal and state laws are constantly changing, and no single book can address all the legal situations you may encounter.

Library of Congress Cataloging-in-Publication Data
Forman, Deborah L.
    Every parent's guide to the law/Deborah L. Forman—1st ed.
      p.   cm.
    "Harvest original."
    Includes index.
    ISBN 0-15-100305-X.—ISBN 0-15-600523-9 (pbk.)
    1. Minors—United States—Popular works. 2. Children—Legal status, laws, etc.—United States—Popular works. 3. Parent and child (Law)—United States—Popular works. I. Title.
KF479.Z9F67 1998
346.7301'7—dc21   97-31994

Text set in Fairfield LH Light
Designed by Susan Shankin

Printed in the United States of America
First edition
E D C B A

For My Parents

CONTENTS

ACKNOWLEDGMENTS

M Y FIRST THANKS go to Allen Wilkinson, who had the idea for this book, recognized the great need for it, and gave me the opportunity to write it. My second thanks go to Diane Sterling, my editor, for her exceptional dedication to the project as well as her skillful editing. Numerous others assisted me along the way. The Whittier Law School provided much-appreciated institutional support, and several of my colleagues—particularly Professors Cindy Alberts Carson and Deborah Cohen-Whelan—took the time to discuss and critique various aspects of the book, as did Arnold W. Forman. I also had the benefit of research assistance from several students during the years while this work was in progress. I must single out three—Alaine Patti-Jelsvik, Christine Markel, and Michael Mosser—for their consistently excellent efforts. The secretarial staff at the Whittier Law School provided valuable clerical help. While I relied on hundreds of judicial opinions and statutes, as well as articles, books, and other materials by legal scholars, practicing lawyers, judges, journalists, advocacy groups, and professionals in psychology and medicine in researching the book, I would like to acknowledge two general sources that proved especially helpful: *The Legal Rights of Children* (2nd ed., Shepard's/McGraw-Hill, Inc., 1994), by Donald T. Kramer, and *Handling Child Custody, Abuse and Adoption Cases* (Shepard's/McGraw-Hill, Inc., 1993), by Ann M. Haralambie.

Finally, I want to thank my family for their lifelong support, my sister for her endless encouragement and her many questions, and my husband for enabling me to devote myself to this project full-time and for providing a most welcome distraction whenever one was needed.

INTRODUCTION

ANNA AND RYAN have one six-year-old son, Elliot, and are expecting their second child shortly. When Anna gave birth to Elliot, she wasn't working. Now she is a buyer for a large national department store. She would like to keep working as long as she can, then take a few months off to care for the new baby. What legal rights does she have as a pregnant woman and new mother in the workplace? Can her employer fire her once her pregnancy begins to show? Is she entitled to any maternity leave? When she returns to work, what child care options will be available to her? Ryan has additional concerns. He has two children by a prior marriage and is worried about how he will be able to continue to pay child support now that he and Anna are having another child. Can he get the amount reduced? Meanwhile, Elliot has been having difficulty in school. Anna and Ryan suspect he may have a learning disability. What kind of services is he entitled to by law?

Anna, Ryan, and Elliot are not real people, but the questions raised in their story are real ones faced every day and regularly resolved without much difficulty by parents across the nation who are well-informed. Millions of parents each year find themselves confronting legal issues concerning their children or their role as parents. Some of these parents come into contact with the legal system because of serious difficulties they encounter as families—charges of child abuse or neglect or juvenile delinquency. But the law's reach goes way beyond such troubled families. Today the law has something to say about virtually every aspect of child rearing, from the decision to start a family to the fate of children after parents die. The law also increasingly regulates parents' and children's interaction with other significant individuals and institutions, such as child care workers, schools, medical care providers, and employers. For the many parents who divorce, the law has an even more immediate impact, since decisions about child custody, visitation, and support are influenced or dictated by state laws and judicial orders.

The law can be a powerful tool to enhance your life and that of your child. It can also, on occasion, be a challenge that you need to overcome. To make the law work for and with you and your child, and to protect your family in situations where the law may be against you, you need to understand your legal rights and responsibilities. In our heavily regulated society, parents cannot afford to remain ignorant of the law.

For decades parents seeking information, advice, and guidance on child rearing have been able to turn to a panoply of popular works like Dr. Spock's classic *Baby and Child Care.* Conspicuously absent from the bookstore and library shelves, though, have been books comprehensively discussing legal issues of concern to parents. This book seeks to fill that gap.

WHAT YOU CAN EXPECT FROM THIS BOOK

Every Parent's Guide to the Law provides a comprehensive overview of legal issues parents may encounter. The first six chapters cover topics that will affect most parents in their daily lives. Chapter 1, "Starting a Family," focuses on legal issues related to pregnancy and parental rights in the workplace. Chapters 2 and 3, in addition to considering matters of child safety, discuss a wide range of issues related to two primary influences on your child's development: child care and education. Chapter 4, "Your Child's Health," addresses legal issues arising from your child's need for medical care. Chapter 5, "Your Teenager and the Law," talks about common issues affecting adolescents, who occupy a position between children and adults under the law. Chapter 6, "Money Matters and Planning for Your Child's Future," examines legal issues concerning your family's finances and, of particular importance, ways of protecting your children in the event of your death while they are still minors.

The next four chapters of the book cover special topics that will bring many parents directly into contact with the legal system. Chapter 7, "Child Custody and Visitation," details the myriad legal issues confronted specifically by parents who are divorcing or were never married, including the special problems faced by gay parents. Chapter 8, "Child Support," likewise focuses mainly on the rights and responsibilities of divorcing or never-married parents, but it also discusses the general duty of support and other issues, such as support of adult children, that apply to married couples as well. Chapters 9 and 10—"Youths in Trouble: Juvenile Crime and Other Transgressions and Parental Responsibility" and "Child Abuse, Neglect, and Exploitation"—concern parents and children who find themselves in trouble with the law, legally liable to others, or victimized by others.

The final two chapters focus on legal issues related to the changing composition of American families today. Chapter 11, "Fathers' Rights," explains the legal issues arising from the evolving role of men within the family as divorce and remarriage, cohabitation, and out-of-wedlock births have become more commonplace. Chapter 12, "Nontraditional Means of Becoming a Parent," addresses the unique legal issues faced by parents who do not have children in the traditional way, including adoptive parents, foster parents, and those who become parents with the assistance of new reproductive technologies like in vitro fertilization.

For each subject covered, you will learn the fundamental principles that govern resolution of the pertinent legal issues. This information can provide answers to many of your questions, help you to protect your rights and those of your children, assist you in deciding whether you have a legal problem that requires professional assistance, and, should that be the case, enhance your comfort level and ability to communicate with a lawyer about your problem.

In addition, you will have an opportunity to learn more about the most fascinating, cutting-edge cases and legal developments affecting parents and children right now. Today's parents are more knowledgeable and savvy about legal issues than parents in previous generations. Millions of people tuned in to the O.J. Simpson trial, *Court TV* has a devoted following, and the print and broadcast media frequently report on legal issues. Not a day goes by without a news story on some case or legislation of interest to parents. You'll find discussions of these highly publicized issues throughout the book.

To get the most out of this book, it is important to keep in mind three points:

1. *The laws of interest to parents and children in many instances vary significantly from state to state.* This means that on a given topic, any two states could have very different laws. For example, one state may require a minor to get parental consent for an abortion, while another may not. *Every Parent's Guide to the Law* covers a very wide range of topics from a *national* perspective. While you will find the laws in specific states mentioned throughout this book, they are intended to serve as examples, not to provide a comprehensive explanation of the law in any one state or in every state. Consequently, on many issues, you will find a number of approaches to a given problem adopted by courts and legislatures across the country.

To find out the law in your state on a particular subject, you will need to consult a lawyer or undertake legal research on your own. If you are interested in doing further research, your county law library or the library at a local law school may have resources and staff that will help you. In some cases, you may be able to find at a local bookstore or public library books that are designed to assist laypeople with specific legal matters, such as calculating child support or writing a will in your state. However, as the next two points explain, you should approach these references with caution as well.

2. *The law is constantly evolving.* Throughout the year, federal and state legislatures pass new laws, and judges decide new cases. Sometimes, the resulting changes are dramatic; often, they are relatively minor. Regardless, to solve a particular legal dispute, you need to have the most up-to-date word on that issue. While much of the law in this book will probably be valid for many years, there is no guarantee that the law pertaining to your particular problem will remain unchanged.

3. *The outcome in a given case is a result of the application of the law to the particular facts of the case.* This means that seemingly minor factual variations can lead to significant differences in outcome. Moreover, the resolution of a number of issues discussed in this book depends largely on judicial discretion. While *Every Parent's Guide to the Law* elucidates the factors that a judge will consider and how he or she might weigh them, ultimately the decision will rest on a particular judge's view of the facts of the case.

For all these reasons, it is best not to think of this book as a do-it-yourself legal manual or as a substitute for a lawyer. While some legal issues are relatively straightforward, or seem that way, many legal problems confronting parents today can be quite complex and are best handled with the assistance of a lawyer. Suggestions for finding a lawyer, should you need one, are included in an appendix at the back of this book.

IMPORTANT BACKGROUND INFORMATION ON THE LAW AND THE LEGAL SYSTEM

The Sources of American Law

Before embarking on your journey through the laws affecting parents and children, it is important to understand certain fundamental principles about the law and the legal system in the United States. As you may already know, our law derives from several sources.

The single most important legal document in the American legal system is the U.S. Constitution. The Constitution represents the supreme law of the land. Other laws, whether federal or state, that conflict with the Constitution are unconstitutional and can be overturned by a court of law if someone challenges them. The U.S. Constitution applies to individuals throughout the country, no matter where they live.

Federal laws, known as statutes, are enacted by Congress with the president's approval or at least his acquiescence. Federal laws apply to all the states and generally take precedence over state laws.

State laws include state constitutions and laws, also known as statutes, passed by state legislatures. In addition, some states have laws created by voter-passed initiatives or propositions. State law can also be created by judges through published judicial cases that establish precedent for other courts to follow. In many states, much of this judge-made law has now been codified. When judges interpret federal statutes, their interpretations likewise become precedent for applying those statutes.

Other sources of law include municipal ordinances—laws passed by local governments such as cities and counties—and regulations promulgated by federal and state agencies.

The Federal and State Court Systems

Just as we have separate bodies of law—federal and state—so, too, we have corresponding separate court systems. Although the two systems overlap, each has its own jurisdiction, or power. Federal courts have limited jurisdiction, which means they can hear only two kinds of cases: (1) those based on the U.S. Constitution or federal law and (2) those in which the parties to the case—known as the plaintiff (the person doing the suing) and the defendant (the person being sued)—are residents of different states. State courts, by contrast, can hear all kinds of cases—whether they involve constitutional, federal, or state law. As a practical matter, though, lawyers usually pursue federal matters in federal court.

Both the federal and state court systems have several levels of courts with different functions. The lowest courts are trial courts. In many states, these are called superior courts, but the name varies. For example, New York is one of the more confusing systems because its lowest courts are called supreme courts while its highest court is called

the Court of Appeals. States often have lower courts with specific jurisdiction over certain kinds of cases—for example, family courts or juvenile courts. Federal trial courts are called district courts.

Most states and the federal government have an intermediate-level
court that hears appeals of rulings made by trial judges in the lower
courts. States often call these appellate courts or courts of appeals. The
highest court in most states is the state supreme court. The state
supreme court typically has the right to choose which cases it will hear.
The highest court in the federal system and in the land is the U.S.
Supreme Court. The Supreme Court has the final say on interpretations of federal and constitutional law and can overturn state laws that
conflict with federal law or violate the Constitution.

Both the federal government and the states also have administrative
bodies that investigate, prosecute, and resolve certain kinds of disputes.
For example, the parent of a disabled student wrongfully denied special
education services can appeal to a state or local education agency. A
woman who has experienced discrimination at her job based on pregnancy can file a complaint with the Equal Employment Opportunity
Commission, which will investigate and pursue a remedy if warranted.

Within both the federal and state systems, there are different types
of actions that can be filed. The two main types are criminal and civil.
All states and the federal government recognize a distinction between
these two types. Whether a case is classified as criminal or civil can significantly affect your rights.

Criminal cases are brought by the state through a district attorney
for state criminal matters or by a U.S. attorney for federal crimes. A
criminal defendant who is found guilty (convicted) faces fines or imprisonment. Crimes are classified as either misdemeanors—relatively
minor offenses—or felonies, more serious offenses.

Civil cases, by contrast, typically involve disputes between private
parties, although government entities, such as school boards, can be
sued under certain circumstances. In civil cases, the plaintiff files a
document called a complaint, which begins the case. The complaint
sets forth the legal claim and usually seeks compensation in the form of

monetary damages, sometimes in conjunction with an order that the defendant change his or her course of conduct (an injunction). Many civil cases are settled or disposed of after pretrial motions made before the court. The remaining cases may be tried before a judge or jury. If the judge or jury finds against the defendant, he or she has been judged "liable" and must pay damages to the plaintiff.

Volumes could be—and have been—written about our legal system, but this brief overview should give you sufficient knowledge to understand the chapters to come. Being a parent in today's world can be a great challenge. The law sometimes makes that job easier, sometimes more difficult, but in either case, as always, knowledge is power. The information contained in *Every Parent's Guide to the Law* will give you that power and transform the law from a mysterious and perhaps intimidating unknown into a system you can understand and confidently navigate.

EVERY PARENT'S GUIDE TO THE LAW

STARTING A FAMILY

FOR MANY PEOPLE, the decision to have a child will be the most significant one they ever make. Having a baby changes your life in innumerable ways. Many of these changes are predictable; others are not. Most prospective parents spend considerable time and energy learning about the medical changes pregnancy and childbirth will bring and pondering the lifestyle changes wrought by parenthood— sleepless nights, increased expenses, and the joy of caring for a new life. Fewer parents contemplate the myriad ways their lives may be touched by the law once they begin the process of creating a family. To help you more fully prepare for the exciting and challenging experience of starting a family, this chapter will discuss those important legal questions that commonly arise for people becoming parents.

LEGAL ISSUES INVOLVING MEDICAL TREATMENT DURING PREGNANCY, DELIVERY, AND BIRTH

Prenatal Care

Obtaining good prenatal care is one of the most important means of ensuring the health of your baby. Failure to receive prenatal care can lead to a host of medical problems for a mother and child, including an increased likelihood of premature birth and low birth weight. Most women receive competent medical care before and during delivery and give birth to healthy children without significant complications. Others are not so fortunate. Some may experience difficulty through no fault of their doctors. Others fall victim to inadequate medical care.

The physician treating a pregnant woman generally owes a legal duty to both the mother and the fetus. This means that if the doctor acts carelessly in treating you during your pregnancy and causes injury to you or your fetus, the physician can be liable for damages. Malpractice in the treatment of a pregnant woman can include, among other things, failure to diagnose or properly treat toxemia (a condition causing swelling and dangerously high blood pressure, which in turn can cause seizures and death to both mother and fetus), failure to perform necessary tests near the time of delivery to determine fetal health and position, and the choice of an improper method of delivery.

The doctor's duty also includes obtaining the mother's informed consent prior to undertaking any procedures or treatments that pose a risk to her or the fetus. Does informed consent require the doctor to warn an expectant mother of every conceivable risk? No, but he must disclose the nature of the procedure or treatment and any significant risks. In addition, the physician should warn you of any adverse effects that could result from ingesting prescription or over-the-counter medications while you are pregnant since many drugs cross the placental wall and can cause harm to a fetus.

What can an expectant mother do if she is injured because of her doctor's negligence? She can sue the physician for medical malpractice. If a court or jury found that the doctor did not act as other doctors in good standing would have in treating her, they may award her damages for any out-of-pocket losses she may have suffered as well as for pain and suffering. If the mother dies as a result of the physician's malpractice, her immediate family can recover damages based on a "wrongful death" statute (a law that allows certain family members to sue when one of them is killed by someone's negligence or other misconduct).

SUITS BY VICTIMS OF DES

Between 1945 and 1971, physicians commonly prescribed the drug diethyl-stilbestrol (DES), a synthetic version of the female hormone estrogen, to pregnant women who were at risk of miscarrying. Sadly, the daughters of these women later developed numerous gynecological problems, including cancer and sterility, when they reached adulthood. These daughters have sued the drug companies who marketed the product and in some jurisdictions have won, even though the injuries occurred before the daughters were born. Suits are now being brought by DES *granddaughters,* but the courts that have considered these claims have rejected them, ruling that preconception injuries are not compensable.

What if the physician negligently causes injury to your fetus? In that case, you can bring an action on behalf of your child after birth to recover money for the damages he sustained while in utero, but different states impose different requirements for bringing this kind of suit. Some jurisdictions allow recovery for such prenatal harm only if the fetus was viable—that is, only if the fetus could sustain life outside the womb—at the time of the injury. Usually viability occurs somewhere around the twenty-sixth week of pregnancy. More states today, though, allow recovery of injuries sustained at any point during a pregnancy. Similarly, in the past, most jurisdictions did not allow the family to sue unless the child was born alive. Today most states allow parents to sue even if the child is stillborn.

A few jurisdictions have even allowed injured children to recover damages when the harm occurred before conception. In one case, a child alleged she was injured by a negligent blood transfusion that her mother received when the mother was only thirteen years old—many years before the child was conceived. The court allowed the suit to go forward, but other jurisdictions have refused to recognize so-called pre-conception lawsuits. Whether you or your child would have the right to sue for preconception harm depends, then, very much on whether you live in a state that recognizes this claim.

In some jurisdictions, when a child is negligently injured during birth, the mother may sue and recover for her emotional distress, shock, and trauma at witnessing the injury to the child. Sometimes the father may also bring suit if he was present during the delivery and aware of the injury-producing conduct. In most states, though, the father will not be able to recover, and the mother may recover only if she, too, suffers physical injury or the threat of physical injury because she is in the "zone of danger."

Genetic Testing, Wrongful Life, and Wrongful Birth

Scientists have made tremendous strides in recent years in detecting potential genetic and congenital abnormalities while a child is still in the womb and in identifying parents who carry traits for genetic illnesses that could be passed on to their children. The availability of these tests has raised perplexing and important legal and moral questions. Parents can now choose whether to carry to term a fetus that suffers from a birth defect identified during pregnancy.

One of the primary tools for diagnosing birth defects during pregnancy is amniocentesis. Amniocentesis is a procedure performed sometime around the fourth month of pregnancy. The physician inserts a long needle into the uterus and removes a small quantity of fluid from the amniotic sac, where the fetus resides during gestation. The fluid is then treated and subjected to a variety of biochemical analyses that can reveal such genetic and chromosomal abnormalities as Tay-Sachs disease, a debilitating and fatal disease that typically afflicts infants of eastern European Jews, and Down's syndrome, a chromosomal defect that leads to mental retardation and other health problems for a child. Amniocentesis is generally considered a low-risk procedure, but complications can arise.

Not all pregnant women are advised to undergo amniocentesis. However, if you are thirty-five or older when you become pregnant or if you have a family history of genetic or birth defects, your physician should advise you of the risks you face and of the availability of amniocentesis or any other test that may reveal potential or existing fetal problems. As we saw, the law requires that you give informed consent before undergoing medical procedures and tests. This means that your doctor should explain the risks and benefits of amniocentesis (or any other proposed prenatal test) to enable you to make a fully informed decision about whether to proceed with the test. *This decision is yours to make.* If you go ahead with the test and it reveals an abnormality, you may then choose to terminate the pregnancy or to carry the child to term knowing of the defect. No one can force you to have an abortion, nor can the state prevent you from having one unless the fetus is viable or unless the abortion would pose serious risks to your health. As a practical matter, it may be difficult to find a doctor willing to perform the abortion as the pregnancy advances. Some hospitals do not routinely perform abortions after twenty-four weeks, others after twenty weeks. Beyond these points, the hospitals may refer the question to a special committee to consider whether to allow the procedure when the fetus is abnormal or the mother's life is in danger.

What if your doctor neglects to inform you of the option of amniocentesis or other screening procedures when she should, and your child is born with a birth defect that could have been detected by the test? Let's consider a couple of hypothetical cases. Mary is a thirty-seven-year-old woman, pregnant for the first time. She gives birth to a child afflicted with Down's syndrome. Mary was never informed of the availability of tests that would have revealed her child's disease. In a somewhat different circumstance, we have Sarah. During her second month of pregnancy, Sarah comes down with rubella, also known as German measles, but her obstetrician carelessly fails to diagnose her condition. She gives birth to a child suffering from birth defects as a result of the rubella.

A number of states have considered cases such as these in recent years with mixed results. Some states have allowed the parents in these situations to sue for what is called "wrongful birth." The claim, in essence, is that had Mary been advised to undergo amniocentesis or had Sarah's rubella been properly diagnosed, each parent would have discovered the birth defect and terminated the pregnancy. Of course, the doctor in these cases does not actually cause the birth defect. He or she simply prevents the parents from discovering the defect and terminating the pregnancy. In states that recognize this type of lawsuit, the parents can usually recover any extraordinary medical and educational expenses they incur because of their child's birth defect. Some states will also allow the parents to recover for their emotional distress at having been denied, through lack of knowledge, the right to choose whether to have a child who suffers from such a condition. Other states have refused to recognize any lawsuit premised on the assumption that the parents would have aborted if they had been informed of a birth defect. The easiest way to ascertain if your state recognizes a wrongful birth cause of action is to consult a lawyer with experience in medical malpractice cases.

Lawsuits have also been brought on behalf of children. These suits are called "wrongful life." In our hypothetical cases, the children's claim is that had the physician acted appropriately in informing Mary of the available tests or in diagnosing Sarah's rubella, the children would never have been born and would thus not have had to suffer the pain and anguish caused by the defects. However, no court has recognized a child's right to be compensated for the very fact of having been born. The courts have refused to say that nonlife is preferable to life and have feared the difficulty of measuring the value of a life, even one that may be marked by extreme suffering and perhaps death in infancy, against the value of never having been born at all.

Let's consider another variation of the wrongful birth lawsuit that has been allowed by some courts. Our hypothetical couple, Callie and Andrew, have three children. Content with the size of their family and concerned about the financial burden of having more children, Andrew undergoes a vasectomy. Unfortunately, the doctor negligently performs the surgery, and Callie ends up giving birth to a healthy fourth child. What recourse does the couple have?

Parents like Callie and Andrew have sued physicians for wrongful birth of a healthy child after the physician negligently performed a sterilization procedure such as a vasectomy or tubal ligation (tying of a woman's Fallopian tubes). In these cases, also called "wrongful conception" cases, the parents sought to avoid pregnancy, but because of the doctor's carelessness, they conceived a child anyway. Some courts have allowed parents in this situation to recover damages related to the pregnancy, including medical expenses, lost wages, and pain and suffering. A few have gone considerably further and awarded damages for the cost of rearing the child until he or she reaches maturity, but other courts have refused to recognize the birth of a healthy child as an injury to the parents worthy of compensation.

Natural Childbirth and Midwives

Most women in the United States give birth in a hospital with anesthesia to ease the pain. In the last two decades, birthing methods such as natural childbirth (without the use of anesthesia) and the Lamaze method have gained in popularity. Some women have even chosen to give birth at home with the assistance of midwives. For some, the home provides a more relaxing and comfortable environment for giving birth, allows the mother and her family more control over the process, and costs less.

According to the doctrine of informed consent, a woman has the right to refuse medical treatment, including drugs, and there is no law requiring a woman to give birth in a hospital, although almost all women do. The difficulty of finding a midwife to assist in a home birth may effectively discourage women from choosing this option, but almost all states allow the use of licensed nurse-midwives to deliver babies. About half the states have laws licensing lay midwives and explicitly allowing them to assist in certain deliveries as well. But in the other states, lay midwives can be prosecuted for practicing medicine without a license.

Only women considered low risk during pregnancy should contemplate home birth. Even then, the qualifications and experience of the midwife should be carefully scrutinized and plans for emergency hospital treatment should be made since unexpected complications requiring medical attention can develop in any pregnancy and delivery.

Cesarean Sections

Almost one in four women will deliver her baby by cesarean section. This figure represents a dramatic increase in the number of babies delivered by this method in the last generation. While the medical condition of a mother or a fetus may justify a C-section delivery, many experts contend that too many unnecessary C-sections are performed. The reasons for this disturbing trend include doctors' fears of malpractice liability, financial incentives (C-section deliveries generate more fees for doctors and hospitals), the myth that having one child by cesarean requires you to deliver all children that way, and the increased use of electronic fetal heart monitoring, which sometimes inaccurately suggests that a fetus is in distress.

While most women advised to undergo a cesarean delivery will do so willingly, some women may refuse because of skepticism that the C-section is medically necessary, fear of surgery, religious objections, or other reasons. Can your doctor force you to have a C-section or any other medical procedure? If your doctor performs a surgical procedure such as a C-section without your informed consent, he has committed malpractice and a battery (an unlawful bodily contact) for which he can be liable. In other words, you can sue your doctor for the invasion of your person and recover damages. A Massachusetts woman won over a million dollars after her doctors performed an unnecessary C-section against her wishes, triggering a latent intestinal infection that led to serious postbirth complications.

Because of this potential liability, some doctors have sought a court order to permit them to perform C-sections or other procedures, such as blood transfusions, when the mothers have objected. In many of these cases, judges have granted the doctors' requests out of concern

LENGTH OF HOSPITAL STAY

In years past, new mothers often remained in the hospital for several days after delivery. More recently, as the medical profession has rediscovered that pregnancy is not an illness and as costs have risen, it has become commonplace for mothers to leave the hospital with their newborns within a day of giving birth, and insurance companies have refused to pay for a longer stay unless documented complications required it. Most women are discharged after a day with no untoward results. However, with increased pressure to keep costs down, some health care payers began urging mothers to leave the hospital within eight hours after the birth. Concerned about possible adverse effects on both mothers and their newborn infants, who may develop problems requiring rehospitalization in that first twenty-four hours, Congress passed federal legislation, effective January 1998, requiring insurance companies to pay for two days of hospitalization for mothers who deliver vaginally and four days for those who deliver by cesarean section, if their doctors deem it necessary. Several states have enacted similar laws.

for the welfare of the fetus. However, some of the cases have been appealed to higher courts with mixed results. A few earlier cases involved pregnant Jehovah's Witnesses who refused blood transfusions or other surgery for religious reasons. The higher court in each of these cases affirmed the trial judge's decision to compel the procedure against the woman's will. Two more recent cases involving forced C-sections have come out the other way. These courts have ruled that the doctor could not perform the surgery without the woman's informed consent.

Whether to compel a cesarean section or other procedure for the sake of a fetus against the will of the mother will most likely continue to be decided on a case-by-case basis. If you have religious or other objections to delivering by C-section, you should make your feelings and beliefs clearly known early in the pregnancy and find out whether your doctor supports your decision philosophically. Of course, there are no guarantees that he or she won't later decide that a C-section is medically necessary and seek a court order to perform it, but good communication between you and your doctor can help to avoid this kind of conflict.

A PREGNANT WOMAN'S DUTY TO HER FETUS

Substance Abuse

Most mothers do everything they can while pregnant to ensure the health and well-being of their child. Unfortunately, though, some women are unable or unwilling during pregnancy to behave in a way conducive to having a healthy baby. Hundreds of thousands of children born each year have been exposed to dangerous substances in the womb because of drug and alcohol abuse by their mothers. These children suffer a wide range of problems, including low birth weight; neurological impairment; learning and developmental disabilities; mental retardation; hyperactivity; difficulty forming emotional attachments; defects of major organs, such as the heart or kidneys; and an overall higher mortality rate. Not surprisingly, women who abuse drugs while pregnant also tend to neglect prenatal care, and if the habit continues after they give birth, the addiction often interferes with their ability to care adequately for the child.

The law has responded to this problem in a variety of ways. In a number of cases involving pregnant women's use of illicit drugs, usually cocaine, district attorneys have brought criminal charges against the mothers after they've given birth. These efforts have proved largely unsuccessful. With the exception of South Carolina, courts considering these cases on appeal have found either that the criminal laws protecting children do not apply to fetuses or that the prosecution violated certain constitutional rights of the mother. However, some counties persist in prosecuting these women, and some judges impose prison sentences instead of probation on substance-abusing pregnant women for unrelated crimes so that their fetuses can be born drug free.

Criminal prosecution is a highly controversial remedy for the problem of drug-exposed babies. Most medical professionals and others working with these women agree that prosecuting them does little to deter them from abusing drugs since they suffer from a powerful addiction. Instead, it merely discourages these women from getting the prenatal care that is critical to any child's health. It also seems unfair to prosecute when pregnant women have very restricted access to drug treatment programs. To make matters even more complicated, going through withdrawal during pregnancy can itself cause serious harm to a fetus.

Much more commonly, women who abuse drugs during pregnancy risk losing custody of their children after birth. Hospitals today often require drug testing for "walk-ins," pregnant women who come to the hospital to deliver their babies and who are not under the care of an obstetrician, since these women are considered high risk. Courts have upheld these policies to protect the children's welfare. Indeed, a few states require hospitals to report drug-exposed infants to child protective services.

In most places, evidence of prenatal substance abuse can give the state grounds for removing a child from a mother's custody immediately after birth. The child is then considered a dependent of the court and placed in foster care or perhaps with relatives until the mother can demonstrate that she has been rehabilitated, is free of drugs, and is fit to parent her child. If the mother cannot prove that she is fit within a certain period of time—usually twelve to eighteen months—she may have her parental rights permanently terminated, and the child may be placed for adoption. (See chapter 10 for further discussion of parental rights and child abuse.)

Although other conduct, such as smoking and drinking alcohol, can cause serious harm to the fetus, no cases have been brought against pregnant women for engaging in these behaviors, perhaps because neither activity is unlawful.

AIDS and Becoming a Parent

Thousands of infants a year are born infected with the human immuno-deficiency virus, or HIV. Given the current state of medical science, it is almost certain that these children will eventually develop AIDS. Babies born with HIV may contract the virus from their mothers during pregnancy or labor or after delivery, possibly through breast-feeding. Experts estimate that a pregnant woman who is HIV positive has a 20 to 30 percent chance of passing the disease on to her child, but encouraging recent evidence suggests that medication can significantly decrease the rate of transmission to as low as 8 percent. For these reasons, many have called for mandatory HIV testing of pregnant women, although no such proposal has yet been implemented. (See chapter 4 for a discussion of HIV testing of newborn babies.)

About half the states also have laws criminalizing transmission of HIV. Some of these statutes could be interpreted to include transmission from mother to child, but no prosecutions of HIV-positive women have occurred at this point, and they are unlikely to occur in the future. Any law that made it a crime for an HIV-positive woman to become a mother would very likely violate the constitutional right to procreate, which is discussed later in this chapter.

PREGNANCY, PARENTHOOD, AND THE WORKPLACE

Today the vast majority of parents—including women—work outside the home. Although progress has been made in ensuring equality for women in employment, by and large the workplace has not been designed to accommodate women's needs as child bearers and as the primary family caretakers. The law has responded by protecting women from discrimination based on pregnancy and providing for limited unpaid family leave for men and women. Unfortunately, some employers, either through ignorance or willfulness, refuse to comply with the law, so it is important for you to know your rights.

Your Right to Get and Keep a Job

Can you be fired for being pregnant? Generally no. Federal law prohibits employers from discriminating against pregnant women. An employer cannot refuse to hire you simply because you're pregnant. In fact, an employer does not have the right even to inquire about whether you are or might become pregnant.

The Pregnancy Discrimination Act, a federal law, protects women from being fired simply because they become pregnant. As long as you are able to work, your employer cannot fire you or force you to take a maternity leave. Moreover, your employer must, at a minimum, treat pregnancy like any other disability. For example, if your employer allows workers who cannot perform some of their job functions because of a medical disability to transfer to a different position, it must allow you the same opportunity. Likewise, if your employer provides for one month of unpaid disability leave if you have to undergo a gallbladder operation, it must provide the same type of leave for you if you become disabled and unable to work because of pregnancy. Pregnancy does not entitle you in most places to any additional leave. Moreover, many employers do not provide paid disability leave, so you would not be entitled to paid leave if you were disabled because of pregnancy.

The Family and Medical Leave Act (FMLA), which took effect in 1993, provides additional protection for some parents. This law requires businesses that employ fifty or more workers to provide up to twelve weeks a year of unpaid family medical leave for full-time employees who have been on the job for at least one year. You may take family medical leave because of the birth, adoption, or foster care of a child; because a parent, spouse, or child has a serious or chronic medical condition requiring care by you; or because you have a serious or chronic medical condition making it impossible for you to fulfill your job responsibilities. If you and your spouse work for the same employer, you cannot both take twelve weeks of leave for becoming a parent; you are limited to twelve weeks combined family leave. This limitation does not apply if you are taking leave because you are suffering from a serious

SINGLE MOTHERS IN THE WORKPLACE

Single mothers have the same right to maternity leave and the same protection against pregnancy discrimination as married women, but they are particularly vulnerable to pregnancy discrimination because of the lingering moral opprobrium that attaches to unwed motherhood. As the text explains, inquiring about the legitimacy of a prospective employee's children and firing, demoting, or forcing a leave of absence on an unwed pregnant woman have all been found to constitute illegal discrimination. However, one court did allow the forced resignation of a pregnant, unmarried program director of a YWCA on the ground that she intended to advocate unwed motherhood to the young people who were her charges. This was considered a legitimate business reason to terminate her.

medical condition and your spouse must take leave to care for you, or because of his own medical condition.

You must provide your employer with thirty days' notice if you can anticipate the need for the leave, as you sometimes can with childbirth or the adoption of a child. If the leave is based on an unexpected serious medical condition related to your pregnancy or childbirth, you should notify your employer as soon as possible. In addition, you will need to provide medical certification—a note from your doctor—explaining the reason for the leave, the date your medical condition began, and its expected duration. You also will need to keep your employer apprised of your status while you are on leave.

Your employer does not have to pay you while you are on leave. However, if your job entitles you to health insurance benefits, your employer must continue to provide those benefits to you during your leave. Your employer also has the right to insist that you take any accrued paid sick leave and vacation time as part of your family leave.

When you are ready to return to work, you have the right to return to your former position or to an equivalent position with the same pay, benefits, working conditions, duties, responsibilities, and skill level as your former position, unless your employer has eliminated your job for a legitimate reason unrelated to your leave. There is an important exception to the reinstatement requirement: If you are deemed a "key employee"—one earning a salary in the top 10 percent of your employer's workforce within a seventy-five-mile radius—you do not have to be restored to your prior position or a comparable one.

The FMLA provides a minimum standard throughout the nation. A few states have laws that allow additional leave for pregnancy, childbirth, and related needs as well as laws that cover smaller businesses. And of course your employer may voluntarily or through a negotiated contract with your union provide for paid or longer maternity or paternity leave.

If you suspect that your employer has discriminated against you based on your pregnancy or has denied you leave to which you are entitled, you can begin by contacting the local branch of the Equal Employment Opportunity Commission (EEOC). The EEOC's job is to investigate and, if warranted, to file complaints against employers who violate federal antidiscrimination laws. You should also contact your state labor or employment department, which should be able to assist you in understanding any specific rights or benefits you may have under your state's law. Of course, you may also want to consult a lawyer. For women who have experienced discrimination, some large metropolitan areas have law offices devoted to issues of concern to you. Although they often limit their cases to large class action–type lawsuits or represent only indigent clients, they may be able to answer basic questions or refer you to a lawyer who can take your case.

Fetal Protection in the Workplace

Some employers have policies prohibiting fertile or pregnant women from filling certain jobs, ostensibly as a way of protecting fetuses from dangerous toxins in the workplace that may cause birth defects. These policies unfairly exclude women from well-paying jobs. The Supreme Court has ruled that such policies constitute unlawful sex discrimination because they apply only to women, even though exposure of men to these toxins can impair their fertility and lead to birth defects as well. An employer cannot require you to undergo sterilization as a condition of employment or refuse to hire you or fire you based on concerns for the health of your unborn child.

What if you don't want to be exposed to toxins that may cause harm to your fetus? Can you insist on transfer to a safer position? Some states, like California, do require an employer to temporarily transfer a pregnant employee to a safer or less strenuous position if the employer can reasonably accommodate the transfer. In other states, the employer has no obligation to grant such a request. However, your employer must comply with Occupational Safety and Health Administration (OSHA) regulations concerning the amount and type of chemicals in the workplace. In addition, your employer may be required to inform you of any chemicals that could harm you or your fetus.

If you work in a position that exposes your fetus to dangerous chemicals or radiation and your child is born with birth defects as a result, can you sue? Courts are only beginning to grapple with this question. A worker who is injured on the job may obtain workers' compensation to cover medical expenses and lost wages but may not sue the employer for negligence. Women generally cannot make a workers' compensation claim for harm caused to a fetus. Because children who suffer prenatal harm are not covered under workers' compensation, logically they should be able to sue for negligence; however, at least one court has rejected this kind of lawsuit.

Help for the Poor and Unemployed

If you are unemployed during your pregnancy, you may be eligible for federal or state public assistance, commonly known as welfare. Some states also have special programs providing free or low-cost prenatal and medical care for the indigent. You should contact your local or state welfare department, which may be called the Department of Human Services or something similar, for further information. If you run into difficulty, you might seek help at a legal aid or legal services office; these offices are more common in large urban areas. Your county bar association may also be able to direct you to lawyers serving the poor.

If you lose your job during pregnancy, you may be eligible for unemployment benefits unless you are fired for good cause. However, if you choose to leave your job *because* you are pregnant, most states will not allow you to claim unemployment benefits. Similarly, you may not receive unemployment benefits while you are on disability or maternity leave.

Breast-Feeding

Pediatricians generally agree that breast-feeding, if possible, is preferable to using formula, in most circumstances. Breast milk provides an infant with all his nutritional needs in the first months of life, protects him against a variety of illnesses, decreases his chance of developing allergies, and, of course, saves money, since formula and related paraphernalia can add up. Breast-feeding also provides health benefits to mothers, including a lower risk of breast and ovarian cancer and postmenopausal bone loss, a decrease in fertility while nursing, and a quicker return to prepregnancy weight. In addition, breast-feeding may strengthen the mother-child bond. With all these benefits, one would think that most women who could breast-feed would, but that is not the case. In fact, breast-feeding declined during the 1980s. Today only 55 percent of American women even attempt to breast-feed. And while many women begin breast-feeding in the hospital, most have stopped by five or six months. The number of working women breast-feeding by that point is particularly small, only 12.5 percent.

No doubt part of the explanation for this trend lies with societal attitudes toward breast-feeding in public and the failure of employers or the government to accommodate the special needs of nursing women in the workplace. There have been reports that women who have attempted to nurse in public—at malls, restaurants, public swimming pools—have been harassed or asked to leave by security guards or the management of the establishments. With incidents such as these, many women are discouraged from breast-feeding. While it is not illegal per se to breast-feed in public, some women fear that they will be prosecuted under the laws prohibiting indecent exposure. In fact, there have been no reports of women actually being prosecuted for, let alone convicted of, indecent exposure because of breast-feeding in public, and most legal scholars believe breast-feeding would not meet the legal definition of indecent exposure. Nonetheless, to counter the perception of vulnerability and deter further harassment, a number of states have passed laws explicitly stating that breast-feeding in public will not be considered public nudity or obscene or indecent exposure. This protection applies regardless of whether the breast or nipple is exposed. While these laws should provide nursing women with security for breast-feeding in public, New York's law goes even further, giving them the right to sue if they are prevented from nursing in a public place. Other states have encouraged breast-feeding by exempting nursing women from jury service.

None of these laws, though, is likely to protect nursing mothers in the private workplace. Nursing mothers may need to take breaks to breast-feed if their child is nearby or, more likely, to pump breast milk. While a very few enlightened large companies have established infant nursing areas where female employees can breast-feed or express breast milk on their breaks, many employers refuse to allow women to breast-feed on the premises or to take time out to pump.

Unfortunately, the law does not give nursing mothers much ammunition to challenge these policies (see box on page 19). While legal scholars have argued that existing laws against discrimination in the workplace can protect some breast-feeding women, these views have thus far found little favor with the courts. In the absence of legislation accommodating their needs, nursing mothers can search out employers with baby-friendly policies, seek protection from their unions, or attempt to negotiate suitable arrangements themselves.

THE RIGHT TO BREAST-FEED ON THE JOB: AN UPHILL BATTLE

In 1981 a federal court identified breast-feeding as a constitutional right in a case brought by a teacher who was forbidden to nurse her three-month-old infant on school premises during her lunch break. But the court went on to rule that the school district was justified in forbidding the nursing based on a policy that prohibited teachers from bringing their own children to school with them. In the court's view, the policy served the important state interest of ensuring a teacher's undivided attention to her students, and this interest outweighed the mother's interest in breast-feeding. Unable to breast-feed at work, the teacher was forced to take an unpaid leave because her baby was allergic to formula and wouldn't take a bottle.

Another civil rights suit, this time brought by a female firefighter in Iowa who sought to nurse at her firehouse, fared better. She obtained an injunction that allowed her to continue breast-feeding while her case was pending, and she won monetary damages. However, her victory was a hollow one; she suffered harassment from coworkers that led her to resign.

HOUSING DISCRIMINATION

As we have seen, becoming a parent can raise significant legal concerns regarding your employment and, if you are a woman, can sometimes subject you to illegal discrimination. Becoming a parent can lead to discrimination in another arena as well: housing. Because some landlords, for a variety of reasons, do not like to rent to families with children, you may face an unlawful eviction attempt or have difficulty finding an apartment.

Fortunately, both federal and state laws generally prohibit landlords from discriminating against families with children. If a landlord refuses to rent an apartment to you or threatens to evict you because you have

---

HOW DO YOU KNOW IF A LANDLORD HAS DISCRIMINATED
AGAINST YOU BASED ON FAMILY STATUS?

The easiest cases involve landlords who advertise for "adults only." Today most landlords know better than to discriminate blatantly in this fashion. However, they may still discriminate in more subtle ways. For example, if a landlord limits occupancy of a one-bedroom apartment to one person, a court may find that to be illegal discrimination based on family status. Rental advertisements that use phrases such as "adult living," "adult community," "adults only," "mature couple or individual," "one child," "no play area," or "singles only" may indicate illegal discrimination and may subject the newspaper that runs the ads as well as the landlord to liability.

---

a child, you may be able to force him or her to rent to you, you may win damages, or you may defend against an eviction based on illegal discrimination. You can bring the action yourself, or a state agency, such as a department of fair housing, can file suit for you.

The law does allow retirement communities and other residential developments for senior citizens to exclude children. In addition, by-laws excluding children from condominium complexes have been upheld by some courts, although the California Supreme Court refused to enforce them, finding that home owners' associations qualify as business establishments and are therefore bound to follow the state's anti-discrimination statute.

FAMILY PLANNING AND STATE INTERFERENCE
IN THE DECISION TO BECOME A PARENT

While this chapter has been devoted to legal issues of concern to those who have or are planning to have children, many parents at some point decide their family is complete and choose to take active means, such as contraception, to limit family size. Others find themselves facing the other side of the coin: government efforts to prevent them from having children. This section explains your legal rights to decide when, and if, you will have children.

Your Constitutional Right to Have—or *Not* to Have—Children

Because the decision to have a child is so important and so intensely personal, the right to bear and raise a child—or to choose not to—receives special protection under the U.S. Constitution. In a series of decisions, the Supreme Court has determined that individuals—whether married or single—have a fundamental right of privacy in decisions relating to procreation and child rearing. When a fundamental right is at stake, the state can prevent the exercise of that right only if it has compelling reasons for doing so and only if the law is very narrowly drawn so that it interferes with the right as little as possible.

Contraception and Abortion

In the last thirty years, this standard has led to the invalidation of a number of state laws that in some way burdened an individual's right *not* to procreate. In two 1960s cases, the Supreme Court struck down as unconstitutional laws that made distribution of contraceptives a crime. In a much more controversial ruling, the Court held in the famous case of *Roe v. Wade* that the constitutional right of privacy encompasses a woman's decision to terminate a pregnancy, although that decision can be subject to state interference to protect the woman's health during the second trimester of pregnancy and can even be prohibited altogether during the third trimester to protect the potential life of the fetus.

Roe v. Wade has come under repeated attack but has not been overturned. Abortion is still legal in all fifty states. However, in a 1992 abortion case, *Planned Parenthood v. Casey,* the Supreme Court allowed the states more latitude in restricting abortion. Under this decision, a state may impose restrictions as long as they do not place an "undue burden" on a woman's choice to terminate her pregnancy. No one really knows exactly what "undue burden" means. But we do know that states can impose, and some now have imposed, twenty-four-hour waiting periods on women seeking abortions, and they can also require distribution of certain literature regarding fetal development to women considering abortion. However, a state may not require a woman to notify her husband.

The contraception and abortion cases deal with laws that interfere with an individual's fundamental right *not* to procreate. As you might expect, there are not many situations where the law prohibits an individual from having a child, but there are some.

Sterilization

The state cannot prohibit you from choosing to undergo an accepted sterilization procedure, such as a tubal ligation or vasectomy, as a means of contraception. In fact, as we saw earlier in this chapter, if a doctor negligently performs a sterilization and that negligence results in the birth of a child, some courts will allow the parents to recover damages, including the cost of rearing the child.

The more controversial question today involves compelled or coerced sterilization. A person generally cannot be sterilized without his or her consent. In the 1920s many states passed laws allowing for eugenic sterilization (sterilization of those considered mentally or socially inferior), and these laws were upheld in the courts. But in 1942 the Supreme Court invalidated a law that required certain criminals to submit to sterilization procedures. Nonetheless, several states still have laws that allow convicted rapists to be castrated instead of serving time in prison, and judges have offered the option in a few cases. To date, no surgical castrations have been carried out for various reasons—the sentences were overturned on appeal, the defendant changed his mind, or no physician would agree to perform the operation. This is likely to change in California unless a recently enacted law is overturned by the courts. The new California law requires repeat or especially egregious sexual offenders to receive injections of a drug that inhibits sex drive unless they voluntarily undergo surgical castration. A recently adopted

Montana law likewise allows judges to order chemical castration for certain sex offenders, and other states are considering similar legislation.

Female criminals have also been considered for sterilization. A Tennessee judge offered a woman convicted of child abuse a prison sentence of ten years or probation if she consented to sterilization. She initially accepted the probation offer but subsequently declined to undergo the procedure.

Although many states still have laws on the books allowing for eugenic sterilization, these are rarely enforced. However, in many states, individuals who are severely mentally retarded may be involuntarily sterilized if a judge determines that (1) they are unable to consent to the procedure; (2) they are sexually active and are incapable of using other means of contraception or taking care of their children; and (3) it is in their best interests.

With advances in contraceptive technology, courts and legislatures are facing new questions about whether they can restrict an individual's right to procreate by requiring use of devices such as Norplant. A contraceptive similar to the birth control pill but much longer lasting, Norplant consists of five thin tubes surgically inserted beneath the skin that secrete hormones preventing pregnancy for as long as five years. One California judge ordered a convicted child abuser to use Norplant as a condition of probation, but, like the castration option for rapists, the sentence was not carried out. There has also been much talk of requiring Norplant as a condition for receiving welfare benefits, but this requirement has not been adopted.

CHILD CARE AND SAFETY

F INDING GOOD, SAFE, and affordable child care is one of the most pressing concerns for parents today. Gone are the days when the mother stayed home to look after the children while the father went off to work. In most married households today, both parents work outside the home for economic as well as personal reasons. For the many single parents rearing children, staying home is rarely an option. Moreover, even in families where one parent does stay home full-time, there will undoubtedly be times when you need to hire a baby-sitter or arrange other child care. The first part of this chapter explores the many legal issues surrounding child care, such as tax and immigration law requirements, licensing and regulation of day care, and ensuring your child's safety when someone other than you or your spouse is the caregiver. The second part, focusing on child safety, explains the law regulating consumer products for children and your legal rights should your child be injured by a defective product.

CHILD CARE: A SURVEY OF THE OPTIONS

The National Association of Child Care Resource and Referral Agencies (NACCRRA) has identified three basic types of child care presently available in this country: 1. in-home care, in which a nanny, baby-sitter, or au pair comes to your home on a regular basis or perhaps actually lives with you; 2. family day care, in which you take your child to the home of a caregiver, who may have children of her own or care for a small group of children; and 3. center care, in which your child goes to an institutional center run by a religious or community organization or a private business. The best type of care for you and your family will depend on many factors, including the age of your child and any special needs he or she may have, your work hours and level of flexibility, your location, and, of course, the cost. There are also important legal issues you should understand before deciding on a particular type of child care or a particular child care provider.

In-Home Care

If you are contemplating in-home care, you will need to understand several issues. Let's begin with your legal responsibilities if a baby-sitter is injured while caring for your child. Suppose Sandra and Max have hired Karina to live with them and care for their two-year-old daughter, Olivia. While bending down to pick up Olivia, Karina injures her back. She has no health insurance and the medical bills for treatment amount to several hundred dollars. Are Sandra and Max responsible for those costs? Probably not. Most workers who are injured on the job are covered by workers' compensation: they can recover limited benefits, such as lost wages and medical expenses, from their employer, regardless of whether the employer was at fault. However, domestic employees, like baby-sitters and nannies, are usually exempt from workers' compensation laws. As a result, not only do you have no obligation to pay for workers' compensation insurance for them, but they can sue you to recover monetary damages for an injury only if your negligence or carelessness causes the injury. However, if you are sued, you are potentially liable for a greater amount of money than in a workers' compensation claim. In our hypothetical case, Karina injured herself through no fault of Sandra or Max, so she cannot recover from them based on negligence.

What if Karina injures her back when she falls down the stairs leading to a basement playroom? Suppose the light in the stairway went out weeks before, and Sandra and Max, though aware of the problem, did not replace the bulb. Under these circumstances, the couple may very well be liable for Karina's medical expenses and any lost wages, as well as for pain and suffering, if they are found negligent for not replacing the bulb. You have a legal duty to use reasonable care to make the premises safe for a baby-sitter who comes on your property, and cases have arisen of baby-sitters slipping on icy walkways or unlit stairways. Home owners' insurance policies usually cover liability for people injured on the premises, but you should check the wording of your policy for exclusions of employees or ask your insurance agent if you are covered in this situation.

In addition to potential liability for injuries sustained by your caregiver, you may be obligated to pay taxes on her behalf. The so-called nanny tax first received widespread public attention in 1993 after President Clinton nominated Zoë Baird for the position of attorney general. During her confirmation hearings before the Senate, it was revealed that Baird had neglected to pay taxes for her children's nanny, and she was forced to withdraw herself from consideration for the post.

Many people are unaware that federal tax laws require them to pay social security and Medicare taxes on behalf of domestic employees, including child care workers, if certain conditions are met. As of 1996, these requirements apply if you pay one thousand dollars a year or more to a household employee, unless he or she is under the age of eighteen and works for you part-time or goes to school full-time. If you have paid that much in any calendar quarter to a nanny who does not work for an employment agency, you may also have to pay federal and possibly state unemployment insurance premiums. Your local unemployment office should be able to provide you with more specific information. While the Internal Revenue Service (IRS) does not require you to withhold income taxes from your caregiver's pay, your state or city may require you to do so. Whether you withhold taxes or not, you will have to provide your caregiver with a W-2 form annually by January 31 so that she can

---

FOR MORE INFORMATION ON TAX ISSUES

IRS Publication 926, "Household Employer's Tax Guide," covers the federal tax issues relating to domestic workers, including baby-sitters and nannies, and Publication 503, "Child and Dependent Care Expenses," explains whether or not you can claim a credit on your income tax return for the money you spend on child care. To obtain these or any other IRS publications or forms, including the form you need to obtain a federal employer identification number, contact the IRS Forms Distribution Center at the following number:

1-800-829-3676

For answers to any questions you may have about your federal tax obligations, contact the IRS at this number:

1-800-829-1040

---

file her tax return for the previous year. To facilitate this, you must get an employer identification number from the IRS (see box above).

Although it may be tempting, you should not pay your caregiver off the books. Doing so is illegal as well as shortsighted. The caregiver might later file for social security, and you could end up paying back taxes as well as interest and penalties that have accumulated over the years.

Since the tax rules and requirements are quite complex and subject to change, you should contact the IRS, your state employment agency (the IRS provides a list of such agencies in its publication on federal employment taxes for household employers), an accountant, or a lawyer to assist you in complying with the law. You can also obtain forms and information directly from the IRS by calling the phone numbers listed above.

Another important issue to consider when hiring an in-home caregiver is his or her immigration status. You are prohibited from hiring undocumented aliens and doing so can subject you to substantial fines or even imprisonment in cases involving fraud. Federal law requires you to verify that your employee is legally able to work here because she is a citizen or has a green card. You must do more than simply inquire; you must complete a Form I-9 provided by the Immigration and Naturalization Service (INS), and your employee must provide some documentation of her identity and eligibility to work, such as a U.S. passport, green card, social security card, or driver's license. To obtain a specific list of acceptable verification documents and other details, as well as the requisite paperwork, you should contact your local INS office.

Additional immigration rules apply if you host a young person from a foreign country, known as an au pair, to care for your child. These individuals, usually women, agree to act as nannies for up to one year for the opportunity to come to America and earn money. In the past, parents could arrange independently to bring an au pair into the country, but today immigration restrictions make that extremely difficult, so you will need to work through a government-authorized program. Generally au pairs range in age from eighteen to twenty-six, have finished high school, and have some experience caring for children. They can work for you up to forty-five hours per week for as long as one year, and you are expected to provide them with opportunities for educational and cultural enrichment. Since they are not permanent residents, you do not need to pay social security taxes on their behalf.

There is one other legal matter you may want to pursue if you hire an in-home caregiver. Some child care experts recommend drafting a contract between you and the nanny. The contract need not be a complex document, but it should describe the caregiver's job responsibilities and specify her wages, hours, and any benefits that you have agreed to provide. The National Association of Child Care Resource and Referral Agencies (see box on page 30), or a local office near you, can provide you with sample contracts.

Family Day Care and Center Care

If you choose to place your child in family day care or center care, you will face a different set of issues. You will not bear any special legal

FOR MORE INFORMATION ON CHILD CARE PROVIDERS

If you would like more information about or assistance in obtaining child care, particularly family day care or center care, contact one of the following organizations. The first two can direct you to referral agencies in your area. The third, which has its own accreditation process, can let you know whether caregivers have specific qualifications and whether their homes or centers meet certain standards.

Child Care Aware
2116 Campus Drive SE
Rochester, MN 55904
1-800-424-2246

National Association of Child Care Resource and Referral Agencies (NACCRRA)
1319 F. Street NW, Suite 810
Washington, DC 20004
202-393-5501

National Association for the Education of Young Children
1409 16th Street NW
Washington, DC 20036
202-232-8777 or 1-800-424-2460

responsibilities yourself, but you will want to be aware of the laws governing the caregivers. Every state regulates family day care and center care, but there are vast differences in the extent of the regulations from one state to another. At one extreme is Massachusetts, a state praised for its child care policies. There the regulations apply whether a caregiver provides family day care for as few as two children or center care for many children. Massachusetts imposes high standards on its caregivers: those who provide family day care must take five hours of training every year, and those who work at centers must complete a vocational training program first and then twenty hours annually of continuing education. Massachusetts also mandates one of the lowest ratios of children to caregiver in the nation: the maximum is three infants, four toddlers, or ten preschoolers per adult. In addition, Massachusetts requires immunizations of all children prior to enrollment, and it conducts both scheduled and unscheduled inspections of centers every two years and family day care providers every three years. At the other extreme is Louisiana, which does not even regulate family day care providers unless they serve seven or more children and which requires no formal training of any caregivers, whether they work in their homes or at centers. Not surprisingly, the ratio of children to caregiver is higher in Louisiana than it is in Massachusetts—as many as six infants, twelve toddlers, or fourteen preschoolers per adult—and while centers there are inspected yearly, family day care providers are inspected only when someone lodges a complaint.

Obviously, with such great differences among states, you will want to find out the specific requirements governing group care providers where you live. The magazine *Working Mother* compiles an annual survey of child care in the fifty states that covers these issues and more. Other parenting magazines regularly run articles on finding child care, and there are a number of books available to help you assess the kind of care you need. For further information, contact one of the organizations listed in the box on page 30.

THE CHILD AND DEPENDENT CARE TAX CREDIT

No matter which type of care you choose for your child, the cost will probably take a significant bite out of your budget. Luckily, the IRS may be able to help. The Internal Revenue Code allows you to take a tax credit up to a certain percentage of your child care expenses, depending on your income, if you pay someone to care for a child under thirteen so that you can work or look for work. You cannot take the credit for money paid to someone you claim as a dependent—for example, an older child who looks after a younger sibling. To take advantage of this credit, you must identify the child care provider on your tax return. If you are a divorced or separated parent with custody of your child but you cannot claim the dependency exemption because you agreed to let your ex-spouse claim it (as explained in chapter 8), you may still be able to take advantage of the child care credit under certain circumstances. IRS Publication 503, "Child and Dependent Care Expenses," explains how the credit works, how to figure out whether it applies to you, and how to calculate it if it does. To obtain this publication, you can call the IRS at the number provided in the box on page 28. You may also want to consult an attorney or accountant for further assistance in claiming the credit.

Another tool for reducing the cost of child care is the "flexible spending account" offered by some employers, which allows you to set aside pretax dollars up to a certain limit to pay for the care. Your human resources or personnel director should be able to advise you whether your employer offers such a plan and, if so, what its terms are.

ENSURING YOUR CHILD'S SAFETY

Once you decide on the type of care you would like for your child, your paramount concern in choosing a particular caregiver will no doubt be the well-being, particularly the personal safety, of your child. A series of high-profile cases involving allegations of widespread molestation at day care centers in the 1980s aroused fear and apprehension in parents who must rely on nonfamily members to care for their children for some part of the day. Although talk shows with nightmarish tales of abusive baby-sitters continue to generate concern, the reality is that many, many more children are abused and molested by family members than by child care workers or strangers. Most caregivers are conscientious individuals who do their jobs responsibly. Nonetheless, it is still critically important that you choose your child's caregiver carefully.

If you plan to hire an in-home caregiver, you should thoroughly check any and all references you can obtain. Ask probing questions of the references. If you are hiring someone from an agency, inquire about the screening procedures the agency uses. While many agencies check references and some states require them to obtain criminal record checks on their applicants, not all do. In states that have no such requirement, each agency devises its own policy. Don't assume that every agency screens its applicants, and don't assume that those that do are as thorough as you would like. It's a good idea to obtain a written file from the agency on any applicant you're considering. The file should provide you with the applicant's driving record, the results of a criminal record check, and any references. You might also call the Better Business Bureau in your area to learn of any complaints made against the agency. Finally, if your financial resources permit, you may want to hire a private investigator or security firm to do a background check to confirm the applicant's education, employment history, and criminal, motor vehicle, and credit record. In some states, you may be able to obtain a background check on a potential in-home caregiver by yourself as well. For example, in Colorado, parents can use a new computer system at their local library to do an instant background check on a prospective caregiver.

If you are pursuing a family or center care placement, you should also ask for references and check them. Inquire how staff members, including noncaregivers like maintenance workers and bus drivers, are hired, and find out what screening process the center uses. Some states require criminal background checks for licensed family and center caregivers. Until recently, though, states ran checks on criminal records only within their own jurisdiction. Now, some states run background checks for records of abuse or neglect in other states, too. Inquire about relatives of the caregivers as well. A national study of day care abuse indicated that 36 percent of the cases involved molestation by relatives of the provider.

Another important way of protecting your child is by regular monitoring of his or her experience and the caregiver's conduct. You should plan to spend some time at the home or center during your child's

SIGNS OF PHYSICAL AND SEXUAL ABUSE

How can you tell if your child has experienced physical or sexual abuse? Since children are not always capable of communicating directly with their parents about abuse, there are few clear answers to this question. However, experts have identified the following as possible signs:

- unexplained or poorly explained bruises, cuts, or other injuries
- pain, irritation, or bleeding in the rectal or genital area
- reenactment during play of odd or inappropriate treatment
- expressions of fear about going to child care or a particular caregiver
- behavior that involves acting out in sexually inappropriate ways or demonstrates unusual interest in sexual matters
- new and unusual manifestations of nervousness, anxiety, or depression—extreme mood swings, withdrawal, excessive crying—or physical symptoms such as stomachaches
- sudden clinginess or fear of separation from you

first few days there, both for her to get acclimated and for you to feel comfortable with the style and conduct of the caregivers. Pay particular attention to methods of discipline. Do not leave your child anyplace where the caregivers use corporal punishment. While you might feel it is appropriate for you to spank your child, it is not a good idea to expose him to physical punishment from others. Find out how naps are supervised, since children are particularly vulnerable then, and how and by whom children are taken to the bathroom, since the National Association of Missing and Exploited Children reports that most day care sexual abuse occurs there. You should also drop by unannounced on occasion to get a realistic picture of a typical day for your child and to assess her interaction with the caregivers. *If the home or center will not allow you unscheduled and unrestricted access to your child, choose an-*

♦ expressions of anxiety about going to the bathroom, removing clothes, or bathing

♦ sudden fear of going to bed or sudden onset of nightmares or bed-wetting

If you observe any of these signs in your child, you should take them seriously and investigate. However, you should not panic or jump to conclusions. These signs are not infallible indicators of physical or sexual abuse; in fact, any one or more of them could result from a whole host of causes that have nothing to do with abuse. Certainly you would not want to ruin the reputation of an innocent caregiver. On the other hand, neither would you want to put your child and others at risk by ignoring potential symptoms of abuse. For this reason, it is very important that you watch for the signs listed above, that you listen carefully to anything your child may say about inappropriate behavior by a caregiver, and, if necessary, that you seek professional assistance (see box on page 294) to determine whether your child has suffered abuse.

other placement. Finally, if your child is old enough, talking with him about his experiences and feelings about his caregivers will provide you with invaluable information.

Even with the best efforts to protect your child, the worst occasionally happens. If you suspect that your child has suffered abuse (see the box on page 34 and above for some potential signs), you should immediately take her out of the situation, carefully investigate the possibility, and seek appropriate medical attention, including examination by a pediatrician and evaluation and counseling by a mental health professional with experience in identifying and treating child abuse (see also box on page 295). If you conclude that your child has suffered abuse or molestation by a caregiver, you should report your concerns to the local child protection and law enforcement agencies as well as to the state licensing bureau. At some point, you may also decide to file a civil suit on your child's behalf for monetary damages, and the district attorney may file criminal charges against the abuser. These subjects are covered in depth in chapter 10.

What if your child is injured accidentally at day care? Consider the following scenario: Wesley is an active four-year-old who attends a local day care center. During playtime one afternoon, he falls off the center's monkey bars, breaking his arm. What legal rights do Wesley's parents have? They may be able to sue the center for negligence. Persons or businesses who invite children onto their premises for a fee have a legal obligation (called a "duty") to keep the premises reasonably safe. This generally requires the caregiver to regularly inspect the premises for potential hazards to children and to supervise the children adequately while they are in the caregiver's charge or on the center's premises. If Wesley was attempting to navigate the monkey bars without any adult nearby or if one of the bars collapsed because the equipment was old and worn out, the center might be found negligent and have to pay damages for Wesley's injury. Of course, accidents do happen. Wesley would be entitled to damages only if the caregiver was at fault in failing to keep the premises sufficiently safe or in carelessly supervising him. Child care centers should be insured for such accidents, and so should family day care providers. Particularly with family care, it is a good idea to inquire about insurance. A successful suit for damages will mean little if the caregiver has no money or assets to pay.

CHILD SAFETY—DANGEROUS PRODUCTS

The road from infancy to adulthood is fraught with peril. Any parent who has seen a two-year-old climb a kitchen chair and attempt to dive-bomb off it knows that growing up can be a dangerous proposition. As a parent, you have a legal responsibility to reasonably supervise and protect your child, a subject discussed at length in chapter 10. In this

THE CASE OF THE HUNGRY DOLL

A product safety case that made headlines in 1997 involved Mattel's Cabbage Patch Kids Snacktime Kids, dolls that featured battery-powered chewing action. Unfortunately, the dolls were prone to overzealous and indiscriminate chewing, and a number of children had their fingers or hair chewed by them. The CPSC and Mattel reached a voluntary agreement that withdrew the dolls from the market and offered forty-dollar refunds to consumers who returned them to Mattel. The agreement does not preclude those injured by the dolls from suing, and one family filed a suit seeking $25.5 million in damages for the psychological harm caused when a doll chewed their nine-year-old daughter's hair to her scalp.

section, we will consider the legal obligations of others, specifically those who produce and sell products for children.

According to the 1996 annual report of the Consumer Products Safety Commission (CPSC), that year 138,097 hospital emergency room visits were associated with the use of toys, and almost half of those involved injured children under five. If we look at all other types of products—nursery equipment, sports and recreational equipment, housewares, to name a few—we see more than a million and a half injuries to children under five requiring treatment in emergency rooms in 1996 alone. What rights do you have if your child is injured by a toy or other dangerous product?

There are two primary and sometimes overlapping avenues for dealing with dangerous products: government regulation and private lawsuits seeking monetary damages. Congress has enacted various laws over the years targeting specific products dangerous for children. For example, the 1953 federal Flammable Fabrics Act led to standards generally requiring that children's sleepwear be flame-retardant, a 1980 regulation banned small parts for products intended for children under three, and the 1994 Child Safety Protection Act requires that toys contain labels warning of choking hazards and indicating the ages for which a toy is appropriate. Unfortunately, these laws are effective only if they are enforced, and unsafe toys continue to be found on store shelves.

The Consumer Products Safety Commission

Established in 1972 by Congress, the CPSC is the federal agency charged with overseeing the safety of thousands of consumer products, and it has been particularly active in investigating and regulating products that pose hazards for children. Since the CPSC has a small budget, it does little product testing itself. Instead, it relies on reports of injuries by consumers to prompt investigation. The CPSC then researches the injuries and sets standards for product safety. Some of these standards are mandatory; others voluntary. Failure to comply with mandatory standards can result in civil fines and criminal penalties, and the CPSC has the power to recall dangerous products. In most cases, the CPSC reaches an agreement with the manufacturer to recall a product or adhere to voluntary safety standards (see box on page 37).

Products Liability—Suing for Damages

While the CPSC plays an important role in product safety, most individuals who are injured by dangerous products will seek redress through lawsuits against the manufacturers of the products. Suppose, for example, that eight-year-old Natalie is playing with a chemistry set that her parents bought for her. The set is labeled "For Children 8 and Up" and contains the following warning: "Use with Parental Supervision." One evening, while her parents are doing the dishes, Natalie decides to perform an experiment in her room. Although she tries to follow the directions, she accidentally mixes two chemicals that she shouldn't mix and an explosion ensues, causing serious burns to her arms. Natalie's parents rush her to the emergency room. Although she is released from the hospital a few days later, she is left with significant

A PERSISTENT PROBLEM: THE DANGERS OF LEAD PAINT

Lead paint is a known carcinogen and can cause severe neurological impairment, including mental retardation, as well as organ damage in children who are exposed to hazardous levels. Although Congress recognized the tremendous harm caused by lead poisoning and banned the use of lead paint in 1977, some four million children are still at risk from housing built before then. Although federal legislation requires the Department of Housing and Urban Development to eliminate lead in public housing, the law does not apply to privately built homes. Fortunately, many states now have laws requiring landlords to eradicate lead paint if they are notified by a tenant of the problem. These laws allow victims of lead poisoning to sue their landlord if the landlord knew of the problem and failed to correct it. A few states mandate removal of the lead paint even if the landlord has not received notice of the problem. These laws provide an important remedy for victims of lead poisoning since it is usually difficult to identify, let alone sue, the manufacturer who produced the paint that injured a particular child.

scarring and will need surgery in the future to correct it. Natalie's parents are thinking of suing for compensation for these costs and for Natalie's pain and suffering and disfigurement. Can they do so?

Product liability cases can be very complex, so Natalie's parents will no doubt want to consult a reputable personal injury lawyer. In preparation for a potential lawsuit, they should take pictures of the product in the aftermath of the explosion as well as of Natalie's burns. They should also keep what's left of the set and all packaging and instruction manuals provided with it. These preliminary steps will assist the lawyer who takes their case.

There are several possible legal grounds on which Natalie might recover damages. First, consumer products generally carry warranties of various kinds, the most important in this case being the "implied warranty of merchantability." This warranty is a promise by a manufacturer that a product is safe for its intended and reasonably foreseeable use. A product violates ("breaches") this warranty if it fails to meet the expectation of safety of the ordinary consumer. In Natalie's case, the explosion might constitute a breach of the implied warranty.

A second basis for recovery might be negligence. To prevail on this theory, Natalie's lawyer would have to prove that the manufacturer acted unreasonably in marketing the product or in failing to provide a sufficient warning. How do you know if the manufacturer was unreasonable? That's a question for the jury to decide. In our hypothetical case, the jury would consider whether the danger of the two chemicals reacting and causing an explosion was foreseeable by the manufacturer and, if it was, whether the risk outweighed any benefit provided by the chemistry set.

A third basis for holding the manufacturer liable would be the defectiveness of the product. There are two main types of product defects: manufacturing and design. A manufacturing defect occurs when a glitch in production leads to a faulty product. For example, if one out of a million soda bottles comes off the assembly line and subsequently explodes, causing injury, that bottle has a manufacturing defect. By contrast, a design defect exists when a product is manufactured exactly as it is supposed to be, but some flaw in the design causes harm. Manufacturing defects are relatively easy cases for the plaintiff (the person suing) to win. Thus, if one of the chemicals that caused Natalie's explosion was not supposed to be included in the set, Natalie will probably prevail. Most cases, though, involve design defects, and these are much harder to prove. Natalie's attorney would have to show that by including the two reactive chemicals, the manufacturer created a product that was unreasonably dangerous. This would require the jury to weigh the risks and benefits of the product, as they would do in a negligence case. While product defect cases purport to hold defendants "strictly liable," meaning that they are liable even though they are not at fault, in practical terms the analysis of whether a product is defective, particularly in its design, often differs little from a case based on negligence.

DANGER FROM AIR BAGS

Sometimes purported safety devices can prove to be dangerous. Hailed as a significant step toward increased auto safety, the installation of air bags, mandatory for all 1998 models, has saved thousands of lives but had tragic consequences for some children. Since 1993 at least forty children have been killed by air bags, which deploy at a speed as high as two hundred miles per hour and with a force as great as 2,600 pounds, and the families of some of the child victims have sued the manufacturers for negligence. In response, the National Highway Traffic Safety Administration (NHTSA) has adopted regulations requiring that vehicles contain labels warning of the dangers of air bags to children and that sports cars and trucks with no backseat have a manual cutoff switch so parents can deactivate them. The National Transportation Safety Board has also issued a recommendation that states enact legislation making it illegal for children under thirteen to ride in the front seat. Meanwhile auto engineers are working on "smart" air bags that will be able to adjust their speed and force according to the height and weight of the passenger.

What can you do to protect your child? According to the National Transportation Safety Board, infants weighing less than twenty pounds should *never* ride in the front seat of a car with an air bag. Children can also be at risk from air bags if they are not wearing a seat belt or if their car seats are improperly installed. Indeed, investigators blame parents in some of those instances for failing to use seat belts. Until the manufacturers modify the air bag design, children should not ride in the front seat of a car if the car has a passenger-side air bag. If you have further questions about air bags and child safety, you can call a NHTSA toll-free hot line at:

1-800-424-9393

While a risk of explosion from a child's toy might seem unreasonable, the defendants can raise a couple of arguments in their defense.

They might claim, first, that Natalie herself was careless in failing to follow directions. In negligence cases and in many defective product cases, the defendants can seek to reduce their liability by showing carelessness on the part of the plaintiff. This is known as "contributory negligence" or "comparative fault." In a product liability case, this kind of behavior by the consumer is sometimes called "misuse." Here it is a weak argument against Natalie since she is only eight and the error was easily foreseeable by the manufacturer. The defendant might also try to avoid responsibility by blaming Natalie's parents for failing to supervise her, as the toy instructs. However, in modern life parents cannot always monitor their children's activities every minute, and manufacturers of products know this. Ultimately, it would be up to the jury to decide whether it was foreseeable that a child would mix the chemicals without adult supervision and whether the risk of explosion and harm outweighed any benefits the chemistry set had to offer.

If the jury found in Natalie's favor, they would award her monetary damages to compensate her parents for the medical bills they had incurred and her for any pain and suffering she had endured as a result of the injuries.

Note that product liability suits, depending on the legal theories used, frequently name other defendants, such as the retailer who sold the product, in addition to the manufacturer. (Strict liability generally applies to everyone involved in distributing the product, and certain warranties apply to the retailer as well as the manufacturer.) This does not allow the plaintiff to recover damages twice, but it may provide another source of funds to pay the judgment.

YOUR CHILD'S EDUCATION

FOR MANY CHILDREN, their educational experience will rank second only to their family life as a significant influence on their development. Children spend many hours each day in school, where they are exposed to the views of teachers, textbooks, administrators, and peers. School offers them an opportunity to master essential information and skills that will enable them to become productive members of society. Without an education, the chance for a successful future is slim. As a parent, you no doubt want your child to receive the best education that he or she can. This chapter will assist you in that endeavor by explaining the myriad laws that govern our schools.

Beginning with compulsory education, we will consider the eligibility requirements for attending public school as well as alternatives such as private and home schooling. Curriculum matters, including competency testing, bilingual education, religious issues, and censorship, come next. A section on maintaining school discipline and safety follows, explaining your child's right to self-expression, a school's right to search students on campus, its legal responsibility for students' safety, and its right to discipline students who misbehave. This chapter also covers the controversial issues of sex education and AIDS in schools; race and sex discrimination, including sexual harassment; and issues regarding gay and lesbian students. The final two sections explain your right to see your child's school records and to obtain an appropriate education for a child who is disabled. Armed with this information, you will be better prepared to participate actively and effectively in your child's education.

COMPULSORY EDUCATION

One of the unique features of American society has been the establishment of a system of free public education for all its children. Although many of us view public education as a right, in fact there is no right to an education under the U.S. Constitution. Most states, though, do provide or recognize one in their constitutions, and all states, of course, offer free public education.

In fact, in every state, education for a certain number of years is compulsory. Children who skip school without parental permission and a legitimate reason (usually meaning a threat to their health or safety) are considered truant and can be charged with a status offense, as we will discuss at greater length in chapter 9. Parents who fail to send their children to school likewise can be subject to criminal charges.

Age and Citizenship Requirements

Most states' compulsory education laws require that children attend school from the ages of six to sixteen, but the rules vary: the lower bound ranges from five to eight and the upper from fourteen to eighteen. Moreover, while children are not generally required to attend school to the age of eighteen, they usually are entitled to do so, and in some states they may attend until they're twenty-one. School districts have the right to set a cutoff date for determining the age of a school entrant. For example, your district may decide that all children who will be six years old by December 15 of a given year may begin first grade in that year. No federal law requires that states offer a kindergarten program, but most districts do.

The right to attend school has historically applied to all children who live in a given school district, regardless of whether they or their

CAN THE GOVERNMENT DENY CHILDREN PUBLIC EDUCATION BASED ON THEIR IMMIGRATION STATUS?

Many people think so, but the law suggests otherwise. In 1994, for example, California voters passed Proposition 187, which, among other things, prohibits children who are undocumented aliens (illegal immigrants) from enrolling in public school. This and other provisions of Proposition 187 have yet to be implemented because a federal district court ruled that denying public education to undocumented children conflicts with federal law. In making its ruling, the court relied on a 1982 Supreme Court case, *Plyler v. Doe*, that struck down a similar Texas law. In the Supreme Court's view, the Texas law denied "equal protection" of the laws to undocumented alien children by singling them out for exclusion. Although it would seem to settle the question, *Plyler* was decided by a 5–4 divided Court. Since the composition of the Court has changed substantially since then, moving considerably to the right, proponents believe a law like Proposition 187 can survive, and they likely will persist in seeking its implementation. Meanwhile, politicians continue to call for similar legislation on a federal level, although none has yet been enacted.

families are citizens or immigrants. This remains the rule in practice today; however, there have been efforts on many fronts to restrict public education to bona fide citizens or legal immigrants, as discussed in the box above.

Although a school district may not be able legally to deny public education based on immigrant or citizenship status, the courts have upheld residency requirements for eligibility in a given school district. This means that a child must actually live within the district. Occasionally children will be allowed to attend school in a different district if they are living there apart from their parents, but not if they're doing so for the purpose of circumventing the district's residency requirement. In other words, you can't send your child to live with Grandma and Grandpa because you prefer their district, although some schools will allow such an arrangement if you're willing to pay tuition. Likewise, if you are divorced and your ex-spouse lives in a different district, you can't just choose the district you prefer; normally your child must attend school in the district where the custodial parent lives.

Recently, advocates of school choice have prompted changes in these rules, and a number of states now allow children to attend schools outside their home district. While the plans vary, transfer usually depends on the availability of space in the receiving school and a determination by the district that no disruption will occur to any desegregation efforts. Districts frequently use random lotteries to select students for transfer; however, public schools offering specialized curricula, known as magnet schools, may employ selective admissions criteria. We'll be talking more about magnet schools later.

Transportation

If the law requires you to send your child to school, does the state have to provide transportation? Not necessarily. You do not have a right to state-funded transportation for your child. Nevertheless, many school districts provide it. In fact, twenty-three million children ride the bus to school each day. In earlier years, when you were in school, you were probably transported for free. Today, in the face of shrinking budgets, many schools have begun to charge a fee, and the courts have allowed it.

If your child's district does offer transportation, it cannot discriminate or act arbitrarily in designing the bus routes. However, it is free to limit bus service to those living a reasonable distance from school. Parents have occasionally tried to challenge bus routes, stops, and schedules in court but with little success. Most courts defer to the district's determination of a reasonable route that balances safety, efficiency, and convenience. The district also has the right to refuse transportation to children who misbehave on the bus. Your child's school should have a policy outlining grounds for suspension of bus privileges and steps required for reinstatement.

CHARTER SCHOOLS—A PUBLIC SCHOOL INNOVATION

About half the states now have laws allowing the establishment of so-called charter schools. These schools are not private schools; they are publicly financed. In contrast to traditional public schools, though, they are independently run by private companies. The group or company operating the schools contracts with a sponsor, who may be a school district, university, or government agency. The contract sets forth standards and expectations for the school. Failure to meet the contractual requirements can lead to revocation of the charter. Parents and educational reformers see charter schools as a way of increasing choice in public education and encouraging innovation. Cities like Detroit; Boston; Houston; Wilmington, Delaware; and Lanikai, Hawaii, have joined the experiment in an effort to revitalize their public schools and reach difficult student populations, and the phenomenon appears to be spreading to other cities and towns across the nation.

Alternatives to Traditional Public Education

The compulsory education laws require all children to attend school, but this does not mean that all must attend public school. You have a right to send your children to private school, and you may even be able to school your children at home.

Private Schools. In a case decided in 1925, the Supreme Court determined that a state could have compulsory education but could not compel parents to send their children to public schools. To do so would violate their "fundamental right" to control the upbringing of their children. About 10 percent of school-age children today attend private schools of one sort or another, many with religious affiliations. Although the state cannot prohibit private school attendance, it can regulate private schools, requiring that their curricula meet certain minimum state standards. The state also generally cannot provide funding for private

---

TUITION VOUCHERS

In recent years a number of legislative proposals have been made to allow tuition vouchers, which would provide parents with a certain dollar amount of education credit to be used toward either public or private school. Proponents argue that these vouchers would give parents greater choice and improve the quality of schools by fostering competition. Critics counter that they would not only violate the Constitution, but would also lead to two systems of education, the public system for the poor, who could not afford private school even with the vouchers, and the private system for the wealthy. Cleveland is one district that has implemented a voucher program using public money to finance private schooling, and the program has been upheld by an Ohio state court. A modified voucher system that allows poor children to receive vouchers to attend private nonsectarian schools has also been implemented in Wisconsin. This system received court approval, too, but amendments extending it to religious schools have not been put into effect pending court review.

---

schools since this would conflict with the First Amendment's prohibition against the government's "establishing" (supporting or fostering) a religion. Any funding that a state provides to private schools must serve a secular purpose and neither advance nor hinder religion. In practice, this standard has allowed public financial support for secular textbooks and transportation but not for teachers' salaries or operating costs of private schools. Most states do not offer transportation to private schools, even if they do provide it to public schools. Moreover, courts have declared direct subsidies or tax credits for private school attendance unconstitutional unless the same subsidies and tax credits apply to parents who send their kids to public schools.

Home Schooling. Concerned about the quality of public education and perhaps unable to afford private education or having religious or cultural beliefs that prevent their children from associating with others outside their group, some parents have turned to home schooling. The Home School Legal Defense Association estimates that half a million children a year are home-schooled; other sources say the number could be twice that. Most states allow home schooling as long as certain requirements are satisfied. Usually parents have to document their home-schooling program with course outlines, lesson plans, hours spent in instruction, and test results. Most often the local school board has the authority to determine whether a home-schooling plan is substantially equivalent to that provided by public schools. The board also has the right to require minimum competency testing of home-schooled students and to revoke permission for home schooling if the children are not making sufficient progress. The state may also require certain qualifications, even a teaching credential, of the home-schooling parent. In cases of divorce, custodial parents with sole custody generally have the right to determine the education of their children, and they may choose home schooling in states that permit it. Noncustodial parents cannot do anything about the decision unless they can show that home schooling poses a danger to the health or welfare of their children.

THE SCHOOL CURRICULUM

Content and Methodology

The content and methods of teaching employed in any given school district are largely determined by the state in conjunction with the local school board. Parents have no right to dictate the curriculum or teaching methods, but they can make their views known and affect policy. They also have a constitutional right to rear their children that may extend to certain curriculum matters. In addition, both state and federal law place some limitations and affirmative obligations on local school boards.

Testing and Tracking. In most schools, your child at some point will be placed in a learning group according to his or her abilities as measured by grades or test scores. This is known as ability grouping. In the younger grades, for example, your child may be placed in a reading or math group with peers who appear to learn at a similar rate and have similar skills. In different ability groups, both the pace and the content of the classes may vary. By junior or senior high, your child may be "tracked" into separate classes or follow an entirely different curriculum from other students according to his or her ability and achievement.

The practices of ability grouping and tracking have generated considerable controversy because they can have a major influence on a child's future educational and vocational opportunities. Critics fear that children tracked into the lower groups will end up working below their potential because of stigma and negative self-image. Mixing children with greater abilities will help these children reach further, the critics argue. Proponents, on the other hand, claim that tracking not only enables slower students to get the attention they deserve but also keeps brighter students from becoming bored.

Ultimately this question is one of public and educational policy rather than law. Courts do not usually get involved in the debate over the wisdom of tracking unless it is a manifestation of racial segregation. There have been legal challenges brought to tracking and to the testing used to determine it on that basis. Some parents have sued, arguing that the tests discriminate against students based on race. In the 1960s a number of courts agreed that certain tests were racially discriminatory, and as recently as 1996 a federal district court in Illinois found that a school district's tracking system fostered illegal racial segregation in education.

Most states today mandate minimum competency testing at regular intervals throughout the school years. In some states, scores on competency tests form the basis for decisions about promotion and graduation. Competency testing, like tracking, has generated its share of supporters and detractors. For those who support the increasingly popular back-to-basics trend, competency testing provides one way of measuring the success of current teaching methods.

Standardized testing is also the primary way that schools select children for gifted and talented programs. Most states have laws that compel districts to identify gifted and talented children and to provide special programs for them. A number of states even require that an individualized education plan be created for every gifted student. Nonetheless, such programs frequently are discontinued because of lack of funds. Can parents sue to compel enrichment for their children? Some have, and in one case the Pennsylvania Supreme Court ruled in favor of the parents. However, the court did not require schools without enrichment programs to develop them; it merely said that schools with such programs already in place had to work within their capabilities to meet the needs of the gifted children. Legal challenges to the criteria for admission to gifted and talented programs have met with little success.

Whatever the methods used, the goal of education, of course, is to prepare our children to become good citizens and productive members of society by teaching them the necessary academic and, to some extent, social skills they will need to cope with the challenges of modern life. Yet for too many children, this goal remains elusive. The National Assessment of Educational Progress for 1994 revealed that only about a third of high school seniors could read proficiently. Too many teenagers cannot work basic math problems, and their knowledge of geography is sorely inadequate. In most areas, if a professional fails to provide adequate service, as defined by standards in the profession, the disappointed party can sue for malpractice. That is not the case in education. Numerous cases have been brought across the nation alleging that teachers and school districts have negligently failed to educate children, but no court has ever accepted this argument. Why? Among other reasons, the courts have been reluctant to define appropriate standards for content and teaching methods; they have found it difficult to prove that any particular teacher or class "caused" a student's failure to learn;

they have disagreed over allocation of responsibility for learning; and they have had a general antipathy toward second-guessing educators.

Even though your child does not have a legally enforceable right to an adequate education, can you as a parent at least choose who your child's teacher will be each year? Many parents would like to, but the law gives you no right to influence this decision. However, in most places, the law does afford you the opportunity to observe classes at reasonable times, and you may be able to informally influence assignment of your child by consulting with the school principal.

Bilingual Education. Undoubtedly one of the biggest controversies in education today—especially in states like California, New York, and Texas—is bilingual education. In 1992 the Department of Education estimated that 2.6 million students had only limited proficiency in English, and some experts suggested that this estimate significantly understated the numbers. By the year 2000, roughly 10 percent of public school children nationwide are expected to have a native language other than English. Federal law, specifically Title VI of the Civil Rights Act of 1964, protects schoolchildren from discrimination based on national origin and mandates that schools provide services that take into account and remedy deficiencies in English. This mandate was affirmed in a 1974 Supreme Court case and by the Educational Opportunity Act of 1974. Yet nowhere do these laws spell out the exact nature of the remedy to be employed. Most people could agree on the general goal: developing proficiency in English as quickly as possible so that children whose first language is not English can be mainstreamed with native English speakers in regular classes. But tremendous controversy surrounds the methods used to pursue this goal.

Initially, schools favored the ESL (English as a Second Language) approach, at least for secondary students. ESL programs provide supplemental instruction in English for students with language deficiencies, but the students take all of their classes in English with the general student population. The theory is that immersion in this fashion leads to rapid mastery of English, greater overall academic success, and, ultimately, assimilation into American society. Critics of the ESL approach point out, though, that by the time some students master English sufficiently to understand their other subjects, they are woefully, sometimes permanently, behind. Critics of ESL also fear that the method contributes to the development of poor self-image and poor cultural identity.

Educators responded to these criticisms with bilingual-bicultural education. In this approach, students are taught subjects in their native language until they reach a level of proficiency in English that will allow them to join regular English-speaking classes. This method is more expensive than ESL and leads to greater segregation of minority-language students. Moreover, many parents and educators feel that integration with mainstream classes takes too long, often years. Nonetheless, Congress definitively declared its support for bilingual, as opposed to ESL, education with the Bilingual Education Act of 1988. This law provides funding to state and local governments to develop bilingual-bicultural programs. Today this remains the prevailing approach, although the form of the programs varies. However, bilingual education has come under strong and consistent attack, and change is likely in the future.

If your child is identified as needing bilingual education, you have the right to know what his level of English proficiency is, how that level was determined, and what programs are available to meet his needs. You also have the right to decline to enroll your child in any recommended programs.

Religion in the Schools

The First Amendment states that "Congress shall make no law respecting an establishment of religion, or prohibiting the free exercise thereof." The first part, the so-called establishment clause, prohibits both the state and the federal government from fostering, supporting, or encouraging any religion while the second clause prohibits the government from infringing on an individual's right to observe his or her religion of choice. How do these seemingly contradictory principles apply to our public schools? The Supreme Court and lower federal and state courts have struggled to establish and maintain a delicate balance between them. Striking the balance in this context poses a particular challenge since parents also have a constitutional right (protected by the Fourteenth Amendment) to direct the religious upbringing of their children, a right that includes sending them to public schools without fear that the children will be subjected to religious teaching or indoctrination.

According to the Supreme Court, a law does not "establish" a religion in violation of the First Amendment if (1) it has a primarily secular purpose, (2) its principal effect does not advance or inhibit religion, and (3) it does not foster an "excessive entanglement" with religion. Laws seeking to bring religious practices, observances, or information into the public schools must be tested against these three criteria. While the lines are sometimes difficult to draw, the Court has resolved a number of specific questions concerning the limits on religion in schools.

School Prayer and Holiday Observances. For many years, public schools routinely started their day with a Bible reading or a prayer. In the 1960s the Supreme Court began to strike down these practices because they violated the establishment clause. Cases continue to arise, but the Court's pronouncements on this point have been fairly consistent. Schools cannot compel students to participate in religious exercises, nor can they allow voluntary prayer. In 1985 the Court struck down an Alabama law providing for a daily minute of silence in school for meditation or voluntary prayer, finding that it had no real secular purpose and did, in effect, serve to endorse religion. Laws in some states allow for a moment of silence, but no mention of prayer has been permitted.

In 1992 the Court revisited the question of prayers in school in a case concerning invocations or benedictions performed during school ceremonies—specifically, commencements. The school at issue had chosen a clergyperson to perform a "nonsectarian prayer" at graduation. Students in attendance were required to stand and remain silent during the prayer, but they did not themselves have to pray. Although the school argued that graduation was a voluntary event, the Court found that it was a highly significant milestone for most children and concluded that they should not be forced to choose between attending a graduation

ceremony and being compelled to suffer exposure to a religious observance. Likewise, coaches cannot end practices with a prayer.

Does this mean that no invocation or benediction is ever permissible at a graduation ceremony? Perhaps not. Some lower courts have allowed prayers at graduation under certain limited circumstances: most
significantly, when the decision to include the prayer has come from the
graduates; when the prayer is to be performed by a graduating senior,
not an outside clergyperson; and when the school remains neutral in
connection with the prayer. Even under these circumstances, though,
not all courts will allow prayers.

The danger of the state promoting an establishment of religion also
arises around the holidays. Can your child's school put on a Christmas
pageant or have the class make Christmas ornaments? Can the school
put up a Christmas tree or Hanukkah decorations? Probably yes if the
primary purpose of what the school does is secular, even if it has a religious basis, too. Practices that have been approved include explaining
the original and modern meaning of the holidays, incorporating religious aspects in the study and creation of music and art (yes, the cho-
rus can perform Christmas carols and the art class can make Christmas
cards), and displaying religious symbols like the tree and the Hanukkah
menorah. Understand, though, that in most other circumstances, the
school cannot insist on the display of religious material; for example, a
South Dakota law requiring that the Ten Commandments be posted in
every class was declared unconstitutional. And students, teachers, and
other staff who do not want to participate in holiday-related activities
are customarily excused.

Although in general a school may not allow religious observances
on campus because of the establishment clause, it also must be careful
not to infringe the free exercise of religion by its students. To accommodate this right, many schools allow students with parental consent to
leave school during school hours for religious observance. For example,
most schools will honor a Jewish family's decision to keep a child out
of school on Yom Kippur. But there are limits. Some states place a ceil-
ing on the number of hours of release time a school may permit for

THE CREATIONISM DEBATE

One curriculum issue that generated considerable controversy in the 1980s was the teaching of creationism. Back in 1968 the Supreme Court struck down an Arkansas law that prohibited the teaching of evolution. Some years later, certain religious groups sought to compel schools to teach creationism—the belief that all forms of life resulted from individual acts of creation by God. Proponents of including creationism in the curriculum argued that failure to do so establishes the "religion" of secular humanism through the teaching of evolution and infringes the right to free exercise of religion of parents and children who believe in creationism. The Court rejected these claims in a 1987 case, declaring unconstitutional a Louisiana law that required the teaching of "creation science" if a class was taught evolution. Similarly, a challenge to a class that discussed witches, goblins, myths, and folktales proved unsuccessful. The objecting parents had claimed that those subjects sought to foster a "pagan religious cult," but a federal court found to the contrary.

religious observance. Moreover, parents seeking to force schools to provide release time have not had much success in the courts.

Religion and the Curriculum. The establishment clause prohibits public schools from providing religious instruction. Bible reading, for example, is impermissible, as is distribution of Bibles to students. However, studying the Bible from a historical or literary perspective may be allowed, and the public school curriculum may include a social studies class that surveys the principles and development of the major world religions. Other curriculum matters that raise freedom of religion issues include sex education, explored in detail later in this chapter, and the creationism debate, discussed in the box above.

Extracurricular Religious Activities. The establishment clause prohibits schools from allowing religious clubs or groups to meet or conduct activities on campus during school hours. If they did, the schools,

and thus the government, would in effect be subsidizing religious organizations and could be perceived as sponsoring those religions. Does
this mean that your child could be prohibited from discussing religion
with friends at the lunch table? No. Schools can't forbid such casual,
informal discussions. Moreover, the Equal Access Act of 1984 requires
secondary schools to open their doors to religious clubs *after* school
hours on the same terms that apply to other extracurricular or community groups. The clubs' religious activities must meet certain criteria,
though: they must be completely voluntary; they must be initiated and
run by the students, not by the school or the government; no nonschool
members may be involved; and they may not interfere with the regular
conduct of educational activities. Primary and middle schools may also
allow religious meetings on campus after hours.

Censorship and Textbook Selection

Over the years, parents in school districts across the nation have sought
at one time or another to have certain books banned from their local
public schools. The books that have come under attack most often are
long-standing classics of American literature frequently included in the
curriculum: *Of Mice and Men, The Grapes of Wrath, 1984, Anne Frank:
Diary of a Young Girl, The Adventures of Huckleberry Finn, To Kill a
Mockingbird, The Scarlet Letter, Black Like Me, I Know Why the Caged
Bird Sings,* and *The Good Earth.* Others, like *The Catcher in the Rye*
and *Go Ask Alice,* are particular favorites of teens. A local school board
has broad authority to choose the content of the curriculum—the
courses offered, the subjects covered, the materials used—and even
the teaching methods employed. However, the school board's discretion
is subject to the demands of the First Amendment, and students have a
First Amendment right to receive information. This right comes into
play in the selection of textbooks for the classroom and the purchase of
books for the school library. Generally, the courts are less inclined to
overturn a school board's decision not to select a book for a school library than they are if the board seeks to remove a book already there.
Some judicial decisions suggest that the board has greater power to
censor material used in the classroom since the classroom is a more

controlled environment than the library, which is supposed to be a place for free exploration of ideas. Regardless of the setting, schools cannot ban a book completely just because the board disagrees with the message or ideas expressed in it or because a parent objects to it. The First Amendment does not allow schools to inflict a "pall of orthodoxy" on the classroom or to deliberately stifle one side of a debate. The board must find that a work is "pervasively vulgar," educationally unsuitable, or inconsistent with the moral standards of the community. For example, a federal court in New Hampshire prevented a school from removing *Ms.* magazine from the school library because some school officials disliked the political tone of the magazine. However, other court decisions have shown greater deference to school board decisions to purge books or other material from the curriculum.

MAINTAINING SCHOOL DISCIPLINE AND SAFETY

Students' Right to Self-Expression: Speech and Dress Codes

In the case of *Tinker v. Des Moines Independent Community School District,* the Supreme Court declared that students do not "shed their constitutional rights to freedom of speech or expression at the school house gate." Yet a student's right to free speech under the First Amendment is not as extensive as an adult's would be outside that setting. Let's suppose Luke is the editor of his high school newspaper. He has written an article about a condom distribution program at a neighboring high school. Although he does not usually do so, Mr. Gray, the faculty adviser to the paper, submits the piece to the school principal for review prior to publication. The principal, believing the piece to be inappropriate and controversial, forbids publication. Does Luke have any legal right to challenge her decision?

The Supreme Court has said that a student's speech is protected by the First Amendment unless it will "materially and substantially disrupt the work and discipline of the school." What exactly does this mean? There are no clear lines for schools to follow. Surely if student speech provokes a riot, the school can penalize the student for it. Indeed, the school does not even have to wait for disruption actually to occur; it can act to prevent it. For example, the Supreme Court upheld a school's refusal to publish an article about pregnant teens at the school, citing concerns about invasion of privacy. Moreover, if the speech is obscene, profane, or patently offensive, the school can sanction or suppress it even if there is no danger of substantial disruption. The school's right to restrict student speech is even greater when the speech bears the imprimatur of the school, for example, at a mandatory school-sponsored assembly. The school can also place reasonable "time, place, and manner" restrictions on speech: in other words, it can dictate when, where, and how the speech is communicated. On the other hand, mere discomfort generated by an unpopular position does not justify suppression or sanction of a student. Nor can a school censor student speech merely because it criticizes the school.

In Luke's case, the answer to whether his rights have been violated by the principal's refusal to publish his article may depend on the jurisdiction in which he lives. Written expression is protected, but school newspapers like Luke's are often part of the curriculum and therefore subject to the review of a faculty adviser. Some legal decisions have stated categorically that a requirement of prior approval constitutes unconstitutional censorship. Others have allowed prior approval but only where there were standard procedures in place, the decision was made promptly, and the rule did not require prior approval of all student work. In Luke's case, submission of the article to the principal is not part of normal procedure. Moreover, in order to suppress Luke's article, the principal should have some evidence of likely disruption from its publication. The mere fact that it concerns a controversial topic is not sufficient, particularly if the article treats its subject neutrally.

Can Luke's school prevent him from publishing an advertisement from Planned Parenthood or a local bar? Most likely yes. The Planned Parenthood ad could appear to be an endorsement by the school, and ads encouraging drinking and other activities illegal for minors are clearly inappropriate in school publications.

Now suppose Heather, one of Luke's classmates on the newspaper, having learned about civil disobedience from her social studies class, decides to protest the principal's decision not to print Luke's article. She refuses to say the Pledge of Allegiance every day in her homeroom. Can the school force her to participate? No. The First Amendment guarantees Heather the freedom to speak, the freedom not to speak, and the right not to adopt particular beliefs. However, to maintain order, the school can insist that Heather stand or sit quietly during the pledge.

Suppose further that another member of the paper, Jamie, has taken to wearing T-shirts from a local store, Condomadness, as part of the protest. The shirts contain the name of the store on the front and an abstract design composed of condoms of varying colors on the back. The principal sees Jamie and demands that he either change shirts, replacing the one he has on with a T-shirt available from the gym, or risk disciplinary action. Can Jamie legally refuse? Probably not. The Supreme Court has protected students' rights to use symbolic speech as a form of political protest. In the famous 1969 case of *Tinker v. Des Moines Independent Community School District,* for instance, the Court upheld students' right to wear black armbands to school to protest the Vietnam War, and another case upheld their right to wear buttons with the word *Scab* during a teachers' strike. But Jamie's case is trickier. While he seems to be engaging in symbolic political speech by wearing the T-shirt, the school can argue, probably successfully, that the shirt crosses the line to vulgar and offensive speech, which it may prohibit. For example, a federal court in Virginia upheld a school's decision to suspend a twelve-year-old for wearing a shirt that said "Drugs Suck!" However, Jamie might fare better in a state like Massachusetts that provides greater protection to student speech than the Constitution mandates. In a 1996 decision, the Massachusetts Supreme Judicial Court found that a school prohibition on wearing Coed Naked T-Shirts that read "Coed Naked Band: Do It to the Rhythm" and "See Dick Drink. See Dick Drive. See Dick Die. Don't Be A Dick" violated Massachusetts law by suppressing speech that was vulgar but not disruptive.

If the school can prevent your child from wearing a vulgar or offensive item of clothing, can it also dictate what your child must wear? It is fairly well settled that schools have the authority to impose dress codes, ranging from unwritten rules requiring "appropriate" dress to explicit rules requiring students to wear uniforms. Courts tend to be more willing to allow these rules (as opposed to rules about hair, discussed next) because the restrictions last only for the duration of the school day. Children can change clothes as soon as they get home if they so choose. Restrictions on dress have become increasingly popular as a way of instilling discipline and discouraging gang involvement. School rules intended to deter gang membership by prohibiting boys from wearing earrings have been upheld after being challenged on the basis of sex discrimination. Other rules forbidding students to wear certain colors or insignia associated with gangs have also been upheld.

Court decisions involving school restrictions on other aspects of personal appearance, namely hair length and facial hair, have been less consistent. About half the courts have found prohibitions on long hair on boys to be unconstitutional, along with similar proscriptions against beards and mustaches, but the rest have upheld them. Some courts reached their decision after balancing students' right to express themselves through their personal appearance against a school's interests in promoting good hygiene, teaching discipline, and reinforcing respect for authority. Sometimes other matters also come into play. In one case, a court held that a school could not enforce its no-long-hair policy against Indian males because long hair is part of long-standing Indian tradition and religious beliefs. Interestingly, a number of federal and some state courts have simply refused to intervene in any constitutional challenges to hair length rules, reasoning that the issue should be resolved by school administrators and parents and that hair length is not a form of communication protected by the First Amendment.

Searches and Seizures on Campus

Drugs and weapons have become a fact of life at many of our nation's public schools, particularly in urban areas. School districts and law enforcement agencies continue to grapple with the most effective means of stemming this life-threatening tide. The challenge is finding a way to rout out possession of these items without turning our schools into prisons and our children into inmates.

DEALING WITH DRUGS AND WEAPONS AT SCHOOL

Drugs and alcohol are probably the items most commonly searched for on campus, followed by stolen money, weapons, and other contraband like cigarettes. In an effort to combat the drug epidemic, schools have resorted to the urine testing of athletes and the use of dogs specially trained to sniff out drugs. Both methods have survived challenges in the courts under certain circumstances.

Drug testing has been particularly controversial, but in 1995 the Supreme Court ruled that random urine testing of athletes was constitutional. In that case, the Court found that the school had an important interest in performing the testing because groups of students at the school openly advocated drug use, behavioral problems had increased, and drug use threatened to impair athletic performance and to jeopardize the safety of athletes and others. The school had tried many other methods before resorting to drug testing, and the testing did not require any students to urinate in front of anyone else. It seems likely that this case will establish the norm for testing programs in other schools. Those that insist on more intrusive testing, such as monitoring students while they produce their samples, or more widespread testing might face further legal challenges.

Public school teachers and administrators are generally considered "state actors," which means that, as government employees, they must act within the bounds of the Constitution. As we have seen in other contexts, though, minors do not enjoy all the same constitutional rights as adults, and events that take place at public school are not viewed in the same way by the courts as events that take place on the street at the behest of the police. Although the Fourth Amendment, which protects individuals against unreasonable searches and seizures, does apply to students in public schools, it applies only in a limited fashion. Normally, police officers must have a search warrant based on probable

The high court has yet to rule on the use of sniffer dogs to detect drugs on students and in schools, and lower courts have disagreed about the validity of these searches. Some courts have upheld dog sniff searches in the absence of reasonable suspicion, particularly searches of student lockers and cars, and even of the students themselves, while other courts have struck down such searches.

Guns and other weapons brought to campus by students pose an even more dangerous problem. Well over a hundred thousand guns are brought to public schools every day, and one study suggests that fifty students a year die as a result of school violence. Most shootings occur on urban, inner-city campuses, but weapons have infiltrated suburban schools in well-to-do neighborhoods as well. If school officials have a reasonable suspicion to believe a student is armed, they have the right to search the student. But in some schools, the problem is so widespread that broader action has become necessary. In New York, for instance, and almost half of the hundred largest districts across the nation, some schools are now equipped with metal detectors. These have been ruled constitutional because the intrusion is minimal and the threat posed to school safety by weapons is so great.

cause to believe a crime has been committed before they can lawfully search a person's property, but there are some exceptions to this rule, most of which we'll be discussing more fully in chapter 9. For our purposes here, you should understand that most states recognize searches at school as one of the exceptions, and the Supreme Court has ruled that this lesser protection is constitutional. Teachers and other school officials can conduct warrantless searches of students and their property, but except in the case of drug testing and the use of metal detectors (see box on page 62 and above), they may do so only if they have a "reasonable suspicion" that a student has committed a crime or an infraction of a school rule and that a search will yield evidence of the violation.

What constitutes "reasonable suspicion"? Well, the answer varies depending on the facts of the case. The school official must have some concrete basis for her suspicion; a mere rumor or hunch will not suffice. In one case, for example, a court found that a school social worker was justified in searching a student after she discovered some money missing from her desk because the student she searched had a criminal record and was the only person with access to the room. In another case, by contrast, a court disapproved a search of the student body—their purses, bookbags, and pockets of male students—after a teacher detected the smell of marijuana in the hallway because there was no evidence linking any particular student to the crime.

When a school official does search a student, the intrusiveness of the search must be commensurate with the alleged offense and the circumstances. Strip searches to find stolen money, for example, have been ruled invalid by more than one court; however, strip searches to find drugs have been upheld in certain cases when school officials had reasonable suspicion that the students were concealing drugs on their person. In deciding whether these searches are reasonable, courts will also consider the age and sex of the students. A search requiring a female student to strip to her underwear in front of a male teacher might be considered overly intrusive, while the same search conducted in the locker room by a female teacher would be permissible. Moreover, a few states have statutes explicitly prohibiting strip searches by school officials.

The right to search based on reasonable suspicion extends to students' belongings, including purses, backpacks, and gym bags, as well as to their lockers. A number of courts have gone further, ruling that school officials may search student lockers even if they don't have reasonable suspicion. To justify these searches, the courts have reasoned that students have only a reduced "expectation of privacy" in their lockers because the school owns the lockers and has the right to control the space. For this reason, courts are particularly likely to uphold locker searches conducted without reasonable suspicion if the school has a written policy explaining to the students that the lockers are owned by the school and subject to search.

School Liability for Injuries on Campus

In the past, schools, school officials, and teachers were immune from liability for negligence or misconduct that caused injuries to students; they could not be sued in court for monetary damages. Many states, although not all, have now abolished in whole or in part that immunity. In these states, if your child is injured as a result of a teacher's carelessness or the negligent maintenance of the school, you may be able to sue. Other states may allow a suit against a teacher or the district if the teacher's error goes beyond negligence to "willful or wanton" misconduct, that is, if the teacher knowingly undertakes a dangerous course of action.

Similarly, if a teacher causes intentional harm—for example, by physically assaulting your child—you may be able to sue her. (Sexual molestation by a teacher is a form of sexual harassment and is discussed later in this chapter.) Unfortunately, the teacher herself may not have any money to pay a judgment, so you may want to sue her supervisor (the principal or superintendent) or the school district. While employers generally can be held legally responsible for their employees' wrongdoing on the job, if the teacher is found to have acted beyond the bounds of her job, her supervisor or the school district will be liable only if they were themselves negligent or at fault in some way, that is, only if they knew or had reason to know of the danger and failed to properly investigate or respond to previous allegations or rumors of abuse. Moreover, some states grant school districts immunity from lawsuits based on negligent hiring, retention, or supervision of teachers. However, a few courts have recognized that exempting school districts from liability unless they are negligent, or immunizing them altogether, would leave many children without compensation for grievous harm and have allowed cases to proceed against the districts.

The law is even less clear when it comes to injuries inflicted on students by other students or outsiders. Some states have found that schools may be liable on the theory that since parents are compelled to send their children to school, schools have a responsibility to ensure the safety of the children in their custody. So if the class bully punches your child in class, breaking his nose, the school may be liable if the teacher failed to exercise adequate supervision, for example, by leaving the classroom unattended. More serious cases may also result in liability. For example, if a high school student is shot or raped on campus, her parents may be able to sue the school for failing to prevent the crime. However, even in states that recognize the liability of schools, the parents may sue only if the school knew or should have known of the danger and did not take reasonable steps to prevent it. Usually, the requisite knowledge is established by evidence of prior incidents on campus reported to the school authorities. But if the school had taken reasonable precautions, such as hiring security guards, it may be found not at fault.

Children involved in athletics at school are among those most likely to sustain injuries at school. In these cases, it is often difficult to sue the school because the children "assume the risk" of the activity. The legal concept of "assumption of the risk" recognizes that certain activities pose risks and that if the participants choose to engage in these activities, knowing the risks, they can hardly expect compensation if a risk occurs. In athletic pursuits, the risks are often quite obvious—getting hit with a baseball during a game, getting injured from a tackle during a football scrimmage, pulling a muscle running track. Moreover, schools often require parental consent before they allow students to participate in extracurricular sports. However, if your child sustains an injury because a teacher or coach failed to provide adequate training, instruction, or supervision or because the school provided unsafe equipment or failed to provide protective gear, you may be able to recover damages.

School Discipline

While we all hope that our children will sail through their school years without a moment of misbehavior, the reality is that many children find themselves in trouble at school at some point. For most children, the infraction will be relatively minor and routinely handled in class or after school in detention. But for a significant number of students, the misconduct will be more serious, perhaps requiring a punishment as severe as suspension or expulsion (see box on page 67). In what ways can a

EXPULSION AND SUSPENSION

Different schools have different definitions of these terms, but expulsion is commonly the more serious sanction. Often it refers to a permanent exclusion from school, at least for the remainder of the term, and in some places, it extends statewide, so an expelled student may not transfer to another school, even one in a different district. A suspension, by contrast, is usually a temporary exclusion for a shorter period of time. In most states, a student is not entitled to any alternative educational services during a suspension or expulsion, and in either case, the punishment is usually noted on the student's permanent transcript.

school discipline a child who misbehaves? And what rights does the child have to defend himself?

All schools have a right to impose measures to ensure the safety of students and school personnel and to maintain order to facilitate the learning process. Courts hesitate to interfere in these matters unless schools seriously exceed the scope of their authority. However, schools must adopt rules that are not arbitrary, and they must enforce them fairly and in the least restrictive way possible. If challenged in court, a school's actions will stand unless they are unconstitutional, as in some of the First Amendment cases we discussed earlier, or unless they are arbitrary or unreasonable.

Teachers have the authority to maintain discipline in the classroom and to exert control over minor matters on a daily basis. With virtually complete discretion, they may admonish students for inappropriate behavior, send them to time-out in the classroom, deny them special privileges, assign them extra work, or impose grade penalties, as discussed in the box on page 68.

By contrast, serious disciplinary matters are most often dealt with by administrative personnel, the principal or vice principal. Suppose eighth-grader Julie is caught smoking in the rest room when she is supposed to

CAN TEACHERS LOWER GRADES
AS A DISCIPLINARY MEASURE?

Under certain circumstances, teachers may lower grades as a sanction for misbehavior but usually only when student infractions are related to classroom performance. For example, teachers may lower a student's grades for frequent absences if they indicate the reason on the student's report card. On the other hand, a court overturned a school's decision to lower a grade after a student violated a school rule against drinking because the lowered grade did not accurately reflect the student's achievement.

be in math class. The principal immediately suspends her for two days. Can he do that? Yes. Possession of alcohol, cigarettes, drugs, or weapons; lewd or assaultive behavior toward teachers; defiance toward school personnel; fighting or other disruptive behavior; vandalism; stealing; truancy; and breaking other school rules can all subject a student to disciplinary measures ranging from detention to transfer, suspension, or expulsion. Schools recently have begun to crack down on students who bring guns to school. Almost every state now has laws requiring a one-year expulsion for this offense, and in 1997 New York City started permanently expelling students seventeen and older who bring guns to school or injure others with weapons. Many schools allow expulsion for students who are convicted of felonies or adjudicated delinquent. Some even permit immediate suspension or expulsion as soon as a student is charged with a crime or becomes the subject of a delinquency petition. Schools also have the right to suspend student participation in extracurricular activities as a disciplinary sanction because of inadequate academic performance—the so-called no pass–no play rule. Even misbehavior off campus that negatively affects a school, such as drug dealing or drinking at a party, can result in disciplinary action.

As a general rule, schools must afford students some basic due process protections when the threatened sanction is suspension or expulsion (see box on page 67). "Due process" refers to those aspects of a law or legal proceeding considered necessary to ensure that the individual is treated fairly. Does this mean Julie is entitled to a trial before she can be suspended? No. According to the Supreme Court, a school does not have to provide a full-scale criminal-type hearing for suspensions of ten days or less. But for longer suspensions and expulsions, minimal due process in most states guarantees the student two rights. The first is the right to be notified both of the charges and of the evidence that will be relied on to prove them. Notice does not have to be in writing, but it should be communicated in a timely fashion so that the student can prepare a response. The second is the right to be heard in response to the charges. This does not require a full, formal adversary hearing, in which the student is represented by an attorney. An informal meeting with the principal may suffice.

Some states go considerably further, at least for major sanctions like expulsion. They may give the student a right to be represented by a lawyer, require that the hearing take place before an impartial fact finder or tribunal, and ensure the right to cross-examine witnesses. These protections are not guaranteed by the Constitution; they depend on state law and on policies adopted by local school boards. Thus there is considerable variation among districts, particularly regarding the right to cross-examine witnesses. The level of formality and the extent of due process required may also differ depending on the severity of the sanction. While most states require that a case be heard before suspension or expulsion occurs, some allow a "summary suspension" for up to five days before a hearing if a student poses a threat to the health, safety, or morals of others.

Remedies for Violations of Students' Disciplinary Rights

What can you do if your child is the victim of an unfair or illegal disciplinary measure? The first step is to try to forestall punishment by availing yourself of any procedural mechanisms provided by the school or

CORPORAL PUNISHMENT

Schools have traditionally had the right to inflict corporal punishment on students to maintain discipline. Today more than half the states have forbidden the practice completely, others if parents object, but many still allow it. According to Department of Education statistics, more than half a million students were subjected to corporal punishment at least once during the 1991–92 school year. In 1977 the Supreme Court heard a case claiming that corporal punishment in school constituted "cruel and unusual punishment" and violated other constitutional rights. The Court disagreed, but it left open the possibility that punishment in a particular case might be so excessive as to violate a student's rights.

Where corporal punishment is permitted, it still must be reasonable, taking into account the age and sex of the child, the child's physical state, the seriousness of the offense, the teacher's reasons, the student's prior behavior and attitude, and the availability of other means of discipline. Courts have tolerated surprisingly extensive corporal punishment. In one case, a court found no violation of rights after a teacher had spanked a nine-year-old seven times in the space of thirty minutes, causing severe bruising. Most states would probably consider punishment that results in serious pain or bruising to be excessive, but cases involving the use of paddles have been upheld in the face of constitutional challenges.

school board, such as the hearings discussed above. But if you believe a sanction has been imposed on your child in violation of the Constitution, state law, or the local school board's own policies, you may want to pursue an action in court. Federal law as well as the law in your particular state may provide a basis for such a suit, depending on the type of violation. Usually you can seek removal of the sanction and reinstatement in good standing if your child did not in fact commit the infraction of which he or she is accused. Monetary compensation for a constitutional violation is available regardless of whether your child is actually guilty, but you may only obtain a token amount (called "nominal damages") unless you demonstrate that actual injury to your child resulted from the violation.

You should also be aware that you may face a substantial obstacle to suing. Most states provide that school boards or at least their individual members are immune from suits, which means they simply cannot be sued. Teachers also have immunity, but as we've seen before, they lose that protection if their behavior is "willful or wanton," that is, if it is malicious or grossly exceeds their authority. If you are thinking of suing, a lawyer, particularly one experienced in education or civil rights law, can advise you on whether and how to proceed.

PUBLIC HEALTH ISSUES

In addition to educating our children, schools today often have the responsibility for tackling serious public health problems faced by young people.

Immunizations and Testing

As a prerequisite to enrolling in public school, all children must receive certain immunizations that protect against highly contagious and serious illnesses. (For more on these immunizations, see chapter 4.) Schools also test children for tuberculosis during the early years of attendance, and they may provide tests for hearing, vision, and color blindness as well.

Sex Education and Condom Distribution Programs

Some of the most important, and most controversial, public health programs provided by schools are those aimed at junior and senior high school students to combat teen pregnancy and sexually transmitted diseases. Many parents believe that they are the appropriate persons to convey information on these sensitive subjects, but many schools have perceived a compelling need to provide education to students on sexual matters, particularly when so many teens are sexually active, teen pregnancy is distressingly widespread, and the number of HIV-infected teens is growing. Consequently, most schools today routinely offer sex education to high school students. Some begin much earlier. Sex education comes in two basic forms: abstinence-only education, which teaches little more than that young people should wait until marriage before having sex, and comprehensive sexuality education (CSE), which covers different types of birth control, in addition to abstinence, and various aspects of human sexual behavior. Approximately seventeen states require CSE, while about thirty encourage development of sex education curricula more generally.

Some parents have objected to mandatory attendance in these CSE classes. In response, many districts now require parental permission as a prerequisite to attendance or allow children to opt out at their parents' request. Although there have been cases challenging compulsory sex education programs without consent or opt-out provisions, courts considering the issue have upheld the programs on two grounds: First, courts have concluded that the state's compelling interest in ensuring uniform sex education for children outweighs parents' constitutional interest in controlling their children's upbringing. Second, courts have found that mere exposure of children to "distasteful ideas" does not violate the right of parents to control their children's religious development, which is guaranteed by the free exercise clause of the First Amendment, as we discussed earlier. A recent case appears to push the concept of "distasteful ideas" to the limit. According to the allegations of the complaint, an AIDS awareness program put on for high school students by a company called Hot, Sexy & Safer Productions contained sexually explicit language, skits, and props; advocated and condoned oral sex, masturbation, homosexual activity, and condom use; and invited participation by the minors in the audience. Nonetheless, a federal court near Boston found the school district had not violated the constitutional rights of parents or students by sponsoring the program, even though no parental consent or opt-out was required.

The desire to interrupt the spread of HIV has prompted numerous school districts and hundreds of junior and senior high schools to distribute condoms to students who request them. A survey of condom programs in the early 1990s revealed that approximately 40 percent did not mandate parental consent prior to distribution, 20 percent did, and 40 percent allowed parents to opt out by preventing their children from utilizing the service. Gallup polls from around the same time indicate that around 60 percent of the parents surveyed supported condom distribution programs, although about 20 percent of those believed parental consent should be required. Still, these statistics indicate that a considerable percentage of parents oppose condom distribution altogether. What can a parent who objects do? Consider the following case. Jason is a sixteen-year-old high school student. While preparing the laundry, his mother discovers a condom in his pocket. When she confronts Jason with it, he claims he obtained it free of charge at school. Angered, Jason's mother calls the principal and lodges a protest with the school board, seeking eradication of the condom distribution program. Can Jason's mom legally challenge the program? If not, can she at least prevent the school from providing condoms to Jason?

In most places, there are no definitive answers to these questions. Condom programs in the public schools raise the same complicated legal issues that sex education programs raise. In addition, minors' rights to make their own decisions regarding health in a very personal matter come into play. Only two courts have addressed the issue so far, and they have reached opposite conclusions. A New York appellate court struck down a voluntary condom distribution program in the New York City public schools. The court found that the program was a health program, not an educational program, and that parental consent for treatment was therefore required. Further, it ruled that failure to insist on parental consent infringed the parents' constitutional right to control their children's upbringing. In the court's view, the state's interest in protecting teens from AIDS through condom use was not overriding because young people can buy condoms elsewhere. Because the program was voluntary, however, the court rejected the claim that it infringed the parents' freedom of religion.

In a second, more recent case, the Massachusetts Supreme Judicial Court came to a different conclusion. The case it heard also concerned a voluntary condom distribution program without provision for parental consent or opt-out. Nonetheless, the court found that since the program was voluntary, it did not infringe either the parents' religious rights or their parental rights. By providing condoms upon student request, the court said, the school arguably was doing nothing but offering a service; it was not compelling, coercing, or mandating that children avail themselves of the service in contravention of their parents' wishes.

While the courts continue to struggle with the extent of parental involvement required in these programs, it seems that sex education and condom distribution at schools may be having an effect on young people's behavior. A recent survey by the National Center for Health Statistics revealed a decrease in teen sexual activity and a dramatic increase in the use of condoms by those who were sexually active. From the 1970s to the 1990s, the number of teenage women saying they had used condoms during their first sexual experience increased from 18 percent to 54 percent.

AIDS in Schools

As the foregoing discussion indicates, the majority of states and most large school districts require schools to provide some form of AIDS education. What about students who have AIDS or are infected with HIV? In the mid-1980s, when news of AIDS entered the public consciousness, many misconceptions were common, and innocent schoolchildren and their families were victimized as a result. Ryan White was one such child. Diagnosed at thirteen with AIDS, which he apparently contracted from a blood transfusion he received to treat his hemophilia, he was prohibited from entering the seventh grade in a public school when his condition became known. He challenged the prohibition in court and ultimately won. Federal legislation now protects HIV-positive children from discrimination in education.

Can a school expel or segregate your child just because he is HIV positive or has AIDS? No. Do you have any legal obligation to disclose your child's status to your school? No, again. You may want to tell certain persons, like the school principal or the school nurse, since one of them may have to administer medication to your child during the school day, but you can make this decision after consultation with your child's pediatrician. You should be aware, though, that even if you choose not to disclose your child's status to his school or school district, in some states the public health department may be required by law to do so if they find out.

Since AIDS is a fatal disease, parents understandably want to protect their children from it. It is important to understand that HIV is not an infection transmitted by casual contact, like a cold or the flu. HIV is transmitted through the intermingling of blood or blood products or other bodily fluids, particularly semen, from an infected person to a non-infected person. The three ways to transmit the virus are through sexual contact, through contaminated blood or blood products, and through contaminated needles. HIV and AIDS are not contracted through touching, hugging, or sharing food. Although transmission through biting is theoretically possible, no confirmed cases have been reported. For these reasons, children who attend school with HIV-positive classmates are not at risk of becoming infected.

RACE AND SEX DISCRIMINATION

Race Discrimination

In 1954 the Supreme Court handed down one of the most important and far-reaching decisions in the history of the Court, *Brown v. Board of Education.* In *Brown,* the Court declared that "separate is inherently unequal" and pronounced the system of legally mandated segregated public schools operating in the southern United States to be unconstitutional. The Court directed those districts with segregated schools to integrate "with all deliberate speed." But only after years passed and violent confrontations occurred at some southern schools did the process of desegregation begin.

Numerous lawsuits were brought based on *Brown* to force school districts to remedy their segregation problems and create fully integrated, unitary districts. The Civil Rights Act of 1964 provided further support for the desegregation effort by depriving segregated schools of federal funds. Unfortunately, these enforcement attempts sometimes proved of questionable efficacy and provoked bitter opposition. As a result, decades later school districts across the country are still trying to fulfill the Court's mandate. While de jure segregation—segregation explicitly required by state law—has been completely dismantled, de facto segregation, or segregation in actual practice or effect, still plagues much of our nation.

One of the most controversial methods of desegregating schools has been busing. To save the time and cost of transportation, school districts usually assign students to the schools that are closest to where they live. In districts with segregated housing patterns, this practice has led to segregated schools. Where these patterns have been the result of de jure discrimination or even de facto segregation resulting from intentional discrimination, some courts have ordered that children be bused from their homes to schools as far as twenty miles away in order to integrate a district. The premise of busing is that if minority children are enrolled in predominantly white schools, their academic achievement will improve simply by virtue of the integration.

In some communities, busing has worked and continues to operate. But today it has largely been discredited as an effective solution to segregation. It is very expensive and apparently has not provided minority students with the expected educational improvements. Many educators now believe minority children are better served by enhanced programs at schools closer to home. Some supporters of busing still remain, though, and their view is bolstered by studies showing not only that integration helps some minority children without harming white children, but also that integrated education helps children of all races learn to live and work together as adults.

Although courts today can still order busing in certain situations, districts that have integrated to the maximum extent possible no longer need to bus their students. Even if de facto segregation remains in these districts as a result of economic forces and housing patterns, as long as those forces and patterns do not reflect intentional discrimination on the part of the district, no busing is required.

Nonetheless, districts composed primarily of one-race schools may be challenged in court. If they are, they must demonstrate that the composition of the schools results solely from demographic forces unrelated to any discrimination and that the schools with predominantly minority enrollment offer substantially the same curriculum, services, and facilities as those with mainly white students. But the existence of a few one-race schools within a district probably will not lead to a court-imposed remedy.

If a court does find impermissible segregation within a school district, it has a number of options for dealing with the problem besides busing. These include changing attendance zones, imposing additional taxes to improve minority schools, and building new schools in strategic areas to encourage integration. A popular method of facilitating desegregation has been the establishment of magnet schools. These schools, found typically in large urban areas, offer special programs designed to draw students of all races from all parts of a district by virtue of their unique curricula. For example, one magnet school may emphasize the sciences while another emphasizes the arts. These schools can be difficult to get into because many employ selective admissions criteria and aim for diversity by adopting explicit numerical targets for students of different backgrounds.

Sex Discrimination

The Constitution prohibits discrimination based on sex. Federal law, specifically Title IX of the Civil Rights Act, expressly prohibits sex discrimination in public as well as most private schools receiving federal funds. In addition, about one-third of the states have equal rights amendments (ERAs) that forbid sex-based discrimination in education. Some states have interpreted their ERA to prohibit any distinction based on sex, but others will allow distinctions in certain situations.

These laws generally prohibit public schools from segregating students by sex, but there are some exceptions. Schools that have been single-sex since their inception may continue to operate that way, as can groups like the YMCA, the Boy Scouts, and the Girl Scouts. Although some districts have attempted to establish separate boys' and

SINGLE-SEX CLASSES—
HELPFUL REFORM OR ILLEGAL DISCRIMINATION?

A number of school districts across the country have begun offering separate classes for girls—some in all academic subjects, others just in math and science. The districts were inspired by research suggesting that single-sex classes may improve girls' performance. Some educators and school administrators believe that single-sex classes also facilitate boys' learning by decreasing distractions, and anecdotal evidence indicates that these classes are generating higher test scores overall. However, the legal status of single-sex classes in public schools is open to question. Some allege that the classes violate the Constitution, Title IX, and state antidiscrimination laws, and a few districts have ceased offering the classes, fearing legal repercussions. Other districts, relying on the fact that single-sex classes are voluntary, serve a legitimate educational purpose, and cover the same course content as coed classes, continue to offer them without legal challenge. The Department of Education has offered conflicting rulings, and no definitive court ruling has settled the matter yet.

girls' schools for gifted children, these have largely been found to be unconstitutional. One such school, the Young Women's Leadership School in East Harlem, New York, opened in 1996, prompting legal challenge by women's and civil liberties groups. Some districts are now offering single-sex classes, but the future of these classes is uncertain (see box above).

The prohibition against sex discrimination in education extends to curricular matters. With a couple of exceptions, which we will discuss shortly, schools cannot offer different courses to students based on their sex. So, for example, a high school cannot prevent Ricardo from taking home economics or Elena from taking auto mechanics. However, informal barriers in the form of guidance counseling and peer pressure continue to inhibit students, especially girls, from pursuing nontraditional educational paths. To encourage students not to be limited by sex stereotypes, some states have enacted laws prohibiting the use of materials that negatively affect children because of their sex, and a number have adopted policies favoring the use of nonsexist teaching materials.

Elementary and secondary school sports is an area in which sex discrimination has been rampant. Consider the following hypothetical case. Ashley is a thirteen-year-old girl who would like to play baseball on her junior high team. The coach has informed her that tryouts for the team are open only to boys. Does Ashley have a legal right to try out for the team?

Times have certainly changed. In the space of one generation, the number of female high school students involved in sports has risen from three hundred thousand to almost 2.5 million. This dramatic change has been made possible largely by Title IX, which prohibits elementary and secondary schools from running separate physical education programs based on sex. A similar rule applies to extracurricular and intramural sports. However, there is a major exception to these laws for contact sports. Since baseball has been recognized as a contact sport by the courts, the coach could legally exclude Ashley. On the other hand, nothing in Title IX prohibits the coach from permitting her to try out and to play if she is good enough. Moreover, in some states that have adopted an equal rights amendment, districts may have to allow girls to participate in contact sports if they are capable of competing.

Ashley might try arguing that the school should have a girls' baseball (or at least a softball) team if girls are not permitted to play on the boys' baseball team. This argument could be persuasive since schools have a legal obligation under Title IX to provide comparable facilities, equipment, practice schedules, and programs to male and female students.

Now let's compare Ashley's case with her brother Matthew's. Matthew is a sixteen-year-old who became interested in playing volleyball after watching the U.S. men's team in the Olympics. Unfortunately, his high school only offers girls' volleyball. Does Matt have a

THE RIGHTS OF PREGNANT STUDENTS

Can a girl be expelled from school or sent to a special class because she is pregnant? No. Title IX and the Constitution prohibit schools from discriminating against pregnant students, as do many state laws. Consequently, schools cannot impose disciplinary sanctions on pregnant students, nor can they compel them to attend special classes separate from the rest of the student body, although they may offer that option. In one case, however, a court did uphold a school's decision to expel a pregnant student from the honor society on the basis that premarital sex was inconsistent with the standards of the organization.

legal right to try out for the girls' team? Possibly yes, since Title IX and other antidiscrimination laws apply to male as well as female students. However, more than one court has refused to allow a boy to join a girls' volleyball team on the grounds that separate women's teams compensate for past discrimination and help to ensure equal opportunity. If boys are allowed to play on girls' teams, the concern is that they will so dominate that girls will effectively be deprived of an equal opportunity to play interscholastic sports.

While gains have surely been made in promoting equality in athletics, much remains to be done. A survey of the top ten high school sports in 1996 by the National Federation of State High School Associations indicated that less than 40 percent of the participants were girls. Moreover, discrimination in high school sports now frequently takes a more subtle form—buying new equipment and uniforms for the boys' teams but not the girls', for instance, or sending cheerleaders and marching bands only to boys' games. The Department of Education's Office of Civil Rights (OCR) has the power to remedy these problems, but it acts only when a complaint is filed, suffers from lack of funding, and apparently has never actually cut off funds to a district for this kind of violation. However, it has prompted changes by schools when persistent parents have fought for them. To contact OCR for more information or to file a complaint, see the box on page 82.

Sexual Harassment in School

A high school student suffers repeated harassment by a teacher and coach, beginning with sexual conversations, fondling, and forced kissing and culminating in forced intercourse between the teacher and student. The school district does nothing.

A seven-year-old girl is taunted on the school bus with lewd comments concerning her sexual organs, urgings by boys on the bus to perform oral sex on her father, and threats to hurt her with rubber knives.

A seventh-grade girl is mocked on a daily basis for over a year by groups of boys who call her "Hot Dog Slut," who make remarks like "I hear you have a hot dog in your pants," and who openly state in English class, "This question is for Jane. Did you have sex with a hot dog?" The school's response to her repeated complaints? "Boys will be boys."

These are just a few of the growing number of cases of students in elementary and secondary school who are subjected to sexual harassment by teachers or, more commonly, by their peers. A 1993 survey conducted by the Educational Foundation of the American Association of University Women (AAUW) revealed widespread sexual harassment by peers in grades eight through eleven. Of the approximately sixteen hundred students surveyed, more than 80 percent reported being the victim of some form of sexual harassment, ranging from sexual comments, jokes, gestures, and looks to being touched, pinched, or purposefully brushed against in a sexual way. Students reported being the target of sexual rumors, being the subject of graphic sexual messages on bathroom walls, and being spied on while dressing or showering at school. While both boys and girls reported being the victims of such harassment, by far girls were the more common targets. About 25 percent of those harassed claimed the harassment happened frequently. A national study conducted in 1992 revealed similar results with almost 40 percent of the girls harassed reporting that they experienced harassment

SEXUAL HARASSMENT ON CAMPUS

What can you do if your child is being sexually harassed at school? The first step, of course, is to create an environment in which he or she feels comfortable telling you about it. Many students don't report incidents of harassment to anyone because they are embarrassed, they do not believe anyone will do anything, or they fear retaliation. If your child does tell you, take the report seriously and complain to the school principal. Your school may have a policy for handling such complaints. If the harassment continues, maintain a written record of all incidents. If the school does not respond adequately to the problem, you can file a complaint with the Department of Education's Office of Civil Rights (OCR) at:

Office of Civil Rights
330 C Street SW, Room 5000
Washington, DC 20202
202-205-5557

OCR will investigate the charge and instruct the school how to respond. If the school still fails to act, you may consider filing suit under Title IX. A lawyer with knowledge of civil rights, education, or personal injury law should be able to assist you.

on a daily basis. Most said they believed that school officials accepted or even condoned the behavior on the theory that boys will be boys and such behavior is the result of "raging hormones" and therefore simply a normal part of the child development process.

Sexual harassment of schoolchildren is not appropriate behavior and is no laughing or trivial matter, particularly for girls. Sexual harassment contributes to the development of low self-esteem and other emotional problems. The victims may suffer from depression, anxiety, fear, loss of confidence, and feelings of isolation, vulnerability, or helplessness, and they may become permanently alienated from school or stop going to class altogether. Moreover, sexual harassment during the formative school years sets the stage for sexual harassment in the workplace. Boys learn that such behavior will go unpunished, and girls come to expect it, believing that it is normal and that the problem is theirs, not the harassers'.

Only since the early '90s has the law really begun to respond to this problem, and the growing pains are evident. Title IX, the federal law that prohibits sex discrimination in schools receiving federal financial assistance, has now been interpreted to include sexual harassment, and it allows victims of harassment to sue a school district and potentially win monetary compensation if the perpetrator is a school employee, such as a teacher or coach. Of the numerous cases of this type that have been brought on the basis of Title IX, some have yielded damage awards in the tens or even hundreds of thousands of dollars. Other laws may also give the victims of sexual harassment a right to sue individual teachers, administrators, and school officials for damages if the individuals knew of the harassment and failed to address it. Constitutional violations may be involved as well. Suits against a school district may be brought if a student can prove there was a custom or pattern of inaction that showed indifference to his or her rights.

The trickier and more common cases involve peer harassment. Unlike cases of sexual harassment by teachers, which are often based on "quid pro quo" claims—claims that a teacher demanded sex in exchange for a grade, for example—cases of sexual harassment by peers are often based on "hostile environment" claims. These claims seek a remedy for conduct or comments of a sexual nature that create an atmosphere so demeaning that it interferes with a student's ability to obtain an education.

While a number of courts have recognized that Title IX can provide a remedy for victims of hostile environment harassment, the courts considering the issue have disagreed on a number of important points. The first issue is the meaning of sexual harassment in this context. Court cases, legislatures, and school district policies have adopted varying definitions, but the definitions often give little guidance. Confused about what constitutes sexual harassment and their responsibility to prevent or remedy it, some school districts have responded by panicking. In the space of a week in the fall of 1996, two districts in different parts of the country each suspended a student, one six years old and the other seven, on the grounds of sexual harassment for kissing a classmate. The districts' overreaction appalled most observers, and both subsequently reversed their position in the face of public outcry. One revised its sexual harassment policy to be more age appropriate, suspending application of the policy to elementary students unless they exhibit a clear intent to commit harassment of a sexual nature. Meanwhile, other schools continue to ignore the problem. That same week a California sixth-grader who had suffered months of sexual name-calling, violent threats, and obscene gestures from a male classmate won half a million dollars from a jury after the school principal and superintendent repeatedly ignored her parents' complaints and she was forced to transfer to another school. Undoubtedly, school districts will continue to struggle with drawing the line between damaging sexual harassment that requires serious disciplinary measures and behavior by young children that warrants education rather than severe sanction.

To assist in this process, in 1997 the Department of Education's Office of Civil Rights (OCR) published guidelines on sexual harassment. The guidelines define hostile environment harassment as "unwelcome sexual advances, requests for sexual favors, and other verbal, nonverbal, or physical conduct of a sexual nature . . . that is sufficiently severe, persistent, or pervasive to limit a student's ability to participate in or benefit from an education program or activity, or to create a hostile or abusive educational environment." Although this definition is still rather vague, the guidelines identify specific factors that can help schools and parents determine when sexual harassment is occurring. Some of these include the number of people involved and their ages; the type, frequency, and duration of the conduct; and the location and context of the incidents. The OCR admits that the guidelines do not provide "hard and fast rules," but they do make clear that a kiss on a cheek by a first-grader does not constitute sexual harassment.

The second issue is deciding when liability can be imposed on a school district for behavior perpetrated by students against other students. Some federal courts (and the OCR guidelines) have said that a school district can be liable under Title IX for peer sexual harassment if it "knew or should have known" about the harassment and failed to take reasonable steps to prevent it. Other courts, including federal appellate courts, have ruled that the victim must prove that the school intended to discriminate on the basis of sex. Yet these courts have not agreed on what constitutes such intent. One court has declared that intentional discrimination is established if the victim proves "active encouragement of peer harassment, the toleration of the harassing behavior of male students, or the failure to take adequate steps to deter or punish peer harassment." But another court recognizes liability only if the district "knew of the harassment and intentionally failed to take proper remedial action." Other courts have applied an even more difficult test: The victim must prove that the school district responded to sexual harassment claims differently based on sex. If the administration punished sexual harassment of boys but ignored sexual harassment of girls, the plaintiff might prevail under this standard. But if the school ignored sexual harassment altogether, the plaintiff would lose.

It will surely take some time for courts to resolve these issues. In the meantime, we can be encouraged that the problem is finally receiving attention.

Gay and Lesbian Issues at School

The treatment of homosexuality and of gay and lesbian students in school is one of the most hotly contested issues in public education today. In generations past, the subject of homosexuality was rarely mentioned in school, and gay students and teachers were virtually invisible. In recent years, as prominent individuals in all walks of life—politics, the arts, entertainment, medicine, law, sports—have identified themselves as gay ("come out," in common parlance) and as the law in many places has shown increasing tolerance toward gays and lesbians in certain settings, issues involving homosexuality have arisen in our schools. This development has been furthered by the widespread adoption of curricula dealing with AIDS, which we discussed earlier in this chapter.

The debate about homosexuality in schools centers on three main issues: curricula concerning homosexuality, support and protection for gay students, and the right of gay teachers to remain in the classroom. With the introduction of sex education and AIDS prevention education, some secondary schools have begun to include discussions of homosexuality in their curricula. As we've already seen, sex education in and of itself causes some parents discomfort; add consideration of homosexuality and the situation can become volatile. In response, a number of states and local school boards, spurred on by conservative and religious organizations, have adopted regulations dictating how schools will—or will not—deal with homosexuality. Some of these rules ban any discussion or mention of homosexuality, period. Others allow discussion of the issue, but only from one of two perspectives: either teachers are forbidden to say anything positive about homosexuality or in any way to indicate that it is acceptable, or they must affirmatively stress that homosexuality is unacceptable.

Restrictions such as these have led teachers to censor their discussions of important matters across the curriculum from history to literature to science. In a New Hampshire town, for example, a high school English teacher stopped showing a film on the life of the great American poet Walt Whitman because it mentions that he was gay. Likewise, Shakespeare's *Twelfth Night* was purged from the curriculum because the play has a character who is gay. A group of parents and civil liberties organizations has sued to stop this kind of censorship, and they make a strong argument that these policies, by requiring schools to enforce and present a particular viewpoint, violate the First Amendment. In another New Hampshire town, an English teacher was fired for distributing books containing homosexual characters, such as E. M. Forster's *Maurice,* in violation of a district policy against mentioning homosexuality "in a positive light." She is fighting her dismissal in court.

FOR MORE ON GAY AND LESBIAN ISSUES

If your child is gay or lesbian, there are a number of organizations that you can turn to for information and help with the problems that he or she may face at school or elsewhere: the Hetrick-Martin Institute offers counseling, outreach programs, an accredited high school, and high school equivalency programs for gay and lesbian youth; Parents, Families, and Friends of Lesbians and Gays provides information, outreach, and support; the Gay and Lesbian Parents Coalition International sponsors conferences, publishes a newsletter for parents and children, furnishes an antihomophobia video for elementary schoolchildren, and offers support; and the Lambda Legal Defense and Education Fund provides advice, support, and referrals regarding legal actions on behalf of gays. The addresses and phone numbers of these organizations are listed below.

Hetrick-Martin Institute
2 Astor Place
New York, NY 10003-6998
212-674-2400

Parents, Families, and Friends of Lesbians and Gays
1101 14th Street NW, Suite 1030
Washington, DC 20005
202-638-4200

Gay and Lesbian Parents Coalition International (GLPCI)
P.O. Box 50360
Washington, DC 20091
202-583-8029

Lambda Legal Defense and Education Fund
120 Wall Street
New York, NY 10005
212-809-8585

Policies restricting discussion about homosexuality may reflect the earnest desire of some parents to control their children's exposure to sensitive issues; these parents feel that certain subjects are more appropriately discussed at home than in school. Other parents, however, fear that discussion of homosexuality or acknowledgment that prominent individuals, real or fictional, are gay will somehow serve to "recruit" their children to that lifestyle. Such fears are unfounded. Although much is still unknown about the cause of homosexuality, most experts (and many gays and lesbians themselves) believe that sexual orientation is established in early childhood and is probably genetically influenced.

Unfortunately, repressive policies regarding homosexuality tend to breed misinformation. Particularly in light of the dangers posed by AIDS, this can be dangerous; students need accurate information. Moreover, repressive policies breed intolerance and ignore the very real needs of gay students. No one knows for certain how many high school students are gay. Some of the students themselves, those who are in a state of confusion or denial or afraid to admit their homosexuality, may not even know they are gay. Nevertheless, researchers estimate that as much as 10 percent of the adult population is gay, and an equivalent percentage of high school students may also be gay. These students are at risk from the hostility and prejudice they encounter at school. A 1990 study of five hundred gay youths found that 40 percent reported suffering violent physical attacks. Gay students also suffer frequent verbal harassment and ridicule that is often ignored by teachers and administrators but would be dealt with harshly if directed at racial or ethnic minorities.

The inhospitability of the secondary school environment to gay students leads to cutting school and, for some, to dropping out. Even more disturbing, a report by the Secretary of Health and Human Services' Task Force on Youth Suicide found that gay young people are two to three times more likely to attempt suicide than their peers and may constitute as much as 30 percent of completed suicides among this group annually. Those studying gay youth and working with this population believe that the suicide rate reflects not the intrinsic quality of being gay, but the tremendous burden of societal prejudice and family rejection shouldered by these young people.

Concerned about the risks to young gays and lesbians, some school districts have undertaken innovative programs to help these students remain in school. A few large urban districts like Los Angeles, Minneapolis–St. Paul, and Seattle have counselors and support groups available for gay students. New York and Los Angeles also have small alternative public high schools for students who have been driven out of other schools by gay bashing. The Eagles Center, a Los Angeles school, even sponsors a prom for gay students.

In some places, gay students now have explicit legal protection from harassment. A number of school districts have adopted antidiscrimination policies on their behalf. At the state level, Massachusetts was the first to ban discrimination against gay students in public schools. It has also implemented a plan encouraging school districts to devise policies to protect gay students from harassment, and it requires sensitivity training for teachers in the state. Other states may follow suit since a twenty-one-year-old man from Wisconsin won nine hundred thousand dollars in 1996 from the Ashland School District as compensation for years of abuse he suffered while in school because he was openly gay. Starting in seventh grade and lasting until he dropped out in eleventh grade, Jamie Nabozny was continually harassed by classmates who hurled epithets like "fag" and "queer" at him, threw objects at him, urinated on him, and beat him. Nabozny attempted suicide and was eventually diagnosed with post-traumatic stress disorder because of the abuse. Although repeatedly informed of the harassment, the administration allegedly did nothing to protect Nabozny. He subsequently sued, and a federal court jury ultimately concluded that his rights had been violated. Before the jury reached a decision on how much money to award him, Nabozny and the school district arrived at a settlement.

Sadly, not all states or school districts have sought to promote tolerance and ease the plight of their gay students. Most districts continue to ignore the problem, and some have actively forbidden gay groups from meeting. In 1996, for example, Utah passed a law banning all gay student clubs after a Salt Lake City school board had banned all student clubs in order to prevent a Gay-Straight Alliance from meeting.

The situation for gay teachers has not been much better than it has for students. Until recently, a gay teacher could be fired with impunity just for being gay, but a few states and municipalities have now enacted laws protecting gays and lesbians from such blatant discrimination based on sexual orientation. While the trend continues in the direction of tolerance, a strong backlash has also been generated with initiatives seeking to prevent gays and lesbians from acquiring legal protection through the legislative process. One such initiative from Colorado was struck down by the Supreme Court. Issues involving gays and lesbians in school and elsewhere will no doubt continue to generate controversy and garner public attention.

SCHOOL RECORDS

The Family Educational Rights and Privacy Act, commonly known as FERPA, gives parents the right to review all official school records and files directly related to their child. FERPA also gives parents the right to contest and seek correction of any inaccuracies in the record. FERPA applies to any school receiving federal funds. These rights belong to parents until their child is eighteen, at which point the rights shift to the adult child. Either parent has the right to inspect the records even if the parents are divorced and one parent has visitation rights only.

What documents or information are covered by FERPA? According to the law, any record "directly related" to a student is covered, regardless of where it came from. Such records would certainly include report cards, standardized test scores, the results of psychological tests and other evaluations performed by school personnel, attendance records, and disciplinary records. If your child is involved in an experimental teaching program at school, you also have the right to inspect any educational materials used in the program. However, you don't have the right to see evaluations of teachers, their notes, or reports of criminal activity at school.

Your child's school has an obligation to notify you of your rights under FERPA and how you might exercise them. You must be allowed to review the records within a reasonable time after making a request, but the law explicitly provides that the school can take up to forty-five days to comply. You also have a right to have the records explained to you, if necessary. Moreover, if you live out of the area and cannot inspect the records at the school, the school has an obligation to provide you with copies, although you may have to pay for them if you can afford to.

It's a good idea to make an appointment to review your child's records regularly. Most of the records will be in your child's cumulative file, but some may be stored elsewhere, such as in the nurse's office or the principal's office if your child has had a recent health or disciplinary problem. If, while reviewing the records, you discover information that you believe is inaccurate, FERPA gives you the right to seek amendment and correction of that information. Note, though, that you cannot seek amendment to challenge a grade your child has received unless you believe it is an error not intended by your child's teacher.

You should request amendment of the record in writing even though you are not technically required to do so. The school must then let you know in a reasonable time whether the record will be changed in accordance with your request. If the school denies your request, you have the right to a hearing. The school should provide you with advance notice of the date and time of the hearing and give you a chance during the hearing to present any evidence supporting your request. You have a right to have an attorney at this hearing, but you have to bear the cost of legal representation yourself. The school must give you a decision within a reasonable period of time. If the school agrees with your request, it will simply amend the record. If it denies your request, you have no right to appeal, but you do have the right to add a statement of disagreement to

---

REPORTING VIOLATIONS OF FERPA

The Department of Education's Family Policy Compliance Office is the agency charged with enforcing the Family Educational Rights and Privacy Act (FERPA). This office should be able to assist you in exercising your rights under FERPA.

Family Policy Compliance Office
600 Independence Avenue SW
Washington, DC 20202-4605
202-260-3887

---

the record. Your statement will accompany any release of your child's records by the school.

In addition to giving you the right of access to your child's school records, FERPA protects the records from unauthorized disclosure. Before the school can release any educational records concerning your child, it must have your consent. The consent should specify which records are to be released and to whom. When releasing the records, the school should inform the recipient that he or she may not disclose them to anyone else without express permission.

Under certain circumstances, however, the school may disclose the records without your permission. For instance, it may disclose them to other school or district personnel with a legitimate educational interest in your child. It may also disclose routine identifying information, such as your child's name, address, and phone number, and the awarding of any degrees. And of course if the records are sought pursuant to a court order or subpoena, the school must generally comply. Even in the last case, though, FERPA requires that you be notified. So if law enforcement has subpoenaed the records, you won't be able to stop the disclosure, but at least you will know about it.

What can you do if your child's school has denied you your FERPA rights by refusing to allow you access to the records or by impermissibly disclosing them without your consent? If a school violates FERPA, it risks losing any federal funding it receives, but FERPA does not give you any right to sue for damages. Some courts have allowed aggrieved parents to sue for damages based on a civil rights violation under a different law, but there is disagreement on this point as well. You can, however, lodge a complaint with the U.S. Department of Education's Family Policy Compliance Office in Washington, D.C., within six months of learning of the violation (see box on page 92). The compliance office will probably be able to convince the school to satisfy your request if it is legitimate. Apparently no school has ever lost its funding for refusing to comply with the office's instructions.

SPECIAL EDUCATION AND DISABLED CHILDREN

As recently as a generation ago, children with physical and mental disabilities of all types languished at home or in institutions without access to any education unless their parents were wealthy enough to afford private schooling. All that has changed dramatically as a result of several federal laws guaranteeing the right of all children to a free public education. The laws establish several fundamental principles: that disabled children have a right to a free public education tailored to meet their individual needs, that they are entitled to due process in the procedures used to assess and develop plans for their education, and that discrimination against them is impermissible. All states are governed by these laws.

Finding Out if Your Child Is Disabled under the Law

If you are the parent of a disabled child, the law that will be of most interest to you in navigating the special education system is the Individuals with Disabilities Education Act (IDEA). Your child has substantial legal rights to receive an appropriate education, but working your way through the bureaucratic process to ensure that your child gets the education to which he or she is entitled may take considerable effort and perseverance on your part.

The first step is to have your child identified as disabled under IDEA. IDEA defines disabled children as those with any of the following conditions who, because of the conditions, need special education and related services: mental retardation; hearing, speech or language, vision, orthopedic, or other health impairments; serious emotional disturbances; autism; traumatic brain injuries; and specific learning disabilities. This definition also includes preschoolers from ages three to five who have physical, cognitive, communicative, social, emotional, or adaptive developmental delays.

Although there has been some disagreement about whether IDEA covers attention deficit disorder (ADD), attention deficit hyperactive disorder (ADHD), and dyslexia, most courts now define these as covered disabilities as well. Courts have excluded some children from coverage, among them those requiring psychiatric hospitalization or round-the-clock nursing care and those who aren't really seriously disturbed but are socially maladjusted or show poor judgment or impulse control.

How do you find out if your child has a covered disability? You may suspect a problem if your child lags significantly behind other students, has trouble listening and communicating, has difficulty interacting with other children or behaving appropriately, seems unhappy, or is anxious about attending school. Any of these may be signs that your child should be evaluated. If you believe your child may have a covered disability, you should contact his school to arrange for the appropriate evaluation. You can usually have your child evaluated even before he reaches school age. Most schools will begin identifying children as disabled as early as three years of age, some even younger, but of course you will need to request the evaluation.

Once the preliminary evaluation is complete, the school may be able to resolve the problem after conducting a prereferral strategy session with you and your child's teacher. Perhaps a tutor is all that is necessary.

If the problem is not amenable to minor adjustment, the school will arrange for evaluation of your child by an interdisciplinary team, including at least one teacher and perhaps a school psychologist or health care worker who can conduct speech, hearing, vision, or other tests that might yield pertinent information. The school cannot conduct this evaluation without your written consent. Some parents have great difficulty acknowledging that their child may have a disability. In cases such as these, some states allow the school to call for a hearing to decide whether your child should be evaluated without your consent. However, anytime the school seeks to evaluate your child, it must notify you in writing of the impetus for evaluation and describe the proposed tests. You should make sure that any testing is performed by a trained professional using approved, validated tests and that the tests accurately reveal your child's abilities and achievements. The school district should not rely on any one test to determine whether your child is disabled.

If you don't agree with the results of the school's evaluation, you have the right to review all records concerning your child and request amendment of those records if you feel they contain misleading or inaccurate information. You can also request an independent evaluation at the state's expense. If the school refuses and convenes a hearing on the matter, the hearing officer may find in your favor and require that the independent evaluation be done. If the hearing officer finds the school's evaluation to be sufficient, you can still have your own evaluation done, but you will have to bear the cost yourself. Nonetheless, the school will be obligated to consider the additional evaluation in planning your child's education.

The Individualized Education Program (IEP)

Once your child is identified as disabled under the law, what services is she entitled to receive from the government? The general standard is that the school district must provide a learning environment that provides some educational benefit. This does not mean that it has to place your child in the program you support or the one that maximizes your child's potential. The law attempts to balance the cost constraints of the state education system against the needs of disabled students. Consequently, all the school district must do is give your child the opportunity to derive educational benefits—in other words, to make more than minimal, trivial progress. In order to satisfy this standard, the school district may have to provide more than a special education teacher and a classroom. Your child's disability may require attendance at a special school or auxiliary services to ensure that she derives educational benefit. These auxiliary services might include transportation to a special school or program; speech pathology, audiology, or psychological services; physical therapy; or certain diagnostic and evaluative medical services.

How do you know which of these services should be provided for your child? Within thirty days of identifying your child as disabled under the law, the school district must develop a written individualized education program for him, usually referred to as an IEP. The IEP is probably the most critical step in the process of obtaining an appropriate education for your child. Every qualified disabled child is entitled to an IEP that will combine instruction with any necessary support services to ensure that the child receives "educational benefits."

What is contained in the IEP? The IEP covers six basic issues:

1. your child's current level of academic performance
2. a description of annual and short-term goals
3. a statement of the specific educational and related services to be provided and a statement regarding the extent of the child's involvement with regular classes
4. projected dates for beginning and terminating services
5. delineation of objective procedures and schedules for evaluating whether the goals of the IEP have been met
6. enumeration of any needed transition services to assist children sixteen and older in moving from the educational environment to the workforce and independent living, if feasible

Who draws up the IEP? The IEP is a group effort, and the makeup of the group is very important. Usually you will meet with your child's teacher(s), a representative of the local educational agency who will supervise the IEP, and any additional persons who have evaluated your child. Your child may also be included if it's appropriate. Both parents have a right to be present at the IEP conference, and both should receive notice of the meeting in sufficient time to enable them to attend and participate. You have a right to be actively involved in drafting the IEP. If you discover the meeting has occurred without you, you should call the school and demand a hearing to obtain another meeting. If either parent is not properly notified and thus fails to attend, the IEP will be subject to challenge. You and the school district must agree on any plan for your child; however, if you cannot come to agreement, there are procedures to appeal the school's decision. We'll discuss those shortly.

What considerations and standards will determine which services will be provided by the IEP? There are two governing principles for the IEP. First, the IEP must place your child in an educational setting with nondisabled students to the extent possible. This is known as mainstreaming. Mainstreaming has been a very controversial approach to educating the disabled. Proponents of mainstreaming argue that contact with nondisabled children facilitates the education of the disabled by stimulating them to learn, that it provides nondisabled children with a valuable opportunity to learn about and interact with the disabled, and that it helps reduce the stigma associated with being disabled. Critics of mainstreaming charge that it provides little educational benefit to the disabled child, causes disruption in the classroom, drains too much of the teacher's energy and attention from the education of the nondisabled, highlights the differences between the disabled and the nondisabled, and is too expensive.

While the goal of the IEP is clearly to mainstream your child if possible, that will not always be a feasible or appropriate alternative. If your child will not be able to benefit from mainstreaming, if any minor benefits will be outweighed by those available in an alternative, segregated environment, or if your child is simply too disruptive to participate in a regular class, a school district can refuse to mainstream.

Related to mainstreaming is the second fundamental principle guiding the IEP: that your child should be taught in the "least restrictive environment" possible. Placements can range from complete mainstreaming to special classes to home schooling to institutional instruction in a residential facility. A mildly retarded child may need a special class to cover academic material but can enjoy lunch and recess with nondisabled children. In some cases, a child could theoretically function in a regular class but would need comprehensive assistance that is more efficiently and effectively provided in a special school. For example, a school district does not necessarily have to provide every deaf student with a personal sign-language interpreter and other technology to enable her to function in a regular classroom if a school with state-of-the-art programs for the deaf is available nearby. Remember, you are not entitled to have your child placed in the closest or best facility; the district need only provide a placement that will result in substantive educational benefit.

Because every child is unique and the law is premised on tailoring education to the needs of the individual, your role in the IEP process is critical. The box on page 99 contains suggestions for maximizing your involvement. You may have to insist that the district focus on your child's individual needs and capabilities. To be an effective advocate for your child, you should fully investigate and understand the nature of his disability, his potential and his limitations, and available educational alternatives. Some children with rather significant disabilities nonetheless can function in a regular classroom with the appropriate assistance. Others will fare much better in a segregated environment. The irony today is that school districts that earlier resisted mainstreaming are promoting it because it is cheaper than the alternative, intensive programs that disabled children may need. Parents currently find themselves fighting *not* to have their children mainstreamed so the children will get the special services and individual attention that will better serve their needs. Meanwhile, financially strapped and dreadfully overcrowded inner-city schools have gone the opposite direction, labeling numerous children as disabled, perhaps excessively,

WHAT CAN PARENTS CONTRIBUTE TO THE IEP PROCESS?

The Council for Exceptional Children provides the following suggestions for maximizing your involvement in the IEP process:

1. Before attending an IEP meeting, make a list of things you want your child to learn so that you are prepared to discuss any differences between your goals and the agency's.

2. Bring any information the school or agency may not already have to the IEP meeting, including medical records, past school records, test or evaluation results, and any notes or personal experiences you have regarding your child's behavior and abilities.

3. Find out what related services are being provided, for example, by professionals other than teachers. Ask each to describe those services and what growth you might expect to see as a result.

4. Ask what you can do at home to support the program.

5. Make sure that the goals and objectives of the IEP are specific and that you understand and agree with each one before signing.

6. Ask for periodic reports on your child's progress. Follow up throughout the year.

7. Regard your child's education as a cooperative effort.

If you and the school cannot agree about your child's needs, ask for another meeting. If conflict still remains, request a mediator or a due process hearing, as described in the text.

to get them into special education classes, reduce regular class sizes, and obtain additional funding.

If your child's needs cannot be adequately met by the public schools, does your child have a right to placement in a private school at government expense? Quite possibly yes. If there really is no suitable public school program to accommodate your child, the district must provide an

FOR MORE ON SPECIAL EDUCATION

To obtain further information about special education or support for your disabled child's educational needs, you should begin by contacting the director of special education in your school district. The department of education in your state may also provide assistance. Numerous national organizations, many with state and local chapters and some focused on specific disabilities, can be invaluable resources, too. A few are listed here.

Council for Exceptional Children
1920 Association Drive
Reston, VA 20191-1589
1-800-CEC-READ or 1-800-232-7323

ERIC Clearinghouse on Disabilities and Gifted Education
1920 Association Drive
Reston, VA 20191-1589
1-800-328-0272
Internet: ericec@inet.ed.gov

National Information Center for Children and Youth with Disabilities
P.O. Box 1492
Washington, DC 20013-1492
1-800-695-0285 or 202-884-8441
Internet:
    e-mail: nichcy@aed.org
    World Wide Web: http//www.nichcy.org

education through private schooling, which may include transporting your child at state expense. The district will be responsible for the costs of the school plus any related costs like room and board and nonmedical care. Moreover, if you choose to send your disabled child to a private religious school at your own expense, the district is allowed to provide funds or services to accommodate her special needs within certain limits. The Supreme Court has held that doing so does not violate the establishment clause of the First Amendment. For example, the Supreme Court has allowed a school district to provide an interpreter for a deaf child attending parochial school.

If IDEA allows school districts to provide services to disabled students attending parochial schools, does it require them to do so? The courts are in disagreement on this point. The traditional view has been that services cannot and need not be provided at a parochial school if comparable services are available at a public school. A district may simply insist that parents transfer their disabled child to a local public school that can provide sufficient educational benefits, or it may instead agree to transport the child from parochial school to public school for special education classes. A few recent cases, though, have ruled that on-site services required on a full-time basis may have to be provided to disabled children in parochial schools even if public school services are available, but at least two of these decisions are on appeal.

The school district must revise the IEP annually. It is not considered a contract between you and the district. The IEP's success will be measured by whether it has given your child a "basic floor of opportunity," not by whether your child has met all the specific educational goals set forth there. The "stay put" rule ensures that your child can remain in the current placement pending revision of the IEP (or be placed in public school pending development of the initial IEP), unless you and the district reach some other agreement. This way, your child will not be deprived of any education while the process is under way.

Your child has the right to receive an education for the same period of time as nondisabled students, which may begin as early as three and last until he is twenty-one, depending on the law in your state. If the district impermissibly cuts off education too soon, your child may be entitled to compensatory education for that period of time. Even if your child completes the standard years of education and meets his IEP goals, though, he is not necessarily entitled to a high school diploma.

Although there has been some disagreement on this point, most courts have affirmed the district's right to require a passing grade on a minimum competency test of all students, including the disabled. In some places, your child may instead earn a "special education" diploma for satisfying the requirements of his IEP.

Discipline and Expulsion of Disabled Students

The law protects your child from being expelled from school for behavior that results directly from her disability. But there is a limitation on this principle: The school is not required to educate a disabled student in a setting where the student poses a danger to herself or others or causes enough disruption to significantly impede the education of other children in the class. In addition, the Supreme Court has said that schools can temporarily suspend disabled students for up to ten days if they pose an immediate danger to others. This does not mean that your child will receive no education. Rather, the district will have to draw up another IEP that prescribes a more appropriate placement, and the IEP may incorporate goals of improvement in behavior. During the ten-day suspension period, if the parents and district cannot agree on a revised placement, the district can seek a court ruling allowing a change, but in order to prevail, it will have to prove that the current placement is "substantially likely to result in injury to the student or others."

When You Don't Agree with the IEP

The law provides for very specific and comprehensive review of agency decisions regarding education of the disabled. If you are dissatisfied with the results of your child's evaluation or the IEP or any other issue related to the education of your child, you have the right to a due process hearing conducted either by the local education agency or by the state. If the local agency holds the hearing, you have the right to appeal to the state for another hearing if the local agency decides against you. The hearing must take place before an impartial official, someone who is not employed by the agency responsible for providing education to your child. The school district should have a list of potential hearing officers for you to review.

You have the right to have an attorney or other advocate at the hearing, and the school district should notify you of low-cost legal assistance that may be available, but it does not have to pay for your attorney. Fortunately, the law provides that if you win your case, either at the administrative stage or in front of a judge, you may be able to recover attorney's fees. But this rule applies only if you win, meaning you obtained the relief you sought and the hearing or litigation was responsible for that success.

Of course there is no requirement that you be represented by counsel. Either way, you have the right to present evidence at the hearing and cross-examine witnesses. You also can stop the school district from using evidence that it did not disclose to you at least five days before the hearing. You have the right to include your child in the hearing and to insist that the hearing be open to the public, but many parents prefer to proceed in private. At the conclusion, you are entitled to receive a written or electronic verbatim transcript of the proceedings and any findings of the hearing officer. The officer must provide you with a final decision within forty-five days after receiving your request.

If you are still not satisfied, you can appeal to the state agency (if your hearing was conducted by a local agency), or you can sue in court. In most circumstances, you will need to go through the hearing process (called "exhausting your administrative remedies") before you will be allowed to sue, although there are some exceptions to this rule. Keep in mind that you may have to sue within a very short time of receiving the agency's decision. The deadline varies by state but can be as soon as thirty days after receiving the decision.

What kind of remedies can you get from suing in court? Not all the states or courts agree. Most will allow you to recover compensatory damages—reimbursement of the costs you've incurred if you succeed in proving that the IEP is unacceptable—and perhaps compensatory education for your child. However, most courts will not allow you to recover speculative damages, such as pain and suffering.

Courts have disagreed about whether you are entitled to reimbursement of costs if you place your child in a private school without the approval of the district. If you do so without going through the IEP and hearing process, you could be liable for the costs if a court concludes that private school is unnecessary. If it concludes that you made the right choice, you may be reimbursed, but don't count on it. Parents who take unilateral action most of the time do not get reimbursed, especially if they acted without any involvement from the IEP team or without giving the school district a chance to meet their concerns. You should carefully consider whether it is worth the risk to make the move before the process is complete.

YOUR CHILD'S HEALTH

EVERY PARENT HOPES his or her child will grow up in good health, and there are many steps parents can take to maximize chances for that outcome. Of course, the most obvious is obtaining consistent, high-quality medical care for your child. Many parents look to classics like Dr. Spock's *Baby and Child Care* or a wealth of other guides by physicians to advise and assist them in understanding their children's medical needs. As with so many other areas of parenting today, though, the seemingly simple act of obtaining appropriate medical care for your child has become complicated by dramatic changes in our health care system and by legal issues related to medical care. This chapter will outline the most significant legal questions you may face in connection with your child's health and will help you navigate the increasingly complex world of health care delivery.

THE PARENTAL DUTY TO PROVIDE HEALTH CARE

Just as parents have a duty to provide food, shelter, and clothing for their children, so, too, they have a duty to provide adequate medical care. Failure to do so can constitute neglect, which could lead to losing custody of your children, termination of your parental rights, or even criminal charges if the neglect is sufficiently severe. Indeed, the duty to provide health care may in the not-too-distant future extend even to providing care before a child is born. Medical research has identified adequate prenatal care as an important factor in the health of children, and although no mother has yet been held legally responsible simply for failure to obtain prenatal care, efforts have been made in rare cases to hold pregnant women accountable for substance abuse and other behavior that has a negative effect on the health of their babies. Child abuse and neglect generally are covered in chapter 10, prenatal harm in chapter 1. Later in this chapter, we will discuss the law's treatment of cases involving parents who refuse to consent to a particular course of medical treatment for their child. Fortunately, these cases are the exceptional ones. Most parents never ponder their legal duty to provide medical care for their children. They eagerly seek medical care; their primary problem is how to pay for it.

Health Insurance

For most parents, the best way to finance their children's health care is through health insurance. Most parents obtain group health insurance through their employer. In some companies, the employer may pay all of the premium, but in many companies today, the employee must pay part of the premium, which is usually deducted from the employee's paycheck. Some employers offer a dizzying array of health insurance options; others provide only one type of plan. If your employer does not offer health insurance, you may be able to purchase group health insurance through your union or other professional organization. You may also be able to purchase individual health insurance directly from various insurance companies. Health insurance obtained this way can be quite expensive, but the alternative could be financial ruin or the inability to obtain necessary medical care for your child.

Fee-for-Service (Indemnity) Plans. Traditionally, most insurers have offered indemnity or fee-for-service plans. Under this kind of plan, you are reimbursed for all medical expenses covered by the plan. Some plans are "basic," generally covering only hospital visits; others, de-

WHAT KIND OF HEALTH INSURANCE PLANS ARE AVAILABLE?

There are three basic types of health insurance plans, each discussed fully in the text. A fee-for-service or indemnity plan reimburses you for expenses incurred by a covered person (your child) up to certain limits and usually after a deductible is met. These plans allow you to pick your own doctor. A health maintenance organization, or HMO, provides health care either in a clinic setting or through a network of physicians. The physicians are paid a salary or a set fee per patient, and members usually must contribute a small co-payment for each office visit. Access to specialists is restricted, so a referral from your primary care physician is usually required. A preferred provider organization, or PPO, allows you to choose from among a number of doctors who have previously agreed to provide care at a certain rate. If you go outside the network, you are still covered, but you pay more.

scribed as "major medical," offer more extensive coverage, with "comprehensive" plans providing the most coverage. With a fee-for-service plan, the doctor typically bills you and then you or someone in the doctor's office submits a claim form to the insurer for reimbursement. Usually, these plans carry a deductible, which means that the insurer will reimburse covered expenses only after you have paid out an amount equal to the deductible. In other words, if the plan carries a $250 deductible, you will have to pay the first $250 of covered medical bills before the insurance company will pay. Bills for services not covered by the plan do not count toward the deductible. Fee-for-service plans often have a family deductible, as well. For example, if your policy has an individual deductible of $250 and a family deductible of $500, if you and your daughter each incur covered expenses of $250, no deductible will apply to charges subsequently incurred by your son.

Once you satisfy the deductible, the insurance company will begin reimbursing you for covered expenses. However, you will probably still have to pay some percentage of the charges, called coinsurance. For example, the insurance company may reimburse you for 80 percent of the "reasonable and customary" fees for a given office visit or procedure. You are then responsible for the remaining 20 percent, or possibly more if your doctor charges an amount greater than the insurance company considers reasonable and customary for that particular treatment. Should the insurance company deny you full reimbursement on the ground that the doctor's fees are excessive, you may be able to challenge that determination. You can also ask the doctor to accept the insurance company's reimbursement as full payment of your remaining balance. Most fee-for-service plans include an annual cap, or limitation, on the amount of money you or your family will have to pay out of pocket in a given year. So, if the cap on your plan is five thousand dollars, when your out-of-pocket costs (including the deductible and any coinsurance payments) exceed that amount, the insurance company will pay any covered bills in full.

Indemnity plans have the advantage of allowing you to choose the physician who will treat your child. However, they also can be expensive, especially for parents. Fee-for-service plans usually do not cover preventive medicine, such as immunizations and well-baby care during the early years of life, both of which are critical to your child's health. Fee-for-service plans also frequently exclude, or refuse to pay for, treatment of preexisting conditions, that is, medical illnesses or conditions that you already have when your coverage begins. Some plans will cover these conditions after a certain period of time has elapsed. For example, if your child received treatment for asthma before you joined a particular health plan, your new policy might exclude treatment for the asthma until after a year has passed. The Health Insurance Portability Act, effective July 1997, protects you from having to go through more than one preexisting condition waiting period (regardless of which type of insurance you have). Once you've satisfied a waiting period with one employer, which now cannot be longer than twelve months, if you switch jobs, you will be covered immediately providing that you did not go without insurance for more than sixty-three days. The law also prohibits group health plans from considering pregnancy a preexisting condition and from excluding treatment of preexisting conditions of adopted children.

Health Maintenance Organizations (HMOs). A second, fast-growing option for medical care is offered by health maintenance organizations, commonly known as HMOs. You may also hear them referred to by the more general term *managed care.* Some states, like California, have been home to HMOs for years. Others are just beginning to see the rise of HMOs. There is little doubt that HMOs or some form of managed care will soon be available throughout the country. Indeed, most experts on health care delivery predict that managed care will dominate the market in the coming years. Depending on where you live, your employer may already have chosen to contract exclusively with an HMO to provide coverage for medical care for you and other employees.

Why are HMOs so popular? First, they are currently the most economical way for employers to provide health care services. The premiums for employers are often considerably less than those for traditional indemnity plans. In addition, HMOs are undoubtedly more economical for users. Your premium will be significantly lower, perhaps as little as 5 percent of the cost of an indemnity plan; moreover, the amount you pay for medical services will often be dramatically less. There is no deductible, and the amount you pay, called a co-payment (co-pay for short), may be only a few dollars per office visit, with certain services provided completely free of charge to you. Hospital charges may even be completely covered. Prescriptions usually are covered and provided at a sharply discounted rate. HMOs emphasize preventive care and often include all the required prenatal care and well-baby treatments, including immunizations and checkups at little or no cost to you.

There are two basic types of HMOs. One type is essentially a self-contained clinic. In this type, all the primary care physicians and specialists are housed in one location, the HMO often has its own hospital facilities, and the doctors receive a salary from the HMO. Organizations like Kaiser Permanente fall into this category. The second type of HMO uses independent practice associations, or IPAs. Doctors who belong to an IPA get prepaid a flat fee by the HMO for every patient who signs up with them. They do *not* get paid by you or the insurer for specific services provided, although, as explained above, you will probably have to contribute a small co-pay for office visits. In this type of system, you will be asked to select a primary care physician, customarily a pediatrician or family practitioner, for your child. This physician will provide most of the services for your child and will act as a gatekeeper to the system, which means that if your child needs treatment from a specialist, the primary care physician will provide a referral to the appropriate specialist in the network. To obtain such a referral, you will usually need to have the primary care physician see your child first. Since the primary care physician plays such an important role in your child's medical care, you will want to select carefully. The primary care physician's office, as well as the customer service department of the HMO, should be able to provide you with information regarding the physician's education, training, and experience. Word-of-mouth referrals from other patients, perhaps coworkers who have used the physician's services for their children, can provide helpful information and evaluation as well.

HMOs offer a very economical way to obtain comprehensive health care for your child. Many members report a high degree of satisfaction with the services provided. However, there are some features common to HMOs that you might find problematic. First, you will have a very limited choice of doctors, and your child's primary care physician will control access to specialists. Second, since HMO doctors do not get paid for the services they provide, they may seek to provide less care. Indeed, many HMOs provide financial incentives, such as bonuses, to participating physicians who limit costs by a certain percentage. These features may make HMOs a poor choice if your child suffers from a serious, chronic illness or from developmental problems. In any case, to ensure that your child is getting the best care possible from an HMO, you will need to be assertive, knowledgeable, and persistent. You will also need to become familiar with the rules of your particular HMO. For example, HMOs typically require precertification for any nonemergency procedure requiring hospitalization. You will have to contact the HMO, inform them of the reason for and nature of the procedure, and wait for approval before your child can be admitted. Otherwise, the HMO may refuse to pay the costs of the treatment. Clinic-type HMOs will require your child to use their hospital facilities and may even require your child to be transferred if he or she has received emergency treatment from a facility outside the plan. HMOs also typically provide only limited coverage for emergency treatment obtained outside the service area of the HMO.

Suppose, for example, that you and your family are vacationing in Hawaii when your child begins to run a fever. The hotel recommends a local doctor who diagnoses your child as having a minor virus. When you return home to Pennsylvania, you seek reimbursement from your HMO. Unfortunately, you're not likely to get it. Many HMOs limit reimbursement for expenses incurred outside the service area to treatment for conditions that could cause serious injury or death. One way to avoid this problem is to call the HMO prior to seeking treatment. An adviser there can instruct you whether to go to an emergency room, which should then be covered, or to wait until you return home. Similarly, if your children do not live with you or within the area served by your HMO, you may have trouble getting the HMO to cover the cost of treatment they receive near their residence.

Preferred Provider Organizations (PPOs). Some companies offer a hybrid of fee-for-service and HMO plans called preferred provider organizations, or PPOs. PPOs contract with physicians to provide care at a previously negotiated rate. If you choose to use one of these preferred physicians, the percentage of your co-pay will probably be less than if you use a physician outside the network. For example, some plans will cover 90 percent of physician services provided by a preferred provider but only 70 percent of services provided by a nonpreferred provider. The premiums for these plans are often just as expensive as those for the more traditional indemnity plans because they preserve options. But they give you the choice of spending less for your co-pay while retaining the flexibility of choosing your own doctor when that seems desirable. For example, some parents might be perfectly comfortable using a preferred provider for routine well-baby care but want to choose their own doctor should their child develop a serious medical problem.

Choosing and Keeping Health Insurance. The information provided here covers the basic features common to fee-for-service plans and managed care. Before committing to a particular plan, you will need to consider carefully the actual terms, benefits, and exclusions (items not covered) of the specific plans offered by your employer or pursued by you directly. *Each plan is different.* If the health care benefit is offered through your employer, your employer probably negotiated with various insurance companies or managed care organizations to offer plans at prices your employer could afford. Consequently, even within an HMO, the specific terms, such as the amount of any office co-pay and the type of services covered, will vary from group to group. Your office administrator will be able to assist you in understanding the various options.

If you have a new job, you may not be eligible for health insurance until you have passed a probationary period. Also be aware that your ability to switch plans, if several are offered by your employer, is limited to a time period known as open enrollment. Open enrollment usually lasts for a month and is offered once a year. If you do not switch during this period, you are locked in to your current choice for the rest of the year. What if your child is born after the open enrollment period? The federal Health Insurance Portability Act now requires insurers offering group coverage through an employer with coverage for dependents— spouses and children, including adopted children and those placed for adoption—to allow dependents to enroll within thirty days of a marriage, birth, adoption, or placement for adoption. Coverage would take effect immediately.

You may lose coverage for yourself and your family if you have individual insurance and the company cancels the policy or if you are covered by group insurance with your employer and you become unemployed or change jobs. If you have a noncancelable individual policy, also called a guaranteed renewable policy, the company cannot cancel unless you fail to pay your premium, although it can continue to raise

DO YOU HAVE THE RIGHT
TO TAKE OFF WORK IF YOUR CHILD IS SICK?

In certain circumstances, yes. It can be difficult to provide necessary care for your child when he or she is sick if you are working outside the home. Day care centers and family care providers frequently refuse to accept children when they are sick, to prevent other children from being exposed to the illness. Unfortunately, the law provides little help for parents in this common situation. However, the Family and Medical Leave Act (FMLA) does give a legal boost to parents who need to take time off work to care for a very sick child for an extended period of time. The FMLA allows parents who work for employers of fifty or more to take up to twelve weeks unpaid leave to care for a seriously or chronically ill child. To qualify as seriously ill, the child must require hospitalization or other inpatient care or be under the continuous treatment of a health care provider for a condition that necessitates recurring absences from school or absences of more than three days. Other specific requirements and features of the law are discussed in chapter I. Your employee benefits coordinator, human resources or personnel department, or office administrator may also be able to assist you in understanding your rights under the FMLA.

the premium. If you have a conditionally renewable policy, the company cannot cancel your particular policy, but it can cancel all policies like yours.

A federal law called COBRA, the Consolidated Omnibus Budget Reconciliation Act of 1985, allows you to continue your group health coverage for up to eighteen months after you leave your job, if the company has twenty or more employees, but you will have to pay the full cost of the coverage for this period. COBRA also applies if your spouse was insured but you are now widowed or divorced. In addition, COBRA permits your child to continue coverage for up to eighteen months after graduation from high school or in some cases college if the group insurance covered her while she was in school. If you become unemployed or change jobs, you have sixty days to elect to continue coverage under COBRA, and if you or your child is disabled, the coverage continues for twenty-nine months, rather than eighteen.

If you are seeking health care coverage on your own, insurance companies and HMOs provide booklets and brochures outlining their plans and have customer service representatives who can answer your questions. Each state also has an agency or commissioner that oversees insurance companies and can provide valuable information about the laws in your state and the various insurance companies operating there.

Dental Care. Finally, don't forget your child's dental needs. Failure to provide necessary dental care for your child can serve as evidence of neglect if it poses a serious risk to your child's health. Tooth decay and gum disease can cause your child chronic and painful problems later in life and can detract from your child's appearance. Dental care and orthodontia can be very expensive. Fortunately, many employers now offer group dental insurance that parallels health insurance, ranging from the traditional fee-for-service plan to the increasingly common HMO. However, not all employers who offer health insurance include dental, and those that do may provide only one dental plan even though they provide a choice of health care plans. If your employer does not offer dental insurance, you may purchase individual dental insurance, but, again, this tends to cost more. Unlike health insurance, most dental plans, including fee-for-service, routinely cover 100 percent of preventive care, including checkups, X rays, cleanings, and fluoride treatments for children under fourteen. Fee-for-service plans often waive any deductible for these services. Although most dental plans exclude cosmetic dentistry, they often cover orthodontia for children.

Tax Deductions and Medical Savings Accounts

If you are uninsured or if your insurance does not cover significant medical costs incurred by you and your children, you might reduce the burden by deducting the expenses from your federal income tax. The tax code allows you to deduct medical and dental expenses if they exceed 7½ percent of your adjusted gross income. This deduction applies to services that may not be covered by your indemnity or HMO plan, such as eyeglasses, hearing aids, and psychotherapy.

You may also have the option of setting aside income in pretax dollars for payment of medical and dental expenses if your employer offers a flexible spending account (FSA). Like a tax deduction, an FSA can apply to costs not covered by your insurance. Usually you will be asked at the beginning of the year to designate the amount you wish to set aside in your FSA. This amount often will be garnered through payroll deductions during the course of the year. If you don't use up all the money in the account (the amount you designated at the beginning of the year), you will lose any remaining balance. Another option for using pretax dollars for health care offered by employers and sometimes combined with an FSA is the cafeteria plan. This plan lets you choose from a number of employee benefits, such as health, life, and disability insurance, to customize your benefits package. You will have to elect which benefits you wish to obtain before the year begins. Usually these elections are irrevocable for the year, but you may change your plan if you have a child through birth or adoption. The rules and limitations governing FSAs and cafeteria plans vary depending on how your employer has set them up, so you will need to consult your office administrator or employee benefits person to learn the details.

Another option for financing medical care, the medical savings account, has received much attention recently but is available only in about fifteen states and under a federal pilot project enacted as part of the Health Insurance Portability Act. Idaho is one state that offers this option. In Idaho, you can deposit up to two thousand dollars per person or four thousand dollars per family in a medical savings account and deduct that amount from your state income tax. If you withdraw money from the account to pay for medical expenses, it remains tax free; otherwise, you have to pay tax and penalties if you are younger than 59½. It is a good idea to buy a supplemental catastrophic insurance policy to go along with your medical savings account if you are participating in a state program like Idaho's, which does not require one. Participation in the federal program, which is limited to the self-employed and businesses with fewer than fifty employees, includes a high-deductible insurance policy.

When You Can't Afford Medical Treatment for Your Child

If you are one of the forty-two million Americans without any health insurance, you may find it difficult to afford the cost of health care for your child. A recent study by the American College of Physicians found that injured uninsured children were more than 25 percent less likely to obtain treatment than those insured. If you are a single parent, unemployed, or married with an unemployed spouse, you may qualify for state medical assistance for you and your child. The federal government's Medicaid program both requires and assists the states to provide free medical care to indigent citizens within certain guidelines. Every state has some program to accomplish this, but eligibility and coverage vary from state to state. Generally, participants in these programs are given a card that enables them to obtain hospitalization or medical care, and the health care providers receive payment directly from the state. However, not every doctor will accept Medicaid patients.

All Medicaid and related programs limit assistance to those who are deemed eligible, often by use of complex formulas based on family income and expenses. The federal government mandates that certain groups be covered, including those receiving welfare or Supplemental Security Income (SSI), federal assistance for the disabled and for blind, disabled, or severely impaired children. However, recently enacted welfare reform has dramatically altered public assistance to the poor and is likely to affect Medicaid, at least indirectly. Given the uncertainties and the variety of programs administered by the states and given the complexity of the calculations states use to determine eligibility, you should contact your local department of welfare or Medicaid program office or your nearest legal services office for information on what aid you may obtain.

YOUR RIGHT TO CONTROL YOUR CHILD'S HEALTH CARE

Informed Consent and Refusing Treatment for Your Child

It is a fundamental principle of American law that every adult of sound mind has a right to decide what will be done with his or her own body. In the context of medical care, this principle underlies the legal concept of "informed consent." A doctor has a legal obligation to explain the risks and benefits of a proposed treatment or procedure sufficiently to enable a patient to make a reasoned decision about whether to undergo it. When the patient is a minor child, this right rests with the parents. Physicians who treat children without obtaining informed parental consent can be held legally liable and forced to pay damages unless they can justify proceeding without it. Let's consider a few scenarios in which that might happen.

Tonya is an eight-year-old child playing at her friend Kimberly's house. During a game of hide-and-seek, Tonya cuts her foot on a rusty fence. The cut is bleeding profusely, so Kimberly's mom takes Tonya to the emergency room after being unable to reach Tonya's parents. The doctor at the emergency room stitches up the cut and gives Tonya a tetanus shot without first getting her parents' consent. Has the doctor violated any rights of Tonya or her parents? Probably not under these circumstances. While physicians who treat children generally need to obtain parental consent, they can act without it in an emergency. Of course if the procedure were a much more serious one that posed greater risks to Tonya, the physician might have had to wait for parental approval, but only if the delay would not jeopardize Tonya's health. In a serious emergency, a physician may not have time to obtain consent if the parents are not present.

Cases involving religious objections to treating children are more complicated than emergencies. Take the case of Bryan, for example, a ten-year-old stricken with leukemia. Bryan's parents are Jehovah's Witnesses, whose religion forbids them to take blood or blood products into their body. Bryan's oncologist, Dr. Sun, has prescribed a course of chemotherapy to combat the leukemia. However, one of the side effects of this treatment is the destruction of red blood cells. Bryan's red blood count has dropped to a dangerously low level, and Dr. Sun has ordered that he receive a blood transfusion. Without the blood transfusion, Bryan will be unable to continue treatment and will most likely die from the leukemia in a matter of months. With continued treatment, Bryan has an excellent chance of recovery. Nonetheless, Bryan's parents refuse to consent, claiming that the transfusion would violate their religious principles.

If Dr. Sun transfuses Bryan without his parents' consent, they could sue her for medical malpractice. However, Dr. Sun could go to court herself, or in conjunction with the hospital where Bryan is receiving treatment, to get a court order allowing her to treat Bryan without his parents' consent. (This petition may take the form of a dependency petition alleging that the child is suffering from medical neglect. The child abuse and neglect system is discussed more fully in chapter 10.) Courts across the nation have decided cases like this one. While they have generally relied on a common set of guiding principles, the results of the cases have varied considerably depending on the facts.

The courts have recognized that parents have a fundamental constitutional right to control the upbringing of their children, and this encompasses the right to consent to any medical treatment. In addition, individuals have a right to freedom of religion protected by the First Amendment of the Constitution. Indeed, there is little doubt that Bryan's parents would have a right to refuse any blood transfusion prescribed for *them,* even if their refusal meant death. However, neither of these fundamental rights is absolute. The state has a very strong interest in protecting children and can intervene for that purpose if necessary. Thus in a case like Bryan's, a court might well find that even though his parents have a legitimately held religious belief preventing them from consenting, the state's interest in protecting Bryan justifies overruling their decision and allowing Dr. Sun to treat Bryan without their consent.

In deciding whether to order treatment over parental objections, the courts will consider the nature of the treatment, the likelihood of its success, and the likely outcome if the treatment is not performed. If the treatment is invasive, painful, and unlikely to result in a successful outcome, a court might allow the parents' decision to stand. In one case, for example, a court upheld a parent's refusal to consent to a dangerous and very painful cancer treatment for a three-year-old that would have provided him a 40 percent chance of survival. But another court ordered that a twelve-year-old suffering from cancer receive chemotherapy and radiation when the treatment had an 80 percent chance of providing temporary relief from her painful symptoms, even though her chances for survival were only 25 to 50 percent. If the child's condition is not life threatening or likely to result in serious irreparable harm, many courts will decline to order treatment over the parents' objections. Even in this situation, though, courts have on occasion insisted on treatment deemed beneficial over the parents' objections if the treatment is less risky than continued inaction.

In Bryan's case, the blood transfusion is minimally invasive and carries little risk, while the risk to Bryan of forgoing the treatment is substantial. Consequently, a court likely would grant Dr. Sun's petition for an order allowing her to transfuse Bryan despite his parents' objections.

Now consider a second scenario, also involving religion. Carrie is a six-year-old child suffering from meningitis, a life-threatening bacterial infection that can be successfully treated with antibiotics if diagnosed early. Carrie's parents are Christian Scientists who do not believe in conventional medicine, preferring instead to rely on faith healing. Carrie dies from the meningitis, and the district attorney charges Carrie's parents with manslaughter. Can they rely on their religious beliefs to defend themselves against the charges?

Probably not. Most states do have laws that specifically exempt sole reliance on spiritual healing from their definition of child neglect, and about half include the exemption in their criminal codes. To avail themselves of these exemptions, the parents must prove that they belong to a recognized religion, and a few states limit the exemption to Christian

Scientists. But even if Carrie's parents can show good-faith reliance on spiritual healing based on a recognized religion, they are still unlikely to prevail. The exemptions for spiritual healing do not constitute a defense against certain criminal charges, including second- and third-degree murder, manslaughter, and reckless endangerment. (Nor do they prohibit a court from ordering treatment over parental objections, as we have seen.) In fact, only three states apply the spiritual healing exemption to charges of murder. Consequently, there have been several cases in which parents who refused to obtain mainstream medical treatment for a sick child based on religious beliefs have been convicted of criminal charges when the child has died. However, it can be confusing for courts, and hence for parents, to ascertain when these exemptions do apply. Therefore, some courts have overturned convictions in these cases on the ground that the law does not sufficiently inform parents what conduct is prohibited (that is, when reliance on spiritual healing crosses the line from permissible conduct to criminal behavior) and thus violates the parents' constitutional right to due process.

Legal Issues in Treating Critically Ill Newborns
Some of the most gut-wrenching cases involve medical treatment of critically ill newborns. Consider the following hypothetical case. Cristina has just given birth to José. Sadly, José is significantly premature, born at a mere twenty-seven weeks. He weights only 950 grams. Birth weights less than 2,500 grams are considered low, and those less than 1,000 grams are considered extremely low. Typical of infants born very prematurely, José suffers from a variety of severe medical problems. Because his lungs are underdeveloped, he cannot breathe without a respirator. He also suffers from brain damage and a severe bowel infection that may eventually make it impossible for him to eat. José's physician does not think he will live as long as a year, and he likely will never be able to leave the hospital. After much agonizing, José's parents would like to discontinue life support. Can they legally do so?

Cristina and her husband face one of the most tragic situations any parent will encounter. Unfortunately, our hypothetical couple is not unique. The wonders of modern medical technology have enabled physicians to keep alive, often by artificial means, premature infants and those with severe congenital or genetic abnormalities who in previous years would have died soon after birth. But medical science has proved less successful in predicting the futures of these children. While some go on to develop normally, many linger for a few weeks or months, never leaving the neonatal intensive care unit before they die. Others survive but with severe impairments that require frequent invasive and painful medical procedures, and they have little chance of leading a life in any way approaching normal. Poor social conditions— including the dramatic increase in births by teenagers, who usually receive little or no prenatal care—and births to substance-abusing women have increased the number of infants in this situation.

The issues surrounding critically ill newborns first gained widespread public attention in 1982 with the so-called Baby Doe case. Baby Doe was a Down's syndrome baby suffering from a defective esophagus that could have been surgically corrected. Baby Doe's parents refused to consent to the operation, and the hospital petitioned the court for an order compelling treatment. Baby Doe's parents prevailed in state court, and the baby died before appeal could be made to the U.S. Supreme Court.

The case received much media attention, and in 1984 Congress responded by passing amendments to the Child Abuse Prevention and Treatment Act defining failure to treat disabled infants as a form of child abuse and requiring doctors to provide treatment if, in their "reasonable judgment," it will ameliorate or correct the infant's condition. The amendments do not give individuals the right to sue. Rather, they permit the state child protection agency to challenge and investigate a hospital's decision not to treat and file suit if the agency believes the hospital is committing medical neglect under the act.

The amendments have been widely criticized by doctors and legal scholars for seemingly excluding any consideration of the quality of life the infant can expect if treatment is provided, for compelling doctors to treat against their better judgment, and for taking the decision away from parents. While some doctors feel compelled to provide treatment because of the amendments, the courts have rarely invoked them.

In fact, the court cases considering these issues since 1984 have barely considered the amendments. Instead, the courts have used one of two approaches to balance society's interest in preserving life with parents' interest in deciding appropriate care for their infants. Some courts have used a "substituted judgment" test. Under this approach, the court tries to figure out what the patient would have wanted to do. While this approach makes sense for adults rendered incompetent and perhaps for adolescents, it doesn't really work well for infants, since they have not achieved a level of functioning that would enable them to make a decision. Other courts have used a different test, ordering continuation or discontinuation of treatment based on whether it is in the child's "best interests." Ultimately, regardless of the standard imposed, the courts in these cases have allowed the parents' wishes to prevail. Some of the cases involved infants; others involved children of twelve and thirteen years of age. Thus, whatever the letter of the 1984 amendments, it seems that most courts will allow parents to discontinue treatment if the decision is supported by medical evidence showing small likelihood of survival or survival in a persistent vegetative or comatose state and if treatment would have little or no ameliorative effect on the child's condition.

Moreover, as a practical matter, most of these issues are resolved without judicial intervention. If the physician and parents are in agreement, the hospital may consult with legal counsel or its ethics committee to ensure that the medical evidence supports the decision and that the parents have been appropriately informed and have made a reasonable decision. If these concerns are met, the decision will be carried out. If the parents want to discontinue treatment against the physician's advice, then the hospital may decide to petition the court for continuation of treatment or to notify the child protection agency so that it can do so. In this situation, it is important for the parents to seek other medical evaluation of their child's condition and to try to convince the hospital ethics committee (if there is one) to support their choice of treatment.

Let's return to newborn baby José. What if José's parents want treatment for José, but his doctors believe treatment would be futile? Physician efforts to discontinue life-sustaining treatment against a family's wishes have not fared well in the courts. There have been only two reported court cases considering this situation, and both ruled, on the basis of different laws, that treatment should continue. One of the cases involved an elderly woman whose husband wanted to continue life support even though she was in a persistent vegetative state and her physicians felt treatment was futile and wanted to discontinue it. The other case, more germane for our purposes, involved an infant known as Baby K. Baby K was born anencephalic, that is, without a brain. Anencephalic infants cannot survive for long, and standard treatment requires only comfort care—food, water, and hydration while the child dies. Baby K's mother, however, wanted the child to be treated with artificial respiration and other procedures that might prolong the infant's life. Her physicians vehemently opposed the futile treatment, arguing that Baby K would never improve or come to function in any meaningful way because she lacked a brain. Nonetheless, the court ruled that the doctors must provide life-sustaining treatment if the baby was brought to the hospital.

It remains unclear how significant the Baby K case will be. Many have criticized it, arguing that compelling treatment in such hopeless situations is itself a form of child abuse because it merely prolongs the dying process with painful, invasive procedures. Clearly, there are no easy answers in these cases. Your views will be informed by your personal moral and religious beliefs and your life experience. As with many issues involving parents and children, the law may provide some rough guidance, but consultation with family, friends, mental health professionals, social workers, and clergy may ultimately prove more valuable in evaluating and resolving these difficult challenges.

Legal Issues in Treating Adolescents
Teenagers bring another voice to the analysis when a legal dispute arises concerning medical treatment. When dealing with newborns and young

children, parents have complete authority, subject to state intervention only if the parents' actions would put the child at serious risk. Adolescents, though, often have and express opinions about their own health care. Moreover, courts and state legislatures have recognized that adolescents possess greater cognitive abilities than younger children and the ability to reason in a fashion approaching adult reasoning. Consequently, the law in many states allows adolescents to make certain health care decisions without parental consent and with a right to confidentiality.

Some states allow adolescents to consent to medical treatment under the "mature minor" doctrine. Under this doctrine, the law presumes that minors of a certain minimum age, usually ranging from fourteen to sixteen, are capable of making some medical decisions for themselves. Some of these laws actually designate the specific age when the child is considered mature. Others require the minor to prove her competence to the physician by showing an understanding of the nature and consequences of the treatment. Most often, these laws allow teenagers to obtain care without parental knowledge or consent for certain specified conditions such as pregnancy, sexually transmitted diseases, contraception, and substance abuse. (The law concerning minors and contraception and abortion is discussed more fully in chapter 5.) Some states have broader laws that allow any minor who can understand and appreciate the risks and benefits of a proposed procedure to consent. Similarly, some states give minors of any age the right to admit themselves to a psychiatric facility or to consent to outpatient mental health treatment without parental consent. Minors emancipated through marriage, enlistment in the military, or otherwise (as discussed more fully in chapter 5) generally also have the right to consent to their own medical care.

When the proposed treatment is complicated, dangerous, controversial, or necessary to save a minor's life, professional prudence will probably lead most physicians to consult the minor's parents. When you and your teenager agree on the appropriate course of treatment, you will be able to follow that course unless the treatment would unjustifiably endanger your child, as discussed above. A trickier problem arises when an adolescent disagrees with his parents' desired course of treat-

ALTERNATIVE MEDICINE

In some cases, parents may resist conventional treatment and seek alternative therapies, not necessarily for religious reasons, but because they believe it to be in their child's best interests. In a 1979 New York case, the Hofbauers rejected recommended radiation and chemotherapy for their seven-year-old son, who was suffering from Hodgkin's disease. Instead, they sought treatment from doctors who practiced metabolic therapy. The court upheld the parents' right to choose the type of therapy for their son as long as they sought care from physicians, the treatment was not completely rejected by all responsible medical authority, they had legitimate concerns about possible toxic side effects of the conventional therapy, and the alternative therapy was less harmful. These cases are rare, though, and courts have reached different conclusions. In a Massachusetts case that same year, a court overruled the parents' decision to eschew chemotherapy in favor of metabolic therapy for their three-year-old child suffering from leukemia. More recently, a similar decision was reached in a Texas case involving a ten-year-old girl suffering from ulcerative colitis. Her parents disagreed with the doctors' recommendation of surgery to remove the diseased colon, and they spirited the child, with an intravenous tube to her heart still in place, to a holistic doctor in Canada. Canadian officials subsequently intervened, ordering the child returned to Texas for the surgery. The Texas court then ruled that the child would be taken into protective custody and given the surgery unless the parents consented.

ment. In 1994 a sixteen-year-old cancer patient ran away to avoid chemotherapy to which his parents had consented. Luckily, the case was resolved without court intervention. The boy returned home, and he and his parents agreed to an alternative therapy. While a court would probably consider a minor's wishes, it is likely the court would ultimately defer to the parents if the physician was in agreement with them about the most appropriate treatment. However, it is also quite possible that a court might find a sixteen-year-old minor sufficiently mature to make his own decision, particularly if the alternative meant forcing painful or otherwise uncomfortable treatment on an unwilling young person. A Florida judge allowed a fifteen-year-old boy to forgo life-sustaining medication and a proposed third liver transplant after a lengthy discussion with the boy, revealing the great pain the treatment causes, as well as testimony from his doctors. However, in a 1991 case, a New York judge sided with parents seeking to compel their fifteen-year-old son to submit to a tumor biopsy. He had refused to undergo the procedure because he had an exaggerated fear of needles. Even the legal guardian (appointed for the boy because he and his parents were at odds) agreed that the biopsy was in his best interests.

One area where parents can override their teenager's opposition to treatment is institutionalization in a psychiatric facility. Disturbingly, parents are increasingly committing their teenage children inappropriately to inpatient mental institutions when they become difficult to control. Most states allow parents to commit their child without her consent if some neutral party finds the commitment medically justified. Some states require proof that the child is dangerous to herself or others; other states, merely that she needs medical treatment. The neutral party need not be a judge. In fact, the Supreme Court has ruled that minors have no right to a court hearing prior to commitment, even though adults are entitled to one, and that a staff physician can satisfy the neutral fact-finder requirement. Moreover, the Supreme Court decision applies only to state-run facilities. Nonetheless, many states have adopted stricter due process protections for minors, some of which apply to private facilities as well.

States take roughly one of four general approaches to voluntary commitment of minors. Almost half the states provide only the minimal due process protections mandated by the Supreme Court, as just discussed, and several of these require those procedures only for public institutions, leaving admissions to private facilities largely unregulated. A second group of states requires that minors of a designated age, ranging from twelve to sixteen, give consent before hospitalization can occur. For example, in Pennsylvania, if a minor is fourteen or older, his consent is required before commitment can proceed, although this protection may be more illusory than real if the consent is coerced by his parents. Some states recognize this danger and require a hearing to determine the voluntariness of a minor's consent to inpatient treatment. A third group of states provides for judicial review of the commitment at some point after admission. The review may be automatic, for example, within a certain number of days of admission, as in North Carolina, or it may be triggered when a minor objects to confinement. Ohio and California allow for judicial review of the commitment, and Michigan requires postadmission judicial review if a minor thirteen or older objects. But even this may be scant protection if the child is unaware of the right to object, doesn't understand it, or is intimidated or ignored by the staff. Finally, a few states will only permit minors to be committed if the procedures for involuntary commitment are followed, but here, too, these more stringent requirements don't always apply to private hospitals.

While some troubled teens may indeed require inpatient treatment in these facilities, perhaps too often exasperated parents, lured by advertisements from profit-driven mental health facilities, inappropriately turn to institutionalized care to deal with their adolescent's problems. Surveys indicate that the rate of "voluntary" commitment has tripled or even quadrupled since 1980, and a Children's Defense Fund study suggests that 40 percent or more of such institutionalizations are inappropriate. Of course, this is an option open primarily to parents with considerable financial resources or comprehensive health insurance, since private facilities are very expensive. Teenagers who are institutionalized at state expense usually have found their way into the juvenile criminal system or are involved in the dependency system as abused or neglected children. These situations are dealt with at length in chapters 9 and 10.

If You're Dissatisfied with Your Child's Health Care

While most physicians are bright, well-trained, and dedicated professionals, you may find yourself dissatisfied with the health care provided to your child. In many cases, parental complaints stem not from incompetency on the part of the doctor, but from perceived lack of service, unresponsiveness, or poor bedside manner. All of these are legitimate reasons for seeking care elsewhere. Confidence in and the ability to communicate with your child's doctor are important to ensuring that she receives appropriate medical care.

What can you do if you have become unhappy with your child's doctor? In years past, the answer to this question was so obvious there would be no need to ask it. You would simply go to another doctor. Today, in the era of managed care, the situation requires consideration. As we saw earlier, if you belong to an HMO, you will often have selected a primary care physician for your child. This doctor may be one of several in an independent practice association (IPA). If so, you most likely will be allowed to select an alternative primary care doctor. However, if you want to switch to another IPA altogether, you may have to wait for the open enrollment period. This is largely a matter determined by the terms of your health plan. In any case, if you have a serious problem with your child's doctor, do not hesitate to contact your HMO or the employee benefits person at your office, who may be able to arrange for you to sign up with another provider. If you belong to a preferred provider organization (PPO), you can choose another doctor in the network or pay more by going outside the plan. Of course, if you belong to a fee-for-service plan, you can see whomever you please.

In most states, you have the right to have your doctor forward your child's medical records to another physician. Many now give parents the right to obtain or review these medical records or at least a summary of them. However, some states do not allow parental access to mental health records or other confidential records concerning treatment of a minor (usually an adolescent) for problems such as drug or alcohol abuse or sexually transmitted diseases. The doctor may charge you the reasonable cost of copying the records.

HEALTH CARE ISSUES AFTER DIVORCE

Divorced parents sometimes face unique problems related to providing their child with appropriate health care. The most common problems involve deciding how costs for medical care will be apportioned between the parents and ensuring that health insurance coverage for the children continues. These issues are discussed in chapter 8. Divorced parents may also have concerns about who gets to make decisions regarding a child's health care.

Parents with sole legal custody generally have the right to make all medical decisions for their children, although noncustodial parents usually have the right to consent to emergency treatment. Parents who have joint legal custody both have the right to participate in major decisions relating to their child's medical care. When parents with joint legal custody cannot agree, mediation may assist them in resolving the issue. As a last resort, the court may make the decision based on the child's best interests. The custody arrangement also determines parental access to medical records. Traditionally, only custodial parents have had the right to examine their children's medical records. Recently, some states have expanded noncustodial parents' rights by allowing them access to the records as well.

While changing physicians can resolve some concerns with the care your child is getting, what recourse do you have if poor care has caused harm to your child? Consider the following scenario: Jamal is an active seven-year-old who broke his arm in a fall off his bicycle. Jamal's pediatrician, Dr. Washington, set the arm, but six weeks later, when the cast was removed, the arm had not healed properly. Jamal may never regain full use of the arm. After consulting with another physician, Jamal's parents learn that the arm was set incorrectly.

In this case, Jamal's parents will want to consider pursuing a claim of medical malpractice against Dr. Washington. This is done by filing a suit against the doctor for negligence in treating the child. A doctor's care is negligent if it falls below the "standard of care"—a standard determined by what other physicians would have done under the same circumstances. Note that if the doctor's treatment was in line with generally accepted norms for your child's particular problem, she will not be held liable even if your child suffered a bad outcome. But if Dr. Washington's treatment of the arm was below the standard of other pediatricians in the area, she could be forced to pay damages for the harm done to Jamal's arm, including pain and suffering, additional doctors' bills, and lost future wages.

In most states, Jamal will not be allowed to sue Dr. Washington during his minority, that is, before he turns eighteen. However, Jamal's parents can bring suit on his behalf. Every state prescribes the time within which a lawsuit must be brought, and that period, called the statute of limitations, depends on the type of suit. A suit for a breach of contract, for example, may have a three-year statute of limitations, while a negligence action may have a one-year statute of limitations. With most types of lawsuits, the statute of limitations is "tolled" during the period of minority. This means that the legal clock stops while your child is a minor. Jamal's parents could wait until he reaches the age of majority; then he could sue in his own name. With medical malpractice actions, though, many states have passed laws that do not "toll" the statute of limitations for minors all the way to age eighteen, although the period typically remains somewhat longer than it is for adults. Thus if Jamal's parents do not file suit within the designated time period, he will be barred forever from bringing the claim to court.

The statute of limitations is just one of many highly technical matters involved in filing a lawsuit. In an effort to protect doctors from frivolous lawsuits, many states have enacted laws that have set up procedural hurdles that must be overcome before you can even file a medical malpractice suit. Consequently if you suspect a physician has committed malpractice on your child, you will certainly want to consult a lawyer.

You should also be aware that many physicians today will ask you to sign a form agreeing to waive your right to sue in court in favor of arbitration. Arbitration has its good points and bad. It is generally less formal and may be quicker than suing in court. Critics argue, though, that the arbitrators are sometimes biased in favor of physicians (many require inclusion of a doctor on the panel) and likely to award lesser damages than a jury.

Some physicians now routinely present arbitration agreements for patients or their parents to sign before an office visit or treatment, and state laws vary in their handling of these agreements for resolution of medical malpractice cases. In some states, a physician cannot condition treatment based on your willingness to sign. You may have the right to rescind, or cancel, the agreement within some set period of time, ranging from a few days to as many as ninety days after treatment. Alternatively, courts in some states will simply refuse to enforce a pretreatment arbitration agreement. Of course, if you don't sign the agreement to arbitrate, you can usually choose to do so at some later point should a problem arise. If you belong to an HMO or PPO, you are probably already committed to arbitrating any disputes by a clause in your policy. Courts have generally, though not unanimously, upheld these clauses.

Suppose Jamal's parents belong to the Good Health HMO. Jamal's pediatrician recognizes that the arm has sustained a break that is difficult to treat and believes referral to a pediatric orthopedist is warranted. Good Health refuses to approve the referral, believing treatment of a broken arm is within Dr. Washington's area of expertise. If Dr. Washington fails to set the arm properly, Jamal's parents may be able to sue not only her, but possibly Good Health as well. This is not a far-fetched scenario. A study by the American Academy of Pediatrics found that 20 percent of surveyed physicians reported that HMOs and PPOs denied some referrals to specialists, and 35 percent of these physicians believed the denial of the referral compromised the patient's care. Moreover, some HMOs and PPOs lack a wide array of specialists for referral. Your HMO should have a grievance procedure by which you can challenge a referral decision to avoid this problem altogether, but reversals are not easily won. A few lawsuits against HMOs have been brought in cases such as these with mixed success, and more are likely in the future.

Public Health Concerns: Vaccinations, Newborn Testing,
and Fluoridated Water

Early in this century, the Supreme Court upheld the rights of the states to compel smallpox vaccination of children over their parents' objection. The Court found that the need to protect the public health from a highly contagious, often fatal disease outweighed any parental rights or religious objections to the immunization. As we near the end of this century, the smallpox virus has been eradicated worldwide, and some states have ceased requiring the vaccination. Other devastating childhood illnesses, such as polio, have become extremely rare due to successful compulsory vaccination programs. Today every state and the District of Columbia require children to receive immunizations for diphtheria, pertussis (whooping cough), and tetanus (the DPT vaccine), as well as polio, measles, rubella, and mumps, before they will be permitted to enroll in school. The national immunization program, Vaccines for Children, assists states in providing free vaccines to children who could not otherwise afford them.

Although the Supreme Court did uphold the states' right to compel immunizations, every state now has statutory exemptions that allow parents to refuse immunization for their children for medical reasons. In addition, in every state except West Virginia, parents may refuse to vaccinate their children based on religious objections. However, parents must provide extensive documentation to obtain an exemption. Failure to immunize your child without obtaining a waiver will result in exclusion of your child from school and put you in violation of the compulsory school attendance laws discussed in chapter 3.

While these immunization laws result in 96 percent of school-age children being properly vaccinated, they do little to help younger children. More than a third of American children are not sufficiently immunized before age two. In some areas, the rate runs as high as 50 percent. To protect your children and others, consult your pediatrician or public health department for a list of the necessary and recommended immunizations as soon as your child is born.

While immunizations have dramatically improved the health of our nation's children, in very rare cases, a child will have an adverse reaction to one of the vaccines, particularly the pertussis part of the DPT shot. Because such immunization is compulsory and because drug companies need to be encouraged to continue to develop and manufacture vaccines, the federal government has established the National Childhood Vaccine Injury Compensation Program for those few children injured by vaccines. Under this program, rather than suing the manufacturer of the vaccine, the child or his parent or other legal representative can file a claim and obtain damages from the government. This program is a no-fault system, which means that the claimant need not show that the manufacturer or anyone else involved in the immunization was at fault; she simply has to demonstrate that the vaccine caused the child's injury.

Schoolchildren must also submit to tuberculosis testing and medical screening for a variety of conditions, such as vision and hearing problems, which vary by state. Parents may object to compulsory medical screening of their children in many states, but some states recognize only religious objections.

The state will have a hand in determining your child's medical treatment long before he or she reaches school age. And it won't be limited to treatment or prevention of contagious diseases. From the first days of your child's life, the state has the power to require certain medical tests. It is standard medical practice and the law in many states that a health care professional administer eyedrops to prevent a condition called ophthalmia neonatorum and perform other tests such as screening for phenylketonuria (PKU), a genetic enzyme deficiency that can lead to retardation. A few states allow parents to object to the drops and the screening tests, some only for religious reasons, but most states do not.

In addition, since 1988 the Centers for Disease Control has mandated blind testing of newborns for the human immunodeficiency virus (HIV) that causes AIDS. The testing is blind because the identity of the child is not noted and the parents are not informed of the test results. So far the purpose of the testing has been solely to gather statistical information about the spread of the disease, but with advances in treating HIV-positive people, there has been a renewed call for open testing. In some places, hospitals must disclose the results to mothers who want them, and New York recently became the first state to require mandatory open HIV testing of newborns.

Depending on where you live, your child may also enjoy fluoridated water to help prevent tooth decay. A few states mandate fluoridation, but in many places, local governments—cities, towns, and counties— have made the decision to add fluoride to the water. Over the years, parents have challenged fluoridation as a violation of their children's rights and their own, but they have not been successful. Courts have recognized the states' power to promote the welfare of children, particularly those in poverty, in a way that is inexpensive and safe.

YOUR TEENAGER AND THE LAW

CHILDREN HAVE LEGAL and constitutional rights just as adults do, but their rights are not the same as those of adults. Young children are considered subject to their parents' control, and numerous laws are designed for their protection. Adolescents occupy a place in between young children and adults under the law. They are still minors and thus subject to a wide range of restrictions on their conduct in areas such as marriage, sexual activity, driving, employment, and access to certain substances like alcohol and tobacco. However, the Supreme Court has recognized that the Constitution does protect adolescents in certain situations, and many state laws recognize that adolescents do have the ability to make certain decisions for themselves.

MARRIAGE

Once you have reached the age of majority, eighteen in most places, you are free to marry. Moreover, the right to marry for adults is considered "fundamental" under the Constitution and entitled to special protection from state interference or restriction. Minors do not share this constitutional protection, and every state has some restriction on their right to marry. To understand the limits on minors' right to marry, let's consider the hypothetical case of sixteen-year-old Tiffany and her seventeen-year-old boyfriend, Adam, who are very much in love and would like to marry. They are still in high school, and their parents adamantly oppose the marriage. Can Tiffany and Adam legally marry without their parents' consent?

Not in most states. Typically, minors sixteen or over may marry, but they must have their parents' consent to do so, and in two or three states, they must also go through premarital counseling because they are underage. Do Tiffany and Adam each need the consent of both their parents? Again, not in most states. Although some, like Georgia, require the consent of both parents if they're married and living together, most states require the consent of only one parent—customarily the one with physical or legal custody if the parents are separated or divorced.

Does it matter whether Tiffany is pregnant? Yes, it does. If she and Adam are expecting a baby and their parents refuse to consent to their marriage, in most states, they may petition the court for an order allowing the county clerk to issue a marriage license without parental consent. In some jurisdictions, though, mere pregnancy is not sufficient to persuade the court to grant such an order; in those jurisdictions, Tiffany and Adam would have to convince the court that marriage was in their best interests.

What about minors under sixteen? If Tiffany and Adam were fifteen or younger, they would not be allowed to marry in some states even with parental consent unless Tiffany were pregnant and the couple also obtained judicial consent. In other states, however, they would be allowed to marry if they had parental consent, judicial consent, or both. In the past, some states differentiated between girls and boys in setting the age at which parental or judicial consent was required, but this distinction has largely disappeared. Although the age of consent traditionally is lower for common-law marriages—as low as fourteen for boys and twelve for girls—only a handful of states still recognize these marriages.

What if Tiffany and Adam, to avoid obtaining parental consent in their own state, go to another state and marry with judicial consent? Will the marriage be considered valid if they return to their home state?

Generally, a marriage validly performed in one state is valid everywhere unless it is against the public policy of the state where the marriage is at issue. Some states might consider underage marriages in violation of their public policy; others will validate the marriage. Conversely, if the marriage is not valid where performed, some states will later validate it if it would have been legal in those states. Either way, if Tiffany and Adam continue to live together once they reach the age of consent, the marriage will be considered valid.

SEXUAL ACTIVITY AND ITS CONSEQUENCES

For many parents of adolescents, teenage sexual activity presents an especially troubling problem. While there is no consensus on the number of minors having sex or the average age for becoming sexually active, 1995 data from the National Center for Health Statistics and the National Institute of Child Health and Human Development indicates that 50 percent of girls and 55 percent of boys age fifteen to nineteen have engaged in sexual intercourse. Parents may object to adolescent sexual activity because they view it as immoral or because they fear exploitation, particularly of girls, or the pregnancy and disease that may result. The rate of teenage pregnancy has increased dramatically in the last generation, but the trend may be abating. The National Center for Health Statistics reported a decline in the rate of teenage births in 1995 for the fourth year in a row. Still, the numbers are staggering. One 1994 study suggests that half a million babies are born annually to girls between the ages of fifteen and nineteen, with almost 12 percent of sexually active girls in that age range getting pregnant each year. Teenagers are also at high risk for a number of sexually transmitted diseases, including AIDS. A 1994 study by the Alan Guttmacher Institute estimates that three million teenagers a year become infected with a sexually transmitted disease, forty to fifty thousand with AIDS. Clearly teenage sexual activity is a social problem of enormous importance. The following discussion will consider what role, if any, the law plays in regulating such behavior.

Statutory Rape

The Supreme Court has never recognized a constitutional right of minors to engage in sexual activity, and such a holding would be extremely unlikely given the current composition of the Court. Consequently, the states are relatively free to pass laws restricting sexual activity by minors. Most states have adopted so-called statutory rape laws as a way of controlling teenage sexual activity and protecting minors, particularly teenage girls, from exploitation. These laws generally prohibit sex with or between minors below a certain age, even if the minors consent. The theory is that individuals below a certain age are too immature and vulnerable to give true, voluntary consent. Violation of statutory rape laws is a criminal offense that can lead to imprisonment.

Let's suppose Andrea and her boyfriend Louis have been dating for most of her freshman year of high school. Andrea is fifteen and Louis is eighteen. Andrea's mother recently discovered that Andrea and Louis have been engaging in sexual intercourse. She would like to put a stop to the behavior, but Andrea insists that she is old enough to do as she pleases and that she loves Louis. Andrea's mother is considering reporting Louis to the police for statutory rape. Can Louis be prosecuted for this crime and would Andrea also be subject to criminal charges?

The answer could be yes to both parts of the question, depending on the jurisdiction. Historically, statutory rape laws were applied only to males; females could not be prosecuted under them. Although the Supreme Court has held that states may treat males and females differently in this way, many states have amended their laws to make them gender neutral, so both Louis and Andrea could be convicted if they satisfy the age requirements for statutory rape.

The age of consent in most states is sixteen, but it is as low as thirteen in some and as high as eighteen in others. In addition, some states now define statutory rape not solely in terms of the age of the victim but also according to the difference in the ages of the participants. For example, in one jurisdiction, it might be a crime to have sex with a fifteen-year-old only if the perpetrator is more than three years older; and in another jurisdiction, it might be a crime to have sex with someone between thirteen and eighteen only if the perpetrator is at least seventeen. In jurisdictions like the first, Louis would not be guilty of statutory rape because he is only three years older than Andrea, but in a jurisdiction like the second, he could be charged. In some states, even if Louis were fifteen like Andrea, they both could face criminal prosecution, since these states consider sex by two underage teenagers statutory rape. Many states have several degrees of statutory rape based on various ages and age differences.

Even if Louis could be prosecuted under his state's law, there is no guarantee that he would be. Statutory rape charges remain very much a matter of prosecutorial discretion. Prosecuting consensual sex between teenagers has not been a high priority for most district attorneys. Prosecutors are usually not inclined to prosecute for statutory rape unless they believe a more serious rape—felony forcible rape—has occurred and they lack the evidence to prove it. True statutory rape cases can be hard to win. The victim often does not want to cooperate because she has feelings for the perpetrator, and juries may be reluctant to convict if the sex was consensual. However, recent statistics suggesting a link between statutory rape and teen pregnancy—one in five mothers under eighteen is impregnated by a man at least twenty years old—and concern over exploitation of teenage girls have led to renewed calls for stricter enforcement, and a number of states have increased the penalties for statutory rape.

If the prosecutor chose to charge Louis with statutory rape, she would need to prove only that Andrea was underage and that sex took place. Statutory rape is a "strict liability" offense. This means that the prosecutor would not have to prove any evil intent on Louis's part nor would Louis be able to claim that he thought Andrea was of consenting age since mistake is no defense. In some jurisdictions, though, Louis might be able to raise a promiscuity defense if he could show that Andrea had engaged in sexual relations with several partners.

Contraception

As we saw in chapter 3, our public schools recognize that many teenagers are sexually active today, and they have added sex education to their curricula to discourage minors from having sex or, in many

MINORS' RIGHTS TO CONTRACEPTION

Although minors' constitutional rights are not coextensive with adults', the Supreme Court has held that minors have a constitutional right to privacy in matters relating to procreation, including contraception. In *Carey v. Population Services International,* the Court struck down a statute that prohibited sale of contraceptives to minors under age sixteen. In order to sustain a restriction on access to contraceptives for minors, the state had to demonstrate a "significant state interest" not present in the case of adults, and it was unable to do so. The state attempted to argue that prohibiting minors access to contraceptives would decrease sexual activity, but it presented no evidence to support that contention.

cases, to provide information on contraceptives so that teenagers can protect themselves from pregnancy and sexually transmitted diseases. Some schools even distribute condoms to minors who request them. While condom distribution programs in schools have been controversial, it is clear that minors do have the right to purchase over-the-counter contraceptives (see box above). In some states, minors can obtain prescription contraceptives as well.

As a parent, do you have a right to notification if your daughter receives a prescription for birth control? This is an issue that has been the subject of some litigation. Reasoning from the Supreme Court's abortion cases (discussed shortly), an absolute requirement of parental consent is probably unconstitutional, but the Supreme Court has not yet decided this issue. The Court did affirm a lower court decision striking down a Utah law that prohibited state-funded services from providing contraceptives to minors without parental consent, but it did not do so on constitutional grounds. A number of courts have also overturned federal regulations requiring federally funded clinics to notify parents of birth control prescriptions provided to minors, although, again, not on constitutional grounds. On the other hand, neither the states nor the federal government has a constitutional obligation to provide financial assistance to clinics to assist needy minors in obtaining birth control. Given the law's protection of minors' rights in the area of contraception, probably the best way to influence your child's decisions regarding sexual activity is to keep the lines of communication open.

Abortion

Abortion is perhaps the most controversial and divisive issue in our nation, and the battle has been waged fiercely over minors' rights in this area. Litigation has centered around two main issues: whether a state can prohibit a minor from obtaining an abortion without parental consent and whether a state can require parents to be notified prior to allowing an abortion to be performed on a minor.

Close to forty states have laws that require either parental consent or parental notification before a minor can obtain an abortion, but about half of these laws have been enjoined (prohibited from going into effect) or struck down as unconstitutional. The Supreme Court has held that minors have a constitutional right to privacy that encompasses the decision to terminate a pregnancy and that states therefore cannot give parents exclusive control over this decision. In the Court's view, a child's interest in terminating a pregnancy outweighs her parents' interest in parental autonomy and control. Nonetheless, the Court has upheld statutes requiring either parental consent or notice so long as they also provide for "judicial bypass" of the requirement. This means that the state must allow a minor an opportunity in court to persuade a judge that she is mature enough to make this decision on her own or that an abortion would be in her best interests even if she is immature. To be constitutional, this judicial bypass procedure must be confidential and expeditious. Let's see how this works in practice.

Danielle is a sixteen-year-old high school junior who is seeking judicial consent for an abortion. She has a steady boyfriend, Roberto, and they usually use a condom when having sexual relations. However, they forgot on one occasion, and she became pregnant. Danielle is a good student, with a grade point average of 3.6, and she plans to attend college. She has discussed the abortion with her boyfriend, who supports her decision, and with a staff person at a family planning clinic, who has explained the medical aspects of the procedure to her. Danielle has also discussed alternatives with an antiabortion group. She does not want to tell her mother because she fears that her mother will be disappointed in her and no longer trust her.

In deciding whether Danielle is mature enough to make the decision on her own, the court will not evaluate whether her parents would consent to the abortion. Rather, the court will focus on Danielle's age, experience, intelligence, and judgment. The court will consider her school record, her ability to consult with adults other than her parents, and her understanding of the procedure and its consequences.

The judicial bypass procedure vests tremendous discretion in the judges who hear these petitions. In some states, the judges deny such requests as a matter of course. Others tend to grant them just as routinely. Nonetheless, the trial judge's discretion is not unlimited. In an Ohio case involving facts similar to Danielle's, the appellate court reversed the trial judge's decision that the minor was not sufficiently mature to obtain an abortion without parental notification. The court found that there was ample evidence that she was mature and well-informed enough to make the decision independently.

In fact, in all but one case appealed after a trial judge denied a minor permission to have an abortion without parental consent or notification, the appellate court has reversed the decision. In that one case, the minor already had undergone one abortion the previous year and had ceased using birth control, even though she said that she planned to attend college and testified that her father had hit her and threatened to cut her off financially if she became pregnant. The court found that she had not demonstrated either that she was sufficiently mature or that a waiver of parental notification was in her best interests.

Although this is the only reported appellate case affirming a judge's refusal to waive notification or consent, there undoubtedly have been many cases in which minors have been denied permission and have chosen not to appeal. Navigating the judicial system is never easy, and minors seeking judicial bypass generally are not entitled to a lawyer to assist them even at the initial stage of the proceeding, let alone if they appeal the decision. Moreover, in some areas, particularly rural counties, judges may refuse to hear abortion petitions for personal or philosophical reasons, forcing some minors to travel long distances just to obtain hearings.

If a state requires parental notification, it may also require a waiting period between notification and performance of an abortion. Waiting periods of forty-eight and seventy-two hours have been upheld. Too long a delay, though, would be considered unconstitutional.

While many people support the idea of parental involvement in a minor's abortion decision through notification or consent, the reality is not necessarily consistent with the goal of bringing families together. Many minors already voluntarily consult one or both parents when considering abortion. Unfortunately, legislatively mandating communication on this issue does not seem to serve a minor's or her family's needs in many cases. In states where the law requires notification of or consent by *both* parents, girls are often accompanied to court for the judicial bypass by their custodial parent, who is separated or divorced from the other parent. Typically, the custodial parent also opposes the other parent's involvement, often because of a history of abuse by the absent parent. Nonetheless, these laws force the custodial parent and the minor to go to court to get permission to terminate the pregnancy.

Faced with the prospect of seeking parental consent, having their parents notified, or going to court, some minors will delay their decision, facing increased risks from abortion as the pregnancy progresses. Some will try to obtain abortions in neighboring states without parental notification or consent requirements. Others will seek out illegal abortions, which can be fatal. Still others may even attempt suicide. The rest may simply decide not to have an abortion. While opponents of abortion see this as a desirable outcome, it is not without risks for a minor. In fact, childbearing by a minor carries significantly greater health risks for her than abortion. Unfortunately, when teenagers become pregnant, there are no easy answers.

Minors as Parents

If an adolescent like Danielle becomes pregnant and decides to keep her baby, she will be treated in almost the same way as any adult parent would. In most states, she will be able to consent to medical care for herself and her child. She will also be obligated to support her child, as will Roberto, because the rules governing child support discussed in chapter 8 apply to minor parents as well as to adult parents. In fact, a few cases have even imposed the support obligation on minor fathers who are the victims of statutory rape by an older woman. In these cases, the courts have found that the child's need for support outweighs any other interests, including protecting the minor parent from wrongful acts of the other parent.

In some instances, though, minor parents may receive different treatment under the law. In a few states, the grandparents of children born to minors can be held financially responsible for child support if the child's parents are unable to provide it. Welfare programs, such as Aid to Families with Dependent Children (AFDC), formerly provided assistance to needy minor parents who otherwise qualified regardless of age. However, in a 1996 effort to curtail the number of teenage pregnancies as part of an overhaul of the welfare system, Congress abolished the AFDC program and gave the states the responsibility for fashioning their own welfare programs within federal guidelines. Federal law now allows states to provide assistance to unmarried mothers under eighteen only so long as they remain in school and live at home with an adult. The states also have the option of denying assistance to unmarried teen mothers altogether. You will need to contact your state's department of social services or public assistance to learn how these changes have been implemented.

RESTRICTIONS ON ADOLESCENT ACTIVITIES

The teenage years are a time for adolescents to begin to assume greater responsibility and broader privileges to engage in adult-type conduct and decision making; nevertheless, teenagers are not yet adults. They are still in need of considerable supervision, and they may be particularly vulnerable to harmful influences and exploitation. The law reflects the changing social and developmental needs of adolescents by allowing them to engage in certain activities with special limitations while prohibiting them from engaging in other activities.

Teenage Drivers

One of the most valued privileges afforded during the teenage years is the opportunity to obtain a driver's license. Becoming a licensed driver represents a milestone for a teenager and his or her parents. It offers the young adult much-desired freedom, and it often yields corresponding benefits for parents, who are relieved of acting as chauffeurs for their children.

Yet the privilege of a driver's license carries with it serious responsibilities both for teenage drivers and their parents. Teenage drivers suffer one of the highest accident rates, and the lethal combination of alcohol and driving falls particularly hard on teenagers (see box on page 146). In addition to concern for their own teenager's safety, parents face liability for harm caused to others by their teenager.

At what age will your child be eligible to drive? Minors in most states are allowed to obtain a driver's license at age sixteen, but they usually need their parents' permission to do so, and they often have restrictions on their license until they complete a driver's education course. They may also be able to obtain a learner's permit or junior license at age fifteen and in some states even at fourteen. These junior licenses carry various restrictions: the driver may not drive in certain locations, at certain times, or without the presence of a fully licensed driver. About fifteen states have adopted rules requiring graduated or multistep licensing of this type for teenage drivers.

In addition to requiring a license, most states today have compulsory insurance laws that require all drivers to carry liability insurance. Adding a teenage driver to your insurance policy will probably significantly increase your premium since teenage drivers are at high risk for accidents. Nonetheless, it is important to obtain adequate coverage because liability for damage caused by your child in a car accident can fall on you.

TEENS AND DRUNK DRIVING:

THE NEW ZERO-TOLERANCE LAWS

Drunk driving is the leading cause of death among fifteen- to twenty-four-year-olds in this country. Since the early 1980s, lawmakers have cracked down on drunk drivers of all ages. More recently states have focused specifically on drivers under twenty-one, since the combination of alcohol and inexperience leads to many more fatalities for this population than for those over twenty-one. More than half the states now have zero-tolerance laws that make it illegal for those under eighteen or twenty-one to drive with virtually any alcohol at all in their blood. Drivers who violate these laws face revocation or suspension of their license, fines of several hundred dollars, community service, and even jail time. According to one study, Maryland's zero-tolerance law has contributed to a significant reduction in the number of alcohol-related accidents among drivers under twenty-one in that state. With this kind of track record, we can expect to see more states follow the trend.

Let's look at an example of how that could happen. Suppose that André is seventeen and has recently obtained his driver's license. While driving his mother's car to the local mall, he runs a stop sign and broadsides a car driven by Shauna. Shauna's car sustains considerable damage, and she suffers serious injuries requiring hospitalization. Shauna sues André and his parents. André has no money or assets. Can his parents be held liable for the damages?

There are several ways in which parents like André's may be legally responsible for auto accidents caused by their teenage children. When a parent signs a minor's application for a driver's license, in most states, she or he accepts legal and financial responsibility for any damage caused by the child's negligence or willful misconduct while driving. These laws "impute" the child's negligence to the parent, which means that the parent need not be at fault in any way to be held legally liable. A few states place a dollar limit on the amount for which the parent can be liable, in which case André's parents might be spared paying the entire judgment if Shauna's damages exceed the statutory limit, but most states allow recovery of full damages. The parent is held "jointly and severally liable" with the child, which means that the injured party, Shauna in our case, can recover all damages from either André or his parents if she is successful in proving that André was negligent.

A second way André's parents may become liable for injuries caused by André's negligent driving is under the "family purpose" doctrine, which is recognized in about half the states. This doctrine can impose liability on parents for the negligent driving of adult as well as minor children. To prevail using the family purpose doctrine, the injured party must show that the negligent child was driving a car purchased for use by the family, that the car was owned and controlled by the parent being sued, and that it was being used by a member of the family for a family purpose and with the express or implied consent of the parent being sued. The doctrine would not apply, for example, if André's mother purchased the car for her exclusive use to go to and from work or if André took the car without permission.

A parent can also be responsible for injury caused by a teenage driver based on "negligent entrustment." Negligent entrustment occurs when someone unreasonably provides someone else with an object that could cause harm to another, often called a "dangerous instrumentality." If André's parents bought or loaned him the car knowing that he was incapable of driving responsibly or had a record of moving violations, mental or emotional problems, or a history of alcohol use, his parents could be liable for their own negligence in providing him with the car, a dangerous instrumentality in André's hands. Other situations involving negligent entrustment are discussed in chapter 10.

Teenage Employment

The right to work, like the right to drive, is a major milestone for teenagers. In response to a long history of cruel exploitation of children by employers, federal and state child labor laws were enacted to prohibit employers from hiring children except in rare circumstances. Today, in addition to federal laws governing child labor, each state has its own laws regulating the employment of children. You should consult your state employment office or department of labor or your local school district to find out the exact requirements and restrictions in effect in your state.

Most states require that a child obtain a certificate from the state before being eligible to work. Usually, the child needs parental consent and proof of age and good health to obtain the certificate. Generally, children under sixteen are prohibited from working in most, but not all, occupations, especially those that may be hazardous. Certain occupations like domestic work (baby-sitting, housecleaning, lawn mowing), newspaper delivery, agricultural work, and entertainment (acting) are often exempt from these age restrictions. Children as young as twelve may be permitted to perform agricultural work; children of any age may work as actors. The range of jobs open to minors between sixteen and eighteen is broader. However, the hours during which minors of any age may work are specifically regulated. For example, state labor laws often prohibit minors from working during school hours or between 7 P.M. and 7 A.M. on school nights. The law may also restrict the total number of hours a minor may work on a given day or over the course of a week. Some may limit work to three hours a day on school days (if the minor is a student) and eight hours on other days. Violation of any of these laws results in penalties against the employer, not the child.

To explore some of the legal questions that arise about teenagers and employment, let's consider the hypothetical case of Caitlin. On her sixteenth birthday, Caitlin gets a job at the local fast-food outlet, serving hamburgers, french fries, and the usual artery-clogging fare two days a week after school and one day on weekends. Concerned about the increase in the minimum wage, her employer offers her a below-minimum wage of four dollars an hour. Has her employer violated the law?

Minors are generally entitled by law to the federal or state minimum wage, whichever is higher. However, some occupations are exempt from this law. For instance, camp employees, newspaper deliverers, baby-sitters, and those involved in fishing may earn less than the minimum wage. In addition, the secretary of labor has the power to issue a special certificate to certain industries staffed primarily by minors, for example, fast-food restaurants, relieving them of the obligation to pay minimum wage. Although critics of the exemption claim that it facilitates exploitation of teenage workers, the employers argue that without it they would not hire teenagers at all. If the fast-food outlet where Caitlin works operates under a special certificate, its conduct is legal.

Now suppose that a few weeks after she begins working, Caitlin's parents insist that she sign over her paycheck to them each week. Are her parents legally entitled to the money? Parents do generally have the right to their children's wages unless the children are fully or partially emancipated, a topic we will discuss shortly. However, some states today require parents to notify their child's employer that they will be receiving the wages; if they don't, the wages belong to the child. Likewise, if Caitlin's parents explicitly allow her to keep her first few paychecks, they may waive their right to subsequent paychecks.

Finally, suppose that six months after she starts working, Caitlin is laid off. Is she entitled to unemployment benefits? There is no age limit on unemployment insurance, but a minor who has been laid off must meet all the usual requirements for receiving the benefit. Part-time workers are generally not eligible for unemployment, so Caitlin, like many teenagers, will be ineligible on this basis. Similarly, all workers, regardless of age, must obtain a social security card, and there are no age restrictions on earning benefits. However, certain occupations frequently employing minors, such as domestic work and work for colleges, do not count toward earning social security credit. Minors are also entitled to workers' compensation if they are injured on the job. However, if they are illegally employed, workers' compensation may not apply. In that case, they may be entitled to sue the employer for monetary damages if the employer was negligent or committed some other wrong compensable under the law.

Illicit Activities

Use of drugs, alcohol, and tobacco by teenagers presents one of our most pressing social and health problems today. Although the lethal combination of drinking and driving appears to have decreased somewhat in recent years, abuse of alcohol by teenagers still remains widespread and the incidence of smoking, particularly by teenage girls, appears to be on the rise. By some estimates, almost one in three teens smokes, and three thousand teens begin smoking every day. Moreover, a 1996 federal study discouragingly reported that illicit drug use appears to be resurgent once again. Among twelve- to seventeen-year-olds, drug use more than doubled between 1992 and 1996, rising from 5.3 percent to 10.9 percent. This increase occurred across the spectrum of illicit drugs, including marijuana, hallucinogens like LSD, and cocaine, and the drug use begins as early as sixth grade. All of this is true despite the existence of laws explicitly designed to protect minors from access to these substances.

Possession and sale of illegal drugs is a crime throughout the nation. In some states, possessing small amounts of some of these drugs, such as marijuana or toluene (the intoxicating ingredient in substances for glue sniffing), remains a misdemeanor, a relatively minor offense that can result in a fine or a short period of incarceration. But possession of sufficient quantities of marijuana and of any quantity of a narcotic, such as cocaine or heroin, or a hallucinogen may result in felony charges—much more serious charges that carry a lengthy mandatory minimum sentence. Various jurisdictions have also passed laws making it a felony to provide drugs to a minor under fourteen on school grounds during school hours. Merely being present when narcotics are being used can subject a minor to misdemeanor charges if the minor facilitates the use or has control over the premises. A full discussion of the juvenile criminal system is contained in chapter 9.

Today in every state, the legal drinking age is twenty-one, and buying, selling, or consuming alcohol below this age is against the law. In some states, even possessing alcohol in public if you are underage is a crime, as is using a false ID to obtain alcohol. Minors are prohibited from working in establishments where alcohol is sold and in some states from even being on the premises unless the sale of alcohol is considered incidental, as it is in restaurants, or the minor is in the company of an adult.

The intent required to violate the law varies by state. Some states make selling alcohol to an underage person a "strict liability" offense. This means that the seller can be liable even if he didn't know the person was underage. States with this kind of law sometimes allow the seller to raise a good-faith belief in a false ID as a defense. In other states, the state must prove that the seller "knowingly or willfully" sold alcohol to an underage person. In most states, the prohibition applies to adults who purchase alcohol for a minor as well as to social hosts; however, some states exclude parents who serve their own children small quantities of alcohol. Large quantities are another matter; in one New York case, the state prosecuted parents who provided their fifteen-year-old with enough alcohol to kill the child.

Sale of cigarettes and tobacco products to teenagers under eighteen is also prohibited in most states, although a few set the minimum age at fifteen or sixteen. Unfortunately, these laws are extremely difficult to enforce because children frequently buy cigarettes from vending machines and possession of cigarettes is not a crime. In an effort to stem the tide of teenage smoking, in 1996 the Food and Drug Administration (FDA) identified cigarettes as addictive drugs and "nicotine delivery systems," thus paving the way for greater regulation of cigarettes and cigarette advertising directed at teens. The FDA plans to implement several new regulations in the coming years, including a ban on cigarette sales in vending machines except in venues limited to adults, like bars and casinos, and a requirement that proof of age be shown. New regulations would also place additional restrictions on print ads, sponsorship of sporting events, and promotional items such as T-shirts and baseball caps. The tobacco industry's initial challenge to these regulations in court has met with mixed results. The FDA's classification of nicotine as a drug has been upheld, but the court struck down the bans on advertising as impermissible restrictions on free speech. The battle

LOCAL EFFORTS TO STOP TEENAGE SMOKING

In an effort to make a dent in the 3.1 million minors ages twelve to eighteen who smoke, a number of cities and towns have passed laws banning sales of cigarettes in vending machines and fining merchants who violate state and city laws prohibiting the sale of tobacco to minors. Woodridge, Illinois, a town outside Chicago, has one of the toughest antismoking enforcement programs in the nation, and it seems to be working. Results of an initial study conducted in 1991 showed a decline in junior high students who admitted to being regular smokers from 16 percent to 5 percent. More recently, a 1996 comparison of Woodridge with a neighboring town showed that a significantly lower percentage of Woodridge high school students regularly use tobacco products than in the past.

Woodridge requires local licensing of tobacco sellers and actively enforces bans on sales to minors by waging frequent undercover inspections and fining violators five hundred dollars. Woodridge also fines any minors caught using tobacco products unless they are under the direct supervision of their parents. While other towns have followed Woodridge's example in enacting stricter laws, they have not emulated Woodridge's consistent enforcement and thus have not obtained the same results.

over federal regulation is far from over. In the meantime, towns throughout the nation are waging their own campaigns against teenage smoking, as the box above details.

Curfews and Entertainment

In an effort to protect young people and the public and to curtail gang activity, a growing number of cities and towns have enacted ordinances imposing curfews on minors. These curfews prohibit minors from being on public streets after a certain hour, usually 9, 10, or 11 P.M., unless they are accompanied by a parent or other adult or unless they have some specified purpose for which the law makes an exception, such as going to or from work. Some cities have also adopted daytime curfews to combat truancy. Many of the curfews have been invalidated as unconstitutional infringements of the First Amendment right to free association, the equal protection clause, and the right to travel, but a few courts have upheld them. Violating a curfew in and of itself does not usually subject a minor to criminal prosecution; rather it is treated as a status offense—that is, misconduct subjecting the minor to the jurisdiction of the juvenile court. (Status offenses are discussed at greater length in chapter 9.)

In addition to curfews, some municipalities have laws restricting access of minors to certain establishments, such as dance clubs, pool halls, and video arcades. Some prohibit entrance at all times; others limit the hours during which minors may be present. These laws have also been challenged in the courts but have largely been upheld. Since they are seen essentially as legislating commercial activity, the state need only show that the law is rationally related to the state's purpose in enacting the statute. These laws are often passed to combat truancy and to protect children from inappropriate influences, like gambling and drugs, and from overspending on video games and the like. Some courts have struck down particular ordinances that don't reasonably serve these goals. For example, a law forbidding minors to enter a video arcade at any time was invalidated because it was not reasonably related to its stated purpose, which was to prevent truancy.

EMANCIPATION

Can your teenager escape the legal limitations of adolescence by becoming emancipated? Yes and no. Emancipation means that a minor is an adult under the law, at least for certain purposes. Depending on whether the emancipation is partial or complete, an emancipated minor may be able to sign contracts or leases, apply for a work permit without parental consent, agree to medical treatment, and establish her own residence. Emancipation also relieves her parents of their obligation to support her. However, emancipation does not eradicate all the disabilities of minority. Minors still are subject to the jurisdiction of the juvenile court for criminal conduct, cannot drink or smoke, must attend school, and remain subject to certain child labor laws.

There are three ways a minor can become emancipated before reaching the age of majority: by marrying, by joining the military, or by obtaining a court order. Traditionally, the last method has been used relatively rarely and often for very specific purposes, such as enabling a child to sue a parent for damages, and emancipation has been granted only after a searching inquiry by the court into whether it is justified. In deciding whether to recognize a minor as emancipated, the court generally considers whether the child resides at home, works for wages outside the home, has control of his earnings, owns a significant asset, or is declared as a dependent on his parents' tax return. Many states require that parents consent to a minor's emancipation, but some do not. When the question of emancipation arises in connection with a claim for child support, the courts often hesitate to grant it, even if the child has supported herself for some period of time.

Emancipation by court order after a full inquiry still goes on, but a significant number of states now offer the additional option of a simplified procedure. In California, for example, a fourteen-year-old need only file with the court a petition asserting that she is at least fourteen, is willingly living apart from her parents with their consent or acquiescence, is handling her own finances, and has income not derived from criminal activity. If her parent signs the petition, no hearing is even held, and within as little as a week, the minor may be completely emancipated. One California study indicates that many simplified emancipations arise out of family conflict and may be prompted by parental suggestion. Although there are no statistics available, this small study suggests that a significant number of emancipated minors struggle financially, end up homeless, or fail to finish high school. Still, emancipation may be an appropriate option for some teenagers and their families.

MONEY MATTERS AND PLANNING
FOR YOUR CHILD'S FUTURE

MOST PARENTS WANT to satisfy their children's material needs and have enough to give them the extras—summer camp, piano lessons, and the like. Most also are concerned with ensuring their children's financial security in the event of their death. To achieve these goals, you will probably want to read one or more of the many books available on financial planning, investing, and estate planning. You may also want to consult with an accountant, a lawyer specializing in estate planning, a financial planner, or perhaps a combination of these professionals to assist you in maximizing your financial position. This chapter is in no way a substitute for any of that research. It will, however, provide you with an overview of important legal issues regarding financial matters of concern to parents, including a child's right to own property, tax issues related to children, and wills and trusts.

YOUR CHILD'S RIGHT TO OWN AND CONTROL PROPERTY

When it comes to money, children have the right to open a bank account and deposit and withdraw money on the same terms as adults. Minors also have the same rights as adults to own real and personal property. Ironically, though, children do not have the right to control their property. That right generally rests with a guardian, custodian (in cases of gifts to minors under the Uniform Transfers to Minors Act), or trustee (in the case of a trust). What this means is that if a minor attempts to sell her property on her own, without one of these agents, she can later repudiate or void the sale, providing that she does so within a reasonable time after reaching the age of majority.

Although you may find it surprising, parents cannot automatically control their children's property, either. To do so, a parent must be appointed by the court as a guardian or conservator of the property. Few parents need to do this, though, because parents do have the legal right to control property they provide for their children as basic support, such as clothing, toys, and books. Traditionally, as you know from chapter 5, parents also have the right to money earned from their children's services. This remains the law in most states today, although the right can be waived if the parent allows the child to collect and spend the wages. Other states presume any earnings belong to the child unless the parent lets the employer know that the wages are to go to the parents.

Because minors cannot legally control their own property and parents do not automatically assume that right, many parents provide money or property to their children by using devices that allow them or another adult to manage it. The two main devices are trusts, discussed later in this chapter, and gifts made according to the Uniform Transfers to Minors Act or the Uniform Gifts to Minors Act, discussed in the box on page 157.

TAX ISSUES

As a parent, there are three primary tax issues you will need to be familiar with: income tax issues that arise with respect to income you or your child earns during your lifetime; estate tax issues that arise on your death; and gift tax issues arising from transfers of property to your

GIFTS AND TRANSFERS OF PROPERTY TO MINORS

Approximately forty states have adopted the Uniform Transfers to Minors Act (UTMA); the remaining states use some version of the Uniform Gifts to Minors Act (UGMA), a similar law. UTMA allows parents to make transfers or gifts of property to their children through a custodian. In other words, the property—which can be money, securities, insurance, real property, or personal property—is given to a designated custodian for the benefit of the child. With a few exceptions, you, as the parent, can name yourself the custodian, but then the property reverts to your estate if you die before your child reaches age eighteen, twenty-one, or twenty-five (depending on your state's version of the law).

Assuming you are the custodian, you have the right to use the money as you see fit for your child's benefit as long as he is under the cutoff age. You can invest the money, but you must maintain it separately from any of your property, and you have a legal obligation to deal prudently with the property. As the custodian, you are entitled to recoup reasonable expenses for your services, but you can't use the custodial property to satisfy your basic obligation to support your child.

Unlike a trust, the money or property in a custodial account is the child's; it does not belong to a separate entity. Thus, the income from the property is taxable to the child. Moreover, a transfer under UTMA automatically becomes your child's property, subject to her control, when she reaches the cutoff date established by your particular state.

Transfers under UTMA are relatively simple and can usually be done at a bank. Once you've established a custodial account, you can then make deposits to the account if you are the named custodian. You should set up the account using your child's social security number, since he will pay taxes on the money. The kiddie tax (discussed in the text) may apply, which means if your child is under fourteen, the income will still be taxed at your rate. If he is fourteen or older, your child will pay taxes at his rate, which is probably much less than yours.

children or grandchildren during your lifetime. Each of these will be discussed in turn in very basic terms and will serve as background for the next section on planning for your child's future after you are gone.

Income Tax Issues

As you are well aware, you must pay federal taxes on your income. Generally, you calculate your federal income tax for a given year by subtracting your deductions and exemptions from your gross income (salary, interest, and dividends), multiplying the result by your tax rate, and then subtracting any tax credits to which you are entitled. The result is the amount you must actually pay to the Internal Revenue Service (IRS).

Claiming Your Child as a Dependent. Can becoming a parent reduce the amount of income tax you pay? Yes, although no one would claim it saves you money in the long run. Raising children is an expensive proposition. Still, federal law allows you to take exemptions for your dependents. To claim the dependency exemption, you will need to meet five criteria:

First, the subject of the exemption must be a dependent. Who is considered a dependent? A dependent is either a full-time member of your household or a relative. Your son or daughter, an adopted child, a child placed with you pending adoption, an illegitimate child whom you have acknowledged, and a stepchild for whom you are providing most of the support all qualify as dependents. Also, a nonrelative who lives with you continuously throughout the taxable year may be claimed as a dependent, assuming all the other conditions are met.

Second, the claimed dependent must be a citizen or resident of the United States, Canada, or Mexico.

Third, you generally cannot claim a child as a dependent if the child is in the armed forces, is attending a military academy, or is filing a joint tax return as a married person, although there are some exceptions to this rule.

Fourth, in general you may not take a dependency exemption if the dependent has gross income in excess of the dependency exemption amount for that year. However, this test does not apply if the dependent is your child and either is under the age of nineteen or is a full-time student under the age of twenty-four.

Fifth and finally, to claim the dependency exemption you must provide more than half of the dependent's support. (Which parent gets to claim the exemption for a child in cases of divorce is covered in chapter 8 on child support.)

You may also get a deduction for dependent child care (discussed in chapter 2) and a tax credit if you have dependents and your earned income is below a certain amount. This credit, called the earned income credit, is subtracted from the amount you owe and is refundable, meaning that you get a refund even if the credit amount is greater than your tax liability. Most employers are familiar with this credit, so if you qualify for it, you may want to consult your human resources or personnel department about figuring it in to your withholding. Moreover, beginning in the 1998 tax year, some families will be entitled to an additional tax credit of several hundred dollars for each dependent child under seventeen.

In addition to the federal government, most states require you to pay income taxes. Although they generally key their deductions to the federal law and define dependents in similar fashion, the tax rate, exemptions, deductions, and credits vary, so you will need to consult the law in your particular state.

Filing Separate Returns for Minors and the "Kiddie Tax." When you become a parent, will your child have to file a tax return? That depends on what her income is and where it comes from. Income flows from many sources. Income from labor is referred to as earned income. Income from other sources is referred to as unearned income, or capital. If your child's income is all earned, then he does not need to file a return unless he makes more than the standard deduction in a given year. Because the amount of the standard deduction varies from year to year, you will have to check the federal income tax table to see if your child's earnings have crossed the threshold. Most summer jobs and part-time work for minors pay relatively little, so your child's earned income probably won't exceed this amount.

On the other hand, if your child has income generated from sources other than work, such as interest from savings accounts or income from a trust, she may have to file a tax return. This is because if your child has even one dollar of unearned income, she must file a return if her total income—earned and unearned—exceeds six hundred dollars.

In addition, the so-called kiddie tax may apply when your child has unearned income. Under the kiddie tax, your child's unearned income is taxed at *your* highest marginal tax rate. For example, if your child has ten thousand dollars of unearned income, normally taxable at 15 percent, and your tax rate is 31 percent, under the kiddie tax, your child's ten thousand dollars will be taxed at 31 percent. The kiddie tax applies if your child is under age fourteen and has more than twelve hundred dollars of unearned income. To simplify your tax filings, if your child's adjusted gross income is between five hundred and five thousand dollars and only from interest and dividends, you can include it in your tax return and can forgo filing a separate return for your child.

Estate Taxes

In addition to income taxes, there are federal transfer taxes, specifically estate taxes and gift taxes. Estate taxes are taxes levied on transfers of money or property to your beneficiaries on your death (known as testamentary transfers), in other words, taxes on your gross estate. Gift taxes are taxes levied on transfers made in the form of gifts to others during your lifetime. Gift taxes are discussed in the next section. Here we consider estate taxes.

Your gross estate for estate tax purposes includes the fair market value of all property in which you have an interest at your death. This amount is multiplied by a tax rate to determine your estate tax liability. You need not be concerned about federal estate taxes unless your estate is valued at more than six hundred twenty-five thousand dollars. Why? Because the Internal Revenue Code provides for an exclusion of the first six hundred twenty-five thousand dollars of your estate (an amount that will gradually increase to $1 million in the year 2006 under the

Taxpayer Relief Act of 1997). You may think that your estate will never approach this size, but keep in mind that the fair market value of your house will certainly be included. And if you own a life insurance policy (that is, if it's in your name and you are the insured), the face value will be included in your gross estate for federal estate tax purposes. It is possible to avoid inclusion of insurance proceeds in your gross estate, but you will have to follow strict requirements in transferring owner-ship of the policy, so you should consult with a lawyer to help you ac-complish this.

If your estate is likely to be subject to estate taxes, you should des-ignate which assets are to be used to satisfy those taxes in your will. (Wills are discussed later in this chapter.) This is important for two rea-sons: First, the estate taxes may be charged to the beneficiaries and thus reduce the amount of money they receive from your estate. Sec-ond, property may have to be sold to satisfy the estate tax obligation.

Most important, though, *if you think the size of your estate will pass the six-hundred-twenty-five-thousand-dollar threshold, you should consult an experienced estate planner or probate lawyer.* There are various legal devices that can help you lower or avoid estate taxes, but they can be quite technical and are beyond the scope of this book.

Also be aware that in almost half the states, your estate or benefi-ciaries may have to pay state death or inheritance taxes in addition to federal taxes. However, the state taxes can at least be credited against your federal estate tax liability, so your estate won't face double taxation.

Gift Taxes and the Annual Gift Exclusion

Are there any tax consequences if you give all your money to your chil-dren while you're alive? Yes. Gifts are subject to federal tax, too. How-ever, the situation is not completely bleak. The Internal Revenue Code allows you to make an annual gift of ten thousand dollars to each of your children or to anyone else you choose free of gift tax. Moreover, you can split the gift with your spouse, which allows you to transfer twenty thousand dollars tax free. For example, under this rule, you can make a gift of twenty thousand dollars to your son and have half of it treated as a gift from your spouse so that it remains within the annual exclusion.

This annual exclusion applies only to gifts of "present interest." This means that the recipient of the gift, your child, has the right to immediate use or possession of the property or the income from the property. If the gift allows your child access to the property only at some point in the future, it cannot count as part of the annual exclusion. This is one of the disadvantages—you really have to give the money to your child, who may not be mature enough to handle it. There are ways to avoid this pitfall—for example, by giving your child the money in trust—but this is a very technical area, so you should consult a lawyer or tax adviser to fully understand the tax implications of the gifts you make.

In addition to the ten-thousand-dollar exclusion, you can make gifts for tuition and medical expenses, but you must make the payments directly to the institution providing the services. This is another way for you to transfer money to your children tax free.

Be careful, though, if you hope to obtain financial aid for your child in college. Financial aid is need-based. If you put money in your child's name, the financial aid formula allows a school to include a greater percentage of her money than of your money in calculating need. For this reason, it is generally ill-advised to put any substantial money in your child's name if you think she has a shot at getting financial aid. If you are considering doing so, you should see a lawyer because the rules governing taxes and transfers to minors are varied and complex.

TAKING CARE OF YOUR CHILD IN THE EVENT OF YOUR DEATH

Understandably, few people want to contemplate their own death, but if you have children, it is critical that you give some thought to the matter. There are three primary devices for providing for your children after you are gone: life insurance, wills, and trusts. Many parents use a combination of these devices to provide posthumous support for their children, but each family is different. A trust, for example, might be a good idea for one family but not for another. *The best way to evaluate the situation for your family is to consult a lawyer.* Many of these devices can get highly technical, especially if you are trying to minimize your tax liability. As you read over the next section, remember that there is no substitute for good legal advice to ensure that your wishes will be carried out in a way that most benefits you and your children.

Life and Disability Insurance

For many middle-class families, their primary asset will be their family home and perhaps some savings and investments. Their main concern should one of them die while their children are still minors will probably be ensuring continued income to support the family at the same relative standard of living, including maintaining any mortgage payments and financing the children's higher education. Many parents purchase some form of life insurance to provide the bulk of this income. Wealthier parents will probably also want life insurance, though it is more likely to be one of several sources of income for the family after the death of one or both of them.

Life insurance has the advantage of providing nearly immediate money because the proceeds, if they are paid directly to your beneficiary and not your estate, do not have to go through probate, a court-administered process that we will be discussing later. You may have other assets, but often it will take some time before they become available after your death. With life insurance, usually all your beneficiary has to do is notify your insurance company in writing, attaching a copy of the death certificate, and the company will issue a check.

There are several types of life insurance that range in cost and offer different short- and long-term benefits (see box on page 164). With so many options and considerations, it will be of considerable help to enlist the aid of a competent and reputable insurance broker, but you will need to guard against agents that seek only to sell. Try to find one that will advise you on the basis of your family's needs. You will want to verify as much as you can the financial condition of the insurance

TYPES OF LIFE INSURANCE

There are numerous kinds of life insurance, each with its own advantages and disadvantages. The two most popular kinds are term-life and whole-life insurance. Term-life insurance, the less expensive option, provides a specific amount of coverage for a set number of years. It works very simply: You pay a premium, determined by the coverage you want, your age, and your health, and if you die during the term of the policy, your beneficiaries are entitled to the face value of the policy. Term-life insurance can be a good idea for young families starting out who have few resources and need to ensure continued mortgage payments and support for young children.

Whole-life insurance is more expensive, but, unlike term-life insurance, it can also be part of an investment plan. In addition to providing a death benefit to support your family, a whole-life policy puts a small part of your premium into a savings account. You can borrow against this amount or withdraw it, even if the policy is canceled. Of course, any money you borrow will ultimately be deducted from the amount paid to your beneficiaries.

There are other kinds of policies—universal life, variable life, and single premium life—that also provide an investment opportunity as well as a death benefit. A reputable insurance broker can explain these options to you in detail so that you can decide which is right for your family.

company providing your policy. You might begin by checking the rating provided for the company by A.M. Best, a financial rating service. Also keep in mind that state regulations vary substantially in this area. Your state's insurance commission may be able to provide helpful consumer information.

Which type of policy is right for you will depend on your total financial plan and your family's changing needs and circumstances. A

HOW MUCH LIFE INSURANCE DO YOU NEED?

Some of you will have life insurance provided by your employer, but it might not be sufficient to meet your family's needs. How do you know how much insurance to purchase? You should certainly try to purchase enough to cover funeral costs, future educational expenses of your children, continuing mortgage payments and other living expenses, money to enable your family to get through the grief period, perhaps without the surviving spouse working, and some money to cover emergencies. Also consider insuring the life of a spouse who is a full-time parent and not bringing in income from a paid job. If the full-time parent dies, the surviving parent will probably have to hire someone to care for the children and might himself need to take some time off from work temporarily. Life insurance would ease the transition.

There are several ways to calculate how much life insurance is necessary to cover these expenses. For example, some experts estimate that a family needs at least 75 percent of its net income to sustain its standard of living after the chief earner dies. This amount is then multiplied by a number contained in a table based on the age of the surviving spouse. This is one of the simpler methods for calculating the amount of life insurance you should have. A reputable insurance broker can explain the various methods available, help you decide which is best for you, and tailor the calculation to your particular circumstances.

policy that serves you well when your children are young may no longer meet your needs as your children mature. Certainly once your children have reached the age of majority or finished their higher education, you will need to provide less protection for them, although of course your spouse will still need sufficient income to maintain his or her standard of living. Different policies also may provide certain tax benefits. A good lawyer or estate planner can help you evaluate how much life insurance you should have (see box on page 165) and where it should fit in your overall long-term financial plan.

Any employed parent should also have a good disability insurance policy. One in three individuals between thirty and sixty-five will become disabled for at least three months. Social security and many states provide a very basic disability benefit for workers who are partially or fully disabled. Similarly, many employers provide disability insurance as a job benefit. However, these benefits together are unlikely to fully replace your income, especially if your income is large. Consequently, you are well-advised to purchase disability insurance to supplement whatever the government and your employer may provide. The cost of the insurance will vary depending on the amount of the benefit, the length of the waiting period before benefits begin, and the duration of the policy. Most important, look for a policy that defines disability as not being able to perform your *current* employment. Some policies will not consider you disabled unless you cannot perform any work at all.

Another form of insurance is provided by the government in the form of social security. If you die, your spouse will obtain survivor's benefits until your youngest child is sixteen, assuming your spouse is under sixty. (If your surviving spouse is sixty or older, she will receive survivor's benefits regardless of whether she is still caring for any children at home.) Benefits will also be provided if your spouse is caring for a child who became disabled before age twenty-two and remains so. However, the amount of these benefits will be reduced if your surviving spouse earns more than a certain amount. Unmarried minor children, including adopted, illegitimate, and stepchildren, will receive their own independent benefit until age eighteen or nineteen if they are still full-time high school students.

Wills

The most important advice anyone can give you regarding planning for your child's future is to make a will. Most people don't and, as a result, leave their loved ones in a vulnerable position. Parents of minor children, in particular, should consider a will an essential item. A will is a document that provides for distribution of your assets upon your death and allows you to nominate a guardian for your children. A will gives you control over your assets and over who will care for your children in the event that both of their parents die. For families with substantial assets, wills can also help you avoid estate taxes.

Dying without a Will. If you don't have a will, it does not mean your spouse or your children will not inherit your money. It means that distribution of your estate will be governed by your state's intestacy laws. What happens to your assets if you die intestate, that is, without a will? Although state laws vary, generally your surviving spouse will inherit between a third and a half of your estate, and the remainder will be divided among your children. If you leave no surviving spouse, your children will divide the entire amount.

Children who can inherit under the intestacy laws include half children and adopted children. Although adopted children generally can no longer inherit from their biological parents once they have been adopted, some states do allow them to. For example, Maine and New Jersey allow inheritance by adopted children from their biological parents if the adoption decree provides for it, which might occur when an older child is adopted after the death of a parent. Many states also have an exception to this rule for children who are adopted by a stepparent.

Children born out of wedlock have always been able to inherit from their mothers. Historically, though, they have not been considered legally related to their biological fathers and therefore have not been able to inherit from them. In most states this rule has changed, in good part because the Supreme Court has declared that states cannot discriminate against illegitimate children. Nonetheless, children born out of wedlock seeking to inherit from their fathers will need to establish paternity. It is much better to do this before the father dies. If a child waits until after her father's death, in many states she will not be able to bring the necessary legal action.

There are many different ways of establishing paternity, as discussed in chapter 11. For inheritance purposes, some states require a definitive determination in the form of a court judgment or a notarized acknowledgment by the father because of their concern about potential fraud or their uncertainty in disposing of an estate. Other states consider less formal or direct evidence of paternity, such as the father's voluntary acceptance of a child during his lifetime or the father's later marriage to the mother.

Like illegitimate children, stepchildren may find themselves unable to inherit. Consider, for example, the hypothetical case of Nathan, the only child of Lauren. Nathan's father and Lauren divorced when Nathan was three, and Lauren remarried when Nathan was five. Her second husband, Brad, hopes to adopt Nathan but has been unable to do so because Nathan's dad will not consent. Nathan is now sixteen. If Brad dies intestate, can Nathan inherit? In the past, in the absence of a will, stepchildren had no legal right to inherit from a stepparent. While this is still largely the case, some states have taken steps to grant stepchildren in limited circumstances the right to inherit from a stepparent under the intestacy laws. Generally, these laws provide that a stepchild can inherit if his relationship with the stepparent began while he was a minor child and continued through the course of the stepparent's lifetime and if the stepchild can prove that the stepparent intended to adopt him but was unable to do so because of legal obstacles. A stepchild may also be able to inherit from an intestate stepparent if no other heirs exist and the alternative would be having the estate revert to the state. Of course, if a stepchild had actually been adopted by the stepparent, things would be different: he would be able to inherit from the stepparent, the custodial parent, and the noncustodial parent's line under the Uniform Probate Code, which is followed in about fifteen states.

Dying intestate is a bad idea because even if you agree with the general distribution provided for by the intestacy laws, it requires your estate to go through a potentially lengthy probate proceeding, during which time your family may have little support. Perhaps even more importantly for parents, dying intestate allows the court to choose a guardian for your children and thus deprives you and your family of making this critical decision yourselves.

Requirements for a Valid Will. As the author of a will, you are known as the testator. To draft a valid will, you must be at least eighteen years old and "of sound mind and memory." This means basically that you understand that you are drafting a will. You must also be doing so voluntarily. If you are under duress or undue influence, the will may be challenged in court and ultimately invalidated.

There are a number of procedural formalities required to ensure the validity of a will. In all but a few states, your will must be in writing and have two witnesses. In some states, the witnesses will be required to testify in court after your death that they saw you sign the will; most states, though, no longer require a court appearance if the signatures are notarized and the will contains a self-proving affidavit—that is, a signed statement made by the witnesses under oath that you did, in fact, sign the document. It is very important that the witnesses be disinterested, which means that they have nothing to gain from your death or by the will. Obviously neither your spouse nor your children should witness your will. In fact, it is best not to have any relative or anyone who will receive money or property under the will serve as a witness. If you have a lawyer prepare your will, she and someone in her office will be able to witness it (as long as the will doesn't leave them anything).

About half the states will accept an unwitnessed handwritten will, called a holographic will, but wills of this sort are very closely scrutinized by the court. If you prepare such a will, it must be entirely in your handwriting; even a typewritten date can invalidate it.

Do you need to have a lawyer to prepare or assist you in preparing your will? Technically, no, but the vast majority of people who have wills do consult a lawyer and with good reason. As we've seen, there are technical matters that could lead to invalidation of a will, and a lawyer can draft a will in language that will be clear and easy for the executor and the court to understand. Some states have statutory wills, forms that are valid if properly filled out, but these are usually for very simple estates and allow no flexibility. Likewise, self-help books and computer programs that contain forms for wills may be helpful to individuals with small estates, but for more complex situations, usually including those that involve minor children, they could end up causing costly problems for your survivors after you are gone. Although hiring a lawyer will cost you some money up front, it probably will reduce the costs paid by your survivors. If you belong to a group legal plan, a will may be provided at little or no cost or at a reduced hourly rate. In some places, legal clinics may be available to assist you in drafting a will. Sometimes you can arrange to have a legal assistant or paralegal do most of the work under the supervision of a lawyer, which will also save you money. If you have a business or a large estate (over six hundred twenty-five thousand dollars) or if you have any reason to believe your will may be challenged, because you are disinheriting a child, for example, you should certainly hire a lawyer. Look for someone with experience in probate and estate planning. Often lawyers will provide an initial consultation free of charge. They may then charge a flat fee for drafting the will in relatively simple cases and an hourly rate for more complex ones.

The more preparation you do, the less your will is likely to cost. You can help keep costs down by compiling a complete list of your assets and debts, whom you intend to name as beneficiaries and for what assets, your proposed guardian and executors, and a comprehensive list of the intended disposition of your money and your real and personal property. Of course, you may want to discuss these decisions with your lawyer; your lists need not be carved in stone. But the more work you do, the less work your lawyer will have to do, and the lower your bill will be. Your local bar association or lawyer referral service can assist you in finding a lawyer for this purpose.

Once you have a will, where should you keep it? The original will should be kept with other important documents (including any trust documents or other estate-planning material) in a secure place. Many choose a bank safe-deposit box, but be careful: in some states, banks automatically seal safe-deposit boxes on the owner's death, so be sure to arrange for someone else to have access in that eventuality. Otherwise your family will have to wait until the box is opened before beginning the probate process.

The Contents of the Will. The will must indicate that by it you are intending to dispose of your property after your death. Beyond that, you have control over the specific contents: to whom you wish to leave what assets (money or property), whom you wish to appoint as executor, and whom you wish to nominate as guardian for your minor children.

Much of the contents will concern disbursement of your assets, with dispositions of money, known as legacies, and dispositions of property, known as bequests. Your assets can be distributed directly to your beneficiaries or, as will be discussed in detail shortly, can be put into a trust for the benefit of others, such as your children.

Can you disinherit your spouse or your children? No and yes. It is almost impossible to disinherit your spouse. All states allow the spouse to take a "forced share" of your estate, usually at least a third, if he or she is not provided for in the will or is given less than the forced share. By contrast, in every state but Louisiana, you are free to disinherit your children; however, you must do so explicitly. Otherwise, most states have "pretermitted heir" statutes that protect against children being inadvertently omitted. Note, though, that about half of these pretermitted heir statutes protect only those children born after the will was executed.

What will you want to include in your will? In addition to providing for distribution of your assets, you may want to direct that certain items of personal property be given to certain individuals, perhaps for sentimental reasons. You may use a tangible personal property memorandum, incorporated by reference in the will, which lists the items and to whom they should go. Many states will accept this as a valid disposition, but beware, some will not; those that won't will consider the list "precatory," which means that the executor should try to honor it but is not legally bound to.

Executors and Guardians. You will also need to designate an executor. The executor is the person who will administer your estate after you die. The executor has tremendous responsibility and often considerable discretion. He is charged with collecting the assets of your estate, preparing an inventory of the property, dealing with claims by creditors (which frequently means paying numerous bills), making the distributions called for in your will, helping the lawyer see the will through probate, making and filing a budget and accounting for the court, and filing any appropriate taxes.

It can be a big job. The person you choose should be honest, trustworthy, and dependable. It may also help to have someone who is experienced or knowledgeable about financial matters, although this is not essential. The executor is free to hire others, such as lawyers and accountants, to assist in managing the property if necessary.

Executors have a right to receive some compensation for performing these many services. This fee, called an executor's fee, comes out of the estate. If you hire an independent, disinterested person (not a family member, a friend who will inherit under the will, or a business partner), she will almost certainly take her allowed fee, but you will not risk a conflict of interest arising. Many families, though, choose a family member or friend who will waive the fee and thus save the estate money. Spouses frequently name each other as executors of their estates; parents often name an adult child. These arrangements can work out fine, particularly if you don't have a large estate (over six hundred twenty-five thousand dollars) or your own business.

You can also appoint more than one person as an executor, which may be a good idea if a trusted family member or friend is inexperienced in financial matters or does not live nearby. Of course if you name coexecutors, there is always the chance they will disagree, which could cause some problems and delay.

Choose carefully and consult with potential candidates before naming anyone executor in your will. If you name someone who does not wish to fulfill the position when the times comes, he can always decline, in which case a successor executor will take over or the court will appoint one. You should always name one or more contingent executors in case your first choice predeceases you or declines to serve.

For parents, perhaps the most important function of a will is to enable you to nominate a guardian for your children should you die before they reach the age of majority. If your spouse survives you, he or she will retain the role of parent. This is true even if you are divorced: when

SPECIAL PROBLEMS FOR GAY AND LESBIAN PARENTS

If you are a gay or lesbian parent and you live with a partner, it is critically important that you and your partner both draft a will if you wish to leave money or property to each other and if you want to nominate your partner as guardian for your children. Although the situation may be changing shortly in Hawaii, at present no state recognizes same-sex marriages. Consequently, individuals in gay or lesbian relationships, no matter how committed or lengthy, acquire no legal rights to property when a partner dies and none regarding any children raised together unless the partner has adopted the children, an option available in some states and discussed further in chapter 12. To protect yourself, your partner, and your children, you should draft a will, being sure to nominate your partner as guardian. Of course, if the children were products of your marriage or other heterosexual relationship, their other parent may have legal rights to custody in the event of your death that supersede your nomination of a guardian. The best way for you to maximize your legal position and that of your partner is to see a lawyer who can thoroughly advise you on all legal aspects of the relationship.

a custodial parent passes away, the noncustodial parent automatically gets custody unless she is proved unfit or has abandoned her child. Nonetheless, it is still critically important for you to name a guardian because of the possibility, however unlikely, that you may both die. Sadly, cases of auto accidents or plane crashes that kill both parents are not unheard of. If you make a will, you can use that document to nominate a guardian. Although a probate court is not legally bound to accept your nomination, most judges will follow your wishes unless someone contests the choice and demonstrates that appointing your nominee as guardian would not serve your child's best interests. In most states, if your children are fourteen or older at the time of your death, they will be able to nominate their own guardian; again, though, the court can reject their choice if it is not in their best interests. The law of guardianship varies by state, but children and their guardians remain subject to the jurisdiction of the court until the children reach the age of majority. Some jurisdictions consider the children wards of the court, with the guardians acting as the court's agents. In either case, the court may review the guardianships periodically to see that the children's needs are being met.

Selecting a guardian is a very personal decision. You will want to consider whether your proposed guardian is capable physically, emotionally, and perhaps financially of taking care of your children. Many parents instinctively want to nominate their parents, the children's grandparents, to serve as guardians. While this arrangement might work out, you should consider that your parents' health will likely decline as they age, and they may not have the energy or physical capability to care for children, especially young ones. Financial considerations can also be important. A struggling relative may not be able to take on another child to raise. If you have sufficient resources and a good life insurance policy, you may be able to lessen the impact of this consideration by amply providing for your child's support.

Whomever you select, before drafting your will, you should discuss your plan with the person to be sure that he wants the job. You should also provide for successor guardians in the event that your first choice is unable or unwilling to assume the role after you die. You can nominate more than one person as a guardian, but this can lead to problems. For example, if you nominate your sister and brother-in-law and they subsequently divorce, your child could be subject to a custody battle.

In addition to nominating a guardian to assume custody of and raise your children, you will need to name a property guardian. As we saw earlier, children can own property, but they can't control it. So if you leave them property in your will and you die before they reach eighteen, they will need a guardian to manage the property. A property guardian is important even if your will leaves all your property to your spouse because your spouse could die before your children reach the age of majority, and in that case the children likely would inherit the property and again need someone to manage it. (Providing money or property for your children in trust, discussed in the next section, is another way of handling this situation.)

Usually parents nominate one person to act as both personal and property guardian so that whoever is raising their children has responsibility for their children's property, just as they would have had. Moreover, if you intend your children's property to support them after you're gone, it makes sense to give the person who will need that support, the personal guardian, access to and control of the funds for the children's benefit. You do have the option of naming a different person or a bank or other financial institution to serve as property guardian, which may be desirable if the personal guardian has little experience with financial matters. But if disagreement arises between the personal and the property guardian, a costly and unpleasant court battle could result. Moreover, institutional guardians generally charge a high fee and may not be able to give your child's finances the personal attention you would prefer.

In most states, property guardians—whether individuals or institutions—have to put up a bond, file documents in court, and comply with numerous legal requirements. Guardians' rights and responsibilities regarding property management are generally governed by state law. For example, your state may limit the type of investments guardians can make or restrict their right to sell or transfer any real property of the children in their care. Guardians do not own the property in their charge, and they must carefully segregate any of their own funds from those of the children in their care. Once the children turn eighteen, control of the property passes to them unless a trust has been set up.

Changing Your Will. As time passes, our life circumstances change. The law governing wills recognizes this fact and allows you to revoke your will, completely voiding it, or amend it by changing specific provisions. To amend your will, you must draft a document known as a codicil to the will. You can't just cross out provisions that you don't like in the original will and add others in the margins. The codicil must comply with the same formalities as the will itself; it must be signed and dated by you before witnesses.

If you want to make substantial changes to your will, it may be better to revoke the old will and draft an entirely new one so that there is no confusion. For example, if you have a carelessly drafted codicil with provisions that vaguely conflict with your original will, your beneficiaries could end up in court with a judge trying to ascertain how to reconcile the two. To revoke a will, you simply write "revoked" on each page of the will and add "superseded by will dated _____." Lawyers disagree about the wisdom of destroying the original will. Some think it avoids confusion; others like to have prior wills available to help interpret subsequent wills, if necessary.

You will want to review your will on a regular basis, perhaps annually, and you should certainly review it whenever you experience a major life change, such as the birth of a new child or grandchild, marriage, divorce, or remarriage; whenever you buy or sell any major assets, particularly real property; whenever your financial circumstances change significantly; and whenever there is a change in the laws of your state or the federal tax laws related to estate planning. You may also need to amend your will if circumstances have changed for your proposed executor or guardian, particularly the latter. If your proposed guardian has married or remarried, for example, how do you feel about her new spouse acting as a parent to your children as well? If he has divorced, will he be able to handle the job as a single parent? Have changes in her health or financial status made it impractical for her to serve as guardian? Has he moved out of the area? If so, do you care about maintaining your child's ties to the community or continued attendance at a particular school? All of these may be signals that you should amend your will to select another guardian. You will have to evaluate your options and discuss the matter with your proposed guardian. Similarly, you may have to amend the will to name a new executor if your original choice has experienced health or other problems that make it impossible for her to serve in that capacity.

LEAVING MORE THAN YOUR PROPERTY—THE HECHT CASE

While the law of wills and trusts may seem rather dry, it has generated some surprisingly fascinating and scandalous cases. One of the most interesting involved a battle over a testator's sperm after his death. William Kane committed suicide in 1991 after depositing sperm at a California sperm bank. His will left the fifteen vials of sperm to his lover, Deborah Ellen Hecht, along with a statement of his desire that she use the sperm to become pregnant after he was gone. She planned to do so, but his adult children by a prior marriage challenged the will and sought to destroy the sperm. After six years of legal wrangling and a decision by the California Court of Appeal that the sperm was property under the probate laws and thus subject to distribution by a will, Hecht was ultimately awarded the sperm. However, while the California Supreme Court declined to review the decision, it also decertified the opinion by the court of appeal, which means that although Hecht won, the case does not establish any precedent for future similar cases that might arise.

Probate. The word *probate* strikes fear in the hearts of many. Costly, time-consuming, and labyrinthine are all descriptions that come to mind for laypersons contemplating the process. Certainly probate can be all these things. The good news is that in many states, the process has been simplified, especially for smaller estates and simple estate plans. Even for larger estates, with good estate planning, probate need not become a nightmare.

Probate is the process by which the court ensures that your estate is distributed to those who are entitled to it, whether by the terms of your will or by the state's intestacy laws. The process involves gathering your assets, inventorying them, paying any debts, taxes, or fees for the administration of your estate, and ultimately distributing your assets to the rightful heirs or beneficiaries.

Most states offer a choice of two types of probate, supervised and unsupervised. Supervised administration requires court approval for the sale of assets, payment to creditors, and other transactions. It is more costly than unsupervised administration and is most often used in estates that are challenged. Of course, if you live in a state that offers only supervised administration, you will not have another option.

Most people prefer unsupervised administration. In general, this type of probate allows an executor to administer an estate without court monitoring and approval. Although the specific requirements will vary by state, the executor usually makes an initial court appearance to begin the process by filing the will with the probate court, but thereafter the executor proceeds independently and provides the final accounting to the beneficiaries. Some states permit unsupervised administration only for estates below a certain amount. Some states also require the written permission of all interested parties before they will allow an unsupervised administration. However, you may be able to designate unsupervised administration in your will.

Even the costs of supervised administration need not be exorbitant. Most of the work of an uncontested probate—filling out forms, cataloguing property, and the like—is within the capability of a diligent administrator, so lawyer's fees can be kept to a minimum. If your executor is up to the task, you may be able to save your beneficiaries a considerable portion of the cost of probate. Some states, though, charge probate fees based on the size of your estate. In these jurisdictions, you would be wise to try to use the available devices (some of which are mentioned briefly below) to reduce the size of your estate and avoid probate for much or all of your property. A lawyer with experience in probate and estate planning can explain these devices to you and advise you on their advantages or disadvantages for your particular situation. Remember that if you don't make a will, in most states your estate will still need to go through probate (unless you have established certain trusts), but the court will determine the distribution of your assets according to the state intestacy laws, and the court will appoint an administrator of your estate.

Trusts

One way to reduce the burden on the property guardian that you appoint and often the best way to protect your child's financial security in the event of your death is to set up a trust. A trust is a legal device through which a person with property—called the trustor, grantor, donor, or settlor—transfers the property to a person or institution, designated as the trustee, to hold, manage, and disburse the property for the benefit of another, the beneficiary. While it may be easiest to understand the concept of a trust by envisioning three different individuals playing the roles of trustor, trustee, and beneficiary, in fact, in some kinds of trusts, the same person could play more than one of those roles. When a trust is created, the trustee gains legal title to the property, and he is viewed as the owner of the property under the law; however, his ability to deal with the property is restricted by the terms of the trust. Of course, if the trustor and the trustee are the same person, the trustor in effect maintains control of the property. Trusts are popular for many reasons: they provide an efficient way to manage money for children; they are a means of avoiding probate in certain circumstances; they sometimes provide tax advantages; and they have a great degree of flexibility.

There are many different types of trusts, and within any given category, the terms of an individual trust may be unique. While it is not possible to discuss all the varieties in detail here, there are two basic features that you should be aware of. The first is that trusts can be revocable or irrevocable. Revocable trusts, as the name denotes, can be revoked by the trustor or changed at any time. These trusts provide maximum flexibility, but they may lose tax advantages that might otherwise accrue. Irrevocable trusts, by contrast, cannot be revoked or amended after creation. When you create an irrevocable trust naming someone else as trustee, you lose control of the property contained in the trust; however, you may accrue some tax benefits. The second major feature that defines the nature of a trust is the time of its creation. Living or inter vivos trusts are created during the lifetime of the grantor. Testamentary trusts, on the other hand, are created by the grantor's will and come into being on his or her death.

The type of trust that will best serve you and your family depends on your financial circumstances, your family composition, and your personal preferences. It may also change over time as your family grows and develops over the years. Parents of young children have very different needs from those of a single elderly person. A good estate-planning lawyer can help you decide if a trust is appropriate for you and can ensure that the trust is properly created.

Living Trusts. Living trusts have received a barrage of publicity, but their benefits have at times been significantly overstated. Perhaps the chief advantage of a living trust for parents is that it allows them to avoid probate for much of their estate. Fearing costly and long, drawn-out probate procedures, many individuals and couples have been attracted to living trusts for this reason. Nonetheless, it is not clear that living trusts are right for all families. Many of the concerns regarding probate have lessened as states have adopted simplified procedures at reduced costs. For example, in New York, probate fees for an estate less than ten thousand dollars were only thirty-five dollars in 1997, and even an estate worth half a million dollars paid only a thousand dollars. A living trust will not necessarily save you or your family money nor will it protect you or your family from creditors. And it won't replace the need for a will to nominate a guardian for your minor children and to dispose of assets not transferred to the trust before your death. In fact, the lawyer fees for drafting and funding the living trust often exceed fees for drafting a will. Living trusts may avoid some of the delay in property distribution inherent in probate proceedings, but here, too, the difference may be minimal.

On the other hand, living trusts do have the benefit of great flexibility. In some states, the trustor can wear all three hats—donor, trustee, and beneficiary—and thus retain control of the property during his lifetime. However, since you control the use of the property even though the trust technically owns it, the IRS will still require you to report any income from the trust on your tax return.

As with all estate-planning issues, *you are strongly urged to consult a lawyer if you wish to set up a living trust.* The appendix provides useful advice for finding a lawyer. Although do-it-yourself kits have proliferated, they could lead to higher costs for your family in the long run. Moreover, if you prepare fully, you can reduce the cost of hiring a lawyer to draft your trust agreement.

Once the trust agreement is drafted, you will usually need to fund the trust. (There are unfunded trusts set up in conjunction with "pour-over" wills, which provide for the estate's assets to pass into the trust at the time of death, but these will not avoid probate.) Funding the trust means transferring title of the assets to the trust. Unfortunately, people sometimes go to the expense and trouble of drafting a trust agreement but never follow through on the funding process, so the trust serves little purpose. Again, a lawyer can be very helpful in explaining why and how to fund your trust.

A revocable trust can be amended by adding a document (called an amendment to the trust) that describes the changes you want. The amendment has to be signed and dated by you, but it does not have to be witnessed. If your trust is properly drafted and has only one beneficiary, you usually do not need to amend it just to add further property to it; you simply alter the title of the property you wish to add. However, if your trust has more than one beneficiary, if you want to add or delete beneficiaries or trustees, or if you wish to change the disposition of your assets, you will need to draft an amendment. To ensure that any change to the trust is done properly, you are wise to consult a lawyer.

Testamentary and Insurance Trusts. Testamentary trusts can be very useful estate-planning devices for families with minor children. These trusts are set up by a provision in your will, and they are funded with assets designated in your will. In addition, parents frequently provide that life insurance proceeds be paid into a trust for the benefit of their surviving spouse or children. By using a testamentary or insurance trust, you can avoid probate for those items transferred to the trust, and you can gain some tax advantages.

Terms of the Trust. A good lawyer can help you decide not only what type of trust to set up but also what terms to include. Parents of young children may want a trust to provide for their children's support and education until the age of majority, perhaps even longer. A general direction to use the trust's assets and income for the "support and bene-fit" of your minor children gives the trustee the most discretion to meet the changing needs of the children. With a revocable living trust, you can always change the terms; but particularly with a testamentary trust, if you limit use of the trust, for example, to education, it will not be available to pay unforeseen medical bills. When young children are in-volved, it can be difficult to anticipate the path they will take and the problems they will encounter. Flexibility will enable the trustee to meet their changing needs.

You will also need to designate the age at which the beneficiaries, your children, will receive the assets of the trust and the point at which the trust will terminate. The age may be anywhere from eighteen on up. Many parents will want the trust to see their children through college and possibly through professional school. If you have concerns about the ability or maturity of your child to manage the assets, you can let the trustee decide when to distribute them, or you can set the age higher—at, say, thirty. Understand, though, that if you give the trustee the power to determine the age of distribution, conflict may arise be-tween your child and the trustee. Another option is to provide that the assets remain in trust until your child dies, at which point they may pass on to your grandchildren. However, be aware that a complicated rule prohibits private trusts from lasting any longer than the life of the beneficiary plus twenty-one years.

If you have more than one child, you will need to decide whether to create one trust for all your children or separate trusts for each. If you do not have a lot of money, you will probably choose to set up a single trust. In one popular arrangement, a single trust lasts until the youngest child completes college or professional school, and then the remaining assets are divided among all the children. Underlying this arrangement is the recognition that older children will already have re-ceived the benefit of more of their parents' financial resources, so pro-viding the younger children with a greater share of the trust may be appropriate. Parents with substantial resources may prefer to set up separate trusts for each of their children. Doing so avoids potential charges of inequality and allows older children to obtain their share of trust assets when they are ready, rather than after the youngest child reaches a designated age.

Finally, but perhaps most importantly, you will need to select a trustee. In revocable living trusts, it is common for the grantor, you, to serve in the capacity of trustee. Obviously that's not possible with a testamentary trust; if you decide to set up this type of trust, you will want to consider some of the same issues discussed in connection with nominating a guardian. With trustees, you have the option of selecting a family member, a friend, or an institutional trustee (a bank or trust company). Each has its advantages. If you have minor children, you will probably want to name your surviving spouse trustee, or at least cotrustee, since she will be raising the children. You will need to select a successor trustee as well, someone to take over the job if the original trustee cannot continue. Family members and friends will often serve as trustee without taking a fee and will usually have a personal interest in properly administering your trust. However, you should evaluate whether the person you select has the knowledge, experience, and persistence to properly manage your trust. You should also anticipate whether the beneficiaries will be able to get along with the trustee.

An institutional trustee will bring substantial expertise to the job but will charge for it. Small estates, those less than two hundred and fifty thousand dollars, may not justify the cost. In addition to objecting to the extra expense, some people are put off by the impersonality of dealing with a bank or trust company employee. If you do decide to appoint a financial institution as trustee, try to get to know the individual who will be handling the work. Realize, though, that employees come and go and institutions change hands. There is no guarantee that the person you discuss your trust with will be the one who deals with your children after you are gone.

Many people appoint cotrustees. You may choose this option to allow for both the personal touch of a friend or family member and perhaps the expertise of a lawyer, adviser, or institution. Or you may simply want to appoint two family members as a check on each other.

Appointing cotrustees may seem like an attractive option, but think carefully before you do it. What if the trustees do not agree on a course of action? How will the dispute be resolved? You can and should indicate in your trust document how disagreements are to be handled, but any conflict between trustees will cause dissension, delay, and potential litigation. Moreover, requiring both trustees to sign off on all transactions can be cumbersome, especially if they are located in different areas or if they do not get along.

CHILD CUSTODY AND VISITATION

ALMOST FIFTY PERCENT of all marriages end in divorce. Of those, about half involve families with minor children. Divorce is a traumatic event for everyone concerned, but particularly for children. Psychological research indicates that children experience divorce as a significant stressor in their lives and often continue to experience feelings of loss, confusion, anxiety, and anger for many years afterward. Divorce also has serious economic consequences for children. Many children experience a precipitous decline in their standard of living after divorce. The legal issues involving children and divorce center on two main areas: (1) custody and visitation and (2) child support. This chapter treats issues of custody and visitation. The next considers child support.

CUSTODY

Divorce brings many changes to the lives of children. The most obvious disruption involves the physical and emotional breakup of the family. In the majority of cases after divorce, children who lived with both parents must adjust to living most of the time with one custodial parent and visiting for short periods with the other, noncustodial parent. Occasionally, children spend significant amounts of time with each parent under a joint custody arrangement.

The best thing divorcing parents can do for their children is to arrive at a custody arrangement that works with as little conflict as possible. The children who fare worst after divorce are those whose parents continue to engage in high-conflict behavior and use their children for their own needs, often as a way of striking back at their former spouses in anger. Custody battles are expensive, emotionally draining, and extremely difficult for children. Fortunately, most divorcing parents work out their differences without going to court; only about 2 percent of custody disputes actually require a trial. Nonetheless, all divorcing parents need to understand the law governing custody and visitation to assist them in reaching a fair settlement that will best serve the needs of their children.

The "Best Interests of the Child" Standard

In all states, courts seek to award custody based on the best interests of the child. Each state has one or more statutes governing child custody that list a variety of factors for the court to consider in determining what custody arrangement will serve the best interests of the child. The box on page 188 provides an example of one such statute. Although these factors provide some guidance for judges and for lawyers, it is important to recognize that the best interests standard is very vague and vests tremendous discretion in the trial judge. It is often extremely difficult to predict who will win a contested custody case. The discussion that follows will explore various criteria relied on by courts in determining the best interests of a child.

Factors in Determining Custody

The Parent-Child Relationship. The ultimate goal of the best interests standard is to place a child with the parent who will be better able to provide him with the love, guidance, support, and discipline necessary to help him grow into a happy, well-adjusted person and a productive member of society. Of critical importance are the quality of the relationship between the parent and the child and the maintenance of stability and continuity in the child's life.

Which parent can better communicate with the child and understand and meet the child's emotional needs on an ongoing basis? To answer this question, courts often look at which parent has the stronger emotional bond with the child. From birth, children develop psychological and emotional attachments to their parents that play a significant role in their development into healthy adults capable of maintaining intimate and meaningful relationships with others. Disrupting this bond can have detrimental, even traumatic, consequences for a child.

Of course, divorce by its nature involves some disruption of this attachment. The key for the courts and for parents is to minimize the disruption. For this reason, a parent who has had temporary custody of a child during separation or prior to litigation of a custody dispute may have a significant edge if the child is functioning well. A parent planning on pursuing custody should maintain a strong and consistent presence in the child's life after separation and while custody proceedings and any appeals are pending.

Because of the importance placed on evaluating the nature of the parent-child relationship, many contested custody cases involve psychological evaluations of the parents and sometimes of the child as well. Often each parent will present evidence of his or her own psychological evaluation—through testimony or a report prepared by a psychiatrist, psychologist, or social worker—but the court may also order an independent evaluation to assist in its determination.

Gender and the Primary Caretaker. The standards for determining custody used to be clearer and more certain. For much of this country's history, custody has been awarded based on the gender of the parent. What people don't realize is that until the beginning of the twentieth century, fathers had a nearly absolute right to retain custody of children after a divorce. Gradually, the pendulum began to swing in favor of the mother, until the courts in most states decided custody cases based on the "tender years presumption." Under this presumption, custody of

A SAMPLE CHILD CUSTODY STATUTE

The usual basis for deciding custody is the "best interests of the child," and most states have laws specifying a number of factors the courts should consider. As an example, let's look at Minnesota's domestic relations law, a particularly comprehensive statute, which lists the following best interests factors:

1. the wishes of the child's parent or parents as to custody
2. the reasonable preference of the child, if the court deems the child to be of sufficient age to express preference
3. the child's primary caretaker
4. the intimacy of the relationship between each parent and the child
5. the interaction and interrelationship of the child with a parent or parents, siblings, and any other person who may significantly affect the child's best interests
6. the child's adjustment to home, school, and community
7. the length of time the child has lived in a stable, satisfactory environment and the desirability of maintaining continuity

children of tender years, roughly age seven and under, was awarded to the mother unless she was proved unfit. With older children, particularly teenagers, a court might award custody of boys to the father on the theory that boys of that age need a male role model.

Today an explicit maternal preference has been abolished virtually everywhere. The Constitution protects against impermissible discrimination based on sex. Although courts have disagreed over whether the tender years presumption can be justified under the Constitution, most states have avoided the problem by precluding reliance on it. A few states, however, still favor mothers indirectly, either by allowing consideration of the age and sex of children or by employing the tender years doctrine as a tiebreaker. In these states, if both parents prove equally fit

8. the permanence, as a family unit, of the existing or proposed custodial home

9. the mental and physical health of all individuals involved; except that a disability ... of a proposed custodian or the child shall not be determinative ... unless the proposed custodial arrangement is not in the best interest of the child

10. the capacity and disposition of the parties to give the child love, affection, and guidance, and to continue educating and raising the child in the child's culture and religion or creed, if any

11. the child's cultural background

12. the effect on the child of the actions of an abuser, if related to domestic abuse ... that has occurred between the parents

13. except in cases in which a finding of domestic abuse ... has been made, the disposition of each parent to encourage and permit frequent and continuing contact by the other parent with the child

The court may not use one factor to the exclusion of all others.

to have custody, a court will award custody of young children to the mother.

The mother may also have an edge in obtaining custody because she is usually the primary caretaker—that is, the parent who assumes primary responsibility for meeting the day-to-day emotional and physical needs of the child. West Virginia has adopted a strong presumption in favor of the primary caretaker; other states consider it a factor that may be given great weight. To identify the primary caretaker, courts will consider which parent prepares the meals, bathes and dresses the child, arranges or provides medical care for the child, coordinates the child's social activities, arranges for baby-sitters when necessary, disciplines the child, and teaches basic skills.

Awarding custody to the primary caretaker serves several goals. It furthers the child's best interests because the parent who has performed these caretaking functions frequently has developed a stronger emotional bond with the child. A history as primary caretaker also suggests that the child will continue to receive the necessary care with less disruption. Moreover, preference for the primary caretaker reflects the greater investment of time and energy that the parent has made in child rearing.

Obviously, the role of primary caretaker may be performed by the mother, by the father, or by both parents. In cases where there is no primary caretaker, courts must rely on other criteria. However, despite increased involvement in child rearing by fathers in recent years, most women today still bear the bulk of the responsibility, and they will benefit most from custody decisions based on who the primary caretaker is.

Even when no explicit or implicit preference for the mother exists in the law, some trial judges, because of their traditional views about the role of women and men in parenting, may continue to favor mothers. Interestingly, though, one study suggests that fathers win 51 percent of the time in contested custody cases that are appealed and result in a published decision. Nonetheless, the vast majority of children of divorce are in the custody of their mothers, mostly as a result of settlements reached by the parents without going to court.

Race. In the 1984 case, *Palmore v. Sidoti,* the Supreme Court declared that race was not a legitimate factor in deciding custody. A trial judge in Florida had switched custody from Mrs. Palmore, who was white, to her ex-husband because after their divorce she had married an African American man. The Supreme Court recognized that the child might suffer stigma from her mother's interracial marriage but nonetheless concluded that to deprive the mother of custody based on race violated the equal protection clause of the Constitution. Unfortunately, there have been cases reported by the news media of judges flagrantly disregarding the Supreme Court's ruling and relying on involvement in an interracial relationship as a basis for denying custody. While such decisions should be and often are reversed on appeal, they cause tremendous damage to children and the families involved in the meantime.

What happens if an interracial couple divorces? Courts have considered race to be a factor in deciding the custody of a child of mixed race, but they have not given it particularly great weight. The concern that a child develop a sense of racial identity with his or her minority background is less important than the quality of the parent-child relationship and the stability of the home.

Religion. The First Amendment to the Constitution protects every individual's freedom to practice his or her religion of choice. Consequently, the courts tread very carefully in this area. A court must refrain from expressing a value judgment preferring one religion over another or religion over atheism. Let's consider a hypothetical case. Robbie is an eight-year-old boy whose parents are divorcing. His mother, Janice, is Jewish; his father, Gordon, is Catholic. Robbie has been raised in the Jewish faith. Is religion a consideration in deciding who should have custody of Robbie?

Some courts will consider evidence of religious training by a parent as a factor in that parent's favor if he shows that continuation of the training is important for maintaining continuity in his child's life. For example, in a 1988 Minnesota case, the appellate court affirmed a custody award to a mother who had been raising her children as Catholics in part because the father intended to convert them to Lutheranism. If the children had not received any particular religious training, religion would not have come into play.

In some cases, religion can work against a parent if it is far outside the mainstream, but only if the parent's unusual religious beliefs or practices are likely to cause physical or mental harm to the child. For example, an appellate court denied a mother custody because she used her religious beliefs as a Jehovah's Witness to justify both her physical abuse of her children and her plan to interfere with the visitation rights of the children's father, who did not share her faith. On the other hand, a Nebraska court's award of custody to a Jehovah's Witness mother was affirmed even though her beliefs prevented the children from participating in various social activities, saying the Pledge of Allegiance, and receiving blood transfusions. Despite these cases, religion generally does not play a significant role in custody decisions and will not likely be determinative in Robbie's case.

Work, Time for Children, and Financial Resources. A parent's employment can work for or against her in seeking custody. Today most married women with children work outside the home, and the number of divorced women who do so is even higher. Indeed, courts in most cases expect women to work after divorce; few women receive alimony and all have an obligation to support their children.

Unfortunately, in awarding custody, some courts nonetheless penalize women who work outside the home. Women who have demanding careers or work long hours or unusual shifts, in the view of some courts, do not have sufficient time to spend with their children. Women are in a particularly difficult bind because men as a rule earn more than women and are more likely to remarry. Hence, although men may work full-time outside the home, they may be able to afford to have a new wife stay at home with the children. As compared to a divorced single mother working full-time, a father may appear in these cases to be the better custodial parent. Moreover, despite appellate court admonitions not to subject women to a double standard, some judges continue to believe that men who work are stable and responsible while women who work are bad or neglectful mothers.

Luckily these attitudes are changing. But it remains the case that time available to spend with children is a legitimate consideration in custody disputes. A parent who works such long hours that she rarely sees her children and performs few if any of the caretaking responsibilities of parenthood may not be able to meet her children's needs adequately. In some cases, fathers really do have significantly more flexible work hours and can spend more time with their children. The challenge for courts is to take into account time available for a child as one factor in a custody decision without letting unrealistic and sexist assumptions cloud the decision.

DAY CARE AS A FACTOR IN CUSTODY CASES:
THE IRELAND CASE

In 1991, when she was a sixteen-year-old high school student, Jennifer Ireland gave birth to a daughter, Maranda. The child's father, Steven Smith, also in high school, had nothing to do with the child during her first year of life but subsequently visited her. In January 1993 Jennifer sued for child support, and Steven countered with a suit for custody. While the case was pending, Jennifer enrolled in the University of Michigan on a scholarship and placed Maranda in the campus day care center. In a decision that caused a furor among women's and children's advocates, the trial judge ordered custody of Maranda switched from Jennifer to Steven so that she could be cared for by Steven's mother, with whom he lived. Declaring that there is "no way that a single parent, attending an academic program at an institution as prestigious as the University of Michigan, can do justice to their studies and to raising of an infant child," the judge concluded that the new custody arrangement was preferable to day care. Fortunately, the Michigan Supreme Court disagreed. It reversed the decision and sent it back to the trial court for reconsideration in light of altered circumstances. However, it instructed that trial judges could consider the appropriateness of a particular day care placement a relevant factor in a custody dispute if it reflected poorly on the parent's judgment.

A related issue that sometimes arises in custody disputes involves the relative financial status of the parents. In general, courts do not consider differences in financial resources relevant to custody. However, those differences may come into play indirectly when the court evaluates the living conditions of each parent and the ability of each parent to provide a stable home. For example, some judges have viewed with disfavor mothers who are on welfare and fathers who have been chronically unemployed. These cases have involved financial situations sufficiently dire to call into question the poorer parent's ability to provide an adequate home for a child, and other factors supporting an award of custody to the other parent have almost invariably been present as well.

A Parent's Health and Physical or Mental Disability. A parent who suffers from a chronic, serious, or life-threatening physical illness such as cancer may have trouble winning custody if the illness significantly interferes with his ability to supervise or care for his child or if the illness creates an unstable home environment. But the court will evaluate the effect of a parent's health in light of the many other considerations discussed here, particularly the quality of the parent-child relationship.

Similarly, a parent who is physically disabled will not automatically be disqualified from having custody. This was not always the rule. For many years, trial judges and courts presumed that a serious physical disability rendered a parent unfit. This view was predicated largely on ignorance, fear, stereotypes regarding the capabilities of the physically challenged, and sometimes outright prejudice. Some courts, particularly at the trial level, continue to adhere to these outdated notions. Fortunately, society's and the courts' views of the disabled are changing.

The trend today is to evaluate a parent's disability as *one* of the factors relevant to whether custody with that parent would serve a child's best interests. The court's emphasis will be on ascertaining the child's needs and evaluating whether the disabled parent is capable of meeting those needs, either alone or with available assistance. For example, in a landmark case, the California Supreme Court overturned a lower court ruling that had denied custody of two children to their father after he was rendered a quadriplegic in an accident. The children had lived with their father continuously since birth, had a strong emotional attachment to him, and had rarely seen their mother in the previous five years. The court chastised the trial judge for adhering to stereotypes about the disabled, for overemphasizing the father's inability to engage in sports and other physical activities with his children, and for over-

CAN YOU BE DENIED CUSTODY
OR VISITATION IF YOU HAVE AIDS?

A number of cases recently have involved attempts by one parent to restrict the other parent's visitation or to obtain custody because the other parent either is infected with the human immunodeficiency virus (HIV) or has AIDS-related complex (ARC) or full-blown AIDS. Because AIDS is at this time a fatal disease and because there are many myths concerning the communicability of the disease, some parents are concerned that exposure to an HIV-positive parent could put a child at risk. In fact, the AIDS virus cannot be contracted through casual human contact. It can be gotten only through exchange of bodily fluids from sexual activity, sharing of intravenous needles, or exposure to HIV-tainted blood or blood products. Consequently, it is extremely unlikely that a child would be exposed to the virus by visiting or being in the custody of an infected parent. Most courts have recognized this fact and have rejected efforts to restrict visitation or modify custody based on a parent's HIV status, even if the parent has developed AIDS.

looking the love and guidance he had provided and was still able to give them. Other appellate courts have likewise reversed trial court decisions that removed children from the custody of parents with various disabilities, including epilepsy, paraplegia, and deafness. Nonetheless, proof that a disability prevents a parent from adequately caring for, supervising, and nurturing a child will support a denial of custody.

A parent's mental health is, of course, also an important factor in evaluating the best interests of a child. A serious mental illness or demonstrated lack of mental stability or maturity can lead to a denial of custody. In fact, some courts still presume that mental illness renders a parent unfit, a presumption sometimes based on prejudice and ignorance. Other courts today do not automatically deny custody to parents who have been mentally ill in the past or who can control their illness with medication. These courts evaluate the effect of the mental illness both on whether a parent is able to care for her children and on whether her illness has adversely affected them. In general, courts view suicide attempts in a negative light and are likely to deny custody to a parent with this history. Evidence that the attempt was in the past and that the underlying condition has been successfully treated may counter this inclination.

As with physical disabilities and mental illness, many courts and judges have viewed mental retardation as presumptive evidence of unfitness in custody disputes. Even today, in choosing between two parents, a court is likely to favor the one who is not retarded on the basis that he will be a better problem solver and will provide more intellectual stimulation for the child and greater assistance with her education. The central question, though, remains what effect a parent's retardation has on his ability to care for a child. If the parent's retardation prevents him from satisfying his child's needs for physical care, comfort, and supervision, he is likely to lose custody, particularly if there is no child care help available.

Substance Abuse and Smoking. Serious problems are raised when a parent abuses or is addicted to drugs or alcohol. A parent who uses illicit substances like cocaine, amphetamines, and even marijuana will frequently lose custody solely on that basis. A parent who is an alcoholic or abuses prescription medications will likely face the same result in a custody fight.

Does this mean that if you smoked marijuana in college ten years ago, you will lose custody of your child? Not necessarily. Evidence of past drug use or problems with alcohol is not determinative in a custody case, but the parent with this history must convince the court that the behavior is a thing of the past and is not likely to recur in the future.

A parent who suspects an ex-spouse of substance abuse may be able to obtain a court order requiring her to undergo drug testing. You should

CAN SMOKING AFFECT YOUR CUSTODY RIGHTS?

One custody and visitation issue that has gotten increasing attention recently is the effect of parental smoking on children. Scientific research indicates that secondhand smoke can cause health problems for children. Growing up in a household with lifelong smokers can substantially increase a child's risk of developing lung cancer. More immediately, secondhand smoke can increase susceptibility to respiratory infections and can exacerbate asthma in children. Consequently, some courts have considered smoking a negative factor in deciding custody when a child has asthma or other respiratory problems. Rather than deny custody, though, a court will more likely prohibit the parent from smoking in the child's presence.

also be aware that substance abuse by a new partner who has contact with your children can also be used against you in a custody dispute.

Sexual Conduct. Judicial attitudes toward parental sexual conduct or misconduct have changed over time. Prior to the advent of no-fault divorce in the 1970s and 1980s, courts considered and harshly judged adultery or postdivorce sexual relations with a boyfriend or girlfriend. Today many courts take a somewhat more liberal attitude toward sexual activity. For example, in one case, an appellate court reversed a lower court that had switched custody from the mother to the father because the mother and her new boyfriend read pornography. The appellate court declared that the sexual conduct of the mother was irrelevant to custody unless it involved or adversely affected her children.

Nonetheless, even today the sexual activities of a parent are fair game in a custody dispute, and more than a few courts have determined in recent years that perceived misconduct (sexual relations outside of marriage) was a strong factor in denying custody. If a parent conducts a relationship discreetly, he is not likely to lose custody solely on this basis. However, if he has numerous affairs or partners of questionable character and exposes the children to these relationships, he puts his custody rights at risk.

What if a parent has a live-in partner or an occasional overnight visit by a steady boyfriend or girlfriend? Most courts will not deny custody on this basis, but a few still presume harm to a child exposed to a nonmarital relationship.

Sexual Orientation—Gay and Lesbian Parents. Many gay parents have children through a traditional heterosexual marriage. They may not have realized their sexual orientation or been willing to admit it, even to themselves, prior to or during much of their marriage. Recognition of their sexual orientation may lead to divorce or may occur during the process of divorcing. How does gay identity affect a parent's right to custody and visitation after divorce? The answer varies considerably depending on where you live.

Historically, evidence of homosexuality in and of itself has been sufficient to deny custody to a parent. Although most courts today refuse to make sexual orientation the sole determinant in custody decisions, sticking instead to the best interests of the child standard, many courts are still very reluctant to award custody to a gay parent. These courts presume that such an arrangement would not be in a child's best interests because of the stigma that attaches to gays and lesbians and because of prejudices and misconceptions held by some judges that gays and lesbians are promiscuous or otherwise of low moral character or that custody by a gay parent will lead a child to choose a gay lifestyle. Despite widespread evidence dispelling each of these notions, some judges cling to them out of ignorance and intolerance.

Fortunately, an increasing number of courts today take a more enlightened view and will not consider the sexual orientation of a parent unless it is shown to have a demonstrated adverse impact on the child. This is sometimes referred to as the nexus approach: the heterosexual parent seeking custody must show that there is a real nexus, or connection, between the gay parent's lifestyle and some harm to their child.

Courts will consider a parent's sexual orientation if there is evidence that the parent flaunts his or her lifestyle or makes the child feel uncomfortable.

Regardless of the jurisdiction, gay parents seeking custody should exercise discretion in pursuing and conducting romantic relationships in front of their children as well as in participating in gay activist endeavors. A gay parent who is living with a new partner should probably be prepared to have the partner testify in court as a potentially significant person in his or her child's life.

The Child's Preference. Does your child have a say in which parent should get custody? Most courts will consider a child's wishes if the child is of sufficient age, maturity, and intelligence and has a persuasive reason for preferring one parent over the other. Generally, children fourteen and older have the right to express a preference, and the court will give their preference great weight. Courts are much less likely to consult children of tender years—those below age seven—and they will evaluate on a case-by-case basis whether to allow children between the ages of seven and fourteen to express a preference and if they do, whether to follow it. Courts consider carefully the reasons for a child's preference. If the child wants to live with one parent because that parents is lax about discipline or because the child has been pressured or bribed with material goods by that parent, the court will likely disregard the child's expressed wishes.

Will your child have to testify in open court to state a preference? It depends. Many judges interview children in chambers, often without any attorneys present, but others require children to testify in court.

In some cases, expressing a preference may help children by providing them with a sense of power and control over a decision that dramatically affects their lives. But having children testify invariably puts tremendous pressure on them by forcing them to choose between their parents. You should consider carefully the benefit to be gained before involving your children so directly in a custody dispute.

Siblings. As a general rule, courts strive to keep siblings together. Siblings develop strong attachments to one another, and sibling relationships become particularly important when parents are divorcing. Siblings are in a unique position to understand the pain and trauma of divorce and can often serve as a great source of support for one another. This rule may also apply to a child who has developed a close relationship with a half sibling by a parent's prior marriage.

Nonetheless, in exceptional or compelling circumstances, a court may order split custody, awarding certain siblings to one parent and the rest to the other. This arrangement might be in the best interests of the children when, for example, one sibling has a very strong attachment to a particular parent and the other siblings do not or when one parent demonstrates a preference for a particular child. It might also be desirable when the children exhibit strong hostility toward one another, not merely everyday sibling rivalry.

Child Abuse. Obviously a parent who abuses or neglects a child will not win custody. In fact, a parent can have his or her parental rights terminated and be subjected to criminal prosecution for this conduct, as we will see in chapter 10. Abuse committed by a new boyfriend or girlfriend of a parent can also lead to loss of custody.

Among the more troubling cases today are those that involve allegations of child sexual abuse leveled against one parent by the other in a custody fight. There is tremendous controversy surrounding this issue. For many years, incest was considered so taboo that no one talked about it. Victims were reluctant to come forward and frequently kept the abuse secret for years, sometimes for their entire lives. More recently, child sexual abuse has come out into the open, and the number of reported cases has increased dramatically. The news media and talk shows are filled with stories of molesting teachers, clergy, and parents. Yet most experts agree that sexual abuse remains significantly underreported.

Allegations of sexual abuse in custody proceedings are particularly controversial because of the highly charged emotional atmosphere surrounding a divorce and because of bias and misperceptions on the part of members of the judicial system. While the number of divorce cases involving allegations of sexual abuse has certainly increased in recent years, there is little agreement about how many actually involve these allegations. Estimates range from 2 to 10 percent of all custody cases. These cases are particularly challenging because sexual abuse is difficult to prove, and a false allegation can cause irreparable harm.

The media have reported sensational stories of parents wrongly accused by bitter and vengeful ex-spouses, but many experts believe that such cases of deliberately false charges are quite uncommon. The perception that a significant number of false allegations are made is misleading because in a large number of cases—perhaps more than half—the court concludes merely that the allegation of abuse is "unfounded" or "unsubstantiated." This does not mean, though, that the abuse did not take place; it only means that it was not proved sufficiently.

In custody cases, the parent alleging abuse has to prove the allegation by a "preponderance of the evidence"; in other words, he or she has to show that the abuse "more likely than not" occurred. This is a much lower burden of proof than is applied in a criminal proceeding. So why are so many cases unfounded, if abuse really did occur? It appears that judges, perhaps unconsciously, require proof closer to the criminal "beyond a reasonable doubt" standard. It can be very difficult to meet this standard because in most cases no conclusive physical evidence of the molestation exists. Consequently, the court must rely on testimony by the child and by experts—psychologists, psychiatrists, and social workers. Unfortunately, young children often make poor witnesses. They may not have the ability to understand what telling the truth means, they may have difficulty remembering events under pressure, and they tend to be very suggestible. Judges in custody cases where allegations of sexual abuse have been made are particularly concerned that a child may have been prompted to make the allegations by a parent intent on undermining the other parent to win custody. Even older children may feel intimidated if they have to testify in court, and they may suffer further trauma from the experience. The problem is compounded because children who have been sexually abused not infrequently recant the allegations even though the abuse did take place.

If you suspect your ex-spouse has molested your child, you should have your child examined immediately by a pediatrician and by a mental health professional with experience in sexual abuse cases. (See the box on page 294 in chapter 10.) How your child is interviewed can have a profound effect on your ability to prove the molestation. You may also have an obligation to report the abuse to law enforcement agencies. For more on this issue, refer to chapter 10.

You should understand that your allegations could have serious repercussions for your ex-spouse, including criminal prosecution, and perhaps some unintended consequences for you as well. In some courts, if you fail to prove your allegation in a custody case, you risk losing custody or visitation yourself. In addition, some states have laws imposing penalties on a parent who deliberately makes a false allegation of sexual abuse. Your ex-spouse may also sue you for libel or malicious prosecution.

These risks should not discourage you from acting if you sincerely believe that your child is being or has been sexually abused by your ex-spouse. On the contrary, you should do everything lawfully in your power to protect your child. However, the risks should caution you to proceed prudently and to seek out professional assistance from pediatricians, mental health professionals, and lawyers who can help you evaluate and present your allegations to the court.

Spousal Abuse. Like the sexual abuse of children, spousal abuse is a problem that has long been kept hidden. Today there is growing recognition of the prevalence of domestic violence and of the great harm it can cause to children. Children who witness their fathers beating their mothers live in terror. Exposure to this kind of violent behavior also frequently leads children to emulate it both as children and as adults. Domestic violence is a generational problem. Abused children often grow up to be abusers. Children whose fathers beat their mothers often grow up to be batterers or the victims of batterers. Spousal abuse also raises grave concerns about the fitness of the batterer as a parent.

Unfortunately, the courts have lagged behind in considering this factor in custody disputes. Too often courts ignore or fail to consider acts of violence against a spouse in evaluating the best interests of a child. But attitudes are changing. Most states now have laws that mandate judges to consider evidence of spousal abuse in awarding custody.

Some states also have special domestic violence laws that allow a court to award custody to an abused spouse, usually the mother. Several states, though, also have so-called "friendly parent" provisions. These laws allow a court awarding custody to take into account which parent is more likely to facilitate a child's relationship with the other parent. While this may be a good idea generally, it works to the disadvantage of battered women since an abused spouse will seek sole custody and often try to limit visitation with the abusing parent. Some states, like Minnesota (see box on page 188), recognize this problem and make an explicit exception for victims of domestic violence. An abused spouse who flees home without her children also faces the added burden of explaining why she left her children.

Increasing public awareness of domestic violence and advocacy on behalf of battered women are slowly changing the law's treatment of spousal abuse in custody decisions and the attitudes of judges deciding these cases. If you are a victim of spousal abuse, your first concern should be your own safety and your children's safety. Many communities have a shelter or hot line specifically for the purpose of providing advice and assistance to battered women. These may be listed in the human services section of your phone book under "Abuse," "Domestic Violence," or "Women's Shelters." Contacting the police, pressing charges against a violent spouse, and obtaining a civil restraining order (also called a protective order) can help your case. You generally do not need a lawyer to obtain a temporary restraining order. If you would like assistance and are without funds, some large urban areas have offices staffed by lawyers, law students, or paralegals who can assist you in filling out the necessary paperwork. Contact your local bar association or legal aid office for a referral. Help yourself and you will be better able to help your children.

Joint Custody

In the mid-1970s a new form of custody appeared on the scene: joint custody, also known as shared custody. Joint custody fast gained popularity, and many states adopted statutes allowing for or even preferring joint custody to the more traditional sole custody arrangement. Within a few years, however, something of a backlash toward joint custody set in. Today, although almost all states have laws allowing joint custody, only a little more than a third still have a presumption in favor of it, and in some of these the presumption applies only if the parents both want joint custody. In the other states, joint custody is simply one option the court can consider.

When people use the term joint custody, they may be referring to joint *legal* custody, joint *physical* custody, or a combination of the two. Joint legal custody, which is more common than joint physical custody, gives both parents the legal right to make decisions regarding their child's health, education, religious upbringing, and other important matters. Joint physical custody refers to a custody arrangement in which a child spends significant amounts of time with each parent, something more than the usual every-other-weekend visits and shared vacations but not necessarily a fifty-fifty division of time. In fact, most couples with joint physical custody don't divide up their time evenly.

Why would someone (or a court) prefer a joint custody arrangement? Joint custody has several potential advantages for children and parents. Most importantly, it enables children to remain involved with both parents after a divorce. Studies indicate that children experience great feelings of loss after divorce, particularly of the noncustodial parent, who is usually the father. Joint custody, especially joint physical custody, may lessen these painful feelings. Since joint physical custody most closely approximates the intact predivorce family, it may help to decrease the trauma of the divorce for children. Yet the research done so far does not indicate that joint custody leads to better outcomes for all children. The result has much to do with the quality of the parent-child relationship, the psychological health of the parents, and the ability of the parents to cooperate.

From the parents' perspective, joint legal custody ensures that even the noncustodial parent will continue to have a say in important decisions regarding the child. Joint physical custody enables the parents to continue to enjoy the rewards of day-to-day child rearing and avoids some of the artificial constraints of traditional visitation. For the parent who would otherwise have had sole custody of the child, joint custody provides much-needed assistance in the difficult job of child rearing and gives the parent more time to develop other relationships. There is some evidence to suggest higher parental satisfaction with joint custody arrangements than with the traditional sole custody arrangement, but the research is not conclusive.

With all these advantages, why do so few families adopt a joint custody arrangement? Joint custody is clearly not for all parents. The most important factor in evaluating whether joint custody is a good idea for your family, and the one that the court will weight most heavily, is your ability to communicate and cooperate with your ex-spouse. Joint custody requires that parents work together to come up with acceptable living arrangements (for joint physical custody) and to reach decisions (for joint legal custody). Usually couples divorce precisely because they have difficulty communicating effectively, solving their problems together, and generally getting along. Unless the parents can set aside their differences and put their child's needs ahead of their own, joint custody will not work.

Recent ongoing research involving about fifty California families in the Joint Custody Project headed by Susan Steinman suggests that parents who can separate their role as spouse from their role as parent, who experience comparatively less anger and depression after divorce, and who are committed to a joint custody arrangement are more likely to succeed. Anger and inflexibility characterize the parents who have failed at joint custody.

Joint custody will do more harm than good if the parents cannot get along in matters regarding their child. If the parents are highly conflictual, their child will be caught in the middle on a near-daily basis. It should go without saying that joint custody is inappropriate where there is a history of domestic violence in a family.

For all of these reasons, many courts are reluctant to order joint custody, particularly if one parent opposes the idea. Some courts, though, recognize that the parents' initial anger may fade and will order joint custody anyway.

True joint physical custody—an arrangement in which the parents share time almost equally, perhaps alternating weekends and dividing up weeknights—poses additional problems. Constant shuttling between two homes can cause a child, particularly one very young, to feel anxious and insecure. For older children, such an arrangement may hinder efforts to establish friendships and become involved in neighborhood and after-school activities.

For this reason, courts are skeptical of "alternate" custody plans that require a child to switch homes on a weekly, monthly, or sometimes yearly basis, although they have been allowed on occasion. Even rarer and less likely to receive court approval are so-called "nesting" or "bird-nesting" arrangements that allow the children to remain in one home while the parents move in and out according to a schedule.

Ultimately, in addition to these psychological and emotional considerations, the court will evaluate whether the parents can pull off the logistics of joint physical custody by looking not only at the proximity of their homes to the school system but also at their financial resources. Joint custody can work, but it takes considerable effort and dedication.

PROCEDURAL ASPECTS OF CUSTODY DISPUTES

Mediation

Although very few custody disputes ever find their way into court, not all divorcing couples can resolve their conflicts by themselves or even with the help of their lawyers. Increasingly, couples and courts are turning to mediation as a way of resolving custody and other divorce-related disputes.

Mediation is an informal process aimed at resolving a particular issue by guiding the parents to the means of solving the problem themselves. Almost half the states now have programs to mediate custody and related disputes. In some states, mediation is now mandatory for couples seeking to go to court over custody. In addition, the number of private mediators has been growing in recent years.

Mediators may be trained as lawyers or as mental health profession-als—psychologists, licensed social workers, or marriage and family counselors. Court-appointed mediators usually have a psychology back-ground. Be aware, though, that in most states mediators are unlicensed, and a private mediator may have no special training. Hence, you should check the credentials of any private mediator you are considering hiring.

What can you expect from custody mediation? Court-affiliated pro-grams often provide an informative orientation session to familiarize you with the process. The actual mediation usually consists of one to four two-hour sessions conducted over the course of a few days or a week. The mediator usually meets with both parents together, but he may also meet with each of you separately. In addition, he may want to meet with your child, either alone or together with you and your ex-spouse, as well as with other important players in the custody dispute, such as stepparents.

Mediation is neither psychotherapy nor legal advocacy. The media-tor's focus will be on helping you to resolve your differences regarding custody or visitation in a way that will best serve your child's needs. A successful mediation will usually result in a written agreement regard-ing the terms of the settlement, although with varying degrees of detail and precision. Finalizing the agreement and preparing the necessary court order are often left to the parties' attorneys.

The mediator does not represent you or judge you. She is an im-partial party, and in most cases anything said during the mediation is considered confidential. However, if the mediator suspects child abuse, she may have a legal duty to report it. Also, if the mediation fails, she may be asked to make a report to the court.

For many divorcing couples, mediation presents an attractive alter-native to a bitter court fight. It is generally far less costly than litigation and less stressful for both parents and children. It also has a high suc-cess rate. A survey of court-affiliated mediation projects in three major cities suggests that the vast majority of cases reach a settlement. How-ever, mediation may not be appropriate in cases involving a history of spousal abuse for obvious reasons: contact with the abusing spouse can put the abused spouse at risk, and she is likely to be intimidated and thus disadvantaged during the negotiations.

Legal Representation of Children

If you and your spouse are one of the few couples who cannot resolve your disagreement over custody without going to court, does your child have a right to his or her own attorney? The answer generally is no. However, in most states, a court has the power to appoint either an attorney or an advocate called a guardian *ad litem* to represent a child in a custody proceeding, which it might do, for example, if a case involves an allegation of sexual abuse, is likely to be especially intense and drawn out, or the parents do not appear capable of representing the child's interests. The child's attorney or advocate is charged with representing and protecting her rights and may conduct investigations, arrange for evaluations, make reports to the court, and participate in court hearings and mediation sessions. In some states, the court can order one or both parents to pay the cost.

VISITATION

When one parent is awarded sole custody, the other parent typically gets visitation with his or her child. The goal of visitation is to preserve the child's relationship with the noncustodial parent since children generally benefit from contact with both their parents. Visitation is considered a right of the child and a right, or in some states a privilege, of the noncustodial parent. Nonetheless, the court has the power to restrict and even deny visitation if doing so is in a child's best interests.

As with custody, most parents reach agreement on visitation without going to court, whether on their own, with the help of their attorneys, or increasingly through mediation. Most often one parent gets sole custody and the other parent is assigned "reasonable" or sometimes "liberal" visitation. Under either of these arrangements, it is understood that the parents will work out the actual details of the visitation schedule. If you believe that you and your ex-spouse will have trouble agreeing on the schedule, and many parents do, you may want to set forth the schedule in specific detail. For example, you may want to indicate in the custody agreement exactly which days the noncustodial parent will visit and who will have the children on specific holidays and vacations. Parents who cannot agree and find themselves in court may end up with this type of arrangement by court order.

The variety of visitation arrangements is infinite, but certain schedules are common. For noncustodial parents who live near their ex-spouses, the most common arrangement provides for visitation every other weekend, with holidays divided or alternating on a yearly basis, and from two to six weeks over the summer. A typical weekend begins at 6 P.M. on Friday and ends at the same time on Sunday, but it may begin when school is over on Friday and end when the noncustodial parent delivers his child to school on Monday morning. Some noncustodial parents also have visitation one evening during the week to enjoy dinner with their children. Courts seem to disfavor arrangements that give the noncustodial parent visitation every weekend, since that deprives the custodial parent of time to spend with her child without the demands of school and work.

If one parent lives some distance from the other, a schedule like this may not be feasible. In that case, the court will usually try to compensate the noncustodial parent by giving him or her much more extensive visitation during the child's summer vacation—usually at least four weeks but often six or seven weeks and sometimes more. Typically, the noncustodial parent in this kind of case will also get custody during the child's spring break and for a significant portion of the Christmas break. Visitation during other holidays, like Thanksgiving, frequently will alternate on a yearly basis.

You should anticipate that as your child gets older, the visitation schedule may need to change. Older children and teenagers frequently get involved in extracurricular school activities, church and community functions, and other social events that may make visitation difficult. The courts will recognize a need for a change in these cases. Nonetheless, they will usually require some continued visitation, and the custodial parent should not purposely schedule activities at times that conflict with visitation if other options are available.

Restrictions on Visitation

The court has the power to place restrictions on the conduct of a non-custodial parent during visitation if they serve a child's best interests. Courts have prohibited parents from having overnight guests during visitation, from allowing an abusive new spouse or boyfriend to be present, and from engaging in behavior like smoking that might cause harm to the child. In one case, a court went so far as to prohibit a noncustodial father from having his preschool-age child accompany him when he flew a small plane, although a different court refused to allow such a restriction. In another case, an appellate court affirmed an order that prevented a noncustodial mother from visiting her child at day care except when parents were invited to attend or an emergency arose. Generally, though, courts avoid placing restrictions on the activities of noncustodial parents.

Religious Restrictions. With many couples intermarrying, religious differences sometimes contribute to the dissolution of a marriage. Other times they take on added significance after a divorce. Let's return to Janice and Gordon, our hypothetical interfaith couple. Recall that Janice and Gordon have one son, Robbie. Janice is Jewish and Gordon is Catholic, and Robbie has been raised in the Jewish faith. Janice now has sole custody, and Gordon has the usual every-other-weekend visitation schedule. Gordon has begun taking Robbie to church on his Sundays. Can Janice stop him? The trend today is against placing religious restrictions on a noncustodial parent. To do so would infringe on the noncustodial parent's constitutional right to religious freedom. Similarly, a court would not force Gordon to attend Jewish services while Robbie was visiting.

To prevent Gordon from taking Robbie to church, Janice would have to prove that Robbie would suffer emotional or physical harm from being exposed to both religions. If she demonstrated, for example,

GAY PARENTS AND VISITATION

As we saw with custody decisions, courts' treatment of visitation disputes involving gay parents vary considerably by and within jurisdictions. When a heterosexual parent objects to visitation in the presence of the gay parent's partner, some courts will restrict visitation to times when the gay partner is not present or will deny overnight visitation altogether if the gay parent is living with a partner. Other courts allow the usual reasonable visitation unless actual harm to the child is demonstrated.

that Robbie experienced severe anxiety, nightmares, or bed-wetting connected to stress over Gordon's attempted indoctrination in a conflicting religion, a court might restrict Gordon's religious activities with Robbie. In one case, the father's religion prompted him to mete out excessive physical punishment, enough to constitute abuse, so consideration of religion was justified. However, without clear evidence of harm, the courts will not impose religious restrictions. In cases where harm has been established, though, the courts have issued orders preventing enrollment of a child by one parent in a religious school in conflict with the religion of the other parent, have prohibited a noncustodial parent from taking a child to upsetting religious services, and on rare occasions have forbidden exposure to conflicting practices or inconsistent principles of another religion. Courts must also take care not to favor one religion over another in setting visitation schedules.

What if Janice and Gordon had signed a premarital agreement stating that any children they had would be raised exclusively in the Jewish faith? Does that change the result? In most states no. For the same reason discussed earlier—protection of religious freedom—most courts will not enforce these agreements. Nor will most states enforce separation agreements that specify the religious observance, training, or education of a child.

Denial of Visitation. In rare circumstances, a court may deny visitation to a noncustodial parent altogether. These cases typically involve physical, sexual, or emotional abuse by the noncustodial parent; a serious risk of kidnapping by the noncustodial parent; or, less commonly, physical abuse of the ex-spouse. Even in these cases, the court will often try to maintain some kind of visitation while protecting the child. Usually the court will provide for very limited "supervised visitation" (see box on page 213). This means that some responsible adult other than the noncustodial parent must be present during the visit. This person might be a court-appointed guardian, the custodial parent, a relative, a court-affiliated social worker, or anyone selected by the court. Some courts have programs that include supervised exchange of children when direct contact between the parents would be upsetting or threatening to the parent or child. Courts have also on occasion ordered noncustodial parents to obtain psychological counseling as a condition of visitation.

Enforcement of Visitation

What recourse do you have if your ex-spouse refuses to let you visit your child in accordance with the terms of your divorce decree? There are several remedies available. Assuming that you or your attorney has tried without success to convince your ex-spouse to comply, you may file a document in court, usually called an "order to show cause," seeking to have your ex-spouse held in contempt. A person will be held in contempt if he has willfully failed to comply with a court order.

There are two kinds of contempt, civil and criminal. Most family law proceedings, but not all, involve civil contempt. Civil contempt allows the court to jail or fine someone who violates a court order. Civil contempt is considered remedial, not punitive—that is, it is designed not to punish the guilty party, but rather to coerce her into complying with the order. A person held in civil contempt is said to "have the keys to her own cell" because she can end the jail sentence or avoid the fine by complying with the order. Criminal contempt, on the other hand, is a form of punishment for failing to comply with a court order. Someone

SUPERVISED VISITATION: THE WOODY ALLEN CASE

In a case that garnered nationwide attention, director Woody Allen sought custody of his biological son, Satchel, and his adopted children, son Moses and daughter Dylan, from their mother, actress Mia Farrow. Allen and Farrow, who were never married, ended their relationship after she found nude photographs taken by Allen of Soon-Yi, Farrow's older adopted daughter. Farrow alleged, among other things, that Allen had sexually abused Dylan. Although the charges were not conclusively proved, the court, strongly disapproving of Allen's relationship with Soon-Yi, awarded custody to Farrow and granted Allen only a few hours of supervised visitation a week with Satchel and none with Moses, a teenager who did not wish to visit his father, or Dylan, who was undergoing psychotherapy. The court left open the possibility of allowing Allen to visit with Dylan during her psychotherapy sessions if a plan was developed for him to do so without interfering with her treatment or welfare. However, no such plan was developed, and two years later, when Allen again sought to obtain visitation with Dylan, the court refused, relying on psychiatric reports that it would not be in Dylan's best interests, particularly since Allen continued to be involved with Soon-Yi. A subsequent attempt to obtain visitation likewise was rejected by the court.

held in criminal contempt must serve the sentence prescribed regardless of whether he is now willing to comply. Even though persons charged with civil contempt may end up in jail, they are not entitled to all the procedural safeguards provided criminal defendants. For example, they usually have no right to a jury trial or to a court-appointed lawyer. In visitation disputes, a court may be reluctant to impose a jail term for a violation of a court order because it might cause the child involved to feel responsible. Nonetheless, if other methods of persuasion have failed, this is an option.

Alternatively, persistent interference with visitation by a custodial parent can constitute grounds for modification of custody. Again, courts hesitate before using this remedy because of potential harm to the child involved, who may be uprooted from a stable custody arrangement. Nonetheless, courts also believe that continuing contact with both parents is in the best interests of the child. Indeed, as we have seen, some states have friendly parent statutes that require the courts to consider which parent will facilitate continuing contact with the other parent when they are deciding custody cases. Consequently, a court can order a change in custody as a remedy for interference with visitation.

Can you stop paying child support if your ex-spouse refuses to let you visit? Generally no. In most states, visitation and child support are not linked; in other words, a custodial parent has no right to prevent visitation to punish a noncustodial parent for failure to pay child support, and, vice versa, a noncustodial parent cannot stop paying as a way to force the custodial parent to comply with visitation. The proper approach is to go to court to enforce the order. Occasionally, a court will suspend child support obligations if the custodial parent is willfully refusing to allow visitation, but this is not the rule in most places. If you act on your own to withhold child support, you can be held in contempt of court yourself.

Some custodial parents have attempted to obtain compensation when noncustodial parents *fail* to visit as scheduled, on the grounds that the custodial parents have to hire baby-sitters, forgo plans, or incur extra costs caring for their children during the visitation period. A few cases have considered this issue, with mixed results.

What if your child expresses reluctance or staunchly refuses to visit his other parent? As the custodial parent, you have an obligation to facilitate the noncustodial parent's visitation. Most courts will not allow you to avoid a finding of contempt for interference with visitation based on your child's wishes, especially if they suspect that your child is reflecting or responding to pressure from you. Citing a custodial parent for contempt in this situation is not an ideal solution since imprisoning her may further alienate the child from his noncustodial parent. For an unusual response to this problem, see the box on page 215.

THE CASE OF THE NUSSBAUM GIRLS:
PUNISHING CHILDREN WHO REFUSE TO VISIT

Enforcing visitation is one of the most intractable problems facing family courts. This problem received national publicity in 1995 and 1996 when two sisters, Heidi and Rachel Nussbaum, ages twelve and eight, respectively, were held in contempt of court for refusing to visit their father. The judge put both children in foster care for a week, then sent the twelve-year-old to a juvenile detention center after she openly taunted the judge when he ordered her to comply with his visitation order. He ordered her younger sister grounded. The decision was highly unusual, and an Illinois appellate court halted the contempt orders the next day. However, in a decision a year later, the appellate court ruled that the judge had the authority to jail Heidi for contempt. The appellate court also ruled, though, that the judge should have considered other alternatives, such as citing the children's mother for contempt, the typical approach, before resorting to imprisoning one of the children.

Even if you believe your child's reluctance to visit stems from abuse by the noncustodial parent or someone else in the noncustodial parent's household, you have no legal right to suspend visitation on your own. However, you can petition the court for a modification of visitation, and you should report the abuse to law enforcement authorities and the local child protective services. (See also the earlier discussion of sexual abuse allegations in custody disputes and the following discussion of parental kidnapping.)

Parental Kidnapping

More than one hundred thousand children are abducted each year by parents, some noncustodial, others custodial. Angry or frustrated over court rulings against them, bitter at their ex-spouses, or suspecting child abuse, these parents kidnap their own children, cutting them off from their other parent, friends, and relatives and leading them into a life of hiding underground. The consequences of parental kidnapping (also referred to as "custodial interference") for the parents left behind and for the children can be devastating. Attempts to recover kidnapped children can be expensive, time-consuming, and emotionally and physically draining, with no guarantee of success.

Until the 1980s the situation was much bleaker. States did not usually recognize custody or visitation orders issued by other states, so abducting parents could simply go into court in a new state and obtain a custody order in their favor. Today, all states have adopted two laws that make this much less likely: the Uniform Child Custody Jurisdiction Act and the Parental Kidnapping Prevention Act. These laws, among other things, require states to enforce custody or visitation orders from sister states without modification.

Parents who kidnap their children are subject to both criminal penalties and civil enforcement actions for contempt and damages. State laws against custodial and visitation interference constitute the primary criminal remedy. In most of the states, parental kidnapping can be prosecuted in state court as a felony. If kidnapping parents cross state lines, they can also be prosecuted in federal court under the federal Fugitive Felon Act. The FBI has policies to make these cases an investigative priority deserving of immediate attention, but the request to involve the bureau generally must come from a state prosecutor seeking to try an abductor on state felony charges.

Some states recognize certain defenses to custodial interference charges, such as when a child is over a certain age (twelve, fourteen, or fifteen, depending on the state) and has accompanied the parent voluntarily. In addition, about half the states allow the accused parent to defend the action by proving that the removal was to protect the child; the other states, however, do not recognize this defense. If you are contemplating kidnapping your child to protect him from suspected abuse, think twice. Seriously consider other options. You can seek an emergency temporary custody order or ask your local child protective services to investigate. The consequences of kidnapping can be grave and can include a prison sentence. If you do act precipitously, also keep in mind that a number of states consider prompt return of a child or prompt notification of the police or the other parent a good defense against the charges or at least a basis for reducing the penalties.

In addition to pursuing criminal charges, the victimized parent can and should pursue civil remedies including contempt proceedings (discussed above) and suits to obtain monetary damages. However, although it may seem strange, a noncustodial parent in most places does not have a right to sue for damages when the custodial parent has prevented visitation.

Of course the most important objective for victimized parents is to recover their children. Numerous state and federal agencies can assist you in this process. The Federal Parent Locator Service, which tracks parents by social security number, tax returns, and job records, can help to locate missing children. To use this service, parents and private attorneys must enlist the assistance of a federal or state agency, such as a court, a law enforcement agency, or the state attorney's office.

The federal Missing Children Act of 1982 provides additional national assistance. Through it, victimized parents can give descriptions of their missing children to the National Crime Information Center (NCIC) and seek assistance from the National Center for Missing and Exploited Children (NCMEC) (see box on page 219).

It is important to respond quickly and effectively if you believe your child has been abducted. Here are some steps to take to begin:

- ◆ File a missing persons report with local law enforcement officials and have descriptive information put in the NCIC computer database. Police are required to do this without a waiting period. If they refuse, call NCMEC or your state's missing children's clearinghouse. Most states have one.
- ◆ Contact local and national parental kidnapping organizations, such as those listed in the box on page 219, and ask for assistance. They have a wealth of information to offer.
- ◆ Distribute photos of your child.

WHAT CAN YOU DO TO LESSEN
THE RISK OF A PARENTAL ABDUCTION?

There are several preventive measures that you can take to protect your child from being abducted by her other parent and to facilitate her return if she is abducted:

- Specify in your custody decree the times for custody and visitation so that the agreement is easier to enforce.
- If you believe that abduction is likely because of prior custodial interference or threats by the other parent, ask your lawyer to include preventive measures in your custody decree or to modify your present custody order. Preventive measures can include prohibiting the removal of your child from the state or country without your prior consent or if there is convincing evidence that kidnapping is likely, requiring the other parent to post a bond (that is, to purchase special insurance).
- Be sure that your child knows his full name, address, and phone number. Teach your child how to use the telephone and how to call 911, the emergency number.
- Give schools, baby-sitters, and day care providers lists of people to whom your child can be released.
- Keep current photos of your child and her other parent.
- Take advantage of programs by local law enforcement agencies and have your child fingerprinted.
- Keep dental and medical records indicating any distinguishing physical characteristics of your child or any medical conditions needing attention.

- Try to generate media coverage of the abduction.
- Contact your child's school. Children can often be traced when their school records are sent to a new school.
- Obtain a custody decree if you do not already have one.

- Maintain information about your child's other parent, including his employment history, bank accounts, credit cards, friends and relatives, and passport number.
- Write to the National Center on Missing and Exploited Children (NCMEC) and ask for their free publications on how to locate missing children, including the invaluable "How to Prevent an Abduction and What to Do if Your Child Is Abducted":

NCMEC
2101 Wilson Boulevard, Suite 550
Arlington, VA 22201-3052
703-235-3900

NCMEC can also advise you on how to recover your child if she is abducted.

- Write to the following organization to obtain further information about international abduction as well as the free handbook "International Parental Child Abduction":

International Parental Child Abduction
2201 C Street NW, Room 4817
Department of State
Washington, DC 20520-4818

- Keep the following toll-free number handy:
1-800-THE-LOST (1-800-843-5678)

This is a hot line operated by the federal government that you may call for reports and assistance if your child is abducted.

Many parents seeking to locate missing children hire private investigators. Be sure anyone you hire is reputable. You may want your attorney to review any contract with the investigator before you sign it or spend any money. Once you make a commitment, provide the identity of the investigator to law enforcement personnel working on the case so that they can coordinate the investigation.

If your child is abducted to a foreign country, additional efforts will be necessary. The United States is a member of the Hague Convention, which provides procedures for recovering wrongfully removed children in member nations. The Department of State's Citizens Consular Services can also be of assistance (see box on page 219).

Custody and Visitation by Third Parties

Stepparent Custody and Visitation. With many parents remarrying and then divorcing for a second or third time, legal questions have arisen about the legal rights of stepparents to custody and visitation. Consider the following scenario. When Cherise was nineteen, she gave birth to a daughter, Jasmine. She divorced Jasmine's father soon after the birth, and he has not seen Jasmine since. When Jasmine was four, Cherise married Leon. Five years later Cherise and Leon are divorcing. Does Leon have any right to custody or visitation with Jasmine?

Leon's chances of obtaining custody are very small. Most states follow a strong presumption in favor of biological parents in determining custody. Unless Leon can prove that Cherise is unfit, he will probably not win custody. There are signs of change, though. Some courts have begun to recognize that children may view stepparents as parental figures and develop strong attachments to them. Disrupting these bonds could prove detrimental to the children. Consequently, a few states have enacted laws granting stepparents the right to seek custody of stepchildren when the natural parents die, and rare cases have allowed stepparents to seek custody upon divorce.

More common are state laws allowing stepparents to seek visitation. Leon will fare better in this endeavor. Traditionally, stepparents have had no legal rights regarding stepchildren once their marriage to the child's biological parent has ended. Today, however, a number of states have statutes that give stepparents like Leon the right to petition the court for visitation. The court decides whether to grant the petition based on the best interests of the child. The willingness of the custodial parent to allow the visitation is a factor in assessing the best interests, but opposition by the custodial parent is not determinative.

In some states that do not have statutes explicitly providing for third-party visitation, courts on occasion have ordered stepparent visitation if it is in the child's best interests and if the stepparent not only acted in loco parentis (in the place of a parent) during his marriage but also developed a relationship with his stepchild. (See chapter 11 for a further discussion of stepfathers' rights.)

Of course, a stepparent will enjoy all the rights and responsibilities of parenthood if she has adopted her stepchild, a topic discussed fully in chapter 12. This may be possible if the biological parent has died, consented to the adoption, abandoned her child, or otherwise had her parental rights terminated.

Custody and Visitation Rights of Partners of Gay Parents. Like stepparents, partners of gay parents have sought custody and visitation rights after their relationships have broken up. Suppose, for example, that Kathy and Rachel have lived together for three years when Rachel gives birth to a child, Trevor, conceived through artificial insemination (discussed in chapter 12). Both Kathy and Rachel act as parents to Trevor. If they split up when Trevor is four, is Kathy entitled to custody or visitation? No. Unless Kathy has adopted Trevor (see chapter 12), she generally has no parental rights or responsibilities. Consequently, she has no right to exercise the traditional functions of parenthood, like consenting to medical treatment; no legally enforceable right to visitation or custody; and no obligation to provide child support for Trevor. Gay partners have tried numerous theories to support a right to custody or visitation, but these theories have largely failed, despite the fact that ongoing contact with a partner who acted as a parent can be critical to a child's well-being.

Decisions in three states, though—Wisconsin, Pennsylvania, and New Mexico—may herald a change in the legal rights of partners in this situation. In 1995 the Wisconsin Supreme Court recognized that a court has the power to grant visitation to the partner of a gay parent after their relationship breaks up if the partner can prove she has a "parentlike relationship" with the child by showing that (1) the biological or adoptive parent agreed to and fostered the partner's development of such a relationship with the child; (2) the partner lived with the child; (3) the partner assumed the obligations of parenthood, such as contributing to the financial support of the child; and (4) the partner played a "parentlike" role for a sufficient length of time to develop a parental bond with the child. If a partner satisfying these criteria can show a triggering event—that the parent substantially interfered with the partner's relationship with the child, for example—he can then seek court-ordered visitation if he acts in a reasonable time. Reaching a similar result, although on different grounds, were courts in New Mexico and Pennsylvania. The New Mexico appellate court held that a custody agreement between two women could be enforceable, and the Pennsylvania court found that the lesbian ex-partner of a mother had acted in loco parentis to the mother's child and thus had the right to seek partial custody.

Nonetheless, since most courts do not recognize the same-sex partner of a parent as a legal parent, families in this position need to do what they can legally to ensure the partner's parental position. Although only Wisconsin, New Mexico, and Pennsylvania so far have granted legal rights to partners once their relationship has dissolved, it is still a good idea while the relationship is ongoing to draft a coparenting agreement setting forth the expectation that the partner be treated equally as a parent. After a breakup, an agreement that specifies a custody or visitation arrangement may also prove helpful, even though most courts won't enforce it yet, because the law in this area is still evolving.

Grandparent Visitation. All states have statutes authorizing a court to award visitation to a grandparent under varying circumstances. Some allow petitions for visitation only in connection with some other proceeding, such as a divorce or adoption. Others allow grandparents to come into court on their own initiative even when the family is still intact.

The right to petition the court for visitation does not guarantee that a grandparent will win. The court will order the visitation only if it is in the best interests of the child. Many courts will require proof that the grandparent has a developed relationship with the child or that the child lived with the grandparent for some period of time. Grandparents often get considerably less visitation than noncustodial parents. Moreover, some courts have resisted recognizing grandparent rights because those rights threaten the rights of parents to determine with whom their children associate.

MODIFICATION OF CUSTODY AND VISITATION

Custody and visitation decisions are not final; they are always subject to modification. However, to encourage stability and continuity in a child's life, courts usually require a parent seeking modification to show "substantially changed circumstances." Some courts, at least in principle, grant a modification only if the present arrangement endangers a child's physical or mental health. In practice, though, courts often modify custody or visitation on a less than compelling basis if they believe that a change serves the best interests of the child.

Circumstances that have justified modification include remarriage either by the custodial parent (if the child does not get along with the new partner) or by the noncustodial parent (perhaps offering the child a richer, more stable family life), a change in employment for either parent, or any evidence that the child isn't faring well under the current custody arrangement. Behavior problems or poor school performance may indicate a need to reconsider the arrangement. Some courts will also grant a modification if the child has reached an age at which residing with her other parent will better serve her needs. It should be emphasized, though, that the legal standard for evaluating whether a modification is justified is designed to discourage modification and thus can be tough to meet. Trivial grounds or a desire to harass or exact revenge on the other parent will not suffice.

Move-Away Cases

One of the most difficult situations divorced parents and courts face is when a custodial parent decides to move a significant distance from a noncustodial parent—to another city, another state, or even another country. The custodial parent may have very good reasons for wanting to move—a better job, a new spouse, the desire to be closer to family— but the move likely will seriously alter or disrupt his child's relationship with her noncustodial parent. Sometimes, too, the custodial parent decides to move as a way of interfering with the noncustodial parent's visitation. Because of the difficulty of reconciling these competing interests, courts across the country have taken different views regarding moves by custodial parents, although the trend today is toward respecting custodial parents' freedom to relocate for legitimate reasons.

Let's look at a hypothetical example. Anita and Martin share two children, eight and ten years old, from their nine-year marriage. They have been divorced for two years, and both are living in South Dakota. Anita has had sole custody of the children, but Martin has exercised his liberal visitation, consistently taking the children every other weekend and one night during the week. Anita has recently remarried, and her new husband has taken a job in Ohio. Anita plans to relocate there with the children as soon as the school year is out. Martin is devastated and would like to stop her from moving. Can he?

It depends on the jurisdiction and the judge, but probably not in South Dakota and not in many other states, either. As with the initial custody and visitation decisions, the court has great discretion in deciding whether a move will be permitted. In most states, the custodial parent, Anita, will be allowed to move if she has a legitimate, good-faith reason for doing so. In order to stop her or to obtain custody in these states, Martin, the noncustodial parent, has to prove that the move would not be in the children's best interests or, in some states, that it would cause detriment to the children.

In deciding whether the move is in the children's best interests, courts will consider the advantage likely to be gained by the move, Anita's motives in seeking to move, Martin's motives in opposing the move, and the ability of Anita and Martin or the court to restructure visitation to ensure Martin's continued access to the children. Here, the move might provide the children with a more stable home life, an additional parental presence, and an improved economic position; and courts have allowed moves when a parent has been offered a better job, is pursuing higher education, or has a new spouse who needs to relocate. However, if Anita were motivated primarily by a desire to thwart Martin's visitation rights, a court might prevent the move. Assuming that she isn't, the court will turn to the problem of protecting Martin's right to visit. Continued access in these cases can often be achieved by providing visitation with the noncustodial parent during most of the summer and other vacations and by allowing visits in the children's new home if the noncustodial parent is in the area. If a revised visitation schedule such as this can be worked out between Anita and Martin, in South Dakota and states with similar laws, she will most likely be free to move to Ohio.

In a few states, such as Illinois, Anita might have more difficulty moving. These states emphasize a child's need for stability and continuity and thus place the burden on the custodial parent to justify a move, rather than on the noncustodial parent to stop it. So if Anita lived in one of these states, she might need to get Martin's consent or a court order before moving. If Martin opposed the move, Anita likely would have to show that the children would gain a real advantage from the move or at least that the move would promote their best interests. A better job or new spouse might not be sufficient under these standards to justify the move, so Anita might well have to choose whether to stay or give up custody of the children to Martin.

Move-away cases raise an additional question: If the move is permitted, who will bear the increased cost of travel by the children? Sometimes courts will decrease the child support obligation of the noncustodial parent to offset the increased transportation costs of visitation. In other cases, the parents will share the added expenses. But there is no set rule. Like most custody- and visitation-related issues, this decision will be left to the court's discretion.

Can the uncertainty be eliminated by including a provision in a separation agreement or divorce decree prohibiting the custodial parent from moving? In general, no. In a few states, the judge will take into account such a provision by placing the burden on the parent seeking to move, but the move will not automatically be denied if sufficient justification is provided. In other states, judges will look only to the relevant statutes and will not consider any restrictions in the separation agreement or divorce decree.

When parents have joint physical custody, a decision by one parent to move constitutes a modification from joint physical custody to sole physical custody. In this situation, the courts often treat the case as one for custody and use the usual best interests test. Joint legal custody does not present the same difficulty. Although a child's residential arrangement is changed by a move, most courts see no problem retaining joint legal custody since decisions about the child's health and education can still be made long-distance.

Because the law in this area is so variable among jurisdictions and so dependent on the facts of a particular case, if you learn or suspect that your child's custodial parent is planning to move out of the area, you should consult a lawyer experienced in family law as soon as possible. She can explain the law governing relocation in your area and advise you on whether and how to oppose the move. It is also a good idea to consider this eventuality at the time of your divorce, even if it doesn't seem imminent. Although a provision in the decree will not necessarily bind your ex-spouse, it may boost your position, as may frequent visitation and active involvement in your children's lives.

CHILD SUPPORT

THE LAW REQUIRES that parents—both mothers and fathers—provide support to their children, regardless of marital status. The duty to provide support encompasses the necessities of life: food, shelter, clothing, education, and medical care, but the law does not specify how much support parents in intact families must provide to their children. In fact, the law will not interfere in parental decisions regarding support in intact families unless the support is so lacking as to constitute abuse or neglect, a subject discussed at length in chapter 10.

When parents live apart or divorce, the situation is different. Courts then become very much involved in determining when and exactly how much child support must be provided, as this chapter will detail. The child support obligations of parents who were never married are the same as those of parents who are separated or divorced. The only difference is that mothers of children born out of wedlock must prove paternity, a subject covered in chapter 11.

SETTING THE AMOUNT

If you are seeking child support from your child's other parent, how much are you entitled to? Traditionally, the amount of support awarded

---

CALCULATING CHILD SUPPORT: AN EXAMPLE

Washington is one of the many states that follows the income shares method of calculating child support. Let's consider a hypothetical example to see how this method works. Suppose Jack and Shelly have two children, ages five and six, at the time they divorce. Shelly is awarded sole custody; Jack gets the usual every-other-weekend visitation. How much child support does each owe? If Jack and Shelly were a real couple, they would fill out a worksheet developed by the state to answer this question. We're going to follow the basic steps of the formula, but we're going to use simplified data.

First, we figure out each parent's net (after-tax) income. This can get a bit complicated if Jack and Shelly have unearned income from savings accounts, stocks and bonds, rental property, and so on, as well as earned income from their jobs. However, for simplicity's sake, let's assume that Jack's net income is $2,500 and that Shelly's is $1,500.

Next we add their net incomes together—getting $4,000—and determine their combined basic child support obligation by consulting a table that projects how much parents of a certain income should provide to their children of a certain number and age. For a couple like Jack

---

has been left to judicial discretion. However, in recent years gross inequities have led states to adopt guidelines for the court in setting appropriate amounts. Although the guidelines vary from state to state, certain principles underlie them in all states. First, as already emphasized, both parents are responsible for child support. Second, child support levels depend both on the needs of the child and on the financial status of the parents.

There are two basic child support formulas. The first formula, used by most states, tries to approximate the income that would be available to the child if the family were intact and then assigns the support bur-

and Shelly, with a combined monthly income of $4,000 and two children under twelve, Washington's table indicates a combined basic support obligation of $473 a month.

Finally, to calculate Jack's and Shelly's proportional shares of this obligation, we first divide the net income of each by their combined net income—getting a factor of 0.375 for Shelly and a factor of 0.625 for Jack—and then we multiply the resulting factors by the couple's combined basic monthly support obligation ($473). We find that Shelly's basic monthly support obligation is $177.38 and that Jack's is $295.63. Now, Shelly is the custodial parent—and therefore presumably is already providing her share. So Jack must pay her $295.63 a month.

Remember, this is a simplified example. In reality, the calculations can get quite complex. Washington's statute, for instance, provides for certain credits to the child support obligation as well as various add-ons like day care and extraordinary health care costs, which are allocated proportionally. It also allows for adjustments when a noncustodial parent has custody for a significant period of time—say, more than 25 percent. If your state is like most, it probably uses a similar method to calculate child support, but the specifics will vary.

den proportionally according to parental income. This is called the "income shares" approach. A simplified example of how this formula works is provided in the box on page 228 and above. The second formula is the "percent of income" approach. This formula, followed by fewer states, sets the amount of child support at a percentage of the paying parent's income, with the percentage determined by the number of children needing support. Some states also reduce the amount of support owed by a noncustodial parent based on the amount of time she spends with her children, on the theory that she is providing support directly to them when they visit.

The parents' ability to pay generally provides the starting point for determining child support. In most cases, ability to pay depends on a parent's actual earnings. However, courts may use the parent's earning capacity instead if it appears that he has deliberately reduced his income to avoid paying child support. Mothers of young children may face the dilemma of being charged with providing child support based on potential earnings when they would prefer to stay home with their children. A few courts have provided an exception for mothers in this situation, but generally the law presumes that mothers, as well as fathers, will work for wages.

According to the status principle, which is usually reflected in the child support formula, children are entitled to share in the standard of living of their parents. With very wealthy parents, courts may deviate from the formula to provide awards consistent with each parent's status; in other words, the child of a wealthy noncustodial parent may receive a large amount of support, beyond what is necessary to meet her needs. The status principle helps to ensure that a child will not live in poverty with her custodial parent while her noncustodial parent enjoys a luxurious standard of living. However, even in cases in which there is a huge discrepancy in the parents' financial resources, courts will sometimes draw the line at requiring payment of exorbitant amounts of money.

Courts may also deviate from the guidelines if a parent can show severe hardship from application of the formula, for example, because of extraordinary health care costs. Child support orders frequently require a parent to provide health or life insurance to benefit a child and to pay all or part of any unusual medical, educational, or child care expenses. Health insurance, in particular, has received much attention in recent years.

Health Care Expenses, QMCSOs, and Health Insurance After Divorce

Divorced parents, like all parents, should have health insurance for their children. (See chapter 4 for a general discussion of health insurance.) Unfortunately, a Children's Defense Fund study found that single-parent households are the least likely of any group to be covered by employer-based health insurance. To avoid problems in this area, it is a good idea to specify in your separation agreement and divorce decree how you will allocate payment for health care and related expenses. Indeed, some states mandate consideration of this issue. The agreement or decree should identify which of you will obtain health insurance for the children through your employer, how you will split deductibles, coinsurance, or co-pays, and, in the event that employer-provided insurance is not available, how you will apportion the cost of individual health insurance for your children. Some states require parents to share the cost of health insurance in proportion to income; others leave it up to the parents or, if they can't agree, the court, which then may assign the obligation to one or both parents. If you live in California, for example, the court must order one or both parents to maintain health insurance for the children if it's available at a reasonable cost, which usually means group insurance, and this includes insurance for vision and dental coverage. In addition, the court must include a provision for an add-on to the basic child support obligation for any reasonable medical expenses not covered by the insurance. These expenses are usually divided fifty-fifty unless one parent can show that the discrepancy between the two parents' incomes is great enough to justify paying proportionally.

You should also know that group health insurance plans provided through an employer have an obligation under federal law to allow either a covered parent or a noncovered parent (the ex-spouse) to enroll his or her child in a plan *if* the parent has obtained a legal document known as a qualified medical child support order, or QMCSO. A QMCSO is a court order, judgment, or decree that provides for child support or health benefits for the child of a participant in a group health plan. To be valid, a QMCSO must contain certain information designated by federal law (see box on page 232). This is a very important document, and you are well-advised to consult a lawyer to ensure that you obtain one and that it meets the law's requirements.

Why is this document so critical? A QMCSO can be invaluable in ensuring health insurance coverage for your children after separation or divorce because it enables a court to order an insurer to enroll your

REQUIREMENTS OF A QMCSO

To be valid, a qualified medical child support order (QMCSO) must contain the following information:

1. the name and last known mailing address of the participant—the covered parent—and the name and mailing address of each child (alternate recipient) covered by the order

2. a reasonable description of the type of coverage to be provided by the plan to each child, or the manner in which the type of coverage is to be determined

3. the period to which the order applies

4. each plan to which the order applies

To make certain that your QMCSO is properly prepared, consult a good lawyer.

children in a plan regardless of certain conditions that would otherwise apply. Specifically, the insurer must enroll the children even if they (1) don't reside with the insured parent, (2) were born out of wedlock, or (3) were not claimed by the insured parent as dependents for income tax purposes. All of these are frequent exclusions contained in employer-provided health policies that can otherwise prevent your children from being covered. With a QMCSO, a parent also has the right to enroll his or her child in a group plan anytime within ninety days of the issuance of the QMCSO, whether the usual enrollment period has closed or not. Another helpful feature allows a custodial parent to receive reimbursement directly from the insurance company if the child is enrolled in the noncustodial parent's plan.

In addition, a federal law known as COBRA (discussed further in chapter 4) requires group health insurers serving employers with twenty employees or more to continue coverage for children of covered employees, even if the children live with the nonemployee spouse after the parents divorce or separate. Coverage can generally continue up to three years unless the covered parent ceases to be employed (in which case the children have only eighteen months of guaranteed coverage), the employer stops providing group insurance altogether, or one of a few other exceptions exists. Your employee benefits coordinator or personnel office can probably give you more information.

Tax Consequences of Child Support

Child support payments are not deductible by the paying parent and are not considered income that must be reported by the receiving parent. This stands in contrast to alimony (spousal support), which is deductible by the payer and must be reported as income by the recipient. Prior to the adoption of child support guidelines, it was common for lawyers to manipulate payment of alimony and child support to take advantage of the different tax treatment of the two. The new guidelines for child support make this much more difficult.

Divorce also affects the dependency exemption (discussed further in chapter 6) since only one parent is allowed to take it. The Internal Revenue Code allows the custodial parent, defined as the parent who has custody for a greater portion of the year, to take the dependency exemption *unless* the custodial parent signs a written declaration (IRS Form 8332, entitled "Release of Claim to Exemption for Child of Divorced or Separated Parents") granting the noncustodial parent the right to take the exemption. In most states, the court can assign the dependency exemption to the noncustodial parent by ordering the custodial parent to execute the release. If the custodial parent does give up his right to the dependency exemption, this loss should be figured into the calculation of child support. A custodial parent who signs the release may still be able to claim the earned income tax credit if the child resides with him for more than six months out of the year. A noncustodial parent who takes the exemption without obtaining this release will have to prove that she provided more than 50 percent of the total support for her child if she is audited.

MODIFICATION OF CHILD SUPPORT

If you lose your job or your ex-spouse wins the lottery, can you get more child support? Most likely yes. Child support orders are subject to modification if the parent seeking modification can show substantially changed circumstances. Examples of some of these follow.

Increased Expenses

Custodial parents may receive an upward adjustment of child support if they can show significant increases in expenses relating to their children. For example, the cost of child rearing tends to increase as children grow older, so a court will consider that a factor in deciding whether to modify a support award. (A lawyer anticipating this change and the inevitable rise in the cost of living over time may include an automatic adjustment clause that would obviate the need to go to court for a modification.)

Job Changes

Child support may also be increased if a noncustodial parent's income has increased—through the lottery or otherwise—on the theory that a child is entitled to share in the parent's improved standard of living. On the other hand, a decrease in a noncustodial parent's income will not automatically lead to a downward modification of child support. Courts scrutinize such changes carefully. If your ex-spouse has been laid off and has been making reasonable and good-faith efforts to find employment for an extended period of time, without success, a court may decrease the amount of support owed temporarily. Other courts have refused to modify based on a temporary decrease in income. Moreover, a noncustodial parent who takes a significantly lower-paying job for personal reasons cannot assume that her child support obligation will decrease. Some courts will allow the modification if the reduced income reflects a good-faith career change, not an attempt to avoid child support, but other courts are less willing to reduce the income available to a child. For example, in one California case, a noncustodial parent who had been a pharmacist decided to attend medical school. Even though his ultimate income would be higher, the court refused to modify his child support payment while he was in school. On the other hand, a Wisconsin court allowed a father to reduce his child support payments when he left a well-paying job to return to school to complete a graduate degree.

Remarriage and Stepparents

Another circumstance that frequently leads to a modification of child support is remarriage. Parents who remarry and have second families sometimes seek a reduction in child support owed to children of their first marriages based on the increased expenses incurred in supporting children from their new family. States vary in their approach to this problem. Some states will not take newly acquired support obligations to children of a subsequent marriage into account at all. Others will consider them a factor. An example should help clarify. Assume that Sam has one child, Jonah, by his first marriage to Ann. He subsequently marries Lisa and they have a child, Chris. Depending on the approach his state takes to the issue, Sam may or may not be allowed to reduce his child support obligation to Jonah after Chris is born. But if Sam and Lisa subsequently divorce, Sam's child support obligation to Jonah will be deducted from his income in setting his child support obligation to Chris. This is because most states allow parents to deduct court-ordered child support obligations arising from previous relationships from the amount of income available in calculating child support awards to children born of subsequent relationships.

The situation becomes further complicated when you consider the income of new spouses. The law does not seek to discourage parents from remarrying, so as a general rule, stepparents do not have a legal obligation to support their stepchildren. However, if the children would otherwise need public assistance, some states do have laws that impose a support obligation on a stepparent who is living with the children and acting in loco parentis. Nevertheless, a stepparent's duty of support does not replace the obligation of the biological parent, and if the marriage ends, the stepparent usually has no further obligation to support the child.

Because stepparents generally have no legal support obligation, most states do not count their income directly in determining child support awards. However, stepparent income can affect the amount owed or received indirectly. If a custodial parent remarries and is supported by her new spouse, her overall living expenses will decrease, so her ability to pay may increase. The same reasoning could apply to a noncustodial parent who remarries. Also, courts in some states may consider a new spouse's income as a reason to deviate from the presumptive amount set by the guidelines.

TERMINATION OF THE DUTY TO SUPPORT

The duty of child support generally lasts until a child reaches the age of majority, which is now eighteen in all but a handful of states, but there are exceptions to this rule that may shorten or lengthen the duration of the obligation.

Your responsibility to support your child can terminate prior to your child's reaching the age of majority if she is considered legally emancipated. As we saw in chapter 5, a child can become emancipated by marrying, joining the military (which may include enrollment in a military academy such as West Point), or otherwise engaging in conduct determined by the court to establish emancipation. For example, in deciding whether to recognize a minor as emancipated, a court likely will consider whether the child resides at home, works for wages outside the home, has control of his earnings, owns a significant asset, or is claimed as a dependent on his parents' tax return. The law generally requires that parents consent to a minor's emancipation, although some state laws allow the court to declare a child emancipated without parental consent. Usually the question of emancipation arises in connection with another legal dispute, such as a claim for child support. Courts often hesitate to recognize emancipation in this context, even if the child has supported herself for some period of time, and they will demand considerable proof of emancipation. Emancipation can be partial or complete and need not be permanent.

You may also be relieved of your obligation to pay child support if your child abandons your home. Parents have a right to insist on compliance with reasonable regulations in exchange for providing child support. In one New York case, a father was allowed to discontinue support to a minor child who was attending college because she moved off campus without her father's permission. If your child refuses to visit you for an extended period of time or if the custodial parent interferes with visitation, in some states you may have a right to discontinue support. However, this is not the norm, and you must go to court to get your obligation suspended. Simply failing to pay will subject you to contempt charges, as discussed below.

POSTMAJORITY SUPPORT

Do you ever have an obligation to support your child *after* he reaches the age of majority? The answer is yes. There are two common situations that may require parents to provide postmajority support: if a child over the age of majority wishes to pursue further education and if an adult child is disabled and unable to support herself.

Support for College

Since many states lowered the age of majority from twenty-one to eighteen, courts have increasingly faced the problem of postmajority support for children pursuing higher education. Many states have laws that require support until graduation from high school, even if a child turns eighteen before that point. There is less agreement among the states about whether parents can be forced to support adult children attending college.

Traditionally, a college education has been a privilege enjoyed only by the elite. Today large numbers of young adults pursue higher education, and some courts have come to view such an education as a "necessary" included in a parent's duty to support, but only when the parent has divorced or separated. Adult children *cannot* go to court to force their parents to pay for their college expenses when their parents are still married and living together.

In cases of separation or divorce, many courts have ordered parents, usually fathers, to pay for their children's college education or, in some states, vocational training, even though the children are past the age of majority. Take the case of Mariko, for example, who is eighteen years old. Mariko has been accepted to a private college and plans to pursue a degree in business. Her parents are divorced, and her father has refused to contribute to her college expenses. Can Mariko or her mother force her father to provide support while she pursues her degree?

Some courts will make this kind of order only if the separation agreement or divorce decree specifies that the parents' child support obligation includes higher education. The Pennsylvania Supreme Court, for example, ruled that compelling divorced parents to provide post-majority educational support violated the equal protection clause of the Constitution because courts cannot order married parents to provide such support. The trend, though, appears to be in the opposite direction, with states more often allowing courts to order payment even if the decree is silent on the subject. Usually the court will consider various factors in deciding whether an award of postmajority educational support is warranted. These factors include whether the parent likely would have provided support had the marriage survived and whether the child had reasonable expectations of receiving a college education; they also include the child's ability to undertake college and to work or otherwise help pay expenses, the parent's ability to contribute support, and the quality of the parent-child relationship. Of these factors, some courts evaluate only whether the child is able to succeed in college and whether requiring support would impose an undue hardship on the parent.

If Mariko's father has been supporting her during her college education, can he stop if she moves in with her boyfriend against his wishes? It depends. In a few cases, the court has allowed a parent to cease support when a child is seriously estranged from a parent. For example, in a 1994 Indiana case, the court relieved a father of his obligation to pay for his son's college expenses because the son had refused to visit for years and had rebuffed his father's recent attempts to re-establish a relationship. In two other cases, though, courts have declared that parents cannot condition support on their children's compliance with parental wishes.

Support for a Disabled Adult Child

The second situation when the law may require parents to support children past the age of majority is illustrated by the following hypothetical case: Mariko's brother Kenji has suffered from schizophrenia since he was seventeen and has not been able to hold down a job. When he turns eighteen, his father stops sending child support. Kenji still lives with his mother. Is Kenji's father obligated to continue to support him?

Probably yes. Both parents have a duty to support an adult child if the child can't support himself because of some kind of mental or physical disability and if the disability existed at the time the child reached the age of majority. This is true *regardless* of whether the parents are married or divorced. This duty comes from statutes known as "poor laws." These poor laws require responsible relatives to provide support to a disabled adult on the theory that she never really reached majority since she was never capable of self-support. In some states, failure to support a disabled adult child constitutes a crime, and the child may have the right to sue her parents. Parents do not have to support an adult disabled child if they do not have adequate financial resources. In addition, in some jurisdictions, a child may have to prove that she is indigent before her parents will be obligated to support her.

The duty to provide support for an adult disabled child frequently arises when a state mental hospital seeks reimbursement for the costs of caring for the child. Many states will allow hospitals to recover from the child's parents if they are financially capable of paying, but some states explicitly relieve parents of an obligation to reimburse state hospitals in this situation. If an adult child is married, the child's spouse can also be liable for the costs of care provided by a state institution.

What if Kenji does not develop schizophrenia until he is twenty-five? Suppose he has a college education and had been working as a bank manager when he became ill. He has now moved back in with his mother and is incapable of working. Under the circumstances, can his father be forced to contribute to his support? In the past, the answer was no. Once a child reached the age of majority, the parental support obligation ceased if the child was capable of supporting himself. Today a few states may reinstate the parental duty of support under the poor laws or under the general child support laws if the child later becomes disabled. Also, if the child was never really emancipated before the disabling injury, the parental duty of support might continue. For example, in a 1995 West Virginia case, the court required a father to provide support to his twenty-year-old daughter after she was permanently disabled in an automobile accident because she had continued to live at home and had remained financially dependent on her mother after turning eighteen. However, most states will refuse to reinstate a child support obligation if a disability occurs after a child reaches the age of majority. In that case, though, the disabled child likely would be eligible for public assistance.

CHILD SUPPORT ENFORCEMENT

Even though the law clearly requires parents to support their children, large numbers of noncustodial parents fail to live up to their legal and moral obligation to do so, leaving many children in difficult financial straits, often poverty. A report of the Census Bureau in 1991 revealed that the poverty rate was 18.3 percent for married couples with children, 19.6 percent for single-parent households headed by men, and a staggering 47.1 percent for single-parent households headed by women. A quarter of our children live in single-parent households. Not all of these children have parents who are divorced. Some never lived with their fathers at all; others have a parent who died. While the reasons for

WHEN CHILD SUPPORT IS INSUFFICIENT
OR UNAVAILABLE: PUBLIC ASSISTANCE

Most children living in poverty live in single-parent households headed by women, in good part because of insufficient or unenforced child support awards. For thirty years the federal government provided financial assistance to single parent families under the Aid to Families with Dependent Children (AFDC) program, but this welfare program was abolished by Congress in 1996. In its place, the federal government now provides block grants to the states to distribute according to their own plans, within certain parameters. Particularly noteworthy are federal requirements that the states limit families receiving welfare to five years of benefits in a lifetime and that most recipients get a job within two years of applying for assistance. Within these guidelines, each state fashions its own plan and level of benefits. Additional support in the form of food stamps, Medicaid, and housing subsidies also can help single parents in financial difficulty. If you are in need of public assistance, you should contact your local social services department to find out how to apply for these programs and others that may be available in your locality.

poverty are many and complex, most agree that lack of adequate child support by noncustodial parents contributes significantly. Approximately one in four women entitled to receive child support gets no payment. About the same fraction receives only partial payment. Only a little more than half the women even have child support orders. Consequently, many efforts have been made at the state and federal level to try to ensure that children entitled to support get it.

In every state, willful failure to pay child support—failure that is deliberate, intentional, or "without justification or excuse"—is a crime. In some states, the crime is considered a misdemeanor; others classify it as a felony, a more serious offense. In either case, conviction can carry fines or imprisonment, or both. A person charged with such a criminal violation is entitled to all the usual criminal due process protections (procedures necessary to ensure a fair trial), including representation by a court-appointed lawyer if she cannot afford one. The only defense to the charge is an inability to pay that is not due to the nonpayer's fault. Criminal prosecution is usually a last resort since sending a parent to jail deprives a child of his parent and cuts off the parent's ability to earn money. Often if the parent pays the debt, the court will suspend the sentence.

Cases of willful failure to pay child support that result in criminal prosecution are usually brought under state law. However, in some cases, failure to pay child support can be a federal crime as well. The Child Support Recovery Act of 1992 makes deliberate failure to pay child support by going to another state a federal crime if the delinquent parent has not paid support for a year or more or if the amount owed exceeds five thousand dollars. Punishment can include fines and a prison sentence in addition to restitution of the unpaid child support.

More commonly, and sometimes in conjunction with criminal proceedings, child support awards are enforced by contempt proceedings. These may be initiated by a custodial parent filing a motion in court or by a district attorney filing one. Child support enforcement cases usually involve civil contempt, which means the parent can purge herself of the contempt charge simply by paying the amount owed.

Before filing a motion for contempt, the custodial parent must know where to locate the noncustodial parent so he can be served (provided) with the legal papers prior to the hearing on the motion. This is often a difficult task. The situation becomes even more complex when the noncustodial parent lives in another state, but the Uniform and the Revised Uniform Reciprocal Enforcement of Support Acts (URESA and RURESA), which all states have adopted, make enforcement of child support orders easier. Under these laws, you can file a petition in your own state, and the court will then forward the petition to the state of your ex-spouse, where a hearing will be held. If the court there finds the parent does owe child support, it will issue an order and take steps to enforce it. Another recent effort to facilitate interstate enforcement, the Uniform Interstate Family Support Act (UIFSA), adopted by about half the states, gives courts even greater power to enforce child support orders and has features designed to streamline the interstate enforcement process, in part by discouraging the existence of multiple support orders in different states.

Although it is possible to pursue an enforcement action on your own, it is ill-advised. There are many practical and procedural hurdles to overcome. Consequently, most parents seeking enforcement must hire a lawyer and finance a search to locate the absent parent—expensive undertakings for individuals who are suffering from a shortage of funds to begin with.

Congress has responded by passing a series of laws pertaining to child support enforcement. The federal government now requires states to establish public agencies that will seek enforcement of child support for welfare recipients and, for a low fee, other individuals who request assistance. These agencies are commonly referred to as Title IV-D agencies, after the section added to the Social Security Act requiring them. Unfortunately, these agencies suffer under a crushing caseload, so there may be considerable delay before your case is resolved. The law also requires states to establish parent locator services to assist in finding absent parents.

Perhaps the most significant reform adopted by Congress is the requirement that all new and modified support orders, whether obtained by Title IV-D agencies or private parties, contain a provision for immediate wage withholding. This requires that notice of a child support order be sent to the noncustodial parent's employer and that the employer automatically withhold the amount of child support owed from the parent's paycheck. The employer then forwards the money to a designated state agency or employee, who disburses it to the receiving parent. If the noncustodial parent is unemployed, a notice is sent to the state unemployment agency and the parent's unemployment benefits are garnished. Once it is fully implemented, this mechanism promises to be a very effective means of collection.

In the meantime, the Internal Revenue Service has the right to withhold child support arrearage (unpaid child support) from tax refund checks. A number of states have a similar provision for state refund checks. Various states also have adopted laws that allow the state to withhold professional or other licenses, even driver's licenses, from individuals who owe child support.

YOUTHS IN TROUBLE:

JUVENILE CRIME AND OTHER TRANSGRESSIONS
AND PARENTAL RESPONSIBILITY

MILLIONS OF YOUNG people today find themselves caught up in the legal system. Hundreds of thousands of children a year, maybe more, run away from home. Gangs, drive-by shootings, teenage prostitution, drug dealing, graffiti, and vandalism are common fixtures of modern urban life. While national crime statistics indicate that the violent crime rate overall has dropped, the same studies reveal a disturbing increase in violent crimes committed by juveniles. In 1992 well over two million juveniles under eighteen were arrested, and more than a third were younger than fifteen. In 1993 juvenile courts handled almost a million and a half delinquency cases, resulting in the confinement of thousands of minors for committing crimes ranging from the petty to the brutal.

Frustrated by these trends, many have called for increased penalties for juvenile crime and for greater parental responsibility. This chapter will detail the operation of the juvenile justice system and the rights of minors involved in the system. It will also discuss the legal liability of minors for harm done to persons or property and the legal responsibility of parents for the misconduct of their children, including the new and popular parental responsibility ordinances.

THE JUVENILE JUSTICE SYSTEM

Until this century, there was no distinction drawn between adults and minors who committed crimes. In 1899, though, the first juvenile court was established, and today every state has a separate juvenile justice system with aims and procedures different from those of the adult justice system (see box on page 247). In your state, this court may be called juvenile court, domestic relations court, family court, or perhaps probate court. In large cities, the juvenile court often occupies its own building or section of the courthouse. In smaller communities, it may consist of a single judge assigned to hear juvenile matters.

What constitutes a juvenile matter? The first criterion is that the juvenile has engaged in some behavior justifying court intervention. This encompasses acts that would be considered criminal if committed by an adult, for example, stealing a car or assaulting someone. Juveniles who commit criminal acts are considered delinquent. Juvenile court also hears cases involving young people who commit noncriminal acts called status offenses. Unlike juvenile crimes, status offenses involve conduct that is *not* illegal if engaged in by an adult. For example, ditching school, running away, drinking, smoking, talking back to parents, sexual promiscuity, and even dating the wrong boy can all subject a minor to the jurisdiction of the juvenile court as a status offender. Some states have laws that list specific activities, like those above, in their definitions of status offense; others define the term very broadly as "habitually disobeying one's parents" or "being incorrigible"; still others combine general and specific proscriptions in their definitions. Although some of these laws have been challenged on grounds of vagueness—because they don't give minors sufficient knowledge of what behavior is prohibited—by and large they have been upheld. In previous years, states often differentiated between boys and girls, but that kind of discrimination has been struck down uniformly.

The second criterion for bringing a case before the juvenile court is obvious: the matter must concern a juvenile. The federal government and most states consider all minors, usually defined as persons under

THE PROBLEMATIC PREMISE
OF THE JUVENILE JUSTICE SYSTEM

The juvenile justice system from its inception sought to rehabilitate and reform wayward young people. Punishment was never the goal. Because the founders of the system saw their first and primary mission as rehabilitation for the benefit of the minor and because minors generally are perceived as having fewer rights and being subject to greater state power than adults, the juvenile justice system operated under much more informal procedures and in private, with an eye toward shielding the minor from the stigma of criminal charges. Minors who committed crimes were considered "delinquent" rather than criminal. While the theory made sense, in practice, minors were caught in an ironic bind: because the system purported to work for their benefit, they were denied important rights and protections accorded adults. At the same time, the system in reality was and is punitive in nature. In a series of cases in the 1960s, the U.S. Supreme Court recognized this dissonance between theory and practice and ruled that minors have some, though certainly not all, of the constitutional rights enjoyed by adults in the criminal justice system. These include the Fourth Amendment's prohibition against unreasonable searches and seizures, the Fifth Amendment's protection from self-incrimination, and the Sixth Amendment's right to counsel.

eighteen, to be juveniles, but in some states, such as New York and Connecticut, the jurisdiction of the juvenile court in delinquency cases extends only to youths under sixteen and in a handful of other states, such as Michigan and Louisiana, to those under seventeen. Some states also specify a minimum age for jurisdiction. For example, in Wisconsin, jurisdiction extends to children ten and over, and younger persons who commit crimes are treated as children in need of protection, also known as dependent children (a subject further discussed in chapter 10). Keep

HOW DO THE COURTS LABEL JUVENILE OFFENDERS?

Juveniles who commit crimes are called delinquents. Children who find their way into juvenile court by committing noncriminal acts, called status offenses, are referred to by a variety of acronyms: MINS (minors in need of supervision or services), PINS (persons in need of supervision or services), CINS or CHINS (children in need of supervision or services), and in some states FINS (families in need of supervision or services). Status offenders are treated separately from juveniles who commit crimes, yet many still lump the two categories together when using the term *delinquent*.

in mind that these age limits may vary within a given state depending on the kind of offense charged, a subject discussed a little later on in this chapter.

What happens if a youth commits a crime while a juvenile but then passes the cutoff age before going to trial? In most, but not all, states, the juvenile court retains jurisdiction to decide the delinquency case and sentence the offender. With status offenses, courts have reached different conclusions about whether a minor who passes the cutoff age while his or her case is pending can still be subject to the juvenile court's jurisdiction.

To help you understand how the juvenile justice system operates, we'll follow two hypothetical cases, the first involving a young man charged with delinquency for committing a crime and the second focusing on a young woman alleged to be a status offender.

JUVENILE DELINQUENCY

In our first hypothetical case, Kevin is a fifteen-year-old suspected of armed robbery of a local convenience store. No one was hurt during the robbery, but close to a thousand dollars in cash was taken. Kevin has never been in trouble with the law before.

Arrest

Because Kevin is fifteen, he will be treated presumptively as a juvenile rather than an adult from the time of his arrest. Technically, juveniles are not "arrested"; they are "taken into custody." However, this distinction is essentially semantic, so we will use the terms interchangeably.

Even though Kevin is a juvenile, the Fourth Amendment to the Constitution protects him from unlawful arrest. The permissible grounds for arresting juveniles are by and large the same as those for adults. If the police have reason to suspect that a crime is afoot, they may detain a suspect, whether adult or juvenile, for a very brief period of time (often called a stop-and-frisk). However, if they want to arrest a suspect, they must have "probable cause"—that is, they must have a reasonable belief, given all the facts and circumstances, that the person has committed a crime. Moreover, if the crime was not committed in their presence, they may also need an arrest warrant. In some states, this requirement applies to juveniles even if the crime is only a misdemeanor. It is difficult to define specifically when there is probable cause to support an arrest warrant or a warrantless arrest. In our hypothetical case, if Kevin was seen simply hanging around or even running in the vicinity of the convenience store, the police may not have probable cause to arrest him. On the other hand, if he was seen running from the store carrying a satchel and he fits the description of the robber, they do.

Assuming that the police do have probable cause to arrest Kevin, they customarily will take him to the station for processing and questioning. Adult suspects are normally photographed and fingerprinted upon arrest. About half the states treat juveniles differently. Some forbid fingerprinting or photographing unless the juvenile consents. Others allow it only if the juvenile is above a certain age or is suspected of committing a serious crime.

Searches

To make a case against Kevin, the police will need incriminating evidence, some of which they may find by searching Kevin's person or his property. This evidence will be admissible at Kevin's trial only if it is obtained legally, for just as the Fourth Amendment protects individuals from unreasonable seizures of their person (arrests), so it also protects them from unreasonable searches of their person and property.

To be reasonable, a search generally must be authorized by a court order, known as a search warrant, but there are a number of important exceptions. When the police initially stop Kevin, for example, they do not need a warrant to frisk him for weapons. Nor do they need a warrant to search him or to inventory anything in his possession once they've arrested him. Moreover, the police may not need a warrant to search other property that belongs to Kevin if he gives his consent. Certainly they would be empowered to do so if Kevin were an adult. However, some jurisdictions question the validity of consent by a juvenile, particularly if there is any hint of duress, coercion, or subterfuge by the police.

What if police want to search Kevin's room and he does not consent to the search? They have a couple of choices. One is to get a search warrant by presenting to a magistrate sworn affidavits demonstrating probable cause that evidence relating to the armed robbery with which Kevin is charged will be found in his room. The other, a trickier alternative, is to appeal to Kevin's parents for consent. Most states presume that parents can give consent to search their child's room on the theory that they and their child share common authority over the room; however, some courts distinguish parental consent for searches of the premises, which they consider valid, from searches of a child's personal belongings, which they consider invalid.

The Right to Remain Silent—Police Interrogation

In addition to searching Kevin, the police no doubt will want to question him. They have the right to temporarily detain him for a reasonable period of time for this purpose, but they must fairly quickly transfer him to a juvenile facility. Regardless of where the police interrogate Kevin, they must respect his right to remain silent, which is guaranteed to juveniles as well as adults by the Fifth Amendment. The police also must advise him of these rights by reading him the so-called Miranda warnings (see box on page 251). Moreover, in many states, juveniles are entitled to additional safeguards against coerced confession. In most

THE MIRANDA WARNINGS

Most of you are probably familiar with the Miranda warnings: "You have a right to remain silent; anything you say can and will be used against you in a court of law. You have a right to have an attorney present; one will be appointed for you if you cannot afford one." Juveniles, like adults, are generally entitled to receive these warnings (although the exact wording may vary) when they are taken into custody and the police seek to question them. If the police fail to give a juvenile suspect these warnings, any incriminating statements the juvenile makes will be inadmissible at trial.

states, the police must notify Kevin's parents of his arrest and the charges against him as soon as possible. Most states also grant juvenile defendants the right to consult with a parent in private and the right to have a parent or other interested adult present during the interrogation. Consequently, if Kevin asks to see his parents, the police in these states are obligated to stop questioning him until he does. Not all states, though, require that a juvenile be advised of these particular rights, so if Kevin does not expressly ask to see his parents in these states, the interrogation may proceed. Likewise, if Kevin's parents are notified but choose not to be present at the interrogation, the police can continue questioning him.

Once Kevin has been Mirandized, he is free to waive his right to remain silent and answer any questions he chooses. However, he must make the waiver knowingly, intelligently, and voluntarily. The validity of Kevin's waiver usually won't come into play until the time of his trial, when the prosecutor attempts to introduce statements that Kevin made after the waiver. At that point, if Kevin's attorney believes the waiver was taken improperly, she will make a motion before the court to exclude these statements from the trial. The prosecutor has a heavy burden of proving that the waiver was valid (see box on page 252).

WAIVING THE RIGHT TO REMAIN SILENT

When juveniles are involved, most courts examine alleged waivers of constitutional rights very closely, more so than with adults, to make sure that the waivers are knowing, intelligent, and voluntary. Some reject a waiver of the right to remain silent out of hand if it was not made in the presence of the juvenile's parents or his lawyer. Others are extremely reluctant to accept it or deem it valid under these conditions. In evaluating the validity of a waiver, the courts will consider a variety of factors, among them the juvenile's age, education, and experience with law enforcement; his physical, psychological, and emotional state; and the length of the interrogation and the conditions under which it was conducted. Generally, the younger the suspect, the less likely a court will be to find a waiver valid.

Notice and the Right to Counsel

Shortly after his arrest, the prosecution should provide both Kevin and his parents with official notice of the charges against him. This is part of his constitutional right to due process of law and is similar to the right he would have were he an adult. The notice must be in writing and must specify the charges brought against him as well as the time, date, and location of any hearings related to the case. The charges must be described explicitly; any acts not enumerated cannot be the basis for a delinquency adjudication. Kevin and his parents must receive notice in a timely fashion so that he can prepare an adequate defense. If Kevin's parents are divorced, both are still entitled to notice, even the noncustodial parent if Kevin has visited with him and his whereabouts are known. The state must make a diligent effort to locate Kevin's parents; otherwise the adjudication may ultimately be overturned. Of course both Kevin and his parents can waive notice, but again the prosecution must show that they did so knowingly, intelligently, and voluntarily. If no notice was given but Kevin and his parents actually show up at the appropriate time and place, they usually cannot claim that the lack of notice violated their rights.

Undoubtedly one of the most important constitutional rights granted to juveniles who have been charged with crimes—perhaps the most important—is their right to counsel. In the 1967 landmark case of *In re Gault,* the Supreme Court decided, among other things, that juveniles have a right to counsel, just as adults do, but the extent of the right varies from state to state. In most states, a lawyer will be provided for Kevin if he cannot afford one; however, some states leave this to the court's discretion and some will charge his parents for the cost of the representation. The right to counsel generally applies to all stages of the proceedings from the time Kevin is taken into custody or once formal charges are filed through adjudication, disposition, and often for the first appeal. The police must inform Kevin of his right to counsel, and an attorney, judge, or other nonadversarial party should explain to him what the right to counsel means.

As with his other constitutional rights, Kevin has the option of waiving his right to counsel, but this is virtually never a good idea. Navigating the maze of the juvenile justice system requires well-trained, skilled professionals with experience in these kinds of cases. No untrained adult, let alone juvenile, could hope to adequately represent herself. Recognizing the critical importance of representation and the vulnerability of minors, a few states categorically deny juveniles the right to waive counsel. Nonetheless, Kevin is allowed to waive this right in most places if the state can establish the validity of his waiver. Some states flatly forbid waiver of counsel unless Kevin has actually consulted with an attorney about it; others require consultation with or sometimes consent by Kevin's parents. Any attempted waiver of counsel should be closely scrutinized by a judge to ascertain that the juvenile was carefully explained his rights, the nature of the charges, and the serious dangers inherent in self-representation. The state must show that Kevin had the intelligence to understand the charges, the possible punishment if convicted, and the consequences of forgoing representation.

Unfortunately, despite the law's mandate, too often judges fail to scrutinize juvenile waivers closely enough; some even actively discourage juveniles from exercising their right to legal representation. A number of studies disturbingly indicate that many juveniles go unrepresented, in large part because they waive their right to representation. Most minors are ill equipped to understand the system and the ramifications of waiving counsel and are incapable of assessing the situation. Often they give in because of parental pressure or because they fear the financial burden on their parents. *If your teenager is in trouble with the law, do not allow her or encourage her to waive this right. The repercussions could be with her the rest of her life.*

The Role of the Attorney

The role of counsel representing a minor like Kevin can be an especially challenging one. Lawyers have an ethical obligation to zealously represent their clients, and this applies to attorneys representing juveniles as well as those whose clients are adults. This duty can cause conflict if, for example, Kevin wants to plead not guilty and his lawyer believes that the plea is not in his best interests. The attorney has every right and responsibility to counsel Kevin about the pitfalls of his proposed course of action and to seek to persuade him otherwise. Ultimately, though, the lawyer is duty bound to follow Kevin's wishes so long as they are not illegal or unethical. This is true even if Kevin's parents are paying for representation and believe that they therefore have the right to control his legal representation. They do not. Kevin is the client, and if he believes his attorney is not adequately representing him because of parental pressure, he can ask the court to appoint a different lawyer.

Preadjudication Hearings and Detention

After Kevin is arrested and perhaps questioned, in some jurisdictions he will be referred to an intake official, frequently a juvenile probation officer, to decide whether there is sufficient evidence to support the charges against him. If there isn't, the case must be dismissed. If there is, the intake officer decides whether the case can be resolved informally or needs to be handled by the juvenile court. About a third of juvenile delinquency cases are resolved without going to court. For a minor first offense, the intake officer or the police may simply issue a warning and release the juvenile. Under other circumstances, they may refer the juvenile to a diversion program for supervision or social services, such as drug treatment or counseling. Diversion programs are usually run by community or social service agencies.

Assuming that Kevin's case is neither dismissed nor resolved, the intake official or the police may consider detaining him. They have the right to do so for a very limited period of time, but this is one of the most hotly litigated issues in juvenile law. Not only does it vary considerably among the states; it is also subject to change. Most states favor releasing juveniles to their parents, but police and intake officials have considerable discretion in this area, and it is not unusual for them to detain juveniles overnight or for several days. In fact, a distressingly large number of juveniles are subjected to unlawful confinement. While some states allow detention only in extraordinary circumstances, in most Kevin can be detained anywhere from one to seven days without a hearing, the usual limit being seventy-two hours.

At that point, Kevin has the right to a hearing before a judge on whether he can be detained further or should be released to his parents' custody. Some states require notice to parents regarding a detention hearing, but the hearing may proceed without them if they cannot be located. In several states, the prosecution initially will have to establish probable cause to believe that Kevin committed the armed robbery with which he's been charged. Then the judge will consider a number of factors before deciding whether detention is justified. Most importantly, the court will consider whether Kevin poses a danger to himself or others or is a flight risk. The court may also take into account Kevin's age and background, the type of offense he allegedly committed, and the condition of the victim. In most states, juveniles are not eligible for bail, nor are they released on their own recognizance. If Kevin's parents cannot or will not take responsibility for him, he may have no choice but to remain in the custody of the state. All told, about 20 percent of juveniles are detained for some period of time, most commonly when a drug offense is involved. Statistically, older, male, or African American juveniles also are more likely to be subject to pretrial detention.

If the police do detain Kevin, where will they keep him? If he is considered dangerous, Kevin will be confined in a secure facility; otherwise he will be sent to a semisecure or nonsecure placement. These options are discussed in the box on page 257.

If Kevin is not detained, he will of course not need a detention hearing; however, he will still appear before a judge in a pretrial proceeding similar to an adult arraignment to determine if probable cause exists to support the charges against him. Like the detention hearing, this proceeding should take place within a reasonable period of time, usually no longer than seventy-two hours after Kevin is taken into custody.

Plea Bargaining and Adjudication

Because the juvenile justice system is premised on the principle of rehabilitation, the terminology it uses is different from that used in the adult criminal system. Recall that juveniles suspected of criminal behavior are technically "taken into custody" rather than "arrested." Similarly, juveniles charged with illegal conduct in juvenile court are not "tried and convicted" of specific offenses, like armed robbery in Kevin's case; they are "adjudicated delinquent." Nonetheless, as a practical matter, the judge in a juvenile adjudication proceeding will need to find that the juvenile actually committed a specified crime before concluding that he or she is guilty of delinquency.

As we've already seen, many cases involving juvenile delinquents are settled without need of a trial, some through informal processing, the remainder by plea bargain. When a juvenile accepts a plea bargain, she pleads guilty in exchange for a recommendation of a particular disposition, or sentence, by the prosecutor. Since the charge is technically for delinquency, rather than a specific offense, the juvenile may still end up with a record as a delinquent; however, a plea bargain may nevertheless

OPTIONS FOR CONFINEMENT OR DETENTION OF JUVENILES

Juveniles believed to pose a flight risk or a danger to society or them-selves will likely be detained in a secure facility. Courts have had diffi-culty agreeing on what *secure* means, but the term generally denotes a setting where the minors are prevented from leaving by guards and locked doors or other physical barriers. Certainly, a county jail or state prison would meet this definition, but in some states, no juveniles are allowed to be confined in prison, and all states generally forbid com-mingling juveniles with adult prisoners. Juveniles housed in adult facili-ties are often victims of sexual and physical abuse at the hands of other prisoners and are at a very high risk for suicide. Nonetheless, in many locations, juveniles are housed in a segregated area within the same facility as adults. As a general rule, there must be a complete "sight and sound" separation. Unfortunately, some institutions accom-plish this separation by placing juveniles in isolation.

Most states have secure facilities that house juveniles exclusively, often euphemistically called training schools. Here, too, the law re-quires separation of juvenile delinquents, in this case from status of-fenders. Some states have also set up boot camps that seek to instill discipline and respect for authority in juvenile offenders.

Juveniles who pose little risk to others or themselves may be con-fined in semisecure facilities. These are less prisonlike than their secure counterparts, but they still have controlled access points to prevent free entry and exit and locked rooms for minors who act out. Juveniles who need even less supervision but cannot return home may be de-tailed in nonsecure placements, sometimes called shelter care, such as foster homes or group homes.

If the court does order confinement, some states will seek reim-bursement from the juvenile's parents for all or part of the cost. Par-ents have challenged these laws in the past but without success.

be in her best interests. Suppose that in Kevin's case, for instance, when the police arrested him, he was fleeing from the convenience store and carrying a thousand dollars in cash but no gun. If the prosecutor offers to let him plead guilty to delinquency based on robbery, rather than armed robbery, in exchange for a recommendation that he be sent to an alternative ninety-day boot camp program instead of the usual juvenile detention facility, he might be well-advised to accept the offer. Alternatively, suppose that the prosecutor is considering transferring Kevin's case to adult criminal court, a subject discussed in the next section. In this situation, a plea bargain might allow Kevin to plead guilty to delinquency in exchange for remaining in juvenile court.

The court can accept a guilty plea and waiver of trial from Kevin as long as he makes it knowingly, voluntarily, and intelligently. Some states provide additional protection for minors by requiring that the juvenile's attorney be present at the taking of the plea. Moreover, the court should explain Kevin's right to a trial as well as the ramifications of a guilty plea and should closely scrutinize the situation to make sure that the plea is voluntary. Be aware, though, that if Kevin does plead guilty as part of a plea bargain, the court does not have to honor the terms of the plea regarding disposition, or sentencing. If it doesn't honor them, Kevin may be able to withdraw his guilty plea in many jurisdictions, but at least one court has refused to grant juveniles this right.

If Kevin's case does proceed to adjudication in court, he will enjoy some, though not all, of the procedural and constitutional protections guaranteed to an adult criminal defendant. For one, Kevin will be entitled to a speedy trial. The federal government defines *speedy* as "within thirty days," but there is considerable variation in the definition among the states (see box on page 259).

For another, Kevin can expect the same burden of proof that the Constitution imposes in an adult criminal proceeding to prevail in his delinquency adjudication. The prosecutor will have to prove beyond a reasonable doubt that he committed armed robbery. Finally, Kevin will have a constitutional right to confront and cross-examine the witnesses against him.

WHEN IS A SPEEDY TRIAL SPEEDY?

Juveniles enjoy the constitutional right to a speedy trial; however, different states define *speedy* differently. For example, in Minnesota, a juvenile is entitled to adjudication within thirty days of arrest if she is being held or sixty days if she has been released. Other states have different limits. In California, they are fifteen and thirty days, respectively; in New Hampshire, twenty-one and thirty days. Some states don't have a clear deadline for commencing adjudication, and failure to meet these speedy trial rules doesn't always result in dismissal of the charges; certainly it doesn't if the juvenile or his counsel caused or consented to the delay.

In addition to these similarities, there will be some important differences between Kevin's adjudication proceeding and an adult criminal trial. Most notably, Kevin will not have a constitutional right to a trial by jury. While about a dozen states may allow him a jury trial, most will not. Those that do generally will leave the matter to the discretion of the court. In addition, more than half the states allow masters, referees, or commissioners, who are not judges but may be lawyers, to conduct delinquency adjudications. A few also allow them to hear pretrial matters.

Kevin will not have another constitutional right that arguably will work in his favor: the right to a *public* trial, which is guaranteed to adults by the Sixth Amendment. The theory behind denying Kevin this right is that confidentiality of the proceedings will safeguard his privacy, enhance his chances for rehabilitation, and reduce the stigma that would otherwise attach to his conduct. Historically, the states have barred the public from attending any proceedings in juvenile court. Today most states as a general rule still close juvenile proceedings to the public, but a judge usually has the discretion to admit people with a legitimate or direct interest in a case or in the workings of the court, including members of the press; and some states allow the judge to open proceedings if doing so is in a juvenile defendant's best interests.

Will Kevin's parents be allowed to attend the proceedings? Generally yes. Most courts allow parents to attend juvenile proceedings, and some even require their presence. Parents can provide important emotional support for a juvenile and can indicate to the judge that the juvenile has their backing. However, the court has the discretion to bar parents from the courtroom, and it might exercise this discretion if, for example, the parents are hostile to their child.

Despite these protections, the current trend is toward more openness in court proceedings in general, including juvenile matters, particularly regarding the news media. There are two issues here: first, whether the press has the right to attend juvenile proceedings and, second, what limits, if any, the state or a court can place on their reports about a juvenile case. Regarding the first issue, a half-dozen states have laws that allow the press to attend unless their presence would harm the juvenile or closure is warranted for other good cause. Several court cases have also ruled that the First Amendment guarantees the media the right to attend juvenile court proceedings, although there is disagreement on this point. Moreover, responding to growing public concern over juvenile crime, about a dozen states have enacted laws guaranteeing the press access for certain crimes, and the laws have been upheld. For example, if Kevin was charged with committing armed robbery in New York or California, the press would have a right to attend his adjudication. Massachusetts allows the public to attend a juvenile trial if the charge is murder; Minnesota, if the charge is a felony and the defendant is at least sixteen years old. A few states also allow the juvenile, his parents, or his attorney to decide whether to open the trial to the public.

The second issue involves whether the state or a court can limit the media's reports on juvenile proceedings, specifically by prohibiting disclosure of the name and likeness of a juvenile defendant. A number of states have such prohibitions or at least permit judges to limit disclosure to protect juveniles. However, in a couple of cases, the Supreme

Court has indicated that the First Amendment guarantees the press the right to reveal the name and likeness of a juvenile defendant, as long as this information has been lawfully obtained. These rulings call into question the constitutionality of prohibitions of identification of juveniles by the press. Nonetheless, after balancing the media's First Amendment rights against a juvenile's interest in anonymity and privacy, the South Dakota Supreme Court in one case upheld a court order conditioning attendance of the press on not identifying the juvenile. Regardless of the law, many publications withhold the names of juveniles charged with criminal or delinquent behavior as a matter of sound professional journalistic practice.

Transfer to Adult Court

Of course, all of the foregoing presupposes that Kevin will, indeed, be tried in juvenile court. There is a real possibility that the juvenile court will waive jurisdiction and transfer Kevin's case to adult criminal court. (This is also referred to as "declining jurisdiction" or "certification of the minor" to adult court.) In the last decade, states have increasingly resorted to this option in the face of rising public outrage at violent youthful offenders who seem beyond rehabilitation and very much in need of punishment.

Ironically, some juveniles may fare better if tried as adults for a couple of reasons. First, they will be entitled to all constitutional and procedural protections afforded adults, including the opportunity for bail and the right to a trial by jury, whose members are often more sympathetic toward young defendants. Second, research indicates that juveniles receive lesser sentences, such as probation and fines rather than imprisonment, in adult court. Nonetheless, because trial as an adult will subject a juvenile to sentencing as an adult, potentially in a prison with a primarily adult criminal population, few juveniles willingly seek transfer to adult court.

Who is eligible to be tried as an adult? More than half the states have laws excluding certain serious offenses from juvenile court jurisdiction. These states send juveniles charged with any of these offenses

JUVENILES AND THE DEATH PENALTY

Can a juvenile accused of a capital offense—like certain kinds of murder in some states—be eligible for the death penalty? It depends on his age. In 1987 the Supreme Court ruled that a state could not execute a fifteen-year-old. However, in a subsequent case, it ruled that the state could constitutionally execute a sixteen- or seventeen-year-old, and a number of men have been executed in the last twenty years for crimes committed at age seventeen, although all were adults at the time of execution. Some forty men remain on death row for crimes committed while sixteen or seventeen. Of course, laws in some states prohibit a death penalty sentence for juveniles.

directly to adult court, and only a few, such as New York, allow them to be transferred back to juvenile court. A few states have concurrent jurisdiction, which means that juveniles can be tried as juveniles or as adults at the prosecutor's discretion. Every state also has procedures for transferring jurisdiction, and these procedures are increasingly being utilized. More than eleven thousand cases were transferred in 1992, an increase of 68 percent nationally since 1989. In most cases, the juvenile court holds a hearing to decide whether transfer is appropriate. In a few, the adult criminal court makes the decision. The transfer hearing must take place before juvenile court adjudication; otherwise prosecution in adult court would be barred by the constitutional prohibition against double jeopardy (which protects an individual from being tried twice for the same crime).

If Kevin has a transfer hearing, the judge will weigh a number of factors before deciding whether he should be tried as an adult. The two most important are Kevin's age and his alleged crime. Federal law allows for adult prosecution of juveniles at thirteen years old for certain enumerated offenses, including crimes involving guns. The states, however, set their own standards. As far as age is concerned, some categorically prohibit transfer to adult court below age fourteen. As for the offense, some states restrict transfer to juveniles charged with felonies while others require it for violent felonies. For example, if Kevin were sixteen and living in Indiana, he would automatically be tried as an adult because he is charged with armed robbery. A third group of states considers several factors besides the nature of the offense: Did Kevin harm persons or property? Was his crime brutal, vicious, or premeditated? Does it indicate a high level of criminal sophistication? What kind of behavior has Kevin exhibited in the past? Does he have a delinquent or violent prior record? What is his physical and psychological condition now? Is he amenable to rehabilitation?

Although proponents of trying juveniles in adult court have been motivated in large part by concern over rising violent crime among juveniles, some research suggests that most juveniles transferred to adult court are charged with property and drug offenses. Judicial transfer decisions have also come under attack as arbitrary and racially discriminatory.

If Kevin is tried in adult court, what happens if he commits another crime before he turns eighteen? Will he automatically be tried as an adult? In some jurisdictions, yes. Others say he has a right to be tried as a juvenile unless a hearing indicates that transfer is appropriate.

The Disposition

Disposition is a critical phase of the proceeding. At this point, the court will determine what steps are necessary to address Kevin's delinquency. Disposition usually takes place in a separate hearing sometime after the adjudication. Under federal law, it must occur within twenty days. Under state law, the timing varies, and it also depends on whether the juvenile is confined or not. In New York, for example, disposition must occur within fifty days of adjudication if the juvenile has been released but only ten days if the juvenile remains confined.

Traditionally, the primary purpose of the disposition phase has been to devise a plan that will rehabilitate the delinquent. While this is still of great importance, many judges today consider other objectives as well, specifically the need to protect the public and the need to sanction the offender, and a number of states have amended their juvenile justice codes to explicitly denote these purposes. In most states, the details of the disposition depend on the discretion of the judge hearing the case. There are few firm guidelines in any of the states, but a state's juvenile code may place certain limitations on the judge's discretion, as will be discussed shortly.

Disposition Alternatives. Generally, the judge will choose among several alternative dispositions after weighing the facts and circumstances of Kevin's case. One alternative, commitment to a state mental institution, would be appropriate only if Kevin were mentally impaired and, as a result, posed a danger to himself or society. A second alternative, suspended adjudication, likely would not be considered appropriate in Kevin's case since he is charged with a relatively serious crime, armed robbery. Suspended adjudication is not a disposition at all. Rather, the court concludes that a juvenile did commit a given offense but delays the official determination of delinquency to give the juvenile a chance to show that he or she can avoid further trouble for a designated period of time. If the juvenile gets into trouble during this time, the original case immediately goes to adjudication and disposition.

A third alternative, probation, is the most common disposition used by juvenile courts. While not necessarily the most appropriate disposition for Kevin, probation would seek to reform him while he remained in his home environment. The length of probation lies within the court's discretion and may even exceed the length of permissible confinement, the most extreme disposition. Although judges have great leeway in devising the conditions of probation, usually they require that the juvenile meet periodically with a probation officer, attend school regularly, and comply with specified curfews. In Kevin's case, the judge may also prohibit any association with persons considered to be bad influences— gang members, other delinquents, substance abusers, individuals carry-

PARENTS AND PROBATION

Some courts have recognized that juvenile delinquency may involve family dysfunction and have adopted creative but controversial solutions. For example, one South Carolina judge agreed to release a fifteen-year-old delinquent girl from juvenile detention to her home on condition that she remain shackled to her mother for thirty days. If the girl had become unshackled, her mother could have been jailed for up to thirty days. In Virginia, if parents violate probation conditions applicable to them, such as participation in counseling, they can face penalties imposed by the juvenile court.

ing weapons—and may even prohibit the wearing of gang colors. In addition, if Kevin has a driver's license, the judge may very well suspend or revoke it, particularly if a car was involved in his offense. Virginia has a law that revokes the driver's license of any juvenile who is adjudicated a delinquent for an offense involving a weapon commonly used in drive-by shootings.

Juvenile court judges are allowed to impose other probation conditions that would not be permissible for adult probationers. For example, since Kevin was carrying a weapon, the judge might order that he submit to random searches of his person and property, such as his locker or backpack. Random drug testing is also a common probation condition in cases where the juvenile has engaged in illicit drug or alcohol use. The court might even require as a condition of probation that Kevin obey his parents. Recently, courts have begun involving parents more in their children's treatment (see box above). However, the court may not impose conditions that would be impossible to meet.

If Kevin is placed on probation and he fails to abide by the terms, what happens? He risks having his probation revoked, in which case he might be placed in confinement or given any other disposition the court deems appropriate. The court cannot revoke Kevin's probation without a hearing and proper notification, and Kevin must have been informed of the terms of his probation in writing. Usually Kevin would have the right to be represented by an attorney at the revocation hearing. In this situation, though, the state need not prove beyond a reasonable doubt that the probation violation occurred; it need only prove by a preponderance of the evidence that it more likely than not occurred.

A fourth disposition that the court can order for Kevin is restitution. This would compel him, or in many states his parents, to compensate the victims of his offense for any damage that he did. The compensation must be consistent with the amount of damage and the gravity of the offense. For example, Kevin's disposition might require him or his parents to return the thousand dollars taken from the convenience store and to pay for any damage done to the store during the course of the robbery. Restitution is most frequently ordered in cases involving property damage, but it may also include reimbursement for medical expenses if a juvenile's actions have caused bodily harm. It may be ordered as the disposition in a case or as a condition of probation; however, the court may be prevented from requiring restitution by a juvenile's parents as a condition of probation if the parents do not have the financial means to pay. In addition to restitution, some states allow the court to impose fines on juveniles or their parents.

Community service, a fifth alternative for Kevin, is an increasingly popular disposition because it helps juveniles learn responsibility and reintegrate into their communities while at the same time providing needed services. The judge can order community service, like restitution, either as the disposition in Kevin's case or as a condition of probation. There is no set limit on how many hours of community service can be imposed, but the number cannot exceed the permissible duration of confinement. At least one appellate court has upheld a disposition requiring a thousand hours of community service in a year.

Confinement, also known as detention, is clearly the most drastic disposition Kevin may face, but here, too, there is considerable variation (see box on page 257). Once confined, Kevin has the same general rights as an adult would have to a safe and clean environment, to sufficient clothing and food, to necessary medical and dental care, to reasonable privacy, and to communication with family members and his attorney. In addition, because the goal of juvenile confinement, at least in theory, is rehabilitation, Kevin should have a right to obtain counseling and treatment to facilitate his reform. Unfortunately, such programs are not often provided.

It is questionable whether confinement is effective in reforming youths. Recidivism rates (the frequency with which criminals commit subsequent crimes) tend to be lower in well-structured community-based programs. Moreover, numerous lawsuits have been brought throughout the country challenging inhumane conditions at juvenile detention facilities. Sadly, it is not uncommon for juveniles to suffer physical abuse at the hands of fellow detainees and staff, to be placed in isolation, and to be given drugs to control their behavior.

If the judge in Kevin's case orders him confined, how long can the confinement last? Traditionally, juvenile courts have used indeterminate sentencing. In most states, this means that the judge would commit the juvenile to the state youth authority for the maximum time allowed by law, and the youth authority then would have the power to decide when he had been rehabilitated and was ready to be released. In other words, the court would not impose a determinate sentence, one of definite duration. With indeterminate sentencing, the sentence could turn out to be longer than it would have been if Kevin had been tried and convicted as an adult.

Indeterminate sentencing has been upheld in court and is still the norm, but it has come under attack in recent years. Increasingly, states are allowing or requiring judges to impose determinate sentences. With determinate sentencing, the judge generally would rely on formal standards to impose a sentence proportional to the nature of Kevin's offense. Some states have guidelines specifying a range of determinate sentences for juveniles that take into account age, prior

THE LEAST RESTRICTIVE ALTERNATIVE

In choosing among alternative dispositions, or sentences, for a juvenile offender, judges in many states are required to select the "least restrictive alternative"—that is, the disposition that least constrains the juvenile's liberty but sufficiently serves the dual goals of rehabilitating him and protecting the public. The judge will evaluate several factors, including any prior delinquency or status offense adjudications; the seriousness of the offense and the juvenile's level of culpability; his age, family situation, and educational record; the setting that will most likely result in his rehabilitation; and any special needs or problems that he has. Ideally, the placement should be as close as possible to the minor's home and provide an array of social, psychological, and educational services.

offenses, and other criteria. Other states impose mandatory minimum sentences for certain offenses or provide administrative guidelines to the state correctional department setting forth the length of a juvenile's sentence.

Under either kind of sentence, Kevin may also be eligible for parole, a conditional release, before the end of his term. Whether he will get parole is a matter usually determined by an administrative body, not the juvenile court. Whether Kevin's sentence is indeterminate or determinate, its duration is limited by the jurisdiction of the juvenile court. Usually the juvenile court retains power over juveniles adjudged delinquent until they reach age twenty-one. In some states, this power, which is known as continuing jurisdiction, can last longer, until the minor is twenty-five or thirty, or it may end earlier, at eighteen. Beyond this point, the juvenile court has no power to assert control over Kevin, although some states, like West Virginia, circumvent this restriction by transferring juveniles to adult facilities when they turn eighteen if they were convicted as adults.

Choosing a Disposition. How will the court decide which disposition is appropriate in Kevin's case? In quite a number of states, the judge will be bound to impose the least restrictive alternative from among these options (see box on page 268). To assist the judge in making this determination, a social worker or probation officer will usually prepare a social history. Indeed, some states require such reports. The social history will discuss in depth Kevin's background—his family history and home environment, school performance, employment history, if any, and any medical conditions that may be relevant. The court also has the power to order a psychological study and even temporary commitment for evaluation.

Kevin's most important ally in obtaining the best disposition will be his attorney. In general, it is unwise for Kevin's lawyer to rely on the social history or on Kevin's family to determine his needs. Rather, she should investigate and prepare her own background report, and when she goes before the judge, she should have a specific recommendation regarding disposition, complete with information on the availability of any programs that she is proposing and on how they will be funded.

Appeal

If Kevin is adjudicated a delinquent for committing armed robbery, he will have the right in most places to legal representation for at least one appeal. Of course, there must be some basis for his appeal. The judge who heard Kevin's case had to make specific findings of fact and law to support his adjudication, and Kevin is entitled to a free transcript of the proceedings. Once Kevin's lawyer has reviewed the transcript, he and Kevin can decide whether an appeal is indicated. In some places, Kevin may appeal a decision to transfer his case to adult court immediately; however, if his case is heard in juvenile court, he generally must wait until after the disposition phase.

Long-Term Effects of a Juvenile Delinquency Adjudication

What effect will an adjudication of delinquency have on Kevin's future? Well, those involved in the juvenile justice system certainly hope that it

will assist Kevin in becoming a well-adjusted and productive member
of society. As a legal matter, in order to protect juveniles from the dele-
terious long-term consequences of their youthful indiscretions, the system has established strong privacy safeguards. In most states, juvenile
police and court records may be disclosed only to statutorily entitled
agencies and individuals or by court order. The relevant records include
the police arrest file, fingerprints and photos of the juvenile, the court
transcripts, and all papers filed in the court proceedings, including any
social histories or psychological evaluations. Authorized recipients of
juvenile records usually include other law enforcement personnel, other
courts, and in some states the juvenile's school or his parents. Federal
law and some states also allow a report of the disposition of Kevin's case
to be provided to the victim, the owner of the convenience store. Only
a few states allow inspection of juvenile records by the public, and even
those states generally place restrictions on which records can be disclosed. For example, Mississippi permits the public disclosure of juvenile court records only if the juvenile has been adjudicated as
delinquent once for certain designated offenses, such as murder, bur-
glary, and armed robbery, or twice for other felonies.

To further insure the confidentiality of a juvenile's arrest, most
states permit the sealing or expungement (also called expunction, era-
sure, or destruction) of juvenile court records under certain circumstances. Although different states define these terms differently, sealing
usually involves storing the records in a locked file or other location
where access is limited while expungement involves deleting the juvenile's and his parents' names or physically destroying the records.

There is little uniformity among the states on the procedures governing the sealing or expungement of juvenile records. In some states,
the police and court records will automatically be expunged after a
specified length of time in certain types of cases, for example, those in
which the charges were dismissed or no adjudication of delinquency resulted. But in many states, the juvenile or his parents will have to bring
a motion seeking to have the records sealed or expunged, and the

courts will consider several criteria in deciding whether to grant it. Most significantly, the judge will want to see that the juvenile has stayed out of trouble since she was discharged from the system. The rehabilitation period is typically two years, but it can be as long as ten years, or it may end when the juvenile reaches a designated age, anywhere from eighteen to twenty-seven. Some states do not specify the conditions for granting expungement in their statutes but instead leave the decision to the court's discretion. In these states, a juvenile may prevail if she can show that she has been rehabilitated, that expungement is in her best interests, and that no valid law enforcement purpose is served by maintaining the records.

What about Kevin? Well, just as some states automatically expunge juvenile records after a certain length of time, so some states categorically refuse to expunge the records of juveniles who have committed certain offenses. If Kevin lives in one of the latter states and armed robbery is one of the offenses, then he is out of luck. If he lives elsewhere, however, he may succeed in persuading the court to seal or expunge his record. Let's suppose he does succeed. Does it matter whether he has the record sealed or expunged? It could. In many, but not all, states, whichever option Kevin chooses, he may thereafter legally represent that he has never been arrested. But in states that do not allow Kevin to make this representation, he may be better off having his record sealed rather than expunged or completely destroyed, especially if it contains exculpatory information. For example, if the record indicates that Kevin was mistakenly arrested or that he was subsequently cleared of the charge against him, then the full story remains available should he need to explain his arrest.

Even though all these methods exist for protecting the privacy of juvenile offenders, information is improperly disclosed with alarming frequency. Although a juvenile delinquency record does not impose any civil disabilities, such as losing the right to vote, that an adult conviction would carry, it nevertheless can impair Kevin's ability to get a job, attend college, or serve in the military. It may even hinder his efforts to obtain a driver's license or housing, although most states have laws ostensibly preventing imposition of these penalties on a minor.

If Kevin finds himself in trouble with the law as an adult, can his juvenile record be used against him? Not usually. In adult criminal cases, a prior criminal record generally is admissible only to impeach the credibility of the defendant if he takes the stand. With juveniles, even this is generally not allowed because the delinquency adjudication is not technically considered a conviction. However, Kevin's juvenile history might be considered at the time of sentencing.

STATUS OFFENSES

Not all young people who find themselves in the juvenile court system have committed crimes. As we saw at the beginning of this chapter, the juvenile court system also handles cases involving status offenders. The process by which status offenders are handled is similar to the process by which delinquents are handled: they are taken into custody, referred to an intake official, subjected to adjudication (trial), and given a disposition (sentence). However, status offenders and delinquents are dealt with separately, and although both enjoy many of the same rights (see box on page 273), there are some important differences in how their cases are treated.

Let's consider our second hypothetical case. Caroline is a bright but troubled fifteen-year-old. For the past year, she has given her parents nothing but problems. Formerly a strong student, she has taken to skipping classes. She uses foul language when talking to her parents and has admitted to engaging in sexual relations with her boyfriend, Randy, a seventeen-year-old dropout who smokes and drinks. Her parents have forbidden her to see Randy, but she has been caught more than once sneaking out of the house after her curfew to meet him. Fed up, Caroline's parents have petitioned the court to have her declared incorrigible.

Caroline's parents are not unique. While relinquishing your child to the court system is a drastic act, unfortunately many parents do exactly

WHAT RIGHTS DO ALLEGED STATUS OFFENDERS HAVE?

Juveniles charged with status offenses, like those charged with delinquency, are entitled to some, but not all, of the protections afforded adult criminal defendants.

They have a right to notice of the charges against them. In theory, the notice should specifically enumerate the dates, times, and places of their misbehavior, but in practice many petitions are often vague in their allegations.

In many cases, they have a right to legal representation after the intake phase, and this representation must be provided at state expense if they cannot afford the fees. Since alleged status offenders have not been charged with crimes, their right to legal representation is not guaranteed under the Constitution, but most states have extended this right to them when an out-of-home placement is a possibility.

In some states, they have the right not to be forced to incriminate themselves if they face the possibility of secure detention. In other words, they must receive the Miranda warnings before the police can interrogate them (see box on page 251).

They can waive their Miranda rights, but the courts will scrutinize any waivers carefully and may not accept them if they were obtained without parental consent or conversely, with parental or police pressure.

that. Other common complainants include schools in truancy cases and law enforcement agencies.

Intake and Adjudication

There are several ways Caroline may enter the juvenile court system. Like a suspected delinquent, she may be brought in by the police. Even though she has not committed a crime, in many states the police may take a minor into custody if they have reasonable cause to believe he or she is in need of supervision, has violated a court order, or is in public and appears to require medical attention. Alternatively, a truant officer may bring Caroline in after finding her at a local teen hangout during school hours. Of course, Caroline's parents can also take her to court.

In our hypothetical case, the process will most likely begin when Caroline's parents file a complaint with an intake person at the juvenile court. The intake person may be a social worker, a probation officer, or simply a clerical worker. The intake session, sometimes called an informal adjustment or preliminary investigation, is critically important. Half of all status offense referrals are disposed of at this stage. If Caroline has been abused or neglected by her parents, the intake officer may reroute her case to the child dependency system (discussed at length in chapter 10). Alternatively, the intake officer may assign Caroline to drug treatment, counseling, or an educational, recreational, employment, or other diversion program; arrange for a guardianship or a third-party custody with a relative's or friend's family; place her in voluntary foster care; or confine her in a state facility or a residential setting. In deciding the appropriate course of action, the intake officer may consider a number of circumstances, including any prior offenses that Caroline has committed, the seriousness of the charges against her, her home environment, her performance in school, and her attitude and likely future behavior.

If the intake officer decides to detain Caroline, a formal petition will be filed and she will be entitled to a hearing before a judge within the next day when court is in session. As in juvenile delinquency proceedings, the judge will determine if there is probable cause to believe that Caroline has committed a status offense. If the judge finds that there is, Caroline will face an adjudication, or trial. In the meantime, the judge can order any of the referrals or placements discussed at the intake phase, possibly even secure detention (see box on page 257).

Recall that juveniles do not have a constitutional right to a jury trial, so Caroline's adjudication will be conducted by a juvenile court judge. At the trial, the prosecution will have to prove either that Caroline committed one or more of the acts forbidden by her state's status offense statute or that she meets the definition of *incorrigible*. Since she is charged with a status offense, not a crime, the prosecution may not have to prove its case against her "beyond a reasonable doubt," as it would in a delinquency proceeding. Instead, it may be required to present only "clear and convincing evidence" or to show by "a preponderance of the evidence" that Caroline has been justly charged. Most likely Caroline's truancy combined with her repeated disobedience, her rude behavior toward her parents, and her sexual involvement with her boyfriend will qualify her as an incorrigible.

Sometimes minors are able to defend themselves against status offense charges by showing that the offenses were isolated incidents. Most state laws require defendants to be "habitually" disobedient or truant. This qualification will probably not help Caroline since she has defied her parents' orders on numerous occasions.

As a practical matter, even if Caroline can somehow defeat the status offense charge, it is likely that she and her parents will be more estranged by the end of the adjudication, and dismissal will simply return her to an environment that not only led her to where she is now but is even more strained than before. For this reason as well as others, it is almost certainly in Caroline's best interests to explore alternatives to a trial on the charges.

A minor's attorney can often persuade the prosecutor to accept an alternative resolution to trial in a status offense case. Again, this might include diversion or an informal adjustment convincing Caroline's parents to allow her to return home or, if that is not a realistic option, to agree to another placement arrangement. Finally, if Caroline were old enough, mature enough, and able to support herself, she might be able to persuade the judge to emancipate her (see chapter 5); however, since she's only fifteen and not self-supporting, this outcome is not likely.

Disposition

If Caroline's case does go to trial and she is adjudged to have committed a status offense and thus to be in need of supervision, care, rehabilitation, or treatment, the judge will have to order a disposition. Usually the disposition phase of the proceeding will be bifurcated—that is, it will

TRUANCY

Truancy forms the basis for a significant percentage of status offender petitions brought in our juvenile courts. The goal of court intervention in these cases is both to keep the minor in school and to deter criminal activity. Courts around the country have developed various approaches to dealing with truants. Some have established truancy centers. Suspected truants are arrested, searched, handcuffed, and taken by the police to one of these centers. Then their parents are called, and the truants are referred to a counseling agency. Other jurisdictions have set up special truancy courts run jointly by the school district and the juvenile court. The truancy court seeks to solve the problems underlying truancy by getting both minors and their parents involved. In some cases, the minors may have quit going to school because of frustration caused by learning disabilities. If so, the disabilities should be identified through proper testing and remedial attention should be provided. In California, minors charged with truancy must be referred to a school attendance review board prior to juvenile court intervention. Elsewhere, alleged truants are tried by a court or jury of their peers, which can order them to attend school or perform some community service. In a few states, truant minors can have their driver's licenses revoked.

take place separately from the adjudication phase—and will be more informal than the adjudication. At the disposition hearing, Caroline will probably have an opportunity to address the court. If she does, she will serve her own interests best by expressing remorse, taking responsibility for her actions, and reassuring the judge that she will not repeat the offending behavior.

The goal of the disposition, at least in theory, is to address Caroline's needs, not to punish her. The judge will consider any available community resources and should choose from among the available alternatives the least restrictive disposition (see box on page 268). The options discussed during the intake phase and as alternatives to a trial (a placement in foster care, a halfway house, a residential treatment facility, or emancipation) would still be available at this stage. In addition, the judge could send Caroline home on probation, perhaps with services provided to her and her family, or commit her to home supervision, imposing restrictions on her activities. The court in many states, particularly those that designate status offenders as families in need of services or supervision (FINS), has the power to order parents to participate in therapy with the minor. In Florida, if a status offender is declared a FINS, the court can order both the child and the parents to mediation. The court can also require the parents to pay some of the costs of services provided to the juvenile. Other states have similar laws.

The most drastic disposition would place Caroline in a secure detention facility (see box on page 276). The presumption against committing status offenders to such institutions is much stronger than it is for juvenile delinquents, and federal law generally prohibits it. However, the trend toward deinstitutionalizing status offenders may be reversing in favor of detaining juvenile offenders of all kinds. Many states now expressly allow secure detention of repeat status offenders, minors deemed to pose a danger to themselves or others in a nonsecure facility, those whose parents are unable or unwilling to provide adequate supervision, and those who have violated previous court orders—for example, by continued refusal to attend school or undertake therapy as required by the court. Moreover, judges sometimes order detention in response to parental pressure. Although these dispositions are frequently overturned on appeal, it is a sad fact that many parents bring status offense complaints against their recalcitrant children because they want to have them confined. Nevertheless, since this is Caroline's first offense, detention is an unlikely outcome.

One disturbing trend, discussed more fully in chapter 4, is for parents with financial means to commit their troubled teenagers inappropriately to mental health treatment facilities. While this disposition is also an option of the court, it is generally reserved for juvenile delinquents who suffer from genuine mental illnesses, not mere status offenders, since confinement is not usually the least restrictive alternative. However, there is evidence to suggest that status offenders who by law cannot be confined in a detention center are sometimes labeled as mentally ill and rerouted to psychiatric facilities.

Runaways

No one knows exactly how many runaways and homeless youths are living on our streets today. Two comprehensive recent studies have attempted to measure this population. A 1990 study estimated the number at more than half a million, including more than a hundred thousand so-called thrownaways, minors forced out of their homes by their parents, while a more recent study suggested that as many as 2.8 million teenagers have had a runaway experience.

Running away constitutes a status offense for which a minor can be taken into custody by the police, yet many runaways are never caught. Often they leave home to escape abuse and neglect only to find themselves living a dreadful life on the streets. Most runaways support themselves through prostitution, drug dealing, or other criminal activity. Many become drug dependent, and they are at very high risk for contracting HIV and AIDS as well as for committing suicide. Alarmed at this appalling situation, Congress enacted and subsequently amended the Runaway and Homeless Youth Act to help local public agencies and private organizations establish shelters for runaway teens. These shelters, located near places that are common destination points for runaways (often major urban centers), serve small groups of youths, and they usually provide a variety of services. Some, called transitional living youth projects, aim to assist sixteen- to twenty-year-olds in learning to live self-sufficiently. Unfortunately, demand for these beds and services exceeds the supply in some areas. Federal law has also provided funds for the development of a national telephone network to enable runaways to contact their families. You can find the toll-free number for

WHAT CAN YOU DO IF YOUR CHILD IS A RUNAWAY?

The National Center for Missing and Exploited Children (NCMEC) lists a number of steps parents can take to help locate a runaway child. NCMEC cautions that the first forty-eight hours after a child is missing are the most critical, so an immediate response is very important.

1. Contact your child's friends, school, relatives, employer, and anyone else who may know his or her whereabouts.
2. Canvas the local mall, video arcade, and other hangouts frequented by your child.
3. Report your child as missing to the police. You should provide them with a recent photo as well as any fingerprints and dental records if you have them.
4. Be sure the police enter your child's name and description into the National Crime Information Center (NCIC) computer. This does not create a police record for your child, and it can assist in locating him or her. If the police will not take the report or provide the information to NCIC, contact the FBI. Contrary to what you may think, the law does not require any waiting period before taking a missing person's report on a minor, although some police departments may have such a policy. Be sure the report is provided to any local or state centers for missing children in your area.
5. Call the National Runaway Switchboard, a toll-free number set up by the federal government that enables runaways and their families to leave messages for each other. This number is 1-800-621-4000. There may also be a local runaway hot line in your area.
6. Prepare posters or fliers with your child's name, description, and picture on them along with contact information. Distribute them at transportation hubs (bus and train stations), hospitals, police stations, and anywhere else in your area that you think your child may have gone.
7. Contact NCMEC at **1-800-843-5678** for additional help.

this network in the box on page 279, along with other steps you can take if your child runs away.

PARENTAL LIABILITY FOR CHILDREN'S ACTS

The previous section considered minors' rights and responsibilities in criminal-type actions brought by the state in the juvenile justice system. Minors can also be held civilly liable to private parties for harm they wrongfully cause. In other words, they can be sued and compelled to pay money, known as damages, to the injured party. What's more, in certain circumstances, parents can be held liable for those damages as well, regardless of whether they were at fault. In fact, parents may even face criminal charges based on the behavior of their children.

Children's Tort Liability
Before a parent can be held liable for a child's conduct, the child must have committed a wrongful act—referred to as a tort—that entitles the injured person to recover damages. If the child caused the injury without any fault, then neither the child nor the parent will be held liable. There are two types of torts: intentional torts—such as assault, battery, or trespass—and negligence.

In most places today, children can be held liable for their intentional torts without any explicit age-based limitations. Even a child as young as four or five can be held liable for wrongfully harming someone, although the person suing will have to prove that the child was old enough to form the intent necessary to commit the alleged tort.

In negligence cases, the law in earlier times exempted children under age seven from liability and presumed that children between the ages of seven and fourteen were incapable of negligence. In most places today, preschool-age children are still considered incapable of negligence, but the law now holds children older than four liable for it. Of course, the standard used to judge negligence on the part of children differs from the standard applied to adults. Children are expected to act as reasonable children of similar age, intelligence, experience, maturity, and training would act. In certain cases, the injured party in a tort case may convince the court to hold a child to an adult standard if the child caused injury or damage while engaged in an adult activity or one considered inherently dangerous. Adult activities include the operation of motorized vehicles or equipment, such as motorcycles, snowmobiles, dirt bikes, and tractors, as well as certain recreational activities, like golf, but they do not include traditional childhood activities like bike riding.

Parental Liability Statutes

Proving that a child acted wrongfully in injuring another person or their property entitles that person to compensation from the child. But does it also mean that the victim can recover damages from the parents? In many cases, yes. All states have laws expressly providing for parental liability under certain circumstances. These statutes impose vicarious liability on parents—in other words, they do not require parents to have acted wrongfully or negligently in any way before imposing liability. While this might seem unfair to the innocent parents, these statutes are designed to provide limited compensation to the injured victims of a child's wrongful acts, since in most cases the child has no resources with which to pay a judgment, and at the same time to encourage parents to control their children. The law does not let the child legally off the hook; the child remains liable to the injured party along with the parents.

Moreover, most of these statutes sharply limit the amount of compensation that parents can be required to pay. For example, in one state, parental vicarious liability for a child's wrongful acts is limited to three hundred dollars in damages. The limit in most states is between one thousand and five thousand dollars, although a few go as high as ten thousand dollars, and California recently raised the limit to twenty-five thousand dollars. Some states impose vicarious parental liability only for property damage, and many others limit compensation to out-of-pocket expenses, such as for property repair or medical treatment, so parents cannot be required to pay damages for pain and suffering.

Parental liability under these laws usually applies only when a child has committed a willful, malicious, or intentional act. To meet this requirement, the child must act deliberately or with intent to bring about harm. Although most states do not categorically exclude even very young children from liability for such acts, in a case involving a toddler or preschooler, it might be difficult to prove that the child actually had the intent to bring about harm, as these statutes require. As for an intentional act committed by an older child, some laws make clear that the parents will be liable even if the child has committed a crime or been declared a delinquent. Indeed, these statutes provide one way of dealing with the pervasive problem of teenage vandalism.

Parental vicarious liability applies only to minor children who are living with or in the custody or control of their parents. In a number of states, the law applies only to the parent with legal custody of the child, so if the parents are divorced and one parent has sole legal custody, the other parent cannot be held liable for the child's wrongdoing.

Except when cars are involved (see chapter 5), parents are generally not held vicariously liable for damage or injuries caused by mere negligence or carelessness on the part of their children; however, a parent may be liable for a child's negligence if the parent was negligent as well, as the next section explains.

Negligent Supervision and Negligent Entrustment

Parents can be liable for harm caused by a child's intentional or negligent acts if the parents are also at fault. In contrast to the vicarious liability just discussed, in these cases the parents become liable based on their own wrongdoing or negligence in failing to adequately supervise or control their child or for giving the child or allowing the child access to some item that poses a risk to others, such as a car, a gun, or matches. Parents need to show particular care regarding a child's access to or use of a firearm. Numerous cases have imposed liability on a parent for providing a child with a gun or failing to take adequate steps to prevent a child from obtaining a gun.

Failing to prevent harm caused by a child does not in itself constitute negligent failure to supervise. Parents are liable only if they fail *reasonably* to control their child. An injured person must prove that the parents knew of their child's specific dangerous tendencies and had the ability to control the child. With minor children, courts may assume that the parents had control. The more difficult determination in this situation is whether the parents had sufficient knowledge of their child's violent propensities. Many courts require that the child have committed similar acts previously or exhibited habitual violent behavior known to the parents. For example, if fifteen-year-old Carl rapes Susana and Susana attempts to sue Carl's parents for negligent supervision, she will probably prevail if Carl's parents know of prior sexual assaults perpetrated by Carl. But if Carl's prior violent behavior consists of a fistfight, she will probably lose.

In rare cases, parents have been held liable for failing to control an *adult* child who physically assaults another, but this is very unusual. Since parents have no legal right to control their adult children, courts usually will not hold them liable for their adult child's torts, even if the parents know, for example, of the child's criminal record, violent tendencies, or mental illness and even if the parents bring a weapon into the house. On the rare occasions when the courts have allowed suit against the parents, the adult children were seriously mentally impaired, living at home, and under the day-to-day care of their parents. Moreover, the parents in these cases knew of their children's history of violent behavior and nonetheless provided access to a weapon.

Criminal Liability

For the most part, parents cannot be charged with crimes based solely on acts of their children unless they actively participate in or encourage the crimes. In cases involving serious offenses, the parents might be charged as coconspirators or accomplices to the crimes; in cases involving less

A GROWING TREND:
THE PARENTAL RESPONSIBILITY ORDINANCE

In 1996 a St. Clair Shores, Michigan, couple was convicted under a parental responsibility ordinance after their sixteen-year-old son committed several burglaries, used illicit drugs and alcohol at home, and kept a stolen handgun in plain view on his bedroom night table. The son had already been arrested once for several church burglaries, and his father had been notified of the problem. The St. Clair Shores ordinance provides that a minor's violation of any city law constitutes "prima facie evidence" of the parents' "failure to exercise reasonable parental control." The ordinance then lists a number of specific "parental duties," such as preventing children from associating with juvenile delinquents or committing any delinquent acts. Parents charged with violations of the ordinance face civil liability, fines, and possible jail time of thirty to ninety days.

In Silverton, Oregon, another town with a parental responsibility ordinance, parents likewise face criminal responsibility for their children's offenses. At least fourteen parents there have received citations with potential fines up to a thousand dollars for offenses committed by their children, including shoplifting, alcohol and drug use, even cigarette smoking. Although most of the charges were dismissed as first offenses, four parents were tried and two of them convicted.

serious offenses, such as truancy, they might be charged with contributing to the delinquency of a minor.

Recently there have been efforts to expand parental criminal liability. Faced with a growing problem of gang violence, California amended its penal code to allow the state to prosecute parents for crimes committed by their children if the parents failed to exercise "reasonable care, supervision, protection and control" over the children. In 1989 the mother of a fifteen-year-old rape suspect was charged under this law. Although her case was dismissed after she completed a parenting program, the law was later upheld in the face of a challenge to its constitutionality. The court explained that the law applies only to parents who know or should know of their children's delinquency, and it requires only that the parents make reasonable efforts to control their children. The parents will not be found guilty if they have tried but failed to control their children. The law also allows parents charged with violating the law to attend a diversion program providing them with education, treatment, or rehabilitation. Successful completion of the program will lead to dismissal of the charges.

While few cases have been brought under this law, many other jurisdictions have recently sought ways to hold parents criminally responsible for their children's misdeeds. More than ten states and numerous local communities have enacted parental responsibility ordinances to serve this purpose (see box on page 284). In New Jersey and the Chicago area, for example, some jurisdictions have devised an innovative approach to parental responsibility for truancy: sentencing parents to attend school with their children. Maryland, on the other hand, takes a more conventional approach to the problem: sentencing parents of truants to up to thirty days in jail or requiring them to pay fines of a hundred dollars a day. Underage drinking is another problem addressed in parental responsibility ordinances. A number of localities require parents to take parenting classes or to pay fines if their children are caught drinking. Some also require them to pay substantial fees to reclaim their cars if their children are caught drinking in them. Parental punishments for other juvenile misdeeds, potential or actual, are even more serious. In Louisiana, for instance, parents can be imprisoned if they permit their child to associate with a gang member, a drug user, or anyone with access to an illegal weapon. And at least eleven states have laws imposing criminal liability on parents who allow their child to have access to a firearm if the child uses the firearm to injure or kill someone (a topic discussed at greater length in chapter 10).

There is little evidence so far that these parental responsibility laws succeed in reducing juvenile crime, but given the current climate of frustration with the perceived rise in juvenile crime and apparent parental irresponsibility or apathy, such laws will probably continue to proliferate. Meanwhile, because they are vague and hold one person criminally liable for the conduct of another, they likely will continue to be challenged on constitutional grounds by groups like the American Civil Liberties Union.

CHILD ABUSE, NEGLECT, AND EXPLOITATION

HUNDREDS OF THOUSANDS of children are abused by their parents or other caretakers each year. Maimed or molested, those that survive carry the physical and emotional scars with them for life. Drug abuse and crime often have their roots in childhood maltreatment. Yet for much of our nation's history, child abuse has been a hidden problem, seldom spoken of or openly acknowledged. In recent years the problem has received increasing attention, particularly in the area of sexual abuse. Famous actors, musicians, and athletes have all come forward with tales of physical and emotional abuse and incest. Increased public awareness has led to efforts by social services, law enforcement, and the medical and mental health professions to combat the scourge of child abuse. Unfortunately, lack of public funds, overloaded caseworkers, a sense of family privacy, and the stigma surrounding abuse all combine to maintain the silence on this issue and to leave many cases unreported and unredressed. Paradoxically, while many children suffer in abusive homes with little or no aid from the state, on occasion innocent families are torn apart by unjustified accusations made by well-meaning but perhaps overzealous social workers or district attorneys.

While the greatest threat to children comes from their own families, children also face danger at the hands of strangers. Child molestation, child pornography, and child prostitution wreak devastation on thousands of our nation's youngsters. Exposure to violence and explicit sexuality through the media—magazines, TV, movies, even computers—causes some parents further concern for their children's well-being.

This chapter will begin with an overview of the law's treatment of child abuse. What can and does the state do to protect children and what rights do you, as a parent, have should you be accused of child abuse? The second part of the chapter will take a look at what you can do to protect your child from exploitation by nonfamily members and from unwanted exposure to violent or pornographic material.

CHILD ABUSE AND NEGLECT

Parents have a constitutional right to raise their children largely as they see fit, without undue state interference. However, the state also has the right to intervene in families to protect children who are in danger. This right comes from the *parens patriae* power that allows the state to act in a parent's place to protect children. The challenge for the law is striking the appropriate balance between respecting family privacy and autonomy and preventing serious harm to children. The law uses two primary means to deal with child abuse: a civil system, also known as the dependency system, which allows the state to investigate reports of child abuse, take custody of children at risk, and seek termination of parental rights if necessary, and a criminal system, which allows the state to prosecute child abusers. Before we discuss these two systems, we must first consider how the law defines child abuse.

What Is Child Abuse?

Child abuse is a broad term that covers a wide range of conduct by family members or other caretakers causing injury to a child. It typically encompasses physical, sexual, and emotional abuse as well as physical and emotional neglect and abandonment. In most states, the statutes that define child abuse use rather vague and general terms such as "nonaccidental conduct posing a risk of serious harm or death to the child" or "willful infliction of bodily injury." Ultimately, the definition depends on the views of the social worker who is investigating an allegation of child abuse and the judge who is hearing the case. These individuals have tremendous discretion.

Physical Abuse. Physical abuse is the most common type of abuse reported. Any injuries inflicted by nonaccidental means can constitute physical abuse, including cuts, burns, bruises, bites, broken bones, mutilation, and death. Infants often suffer severe injury from being shaken by parents who do not realize that because a child's neck muscles are weak and his head relatively large, shaking can cause hemorrhaging, spinal cord injury, eye damage, and potentially fatal head injuries. Many states define physical abuse, like child abuse generally, in vague terms such as "unjustifiable physical pain" or "great bodily harm or death," while others enumerate specific injuries that qualify as physical abuse if caused intentionally by a parent.

Parents frequently wonder whether spanking is considered child abuse. While there are other countries that adhere to this view, here most states recognize, either explicitly or implicitly, that parents have a right to discipline their children by reasonable physical punishment. The key word here is *reasonable.* The use of excessive force on a child even to discipline her is considered child abuse. Punishment that poses a substantial risk of death, disfigurement, or serious bodily harm is likely to be viewed as excessive, but beyond these parameters, it is all a question of degree. In determining whether physical abuse has occurred, social workers and judges will often consider the extent and seriousness of visible signs of injury, such as bruises, burns, and lacerations, as well as the amount of pain that a child likely suffered in sustaining the injury. Florida's child abuse statute, for example, provides a list of specific injuries that may indicate excessive punishment (see box on page 290). Some courts also consider the need for the punishment as well as its severity. In one case, an appellate court affirmed the conviction of a father who struck his son twenty to thirty times because the boy wet the bed. Ultimately, though, there is simply no way

WHEN IS CORPORAL PUNISHMENT EXCESSIVE?

Although many states do not specifically answer this question in their laws, Florida provides that corporal punishment may be considered excessive when it results in any of the following or other similar injuries:

a. Sprains, dislocations, or cartilage damage

b. Bone or skull fractures

c. Brain or spinal cord damage

d. Intracranial hemorrhage or injury to other internal organs

e. Asphyxiation, suffocation, or drowning

f. Injury resulting from the use of a deadly weapon

g. Burns or scalding

h. Cuts, lacerations, punctures, or bites

i. Permanent or temporary disfigurement

j. Permanent or temporary loss or impairment of a body part or function

k. Significant bruises or welts

to clearly delineate when conduct crosses the line from legitimate discipline to impermissible abuse. To make matters more difficult, where that line is drawn varies depending on the socioeconomic status, culture, and family background of the people evaluating the situation.

Physical abuse can be difficult to prove. Witnesses are rare, so judges must rely on circumstantial evidence. The injuries themselves are often the strongest proof of the abuse. Doctors can testify that injuries like those sustained by a child while in a parent's care probably would not occur by accident.

Sexual Abuse. Sexual abuse—including fondling, touching of the genitals, oral-genital contact, and penetration—is perhaps the most difficult kind of child abuse to prove for a number of reasons. First, in most cases, sexual abuse rarely leaves physical evidence, and even when it does, the evidence—genital abrasions, for example, or venereal disease—does not necessarily help to identify the abuser. Second, the victims frequently don't reveal the abuse to anyone, or they delay in reporting it, in many cases for years. Incest often begins during the elementary school years, perhaps with fondling, and escalates in the adolescent years, at which time some children will finally disclose the abuse. Others continue to carry the secret with them into adulthood. Third, victims of sexual abuse, particularly young children, tend to recant their accusations even though the abuse actually did take place. This phenomenon is so commonplace, researchers have a name for it— the sexual abuse accommodation syndrome.

Sexual abuse is also difficult to recognize because many people still find it impossible to believe that family members could engage in such awful behavior with their children. Moreover, sexually abusive parents are hard to identify because they're not usually pedophiles, individuals who get their primary or exclusive sexual gratification from molesting children. In fact, sexual abuse crosses all socioeconomic lines, and the perpetrator may be the father next door.

Even the spouse of an abuser may be consciously unaware of the abuse because of denial, the psychological mechanism that enables people to block out emotionally disturbing and traumatic events. In other cases, the mother may know what is going on but be powerless to stop it for a host of reasons; she herself may be a victim of spousal abuse. In some cases, of course, the other parent is truly unaware of the abuse and once apprised of the situation acts to protect her child. On the other hand, if the other parent is aware of the abuse but has made no effort to stop it, she may also be held responsible for the abuse and could lose custody of her children, as will be explained later.

How do you know if your child is being sexually abused by your spouse, your child's other parent, or someone else? Of course listening to your child and promoting open communication may create a supportive environment where he or she will disclose the abuse. In many cases, though, the child has been threatened, feels fear and shame, or otherwise is not able to reveal the abuse. In these cases, parents should pay attention to any physical signs of abuse, such as rectal or genital bleeding, difficulty walking or sitting, itching in the genital or rectal area, torn or bloody underpants, or the presence of sexually transmitted diseases (see also box on page 34). Behavioral changes can also indicate sexual abuse. The American Medical Association Diagnostic and Treatment Guidelines on Child Sexual Abuse enumerate a number of possible behavioral indicators of sexual abuse, including some that are more specifically linked to the abuse, like persistent sexually precocious behavior, and others that are more general:

- extremes of activity, such as hyperactivity or withdrawal
- poor self-esteem
- poor peer relationships
- general feelings of shame or guilt
- distorted body image (distorted drawings)
- regressive behavior
- bed-wetting or soiling
- fear or phobia, especially of adults
- pseudomature behavior
- deterioration in academic performance
- eating disorders
- sexually provocative behavior
- compulsive masturbation
- sexual abuse of a sibling, friend, or younger child
- sexual promiscuity
- becoming pregnant
- running away
- attempting suicide

It is very important to understand that these behaviors may arise in response to a wide range of stressful events that have nothing to do with sexual abuse, such as a divorce or death in the family. For this reason, you should be careful not to jump to conclusions based on the presence of one or more of these behaviors, especially if a general indicator like low self-esteem appears in isolation. If you suspect that your child has been sexually abused, you should have him evaluated as quickly as possible by a competent pediatrician and mental health professional with experience in diagnosing and treating sexual abuse (see box on page 294).

Emotional Abuse. Emotional abuse can be just as devastating to a child psychologically as physical abuse. Most states recognize emotional abuse as grounds for removing a child from her home, although fewer include it as a criminal offense. As a practical matter, though, few cases involve emotional abuse exclusively, in good part because few people agree on what constitutes emotional abuse and the law rarely provides much guidance. Terrorizing or corrupting a child, demeaning him, calling him foul names, and screaming at him, if sufficiently severe and chronic, can rise to the level of emotional abuse. Since it is difficult to determine when this type of conduct crosses the line into abuse, some courts will focus on the behavior's effect on the child. For example, the court may look to see whether the child manifests any symptoms of mental disorder, such as extreme depression, anxiety, or aggressive behavior, as a result of the parent's behavior.

Neglect. The law protects children from parental neglect as well as abuse. In fact, research reveals that almost half of all substantiated or indicated child maltreatment cases involve neglect. Neglect can take many forms, including physical, emotional, medical, and educational neglect.

Physical neglect occurs when a parent fails to provide for a child's basic needs for food, clothing, shelter, or supervision. Unfortunately, many children go wanting in these areas not because their parents are neglectful, but because they live in poverty. The mere fact that a child is poor does not mean that the child is neglected and should be removed from her home. The state must show that there is an actual risk of harm to the child and that the parent has refused or misused available services. For example, if six-year-old Phillip is reported to be malnourished and homeless, the social service agency has an obligation to provide assistance to his family, as discussed further below. Some parents may be unaware of available services or have difficulty navigating the public assistance bureaucracy. However, if Phillip's mother has been receiving

TIPS FOR OBTAINING PROFESSIONAL HELP
IF YOU SUSPECT SEXUAL ABUSE

The National Center for Missing and Exploited Children (NCMEC) recommends that you consider the following advice in choosing a therapist or physician for evaluation and treatment of possible sexual abuse:

1. The therapist should have an advanced degree, either a master's (M.S.W., M.S., M.A., M.F.C.C.) or doctorate (M.D., Ph.D., Psy.D.) in a mental health specialty, such as psychiatry, psychology, social work, or counseling, and should be licensed to practice in that field by your state. The therapist should also have experience and special training in evaluating and treating child sexual abuse.

2. The physician should be board certified in a specialty related to children, such as pediatrics, obstetrics and gynecology, or family practice, and should have experience in evaluating children for sexual abuse.

3. Both the therapist and physician should understand the legal issues surrounding child sexual abuse, since they may be involved in reporting the abuse, collecting evidence, and testifying in court.

food stamps and trading them for drugs or using them for items other than food for Phillip, she may be considered to be neglecting him. Likewise Phillip's mother may be guilty of neglect if she is apprised of the availability of financial or housing assistance and fails to pursue it.

Children who live in filthy homes may also suffer from neglect. The standard in these so-called dirty home cases is fairly extreme. Parents who are poor housekeepers or who simply fail to vacuum on a regular basis are not likely to be accused of neglect. On the other hand, parents who have food rotting in their kitchens or animal feces, toxic substances, broken glass, or other dangerous materials lying around their houses likely will be considered neglectful, as will those who rarely bathe their children and regularly dress them in soiled clothing. Since

To find professionals with these qualifications and experience, you can call social service and court agencies serving children in your area; local psychological, psychiatric, or pediatric referral organizations, including any universities or medical schools nearby; rape crisis or domestic violence centers; victims' assistance programs; or child abuse hot lines.

If *you* are having trouble controlling your emotions and have been or are in danger of abusing your child in any way, you can contact Parents Anonymous, a support group for parents that has local chapters throughout the country. The national office can direct you to the one nearest you. Their number is:

909-621-6184

Help is also available toll free from the Boys Town National Hotline, which provides telephone counseling twenty-four hours a day for both parents and children in need of assistance. The number is:

1-800-448-3000

Don't wait to call!

social workers have considerable discretion in identifying neglect, in cases of this kind, there is always the danger of middle-class or cultural bias leading to intervention that may not be warranted.

Another form of physical neglect is failing to provide adequate supervision for your child. Today, with most mothers working outside the home and a dearth of safe and affordable child care, some parents are forced to leave their children alone after school or during the evenings. A 1990 survey found that 44 percent of children age five to twelve whose parents worked went unsupervised after school. At what age is it safe to leave your child alone and for how long? Although some child care experts recommend care for any child under nine or ten, and other experts recommend care for even older children, the need for supervision

SUBSTANCE ABUSE

Parents who abuse drugs or alcohol are at particular risk for neglecting, as well as abusing, their children, since they often spend their money on drugs or drinks, show poor judgment, lack the capacity to pay adequate attention to their children's needs, expose them to criminal behavior, and fail to supervise them. Substance abuse during pregnancy can constitute evidence of abuse or neglect in some jurisdictions if harm to the child can be established and especially if the drug use continues after birth. This subject is further discussed in chapter I.

depends on the individual child, and the law in most states provides no definite answer to this question. In Oregon, a parent who leaves a child under ten in a place likely to endanger the child's health or welfare can be charged with criminal negligence; and in Texas, an unusual law makes it a crime to leave a child under the age of seven in a car longer than five minutes unless he is accompanied by someone at least fourteen. Elsewhere, and under other circumstances in Oregon and Texas, it is up to the court to determine whether a child who has been left alone has been neglected. In making its determination, the court generally will consider whether the parent acted reasonably, taking into account the age, needs, and abilities of the child, the character of the neighborhood where she lives, her emotional reaction to being alone, and the presence or absence of other adults to supervise the child.

Of course, many states do have specific laws imposing responsibilities on parents to protect and supervise their children in dangerous situations. In all states, for example, it is illegal not to use an approved child safety seat while driving with a child of a certain age or weight, usually under four years old or forty pounds. In a few cases, parents who failed to use safety seats have been criminally charged when their children were killed in auto accidents. (See box on page 41 for a discussion of protecting children in vehicles with air bags.)

Another dangerous situation arises when parents are careless about storing their firearms. In an effort to reduce the hundreds of accidental gunshot injuries and deaths to children each year, some states have adopted laws regulating the storage of guns and ammunition. In one of several cases brought under such laws, a Connecticut minister was charged in 1996 with criminally negligent storage of a firearm after one of his sons accidentally shot the other with the father's shotgun.

In addition to physical neglect and inadequate supervision, parents can harm their children by emotional neglect, which may include isolating, rejecting, or ignoring the child. Emotional neglect can be very damaging, but like emotional abuse, it is difficult to establish in part because child-rearing styles vary greatly and, again, people don't agree on what the term means. Emotionally neglecting an infant by providing little or no nurturing or affection can lead to a condition known as "failure to thrive." Babies who suffer from this condition are born at a normal weight but do not grow or develop as expected for no discernible physical, medical, or organic reason. Failure to thrive can be detected by placing the child in a controlled environment, such as a hospital or an alternative home, and seeing whether the child eats and gains weight normally. In these cases, observations of the parent-child interaction may reveal that the parent has not bonded with the child.

Failure to provide necessary medical care can also be considered neglect justifying state intervention. Sometimes parents simply don't have the knowledge or experience to understand when a child needs medical attention. These parents may be helped by educational assistance and training. Other cases frequently involve religious objections to certain types of treatment. In these cases, discussed at greater length in chapter 4, the state will often obtain a court order permitting necessary treatment or designating someone other than the parent to be the medical decision maker for the child. It is not usually necessary to remove the child from his home.

Parents have a legal obligation to educate their children, too. Failure to send a child to school can constitute educational neglect, unless an approved home-school plan is in place (see chapter 3), and parental tolerance of or complicity in truancy can lead to criminal charges against the parent as well as the child (see chapter 9). Keeping a child from school may also be a signal that some form of abuse is occurring.

Finally, parents who leave their children for extended periods of time without support or contact may be judged to have abandoned them. Some states presume that no contact or support for six months or a year constitutes abandonment, but a court might reduce that time if there is other evidence that a parent intends to abandon a child. Many parents rely on extended family and friends to care for their children for days, weeks, months, sometimes even years. These parents have not abandoned their children under the law if they maintain a relationship with them. Very infrequent or sporadic letters or phone calls, though, may not be enough to preclude a finding of abandonment.

Now that we understand what child abuse is, let's see how the legal system responds to it.

The Dependency System

Most cases of child abuse and neglect are brought to court by social workers who file petitions on behalf of the state asking that children in need of protection be made dependents of the court. The dependency system is a civil system, not a criminal system. Its goal is not to punish the abusing parents, but to ensure the safety of their children, to reunite the children with their parents if possible, and if not, to terminate the abusers' parental rights and free the children for adoption. A hypothetical case will take us through the various stages of the process.

Emily is a bright seven-year-old with curly brown hair and big brown eyes. She is also an unusually aggressive child. Ms. Chang, her second-grade teacher, has noticed that Emily has been acting out in class, kicking and biting the other students and generally being disruptive. She also has noticed unusual bruises on Emily's arms. When she asks Emily how she got the bruises, Emily says she fell. A few days later, Emily comes to school with a black eye. She says she walked into a door. Ms. Chang suspects that Emily is being abused, so she calls the Department of Children's Services and explains what she has seen.

The legal system's involvement in a child abuse case begins when someone like Ms. Chang reports suspected abuse to the local child welfare agency. These agencies go by different names: Child Protective Services, the Department of Social Services, the Department of Children's Services, and others. The appropriate agency can usually be located by looking in the local government section of your telephone book or by calling your local police department.

Every state has laws that require certain classes of persons to report suspected child abuse. As a teacher, Ms. Chang would be designated a "mandatory reporter" in most states. Also required to report are other school personnel, doctors, health care workers, law enforcement agents, social workers, mental health professionals, child care providers, and in about half the states, members of the clergy. A few states also include lawyers, and some require *any* person to report suspected child abuse.

These reporting laws are exceptions to the usual privilege of confidentiality that applies to some professions. Ordinarily, doctors and mental health professionals, for example, cannot disclose information obtained about you in the course of treatment unless they have your permission. However, when it comes to child abuse, not only *can* they reveal confidential information if they suspect child abuse; they have a legal obligation to do so. Court decisions in some states also require certain professionals, usually psychiatrists and psychologists, to warn anyone who has been identified as an intended victim of one of their patients.

Failure to report suspected child abuse by those mandated to do so is a criminal offense, usually a misdemeanor. If Ms. Chang failed to report her suspicions about Emily, she could face a fine or imprisonment. As a practical matter, though, prosecutions for failure to report are rarely brought. Failure to report could also subject Ms. Chang to civil liability, requiring the payment of damages.

Most reporting laws require the reporter to make an immediate oral report to the appropriate agency and to follow up with a written report.

Ms. Chang does not have to be certain that Emily is being abused, nor does she have to have definitive proof of the abuse. Moreover, she is under no obligation to investigate to find out whether abuse has actually occurred. In most states, all she needs before she can and, in fact, must report is a reasonable suspicion that Emily has been abused. What if it turns out that Emily really did fall down and sustain those injuries, that there was no abuse? Can Ms. Chang be held liable for damages to Emily's family or criminally charged for reporting her erroneous suspicions? The answer is generally no. Reporters of suspected child abuse are granted immunity for their reports: they cannot be sued or prosecuted even if the suspicion is ultimately unfounded or false. In some states this immunity is absolute, meaning Ms. Chang will be protected regardless of her motives. However, in many states Ms. Chang would be able to claim immunity only if she acted in good faith. Since she had credible reasons to suspect child abuse because of the nature of Emily's bruises and Emily's unconvincing explanations, she would have no trouble showing good faith. But if Ms. Chang had intentionally made a false report of child abuse, she would no longer be protected by immunity, and in some places, she could face a civil suit and even criminal penalties. This immunity would also apply if Ms. Chang were a so-called permissive reporter, someone who voluntarily chooses to report suspected abuse but is not required to do so by law. While the law mandates that certain people report suspected child abuse, it usually allows any citizen to make a report and receive immunity for doing so as long as he acts with reasonable suspicion of abuse and in good faith. Needless to say, a child abuser cannot report herself and then claim immunity.

Temporary Custody. Once Ms. Chang has reported the abuse to the child protection agency, it becomes the agency's responsibility to investigate the allegations. If the social worker assigned to the case believes that Emily is in imminent danger of serious bodily harm or death, he has the power to take emergency temporary custody of her to protect her until he can complete an investigation. Generally state social workers, law enforcement personnel, and sometimes hospitals have the power to take temporary custody of a child without first getting court approval if the child is in immediate danger. As agents of the state, they do not even have to notify the parents before removing the child. But this power exists only in an emergency; if the state has time to get a court order, it has an obligation to do so.

Usually when a child like Emily is taken into custody, she is placed in foster care. Foster care can mean a group home or, more commonly, the home of foster parents who have agreed to house and care for children temporarily in need and who receive financial assistance from the state to do so. Although foster care may be an improvement over the days when children without homes were warehoused in orphanages or other institutional settings, it is far from ideal. In some cases, the disruption and trauma caused by removing a child from his family may prove more damaging than leaving him with them. For this reason, parents should suggest placing their child with a relative or family friend whom the child knows. The caseworker may agree to such an arrangement if the suggested placement is with an appropriate caretaker who will be willing to enforce any restrictions on parental visits that may be imposed.

As an alternative to removing a child from her home, a nonabusing parent or a representative of the child, including the child protection agency, may seek a civil protective order (CPO). The CPO would require the allegedly abusive parent to leave the home pending investigation and resolution of the charges. This would be appropriate only if the parent or caretaker remaining in the home were capable of protecting the child and enforcing restrictions on the abusive parent's visitation.

If the state removes Emily from her parents' home without a prior court order or hearing, the child protection agency must file in court within a relatively short time what is often called a dependency petition. This petition will prompt the court to hold a protective custody hearing (also called an emergency placement or shelter care hearing). Dependency cases are most often heard in family or juvenile court, where the proceedings are generally closed to the public. Sometimes statutes provide specific deadlines, as short as twenty-four hours or as long as ten days, within which the protective custody hearing must be held. However, in some states, Emily's parents would have the responsibility of asking that a court hearing be held. As a rule, they should request one as soon as possible because the longer Emily remains in foster care, the less willing social workers will be to move her. Emily's parents must be notified of the time and place of the protective custody hearing and must have an opportunity to challenge the dependency petition. Although the state is not necessarily obligated to appoint an attorney for them at this point if they are indigent, many states will do so. Since dependency cases can result in loss of custody and ultimately permanent and complete termination of parental rights, *any parent whose child enters the dependency system should have a lawyer, ideally one who is experienced in abuse and neglect cases.*

At the protective custody hearing, the court will consider whether the child protection agency has a basis for maintaining custody of Emily, but it will not make a formal decision about whether she has been abused or neglected or is at risk. Through overzealousness or incompetence, agencies at times abuse their authority, violating the rights of parents and risking trauma to children. This hearing is primarily to ensure that the agency has not abused its authority in removing Emily from her parents' home. At the protective custody hearing, the court may order that Emily or her parents undergo psychiatric evaluation and that the agency provide certain services to the family.

Usually, the court will also appoint an attorney or guardian *ad litem* (GAL) to represent Emily at this point. Recognizing that a child's interests may differ from those of both her parents and of the child protection agency, virtually all states now require that a child be represented by either an attorney or a GAL. Some states specify which type of advocate will be appointed; others leave it to the court's discretion. The different roles lawyers and GALs play are discussed in the box on page 303.

The Dependency Trial. Emily's case, like many, may be resolved by a voluntary agreement or settlement between her parents and the child protection agency that gives the agency the right to monitor her family

LAWYERS FOR CHILDREN AND GUARDIANS *AD LITEM* (GALs)

Most states grant children the right to be represented by either an attorney or a guardian *ad litem* (GAL) in a dependency proceeding. What's the difference? GALs do not have to be lawyers; often they are laypersons who volunteer to represent children in need. In some jurisdictions they are called CASAs—court-appointed special advocates. A GAL's role is to represent a child's best interests and to work with the child protection agency to achieve the best outcome for the child.

A lawyer's role in a dependency proceeding traditionally has been somewhat different, and it has been the subject of considerable controversy. Under their rules of ethics, lawyers are bound to zealously represent the wishes of their clients. In theory, this rule applies to lawyers representing children as well; however, many states' laws are ambiguous on this point, and lawyers may find it difficult to adhere to the rule when their clients are too young to adequately express their wishes or to make a considered judgment about what course would best serve their interests. Others believe that an attorney should act in a child's best interests even if it means going against the child's express wishes. For example, if a child wants to return to a home where she has been sexually abused, her lawyer might argue for an alternative placement. In fact, California has recently enacted legislation prohibiting attorneys for children in dependency proceedings from advocating any position that would put the children in danger.

In either case, the court often listens closely to the views of a child's representative, so it is important for the lawyer or GAL to investigate the charges and explore alternative approaches to protecting the child with as little trauma and disruption as possible. It is also wise for parents seeking to regain custody of their child to work cooperatively with his lawyer.

situation or even retain custody of her. Indeed, the vast majority of child abuse reports do not involve the court at all. But if her parents and the agency do not settle, the next phase of the dependency process involves a trial, usually called an adjudicative hearing. The trial may take place weeks after the filing of the original dependency petition, but it should be expedited if Emily has been removed from her home. At the adjudicative hearing, the state must prove that Emily has been abused or neglected. The state does not have to prove the abuse or neglect beyond a reasonable doubt, as it would in a criminal case. In most jurisdictions, the state can prevail if it shows that the abuse more likely than not occurred; in others, the state must prove its case by "clear and convincing" evidence.

The trial itself will be less formal than a criminal trial, but the state still must present evidence supporting its position, and Emily's parents must be given the opportunity to present evidence on their behalf and cross-examine witnesses. The court cannot simply rely on the social worker's report to reach its conclusion. As we discussed earlier, it is often difficult to prove abuse, especially sexual abuse; there are rarely eyewitnesses and children often make poor witnesses. Young children, particularly, may have difficulty articulating what happened and may confuse fact and fiction. Children of all ages may be intimidated by their abusive parents and concerned about damaging their families and having to leave home. To bolster its case that Emily has been abused, the state may present medical testimony, psychiatric evaluations of Emily and her parents, evidence of prior episodes of abuse of Emily or her siblings, and lay testimony from teachers, scout leaders, and friends who have observed the family. It does not have to prove that Emily's parents actually intended to abuse her; the court can infer that from the abuse itself. To defend themselves, Emily's parents may present testimony either to counter the inference that her bruises resulted from beatings or to show that the incidents were extraordinary and are unlikely to happen again.

If the court finds that the state has not proved abuse or neglect, it will dismiss the petition, and Emily will be returned home. If the court finds there has been abuse or neglect, it must then hold a dispositional hearing to consider placement. This hearing usually occurs some time after the trial. At the dispositional hearing, the court will consider where Emily should be placed and what services the agency should provide. Often, though, the agency and the parents decide on a disposition by agreement, without needing a full hearing, and the court essentially rubber-stamps the arrangement unless the child's attorney objects.

Deciding on a disposition for a child like Emily is critical. Many states have laws that enumerate the various placement options. If the court concludes that Emily has been abused but is not in danger of serious harm from her parents, she may be returned home under agency supervision. The agency will then have an obligation, at a minimum, to monitor the situation and report to the court on progress being made by the family. They may also have to provide services to assist the family in adequately caring for Emily. In these situations, the agency may actually retain legal custody of the child even though the parents have physical custody. This allows the agency to immediately remove the child without a protective custody hearing should the need arise again.

When a child cannot safely be returned home, foster care is probably the most commonly used placement, and nearly half a million children are currently in foster care. Unfortunately, foster care is far from ideal. Separating children from their parents, even abusive ones, can be traumatic, and placing them with strangers can intensify the harmful emotional and psychological effects. Children often have difficulty adjusting to a new home, and foster care is very expensive for the state. Moreover, children in foster care are at considerable risk of suffering further abuse at the hands of their foster family. For these reasons, all parties would be well served by seriously exploring alternative placements with suitable relatives (sometimes known as kinship foster care) or a family known to the child.

Placement with relatives has become much more common in the last decade. Some states require that the agency social worker ask the parents if placement with relatives is an option; others, like New York, explicitly prefer placement with relatives to foster care. Placements with relatives often are not subject to all of the same rules governing regular foster care homes. For example, in New York, instead of having to go through the normal licensing procedures, which typically take several months, relatives can get emergency approval and take a child within twenty-four hours if a home study is done. Final approval is also expedited. This has the benefit of facilitating continuity in the child's care, but it has a downside as well; there is no assurance that the relatives will be able to offer the child a suitable, loving environment and appropriate attention and guidance. In many places, relatives who take temporary custody of children involved in dependency proceedings may be eligible for the same financial assistance received by foster parents, but some evidence suggests that they receive inadequate assistance to do the job properly.

In cases that involve a child who needs intensive psychiatric treatment, institutionalization might be necessary.

In addition to deciding where Emily will live while she is a dependent of the court, the court will probably establish visitation rights for her parents. Frequent visitation by parents is a strong indication that they will eventually regain custody of their child. For this reason, it is important to seek a placement that is within reasonable proximity to the parents. In many cases, the court will allow visitation only if it is supervised. Supervised visitation can consist of meetings in the presence of a social worker or sometimes with a family friend or relative.

The court may also order the agency to provide reasonable reunification services. States have an obligation to try to reunite families if possible. This means that the state may have to provide certain services such as in-home assistance, parenting classes, emergency day care, or psychiatric, medical, or vocational counseling to rehabilitate the parents to the point where they can regain custody of their child. The social worker may also need to facilitate visitation, perhaps by providing transportation for the parent or child, or help the parent obtain benefits like welfare from other agencies. Of course, in some cases, the parents are not capable of rehabilitation and such services would be futile. The state is obligated to provide only "reasonable" services. The state is not required to use its "best efforts" to provide such services. So if, for example, Emily's father abused her because he had a mental disorder that was not treatable, the state would not be obligated to provide twenty-four-hour in-home care. Moreover, if a given locality does not have the necessary services available, the courts have held that the law does not require the government to create them. To make matters worse, even when the law requires that services be provided, some research indicates that judges do not seriously scrutinize whether they actually have been.

Most cases are deserving of some effort at reunification, so many states require the agency to develop a case plan with this as the goal whenever a child is removed from his home; in other states, the parents or the child's representative can request a plan. These plans spell out what services the agency will offer to assist in reunification and what steps the parents need to take to become sufficiently rehabilitated to regain custody of their child. One kind of case plan that is becoming increasingly popular is a contract in which the agency and the parents each agree to fulfill certain responsibilities to enable the child to return home. Like any other kind of case plan, the best and most effective contract is very specific. For example, a contract might require that a parent become employed, obtain a stable residence, and attend a parenting support group, and the agency might agree to provide child care while the parent is attending the support group or getting other assistance. Contracts or other case plans sometimes become part of the court order; however, they do not bind the court in making its ultimate determination about the fate of a child. Nonetheless, if a parent successfully fulfills all the required conditions of a plan, a court will often be persuaded that his child can be returned home. By the same token, a parent who fails to make progress in completing the steps laid out for rehabilitation is much less likely to regain custody of her child.

To ensure that the child does not slip through the cracks, the court, or sometimes a less formal body, will monitor the progress of the case plan and adjust the disposition arrangement, if necessary, by holding periodic hearings. These review hearings normally occur semiannually or annually, depending on the locality. They give parents the chance to demonstrate their rehabilitation and their compliance with the case plan or previous court orders. They also allow the parents or the child's representative to point out any failure by the agency to provide services.

Permanency Planning. The law recognizes that a child has fundamental needs for stability, security, and emotional attachment to a parental figure. These needs may be at odds with the desire to rehabilitate the child's parents or find a better placement. Federal law requires that the state develop a permanent plan for any child who has been in foster care for eighteen months. Many states require permanency planning even sooner. For example, in California, a permanent plan must be devised within one year of the dispositional hearing and no more than eighteen months from the time the child was removed from his parents' custody. California law also requires periodic hearings once the permanent plan is in place.

What is permanency planning? In Emily's case, permanency planning could mean returning her home or placing her in long-term foster care. Long-term foster care or a guardianship may be appropriate when ongoing contact between Emily and her parents is desirable but her parents are not expected ever to be able to regain custody of her. The most drastic plan would seek termination of Emily's parents' rights so that she would be free for adoption. When parental rights are terminated, a foster family with whom a child has developed a close relationship will, in some places, get preference if they seek to adopt the child.

Termination of Parental Rights

Termination of parental rights results in a total severance of the legal parent-child relationship. The parent no longer has any rights to custody, visitation, control, or even information about his or her child. Because the right to rear one's children is constitutionally protected, the state must demonstrate compelling reasons for completely destroying a parent-child relationship and must provide the parent with due process—certain procedures deemed necessary to ensure fairness. This means that the parent has a right both to be notified of the state's efforts to terminate parental rights and to have an adversarial hearing before a judge to challenge the state's petition. In cases where the

THE GREGORY K. CASE

In 1993 the Gregory K. case made headlines when twelve-year-old Gregory Kingsley sought to terminate his parents' parental rights. Although the media depicted the case as that of a child "divorcing" his parents, it actually was nothing more than an attempt by the child to bring a termination petition in his own name in a dependency proceeding. Moreover, the Florida appellate court ultimately ruled that Gregory, as a minor, could *not* bring the suit himself and that his attorney, foster parents, or the state would have to petition for termination. This is the rule followed in most places. However, the court also ruled that since Gregory's mother had abandoned him, her parental rights should be terminated, and since Gregory's father had given his consent and was, in any case, now deceased, Gregory's adoption by his foster parents was subsequently approved.

whereabouts of the parent, typically an unmarried father, are unknown, the state must make diligent efforts to locate him in order to provide notice of the termination proceedings. If the state fails to make the necessary effort, the parent can later challenge the termination. Parents do not have a constitutional right to be represented by an attorney at state expense in every termination case, only those that are particularly complex or can subject the parent to criminal charges, but most states require or allow the court to appoint an attorney for an indigent parent.

Who may petition to terminate parental rights? In most abuse and neglect cases like Emily's, the state seeks to terminate parental rights in order to free the child for adoption by a loving family. In many states, though, private parties who have an interest in a child's welfare can also petition for termination. These include the child's attorney or guardian *ad litem,* the other parent, foster parents who have formed a "psychological family" with the child, and, in some states, the child himself. While most states do not recognize a child's right to petition for termination of parental rights in his own name ("divorce" his parents), a few states, such as Arizona, do (see box on page 309).

Although the specific statutory grounds may vary from state to state, to terminate a parent's rights, the petitioner must prove that the parent is unfit because she (1) has abused or neglected the child and is likely to continue to do so, (2) has a physical or mental disability or substance abuse problem that prevents her from adequately caring for her child presently and in the foreseeable future, or (3) has abandoned her child. Once one of these grounds is established, the petitioner must also demonstrate that termination would be in her child's best interests.

Because parental rights are so important, the state must meet a higher standard of proof in termination cases than in the usual civil case: it must prove by at least clear and convincing evidence that there are grounds for terminating a parent's rights and that termination is in a child's best interests. Some states go even further and require that the state prove its case beyond a reasonable doubt, the standard used in criminal proceedings. The burden is on the state to prove the parent's unfitness.

As you can see, the grounds for termination essentially cover the same conduct as the grounds for establishing a dependency action initially. The key difference is one of degree and potential for rehabilitation. Usually, termination proceedings follow a period of time during which the parent received the rehabilitation services set forth in his case plan or contract but failed to make sufficient progress toward remedying the problems that caused him to lose custody in the first place. Let's consider how this works for each of the grounds listed above.

In deciding whether to terminate parental rights in cases involving abuse or neglect, like Emily's, the court will evaluate whether violence is likely to recur or neglect to continue. If Emily's parents can show that they complied with the case plan by attending parenting classes and undergoing counseling and they admit the abuse, the court may find that they have been successfully rehabilitated and return Emily to their custody. But if Emily has sustained other bruises or her parents' behavior during the dependency period suggests that the abuse will continue, the court will probably find grounds to terminate Emily's parents' rights. For instance, if Emily's father beats her when he drinks and he continues to drink while Emily is in foster care, his parental rights probably will be terminated. On the other hand, if he enters a treatment program and regularly attends Alcoholics Anonymous meetings, his chances of regaining custody of Emily will improve substantially. When a parent has neglected or abused a child because of a substance abuse problem, the court will consider whether the parent has successfully completed treatment and has a support system to help her stay sober.

It should be noted that even if Emily's father was the actual abuser, her mother may also risk loss of custody and termination of parental rights if she was aware of the abuse and failed to take steps to protect Emily. Unfortunately, Emily's mother may have been the victim of spousal abuse as well. In this case, some courts will excuse a mother's failure to protect her child, but others will not.

Physical or mental disabilities such as mental retardation can also render a parent unfit and lead to termination of parental rights. Each of these disabilities alone is insufficient to support permanent termination of parental rights without proof of some independent ground, such as abuse or gross neglect. Before ordering this drastic remedy, the court will assess the availability of services to assist the parent, the needs of the child involved, and the benefits of a continuing relationship between the parent and child versus the benefit from permanent termination and the possibility of adoption. As always, the state has an obligation to provide reasonable training and assistance to rehabilitate the parent to the point where she can function adequately, if possible. Unfortunately, while adequate home child care would enable many physically disabled and some mentally retarded parents to fulfill their parental duties, the dearth of affordable services leaves too many vulnerable to charges of unfitness. In addition, prejudice against the physically disabled and mentally retarded leads social service agencies to pursue termination of parental rights and adoption more vigorously than family reunification or preservation. Ultimately, the question is whether the parent is inherently unable to fulfill his responsibilities or the state has failed to provide adequate services or training to enable him to do so.

Parental rights are also subject to termination for abandonment and nonsupport. This issue often arises when a custodial parent remarries and her new spouse wishes to adopt her child. Let's suppose, for example, that Miguel's mother and father divorce when he is two and that his mother remarries when he is three. He is now almost five, and his stepfather wishes to adopt him legally. Miguel's father visited with Miguel sporadically in the year before his mother remarried but has not communicated with Miguel at all for the past year. Can Miguel's father's rights be terminated based on abandonment and nonsupport? Yes, so Miguel's stepfather will be able to adopt him without his father's consent.

Now let's assume that Miguel's mother, emotionally distraught, unemployed, and unable to care for Miguel after his father leaves them, places Miguel in the care of her mother while she gets help for her emotional problems and finds a job. A year later, when she remarries, she goes to reclaim Miguel. Can Miguel's grandmother stop her, claiming abandonment? Probably not if Miguel's mother has continued to see, call, or communicate with Miguel throughout the year. A parent who places a child in the care of a friend or relative for an extended period of time has not abandoned the child if the caretaker is fit and the parent maintains contact with the child.

Termination of parental rights can also occur when a parent is incarcerated. A parent who commits certain felonies will likely lose parental rights solely because the very nature of the crime indicates unfitness. For example, fathers who kill mothers of their children frequently—though incredibly not always—have their parental rights terminated. In most cases, though, a criminal conviction alone will not suffice to support a termination of parental rights. Courts will look at a variety of factors, including the parent-child relationship, any history of abuse or neglect, chronic criminal activity, the age of the child, and, most critically, the length of the sentence and any possible eligibility for parole. If the parent will be imprisoned for many years, the court will probably grant termination to enable the child to be placed in a permanent home. Parents who can place their children with relatives while serving their sentence may avoid this outcome. Incarcerated parents have a right to receive notice of a termination hearing and to be represented there, but they do not have a right to be physically present; they may, however, testify by phone or deposition.

Once the grounds for termination have been established, the termination proceeding moves into its second phase, the disposition. At this point, the judge considers whether termination is in the best interests of the child. To decide whether it is, the court will evaluate the child's age, needs, and wishes; any danger the parents pose; the child's attachment to any alternative caregivers; the availability of programs to assist the parents; the stability of the home compared to alternative placements; the quality of the parent-child relationship; any mitigating factors concerning the parents' past behavior; and the adoptability of the child.

If the judge finds that termination is not in the child's best interests, she may put him into long-term foster care or a guardianship that enables the parents to maintain contact. If the judge finds that termination is in the child's best interests, she must decide what placement is most appropriate. At this point, third parties, such as relatives or foster parents, may intervene to seek custody, and the child may be made available for adoption. As long as the child remains in the care of the social service agency (which includes foster care), the court will continue to monitor the case periodically.

As evidence of the large number of children spending long periods of time in foster care has come to light, some children's advocates have argued for expedited and easier terminations, rather than prolonged, ostensibly futile efforts to reunify children with abusive or neglectful parents. But termination is no panacea for some of these children, for, sadly, evidence also shows that abused and neglected children freed for adoption don't necessarily end up finding permanent homes. Instead, they remain in foster care until they "age out" of the system— that is, until they become old enough to leave. Policy makers, legislators, judges, and social workers will no doubt need to carefully consider how best to improve the lives of these children.

Central Registries

Most states maintain a central registry containing child abuse and neglect reports. When Ms. Chang, Emily's teacher, reported her suspicions of abuse to the child protection agency, a report likely was made to the state's central registry. In some localities, the report is made directly to the registry; in others, it is forwarded to the registry by the child protection or law enforcement agency that initially receives it. The central registry might later add information on services provided to the family and the ultimate disposition of the case. Significantly, though, the initial report usually enters the registry before the allegations have been investigated or substantiated.

The purpose of the registry is to aid in detecting child abuse, since a record of reports on a parent may reveal a pattern, suggesting that a given injury to a child may not be accidental. The registry can be especially helpful in monitoring abuse when families move from one location to another, particularly out of state. The registry also enables the state to screen people who seek to adopt or serve as foster parents and to collect valuable statistics on child abuse. Many states allow employers of child care workers to access the registry, and some even require them to screen employees by checking the registry.

While child abuse registries serve laudable goals, they can cause problems for parents about whom unsubstantiated reports are made. While some states include only substantiated reports in the registry, others include any reports for which there is "some credible evidence" or "substantial evidence" of abuse or neglect. Neither of these standards is as stringent as the standard for proving that a parent has indeed abused or neglected her child in a civil dependency case or a criminal case. Nonetheless, the parent will be listed as an abuser in the registry.

Most states have procedures for expunging, or removing, a parent's name from the registry, but this can be a difficult and time-consuming process with no guarantee of success. Some states provide for automatic expungement when a child reaches a certain age, usually eighteen, but New York delays expungement until the child is twenty-eight. Others require automatic removal after a set number of years—seven in Maryland, for example—if no other incidents are reported. Parents wrongly suspected of child abuse will undoubtedly want their names removed much sooner. Usually the law provides for an administrative hearing to appeal inclusion in the registry, but only after the child protection agency has completed its investigation. Moreover, unless there is no evidence to support an allegation of abuse, in many states the hearing board is likely to deny a parent's request for expungement. Sometimes a parent can further appeal to the courts and prevail. In one Florida case, for example, a parent successfully appealed the denial of his request to have his name expunged from the central registry. The appellate court found that the mere existence of bruises resulting from disciplining his child did not constitute substantial evidence of excessive punishment indicating abuse. Cases have also been brought by parents challenging the constitutionality of these registries with mixed success. In one case, a supervisor at a group home for wayward boys was fired after his employer discovered from the registry that he had been accused of physically abusing one of the boys and that the report was described as "indicated." After a long process, the agency expunged his name, and the court found that his rights could have been violated.

Tort Liability of Social Workers and State Agencies

What recourse do you have if you are wrongly accused of child abuse and your child is removed from your home? Aside from fighting to regain custody of your child through dependency proceedings and seeking expungement of your name from the central registry, in rare cases you may be able to sue the social worker or the state agency responsible for the grievous error.

Traditionally, it has been very difficult to sue state agencies and their employees in this type of situation. Often courts have determined that an agency owes no legal duty to a particular individual. Many, though not all, courts now recognize that agencies may assume a duty to a child in certain circumstances. For example, an agency that takes custody of a child assumes a duty to use care to ensure that the child does not come to harm while in the state's control. So if the child protection agency removed Emily from her home and placed her in foster care, the agency could be liable to Emily for damages if the foster parent abused her. Likewise, there have been cases when a child or a parent has won damages against a state agency for failing to investigate allegations of abuse by the child's other parent.

Even in these cases, though, many states provide immunity for the social worker. As we saw with mandatory reporters, courts take different views on the extent of immunity enjoyed by social workers. Some states grant social workers absolute immunity for their actions in investigating and responding to child abuse allegations. This means that they cannot be sued, period. Other states provide only qualified immunity. In these states, a social worker can be liable for negligence in investigating a child abuse allegation, but only if he acted in bad faith or in violation of statutory requirements or agency policies. Federal court decisions in civil rights actions alleging that social workers violated parents' constitutional rights in removing children from their homes have likewise led to varying results with some courts granting social workers absolute immunity and others only qualified immunity. In a civil rights action, qualified immunity protects only those who have acted in good faith, meaning that they do not know or have reason to know that their conduct violated a parent's rights. But this may provide little protection. In one court's view, this standard protects "all but the plainly incompetent or those who knowingly violate the law."

While suits for damages by injured parents or children are often difficult to pursue, children's advocacy groups in many states have filed class action–type suits against state child welfare departments, alleging that they failed to protect the children or to provide needed services to the families. These lawsuits have resulted in court orders governing the departments.

Criminal Penalties

In all states, child abuse and neglect are criminal offenses, often felonies with possible sentences of up to twenty years, as well as grounds for dependency proceedings. Only a small percentage of child abuse reports results in prosecution, though. To convict a parent of criminal child abuse, the state must prove that the parent committed the offense beyond a reasonable doubt. Every state has its own particular statutes defining criminal child abuse and neglect. Most require that a parent commit the abuse knowingly or willingly, especially for felony child abuse. This standard includes cases in which a parent explicitly intends to cause pain or physical injury to her child, knows that serious injury will result, or engages in punishment that is clearly excessive. In some states, a parent must actually inflict serious physical or psychological injury to be prosecuted. A few even delineate specific injuries that must be proved to convict a parent, such as fractures, injury to certain body organs, or injuries necessitating medical treatment. Usually, though, a parent can be convicted if the abuse endangered her child or was likely to have caused death or serious bodily harm, even if the harm didn't actually occur. A parent may also be convicted if she knew of abuse committed by someone else, such as her boyfriend or the child's father, and did nothing to stop it.

Parents accused of child abuse may raise the defense of corporal punishment (see box on page 290), since parents have a right to discipline their children. However, this right is limited to reasonable discipline or punishment. Any punishment likely to cause serious pain or injury will probably not be considered reasonable. For example, throwing a child against a wall or dunking the child in scalding water, even if done ostensibly for the legitimate purpose of disciplining the child, would still constitute criminal child abuse.

The district attorney is more likely to bring charges against a parent who has sexually abused his child, particularly if the abuse is severe and prolonged, than with other kinds of abuse, but she is still less likely to prosecute in cases of intrafamilial abuse than of molestation by nonfamily members. In the past, the law required corroboration before a sex abuse charge could be brought. Today the law is less stringent in many places, but as a practical matter, prosecutors are unlikely to pursue a case without it.

PARENTAL LIABILITY FOR HARM TO CHILDREN

Can a child abused or neglected by his or her parent sue the parent? Traditionally, the answer to this question has been no, based on the doctrine of family immunity. This doctrine, which was designed to protect family harmony and prevent collusion or fraud, prohibits family members from suing one another.

Some states still retain family immunity, but most now allow children to sue parents in varying circumstances. Children in many states can sue parents in connection with damage to the children's property or accidents that are unrelated to the family relationship—particularly auto accidents. A child also can usually sue a deceased parent, since there is no longer any danger of disrupting the parent-child relationship.

States that have abolished family immunity still frequently prevent a child from suing for acts involving the exercise of parental authority or discretion, such as decisions regarding food, medical treatment, or discipline. But decisions related to supervision of the child, which might give a third party injured by the child an action against the parent for negligent supervision, fall into a gray area where courts have reached different results.

Even states with family immunity generally make an exception for intentional, willful, or malicious acts of a parent, such as physical or sexual assaults. Some cases have been brought and won by children supported by their nonabusing parents. Many more cases have been brought in recent years by adults who believe they were sexually abused as children, some resulting in large damage awards. In a number of these cases, the child has also sued the other parent or spouse of the molesting parent for failing to protect him. For example, a jury in Minnesota awarded a twenty-one-year-old woman $2.4 million in damages because her father molested her as a child. Although the father was held solely liable for the $1 million in punitive damages, the mother was held jointly liable for the $1.4 million compensatory damages portion of the award.

These lawsuits are not easy to win. One of the primary legal problems with them is the statute of limitations. All states have laws governing the time within which a lawsuit must be filed, as explained in chapter 4. The statute is usually "tolled," or suspended, during the period of minority and does not begin to run until the child turns eighteen. Nevertheless, it still poses a problem for survivors of sexual abuse. In some cases, the victim has been aware of the abuse all along but does not realize until well into adulthood that it has caused physical and emotional injury. In other cases, the victim claims to have repressed all memories of the abuse because of its traumatic nature and to have "recovered" the memories while undergoing psychotherapy or experiencing some subsequent trauma. With either type of case, the victim is often not ready to sue until after the statute of limitations has already "run," meaning the deadline for filing suit has passed.

In an effort to allow victims of incest to seek damages from their molesters, many states have enacted laws extending the statute of limitations for childhood sexual abuse. For example, Vermont gives the plaintiff six years from the date he discovers the injury to file suit. So if he doesn't remember the abuse until he is twenty-five, he has until thirty-one to sue. Other states give the plaintiff until a certain age to file suit; in Connecticut, for instance, the age is thirty-five. In states without such extensions, many victims would be barred from suing by the time they realized they had grounds. Even in states that have extended the statute of limitations, courts have disagreed about how to apply these "delayed discovery" rules, as they are sometimes called. Victims who were aware of the abuse prior to adulthood have had the more difficult time being able to take advantage of the extension. Those who repressed the memories of the abuse fare somewhat better in overcoming the statute-of-limitations hurdle, but these are the cases that have come under the most attack on substantive grounds.

As more and more people have come forward with recollections of abuse, a skepticism has arisen regarding the validity of the recollections. Some now claim that the memories have been implanted in these individuals by their psychotherapists, who have essentially brainwashed them into thinking that they were abused. In a few cases, parents who alleged that they were wrongfully accused of abuse based on "false memories" were allowed to sue the treating therapists. False memory

RECOVERED MEMORIES AND THE FRANKLIN CASE

In 1991 George Franklin was convicted of murdering eight-year-old Susan Nason in 1969 and sentenced to life in prison primarily because of the testimony of his daughter, Eileen Franklin-Lipsker, ostensibly an eyewitness to the crime. What made the case so remarkable was that Eileen's testimony was based on memories recovered twenty years after the event. Observations of her own daughter during a period when Eileen was undergoing therapy triggered the recollection that her father had molested and murdered her playmate, Susan, when Eileen and she were young girls. The trial and conviction set off a storm of controversy as experts and the public debated the validity of recovered memories. The controversy did not subside after a federal court overturned the conviction based on several errors that occurred during the course of the trial, none of which directly involved the validity of Eileen's recovered memories. The court did *not* rule that Eileen's recovered memories were inadmissible or unreliable. Rather, the court maintained that it was up to the jury to evaluate the credibility of her testimony and that of the experts who testified. However, the court also found that the trial judge had erred by refusing to let the defense bring in newspaper articles from the time of the murder to show that Eileen could have learned the details of the crime from those sources, not from witnessing the incident. The district attorney declined to retry the case after learning that Eileen had recalled the murder while under hypnosis, making her testimony inadmissible under California law, and that she claimed to recall another murder by her father that he could not have committed. It remains to be seen whether other cases involving recovered memories in the absence of corroborating evidence will succeed.

syndrome, as it is called, is *not* a scientifically recognized or validated phenomenon, nor is there sufficient evidence at this point to suggest that false memories afflict a significant number of individuals. On the contrary, empirical evidence supports what mental health professionals have long recognized: namely, that childhood trauma can lead to repression, amnesia, and dissociated responses (an inability to integrate feelings, thoughts, and actions in the usual way). No doubt research will continue in this troubling area, and judges and juries will have to decide whether recovered memories are sufficiently credible to support an award of damages or a criminal conviction. Some of the difficulties encountered in the first criminal case to rely on them—a California murder case—are discussed in the box on page 320.

EXPLOITATION OF YOUR CHILD BY OTHERS

Child Molestation

It is one of a parent's worst nightmares: a child sexually molested by a stranger or by a teacher, coach, clergyperson, caregiver, relative, or family friend. To protect children from this nightmare, the law provides two ways of deterring the molester. First, a criminal action can be brought by the state, and the molester can be sentenced to prison for violating the criminal law. Second, a civil action can be brought on behalf of the child, and the molester can be forced to pay monetary damages to compensate the child for the wrong done. Let's look at both of these ways.

Criminally Charging a Molester. Every state has laws prohibiting sexual conduct of all kinds with children below a certain age. Child molesters can be charged with rape, sodomy, sexual abuse, or assault, depending on the behavior engaged in.

Unfortunately, precisely because the victims are children, molestation cases can be very difficult to prosecute and win. If your child has been molested, the district attorney will decide whether there is sufficient evidence to bring criminal charges against the molester. The prosecutor must be able to prove the crime beyond a reasonable doubt, so unless he can do that, even if he believes that your child has suffered molestation, he may have to forgo bringing charges.

If the prosecutor does file charges, he will have to decide whether to have your child testify. In the past, many states presumed children under a certain age (fourteen or in some states ten) were "incompetent"—a legal term meaning that they were deemed incapable of testifying in court. Today no state absolutely bars children from testifying. In most places the decision depends on the ability of the individual child to tell the difference between truth and falsity and to understand questions and articulate answers regarding facts and impressions. Children as young as three have testified in molestation cases, but there are no hard-and-fast rules. The decision ultimately rests with the trial judge.

The prosecutor may feel that your child's testimony is necessary to prove the case against the defendant. You may rightly be concerned, however, that testifying in open court will cause further emotional damage to your child. Testifying in court can be a frightening and intimidating experience for adults. For children, the fear and anxiety are significantly increased, particularly when they are forced to relive a traumatic molestation and subjected to cross-examination, all in the presence of the perpetrator. In an effort to minimize some of this trauma, courts have made a variety of adjustments for child witnesses. The prosecutor should and probably will familiarize your child with the courtroom prior to testifying, and you or another trusted adult may be able to sit with her while she testifies. If the court is convinced that testifying will cause emotional harm to your child, some will let her testify by closed-circuit TV or videotape rather than in open court. She will still face cross-examination but will not have to see the jury and, in some cases, may be out of the presence of the accused molester. The right to petition the court for this accommodation in federal court was established by the 1990 Child Victims and Child Witnesses Rights Act and has been upheld by courts against the challenge that it violates a defendant's constitutional right to confront his witnesses.

Because the reliability of children's testimony is always open to question, it is critically important that your child be examined by medical, mental health, and law enforcement professionals trained in child abuse. Otherwise, your child may be subjected to repetitive, leading, or suggestive questioning by unskilled interviewers that can render any future testimony unreliable and hinder prosecution of your child's abuser. You will also want, of course, to obtain treatment for your child in the form of counseling by a mental health professional. See the box on page 295 for help in this regard.

Bringing a Civil Suit against a Molester. You also have the right to bring a civil suit for monetary damages on behalf of your child and sometimes yourself against a molester for committing assault, battery, or false imprisonment or for intentionally inflicting emotional distress, depending on the particular facts of the case. The suit will have a much greater chance of succeeding if the perpetrator has been convicted in criminal court, but that is not a prerequisite for a civil suit since the burden of proof is less than in a criminal case. In a criminal prosecution, the charges must be proved "beyond a reasonable doubt"; in a civil case, by contrast, the plaintiff can prevail by proving her case by "a preponderance of the evidence," which means in this case that the molestation more likely than not took place. Of course, many of the concerns regarding testimony by your child will still exist, and you will want to consider whether it will help or harm your child to go through the process. You will also want to investigate whether the defendant has any assets with which to pay a judgment should you prevail. It probably will not be worth suing a poor or bankrupt defendant.

Megan's Law—Community Notification of Sex Offenders. In 1994 seven-year-old Megan Kanka was brutally kidnapped, raped, and murdered by a man living down the block from her who had a history of sexual offenses against children. Outraged by this crime and others like it nationwide, New Jersey joined a number of states in enacting legislation that requires convicted sex offenders to register with the state and allows communities to be notified of the identities and addresses of offenders in their area. While Megan's Law, as it is now known, went further than many by mandating, among other things, that dangerous sex offenders provide a DNA sample and submit to lifetime community monitoring after their release, it was not the first and will not be the last to require registration and some form of community notification. As we've already seen, most states have central registries containing reports of child abuse and neglect. In addition, almost all the states require certain sex offenders to report their current addresses to a central state registry, and the federal government is establishing a national computer registry to track sex offenders. Fewer states provide for community notification, but that is likely to change. By federal law now, states lose 10 percent of their federal funding for crime-fighting programs unless they provide notification when necessary to protect the public. Individual states are free to establish more stringent and comprehensive schemes as long as they meet the minimum requirements of the federal law.

Although current state laws vary widely in their details, they share some features. All require convicted sex offenders to notify a law enforcement agency when they are paroled or released, take up residence in a state, or change their address. Depending on the state's particular definition, sex offenders may include persons convicted of indecent exposure or loitering near public rest rooms as well as rapists and child molesters. States differ in their treatment of juvenile sex offenders. Some exempt them from registration; others treat them the same as adult offenders. Some states require registration for a set period of years, at least ten to comply with federal mandate. Others require registration throughout an offender's lifetime.

From your perspective as a parent, undoubtedly the most significant aspect of these laws is community notification. Here, too, states have adopted a variety of models. Many have limited notification to law enforcement agencies and make it a crime to disclose the information to unauthorized persons, but the federal guidelines will likely prompt these states to expand notification. Others already provide for community notification or public access to the registry. Notification may be made by fliers, public announcements in newspapers, or signs describing the offender, his address, and his crimes. Louisiana requires the offender to provide the notification himself. More commonly, and under the federal guidelines, law enforcement agencies decide whether community notification is warranted for a particular offender. Other states designate the individuals entitled to notice, usually victims and those working with children, such as schools and child care providers. At local police stations in California, interested persons can look at books or CD-ROM containing pictures of registered sex offenders who are believed to pose a continuing danger to society, but they do not have access to the offenders' addresses. New York, California, and other states have also set up 900 telephone numbers that enable members of the public with a legitimate interest to check on the criminal histories of registered sex offenders for a fee.

Laws governing sex offenders were passed with the aim of protecting the public, particularly children, its most vulnerable members. However, they have provoked considerable controversy and several legal challenges, some of which have not yet been resolved. While most courts have upheld these laws, many believe they are ineffective and do more harm than good. States have insufficient resources to monitor the registries and assure compliance. Surveys in some states reveal that a large percentage of offenders never register and those that do use fake addresses or fail to keep their addresses current. Most states provide little penalty for failing to register and have no time or money to enforce compliance anyway. At the same time, those who do register and are identified to the community are frequently subject to vigilantism and harassment, which may drive these offenders and others underground and hinder their ability to reintegrate safely into society. Moreover, registration and notification may give the public a false sense of security. By all accounts, most sexual abuse of children is perpetrated by family members and friends, and most child molestation, regardless of the perpetrator, is never reported. Hence many child molesters are still at large. Do not assume that Megan's Law or one like it will protect your child.

Laws against Child Pornography

Child pornography is a multimillion-dollar criminal enterprise that involves children in emotionally devastating and sometimes deadly activities, including performing in movies and videos and modeling for photographs. These criminal activities subject children to AIDS and other sexually transmitted diseases, drug abuse, beatings, and other serious physical injuries. They also cause lasting psychological trauma to their victims: the interruption of normal psychological and social development, the inability to develop healthy sexual or intimate relationships during adulthood, and, particularly pernicious, the tendency to perpetuate the abuse on their own and other children. Recognizing the grave consequences of these activities, the federal and state governments have taken steps to destroy the child pornography industry, but much remains to be done to protect children.

In 1978 the Sexual Exploitation Act went into effect. This law, together with later amendments passed during the 1980s, serves as the bulwark of federal prosecutions for child pornography, making it a federal crime to transport through interstate commerce visual depictions of sexually explicit conduct involving minors (children under eighteen). Pornographers meet the interstate commerce requirement if they knowingly use the mails, computers, or any other service that crosses state lines to transport or receive pornographic material, including undeveloped film sent for processing.

A pornographer does *not* have to know that a child is a minor. However, if arrested, he may be able to raise as a defense that he made a "reasonable mistake of age." In other words, if he can show by clear and convincing evidence that he reasonably relied on false identification provided by the minor and that the minor—by appearance, behavior, or experience—seemed to be older, he may escape conviction.

While the original Sexual Exploitation Act targets those who use minors in the production of child pornography, subsequent amendments have expanded the law's reach to include those who buy, sell, or transfer custody of children for the purposes of making pornography and those who knowingly advertise, offer to buy, or receive child pornography or possess it with intent to sell. A pornographer does not have to have a commercial purpose. The amendments cover private as well as public transfer and reproduction of child pornography. This is particularly important because much of the market for child pornography consists of pedophiles who use, trade, and exchange material for their private collections, not for commercial purposes or profit.

Parents who exploit their own children in pornographic enterprises can also be prosecuted. Does this mean that if you take an innocent photo of your three-year-old naked in the bathtub, you have committed a federal offense? No. The child pornography laws apply to lewd or lascivious exhibition of a child's genital or pubic areas or to visual depictions of children engaged in sexually explicit conduct, specifically defined as sexual intercourse, whether oral, genital, anal, or any combination of these; bestiality; masturbation; or sadomasochistic abuse. The first category, lewd or lascivious exhibition, is rather vague, but at least one court has defined it to include depictions that call attention to the genitalia or pubic area in order to sexually stimulate the viewer. Other courts have considered six criteria to distinguish child pornography from permissible depictions of children:

1. whether the focus of the picture is genitalia,
2. whether the pose or setting is sexually suggestive,
3. whether the pose or attire is unnatural given the child's age,
4. whether the child is clothed or naked,
5. whether the picture suggests sexual coyness or willingness on the part of the child, and whether the producer of the picture intends it to elicit a sexual response in the viewer.

Clearly by these criteria your bathtub photo of your three-year-old does not constitute pornography. However, the line between pornography and art can be blurry and very much depends on one's point of view, as a few parents have discovered. In one case, a professional artist had her children removed from her home by social services after the photo developer discovered numerous nude pictures of her two preschool-age children. The department investigated over several weeks and after a court hearing, ultimately found no abuse and returned the children home. In another case, a father was arrested after he took more than one hundred nude photos of his daughter for an art class. Criminal charges were ultimately dropped after he agreed to a counseling program.

Unfortunately, there are no black-and-white rules in this area of the law. Nudity in and of itself does not necessarily equal lasciviousness under the law; on the other hand, a picture of a clothed or partially clothed child could be pornographic based on other criteria. The vagueness of the law is part of what makes pornography so difficult to regulate and what causes so many people concern about infringement of our constitutional right to free speech.

Nonetheless, child pornography laws have been upheld repeatedly in the face of constitutional challenges arguing that they impermissibly infringe the First Amendment. In fact, the Supreme Court has ruled that child pornography is not speech protected by the First Amendment. Moreover, the Court has recognized that the states have a compelling interest in protecting children from exploitation by destroying the market for child pornography.

In addition to federal laws, laws in every state criminalize sexual exploitation of children by the production, distribution, and often possession of child pornography. Some state laws specifically define the prohibited acts; others rely on general terms like the "lewd and lascivious exhibition of genitalia" discussed in connection with the federal law. About half the states limit child pornography laws to depictions of children under sixteen. In most of the rest the age is eighteen, while in a few it's seventeen. Recent legislation in several states prohibits the transmission of computer images of minors engaged in sexual activity as well as the use of computers to depict, advertise for, or otherwise solicit sexual conduct with a minor.

Unfortunately, prosecution under either federal or state law often proves difficult. Because pornographic material circulates in a secretive, underground market, it is hard to trace. The children depicted are also difficult to identify, making it hard to prove their age. When a child is identified, he or she may not want to relive the trauma by testifying, particularly when a parent has been involved. Some states have attempted to deal with these issues by establishing a presumption that the child is underage, allowing experts to testify as to age, and rejecting the "mistake of age" defense. Federal regulations now also require states to make sexual exploitation a mandatory reportable offense, thereby requiring doctors, teachers, and others who suspect it to notify the police or child protective services so that the children involved can be eligible for social services.

Individuals who are convicted of violating child pornography laws face large fines and potentially lengthy prison sentences.

Child Prostitution

The child prostitution industry exploits hundreds of thousands, some estimate millions, of male and female teenagers. As with child pornography, both federal and state laws have provisions designed to abolish this industry. The federal Mann Act prohibits transportation of minors across state lines for the purposes of prostitution or any other criminal offense, whether the minors know why they are being transported or not. Adult prostitution, of course, is illegal in almost every state. Most states criminalize child prostitution as a separate, more serious offense, and they ban promoting, forcing, urging, or profiting from it. Those involved might also be charged with contributing to the delinquency of a minor. In addition, some states have special laws targeted at parents or guardians who allow their children to engage in prostitution.

As in pornography cases, prosecution for prostitution offenses often proves difficult. In some states, the prosecutor has to prove that the defendant knew the prostitute was a minor. More problematic, many minors refuse to testify against their pimps, fearing retaliation. Often these children have become addicted to illegal drugs, and they depend on their pimps to feed their habits. Like their pimps, the children are violating the law by engaging in prostitution, but if caught, they are less likely to be prosecuted criminally than to be treated either as neglected children or as runaways, a subject discussed in chapter 9.

Protecting Your Child from Indecent, Obscene, or Violent Material

Pornography. Children today are bombarded from all sides by sexually explicit and violent material. Myriad forms of communication and broadcast media—books, magazines, television, movies, radio, music, telephones, computers—provide an incredible array of aural, visual, and verbal depictions of sex and violence. The law has responded by attempting to restrict access to some of this material, but the ability of the government to protect children from exposure is appropriately limited by the First Amendment, which protects against impermissible government restrictions on speech. The Supreme Court has ruled that obscene speech is entitled to no protection under the First Amendment, and thus it is subject to significant state regulation. However, defining *obscenity* and applying the definition to particular items has proved very challenging for the courts.

Obscenity is not the same as pornography. Words or pictures can be pornographic without being obscene. The Supreme Court has defined *obscenity* as material that appeals to the prurient interests of the viewer, depicts sexual conduct in a "patently offensive way," and "taken as a whole, lacks serious literary, artistic, political, or scientific value." This definition usually includes material that explicitly depicts intercourse, oral sex, masturbation, other sexual activity, the excretory functions, or genitalia in a lewd manner. But again, law enforcement agencies and courts struggle to distinguish obscene pornography from art, erotica, and merely indecent material, a distinction that ultimately is based on a subjective value judgment.

When it comes to children, though, the Supreme Court has different standards. It has interpreted the First Amendment to allow states considerable latitude in protecting minors from pornographic material that would not be considered obscene for adults. The Court recognizes that the state has a legitimate interest in protecting children from exposure to pornography and protecting parents' interests in rearing their children. Although the Court itself has not concluded that a causal link exists between minors' exposure to pornography and inappropriate or violent behavior, it has found that a state may draw that conclusion and legislate accordingly, and the states have done so.

Most states ban the sale or distribution of pornography to children under eighteen, but a few place the age cutoff at seventeen. Some states specifically exclude parents from these laws, recognizing that parents may have diverse opinions about what constitutes indecent material and whether and at what age to allow their children access to it. Moreover, some states allow a defendant to claim as a defense that a parent accompanied the minor during the purchase. Many laws also ban the display of indecent materials, but some of these laws have been struck down as unconstitutional because they have the effect of restricting access by adults as well as children.

Movies, Videos, and Television. Parents today must be concerned with more than magazines at the local convenience store. Pornographic, indecent, or violent material in the form of movies, videos, television programs, popular music, and computer images may pose a greater threat to the moral and social development of our children than magazines and books. While the law has attempted to respond to this problem, ultimately the best protection of children will come from vigilant parents who monitor their children and communicate with them about the information they receive from these various sources.

The government does not regulate the movie industry; however, newspapers increasingly provide reviews of movies based on their suitability for children of various ages, and movie producers have voluntarily established a rating system familiar to most of us. Movies rated R will not admit children under seventeen without a parent or guardian. X-rated and NC-17 movies are completely off-limits to children under seventeen (eighteen in some states). Movie theaters will allow minors to view PG-13 and PG movies without parents in attendance, but the ratings at least give parents some guidance about the content of the movies. Some parents may feel even some G-rated movies are unsuitable for very young children.

Children may also encounter unsuitable viewing material at the local video store. In most states, video stores segregate adult or X-rated movies and will not rent these films to children under eighteen, as required by law. Some video stores, like Blockbuster Entertainment, market themselves as family oriented and refuse even to carry X-rated films. However, video stores stock numerous R-rated movies, including extremely violent horror movies, commonly known as slasher films. Often the stores impose no restrictions on rental of these movies. Indeed, a Missouri statute that attempted to prohibit rental or sales of such films to minors was struck down as unconstitutional because it failed to describe sufficiently what type of violence was considered harmful to minors so that the offending works could be identified. If you are concerned about the availability of certain movies to your children, you should consult your local video store about its policy. You can always choose not to authorize rental to your children on your account, and some stores will allow you to selectively block rental of R-rated movies.

Children do not need to leave home to be exposed to sex and violence. Studies estimate that children watch twenty-five hours of television a week on average, and some watch as much as eleven hours a day. Television programming presents numerous shows depicting sexual activity in various degrees of explicitness and, perhaps even more disturbing, graphic violence, often with little or no discernible purpose other than to titillate. The American Psychological Association estimates that children view more than one hundred thousand violent acts and thousands of murders on television before reaching their teenage years. A 1994 study by the Center for Media and Public Affairs found 2,605 acts of violence on television in a single day, and a 1996 study by four universities found violence in more than half the programs on TV and 85 percent of the premium cable channels. Numerous studies suggest a link between television violence and antisocial behavior. Not surprisingly, a 1993 poll found that 80 percent of Americans believe television violence is harmful to society.

Congress has taken some steps over the years since the introduction of television to try to protect children from explicit sex and violence in TV programming, but at every step it has had to be careful not to infringe the First Amendment guarantee of free speech. To protect the viewing rights of adults, the Federal Communications Commission (FCC), the agency charged with responsibility for licensing and regulating television networks, has required networks to offer a "safe harbor," a period during which programs deemed generally unsuitable for children may be aired. The safe harbor operates between 10 P.M. and 6 A.M. on the premise that children are less likely to be watching TV during those hours. Today, however, children watch television around the clock, and the safe harbor seems to many people to provide inadequate protection.

In 1990 Congress passed the Children's Television Act to encourage networks to offer more educational and less destructive TV programming for children, but the networks by and large failed to respond. After several years, the FCC approved an agreement by broadcasters to adhere to a minimum standard for children's educational programming. Although the standard is a mere three hours a week, it is a start.

A few years later, Congress tried again, passing the Telecommunications Act of 1996, which, among many other provisions, requires television manufacturers to equip all televisions thirteen inches or larger with an electronic V-chip by 1998 and requires the broadcast industry to develop a ratings system to go with the chip. The V-chip will allow parents to block out programs that the ratings system determines may be too violent, sexually explicit, or indecent for children; however, it will not let parents block out specific programs. Broadcasters have voluntarily developed a ratings system for the V-chip that is already being displayed on screen and in TV listings for many programs. The system designates general programs by one of four ratings: TV-G (suitable for all), TV-PG (parental guidance suggested because of some sexual or violent content), TV-14 (not suitable for those under 14), and TV-M (for mature audiences only). Children's programs are rated either TV-Y (suitable for all) or TV-7 (may be frightening to children under seven). The ratings are displayed in an icon on the TV screen during the first fifteen seconds of the program and in program listings. Initial response to the ratings has been quite critical. Parents polled by the *New York Times* in Alabama, California, Indiana, Texas, and New York City largely found the ratings irrelevant, and many parents have complained that more specific ratings regarding sexual or violent content are needed. Moreover, there is some indication that labeling may actually attract minors to programs deemed unsuitable for them. Congress has yet to ratify the system for use with the V-chip.

Cable operators have been subject to less government regulation than the broadcast industry because they allow parents more control over access. Parents with cable service can arrange to have channels that offer adult movies and entertainment, such as pay-per-view, blocked, or they can use a lockbox or parental key that enables them to selectively block certain channels for their children. Cable guides frequently provide warnings about the content of programming potentially unsuitable for children. And of course parents can exercise control by choosing not to subscribe to channels with sexually explicit programming, such as the Playboy Channel.

Music. Exposure of minors to sexually explicit or violent material has also been an issue for the music industry. Public concern with the effect of certain forms of popular music on young people has surfaced sporadically throughout this century, but particularly since the advent of rock and roll in the 1950s and '60s. In the mid-1980s the concern became politicized and gained new momentum with the creation of the Parents Music Resource Center, led by Tipper Gore, which waged war on what it deemed offensive and harmful rock music lyrics.

When numerous state legislatures considered requiring labeling on music similar to that used on movies, the music industry responded by agreeing to voluntarily apply a warning label, "Parental Advisory—Explicit Lyrics," to help parents protect their children from exposure to potentially unsuitable sound recordings. Neither the federal government nor any states require such labeling. However, a number of states include music in their "harmful to minors" statutes, and these laws, which prohibit vendors from knowingly selling, loaning, or in some cases displaying explicit sexual materials, have usually, though not always, been upheld by the courts. Nevertheless, few cases have been brought under these laws, and none has resulted in a conviction. Suits by individuals for harm allegedly caused by offensive lyrics have likewise been unsuccessful (see box on page 335).

MUSIC RESPONSIBLE FOR TEEN SUICIDES? COURTS SAY NO

In the 1980s two families whose sons had committed suicide filed lawsuits against musicians and the record companies that produced their recordings. One sued Ozzy Osbourne, the other Judas Priest. Both suits alleged that the teenagers had committed suicide after listening to the works of these artists and that the music, in fact, had provoked the suicides. Both suits were ultimately dismissed by the courts. In the case against Judas Priest, a Nevada court found that although *Stained Class* contained the subliminal suggestion "do it," the suggestion was not placed on the album intentionally and did not cause the teenager's suicide. In the Ozzy Osbourne case, a California court found that the lyrics were protected by the First Amendment, so the boy's family could prevail only if they showed that the music not only was intended to prompt imminent suicide among its listeners but also was likely to do so, which the family could not do. The court further concluded that regardless of the First Amendment issue, the family could not recover because the harm to their son was simply not foreseeable by the musicians and their record company.

Pornography and Child Exploitation on the Internet. One of the newest problems facing parents is how to monitor and restrict their children's exposure to unsuitable information and dangerous people on the Internet. The Internet is a massive network of computers linked worldwide. As many as twenty-five million people, including children of all ages, now use the Internet, which provides access to a wealth of databases, web sites, bulletin boards, and chat rooms throughout the world. Not all the information and contacts available through the Internet are appropriate for children. In fact, individuals schooled in surfing the Net can gain access to pornography of all types, though exactly how much remains a subject of considerable debate, as does the question of how easy it is for children to find. Some researchers have pointed out that not all Internet sites related to sex are pornographic; some are informational. Those that are adult oriented sometimes have warning labels or require use of a password, disclosure of a user's name and address, or proof of age, such as a photocopied driver's license, before allowing access. Moreover, downloading and printing the graphic images available at some sites requires considerable skill.

Congress reacted to concern over pornography on the Internet by enacting the Communications Decency Act of 1996 (CDA). The CDA makes it a crime to use an interactive computer service to send, display, or make available to a minor any communication that depicts or describes sexual or excretory activities or organs in obscene, indecent, or patently offensive terms. Violators can be fined or imprisoned unless they can show that they took reasonable precautions to restrict access to obscene or indecent material to adults, such as by requiring use of a verified credit card or adult personal identification number. The CDA has not gone into effect, however, because the Supreme Court found that key provisions violate the First Amendment of the Constitution.

Access to pornography is not the only potential danger for children using the Internet. Pedophiles and child pornographers also use the Net, and they have lured children they meet on-line to face-to-face meetings and, in some cases, molested them. Suggestions for protecting your child in cyberspace are provided in the box on page 337.

Dial-a-Porn. Another means by which young people can access pornography is through the telephone. So-called dial-a-porn numbers have proliferated in recent years. These numbers, usually beginning with 900 or 976, can be very expensive. Some services advertise an 800 number, giving the appearance that the call will be free, then switch the caller to a 900 number. Shocked parents have received phone bills with hundreds of dollars in calls to these numbers placed by their children. To protect parents from such unexpected charges

HOW TO PROTECT YOUR CHILD
FROM DANGERS IN CYBERSPACE

There are software programs available, such as SurfWatch, Net Nanny, and CyberSitter, that will enable you to monitor and restrict your child's access to sites on the Internet, limit sources of E-mail to specific users or categories of user, and block access to offensive material. In addition, some on-line services have adopted measures to screen indecent or obscene material by looking for designated words, such as *sex* or *erotic*, or to block access by certain family members. America Online, for example, provides a service that limits access to designated "kids-only" locations and, like others, requires use of a credit card to open an account. On-line services are also working to develop a ratings system similar to the one used by filmmakers.

To protect your child from dangerous people she may meet on the Internet, the National Center for Missing and Exploited Children (NCMEC) recommends monitoring your child's use of the computer and establishing rules for it. Instruct your child never to disclose identifying information—such as his name, address, phone number, or picture—to others through chat rooms or bulletin boards; never to agree to meet another computer user face-to-face without your permission; and never to respond to any disturbing, obscene, threatening, or harassing messages but instead to report them to you so that you can alert your on-line service provider.

and to protect children from exposure to pornography, the law prohibits use of dial-a-porn numbers by minors. Services that knowingly provide obscene or indecent proposals, suggestions, or communications to a minor over the telephone, even if the minor initiates the call, violate federal law. Moreover, FCC regulations mandate dial-a-porn providers either to use scrambling devices that require the caller to have a descrambler or to limit access to adults by requiring use of a credit card or a special access code. Ultimately the easiest way to protect your child may be to block the 900 or 976 lines. Many telephone companies will do this for free.

FATHERS' RIGHTS

FOR MUCH OF this century, the role of the father in the family has received little attention from social scientists, lawyers, and legislators. In the last decade, though, society has seemingly "discovered" the father. The women's movement, with its challenge to traditional sex roles, has encouraged young men of today to take a more active role in parenting, and more and more men are assuming child care responsibilities and seeking custody of their children after divorce. In an apparent paradox, though, research and the media have thrown a spotlight on the millions of men who have abandoned or never assumed their parental responsibilities, and lawmakers are increasingly focused on compelling these absent fathers to fulfill their parental obligations.

ESTABLISHING PATERNITY

The starting point for discussing fathers' rights and responsibilities is the establishment of paternity. Most married men probably give little thought to this issue since the man married to a woman when she conceives or bears a child is usually the child's biological father and is, in any case, presumed under the law to be the child's father, as will be explained further. For the unmarried father, the situation is considerably more complex. The law sometimes treats an unmarried man seeking to *assert* parental rights differently from an unmarried man seeking to *avoid* parental responsibilities. Moreover, an unwed father's rights are largely determined by whether the mother is married to someone else at the time of conception or birth of their child.

Let's consider the hypothetical case of Nick and Vanessa. Nick and Vanessa have been romantically involved for a year when Vanessa tells Nick she is pregnant. Nick is not convinced he is the father of Vanessa's child since he knows she has been seeing other men besides him. Neither Nick nor Vanessa wants to get married, and they stop seeing each other. Six months later, Taylor is born. Vanessa would like to obtain child support from Nick. As discussed in chapter 8, both parents have an obligation to pay child support, regardless of whether they're married. However, since Vanessa and Nick aren't married, she will have to prove that he is Taylor's father before a court will order him to pay child support.

The Paternity Suit

The primary means of establishing the male parentage of a child born out of wedlock is by a paternity suit brought against a man commonly referred to in legal jargon as the "putative father." A paternity suit is a civil action that can be brought by the mother or by the state if public assistance is involved. In some states, a child can also bring a paternity action through a guardian. In fact, some states require that the child be included ("joined") as a party in any paternity action and that an attorney or other representative be appointed to represent the child's interests. While the father does not have a constitutional right, in most places, to a jury trial in a paternity action, about half the states grant him such a right. The states also allow any of the other parties to request a jury trial. States are divided, too, on whether the father has a right to counsel, meaning the government will bear the cost of a lawyer if the father is indigent. Although most states refuse to recognize this right, many give the court discretion to award attorneys' fees to the prevailing party in a paternity action.

When can a paternity suit be filed? It can be filed even before a child is born, but it usually will not be resolved until afterward, when blood tests become available. It can also be filed later, but it generally must be brought while the putative father is alive. The statute of limitations (that is, the law determining the time within which the suit must be brought) varies widely by state. It can be as short as a few years, in a "reasonable time," or without any limit. In many states, a paternity action can be brought until a child is eighteen.

Proving Paternity—Blood Testing. The burden of proof in a paternity action ranges from a "preponderance of the evidence," meaning that a man is more likely than not the father, followed by most states, to "beyond a reasonable doubt," the standard used in criminal cases. The most common and effective way of proving paternity today is through blood tests, although these are not always necessary, as we will see shortly. A variety of tests are available that can prove or disprove paternity to different degrees. Virtually all states now admit various blood grouping tests as evidence to disprove paternity. The oldest and least accurate test looks at red blood cells and groups blood according to type (A, B, O, or AB) and Rh factor (positive or negative). This type of test can indicate that there is about a 75 percent likelihood that a particular man is *not* the father, but it does not conclusively prove that a given man *is* the father. Much more accurate is the human leucocyte antigen (HLA) test. This text examines white blood cells and can exclude a man as the father to a better than 99 percent certainty. In most states, this kind of proof is viewed as conclusive evidence denying paternity. HLA tests can also be used to *establish* paternity in most states, since they can identify a father with 90 to 99 percent certainty, although this use is less universally accepted. In most states, even evidence of a 97 or 99 percent likelihood of paternity creates only a rebuttable presumption of paternity; the alleged father can still introduce evidence showing that he could not be the father—evidence that he is impotent or sterile or that he did not have sexual relations with the mother, for instance. If he does, the judge or jury has to weigh that evidence against the blood test results and decide.

The most recent type of test used in paternity cases, and certainly the most accurate, is a DNA test. Each person's DNA is unique. When subjected to special processing, DNA makes a pattern like a bar code. Scientists can read and analyze a child's DNA fingerprint and compare it with the DNA fingerprints of the mother and putative father, taken from blood or other tissue samples, and ascertain whether the man is the biological father. DNA testing, unlike HLA testing, yields an extremely high degree of accuracy in identifying, as well as excluding, a man as the father. DNA testing is more expensive than blood grouping testing, and courts have just begun to consider whether it should be admitted as evidence, but the trend is strongly in favor of allowing it.

The court has the power to order that Nick, as well as Vanessa and Taylor, undergo the necessary blood tests. Under certain circumstances, however, the court may not do so. For example, if Vanessa had been married to another man at the time Taylor was conceived or born, the court might refuse to order the testing or require a showing of good cause before doing so because, as already mentioned, her husband would be presumed to be Taylor's father. If Nick refuses to submit to a blood test, the court can enter a default judgment against him, in which case he will automatically be judged to be the father. Blood testing can be expensive, and more than one court has held that it is unconstitutional to deny an indigent alleged father the opportunity to use blood tests to exclude him as the father. So if Nick cannot afford to pay for the tests himself, the state may be obligated to bear the expense.

The Consequences of a Paternity Determination. Once Nick's paternity is established, the court will undoubtedly order him to pay child support for Taylor. Nick will find, though, that in addition to imposing parental responsibilities on him, the paternity judgment will give him all the rights of fatherhood as well. An unmarried man who lives apart from his child's mother but is legally determined to be the child's father, whether by blood tests or the methods discussed in the next section, has the same right to custody and visitation as a married father after separation or divorce. As a practical matter, though, few courts are likely to award sole custody of a newborn or infant to an unwed father.

If Nick hopes to win custody, he will need to demonstrate regular and frequent visits and support. Expert testimony by a psychologist or psychiatrist regarding his ability to parent and his relationship with Taylor will also be helpful, as will evidence that he attended child care classes. Even with all this, though, chances are slim that Nick would win custody from Vanessa if she was a fit mother.

Although Nick would face an uphill battle to win custody, visitation rights are often granted as part of the paternity proceeding. However, an unwed father of a newborn should recognize that there may be limits on the duration and circumstances of visitation dictated by the developmental needs of the child. For example, an overnight visitation would probably be inappropriate if the mother was breast-feeding.

Other Ways of Establishing Fatherhood for Unwed Fathers

Let's consider a slightly different scenario now. Suppose that Nick reacts positively when Vanessa tells him she's pregnant and that the two move in together but never marry and never establish Nick's paternity through blood testing. When Taylor is five years old, Vanessa is killed in an automobile accident. Will Nick automatically get custody of Taylor?

In the past, unwed fathers like Nick had no rights regarding their children, and the children labored under the social and legal stigma of illegitimacy. Today at least some unwed fathers, often called "presumed fathers," have a constitutional due process right to be involved with their children and are protected under various state laws from being deprived of their children by the state without justification. In the famous 1972 case of *Stanley v. Illinois,* the Supreme Court considered a situation similar to Nick's. Peter Stanley had lived with Joan for eighteen years and had three children with her. When Joan died, the children were automatically made wards of the state under Illinois law. Stanley challenged the law that deprived him of his children without even a court hearing to determine his fitness. He won. The Court recognized that Stanley had a constitutional interest in the care and custody of his children even though he wasn't married to their mother. Subsequent Supreme Court cases have explained that this right exists because Stanley had a developed relationship with his children. The law is less clear when no such parent-child relationship has actually developed. In our hypothetical case, Nick should get custody of Taylor because he has lived with Taylor since Taylor was born.

Changing the scenario again to examine another aspect of the issue of paternal rights, suppose that Nick is thrilled when Vanessa tells him she is pregnant, that he even wants to marry her, but that Vanessa declines his offer and tells him she wants to raise the baby by herself, with no help or interference from him. What are Nick's legal rights regarding Taylor?

The Uniform Parentage Act (UPA), a law adopted in some form in eighteen states, provides four ways of becoming a presumed father with recognized parental rights. The first, a way accepted by all states, is by being married to the child's mother at the time of birth or conception. Second, a man is presumed to be a child's legal father if he marries the mother after the child's birth, but only if he also does one of the following: consents to being named as the father on the birth certificate, acknowledges his paternity in writing and files the document with the court or the Bureau of Vital Statistics, or agrees in writing to pay child support. Given Vanessa's stand against marriage in our present scenario, neither of these first two ways is open to Nick. He will almost certainly have to take some other action to establish himself as Taylor's father so that he can seek custody or visitation.

A third way for a man to become a presumed father under the UPA is by "receiving" his child into his home and openly holding himself out as the child's father. What does this mean in Nick's case? Well, Taylor must be physically present in Nick's home at some point, and Nick must also tell people that Taylor is his son. This way might be open to Nick, but since Vanessa has said that she does not want any help or interference from him, she likely will refuse to let Taylor visit Nick in his home. Finally, a man will be presumed to be a child's father under the UPA if he files a written acknowledgment of paternity with the court or the Bureau of Vital Statistics. Happily, this Nick can do. In some states,

VOLUNTARY ACKNOWLEDGMENT OF PATERNITY

In an effort to improve child support collection, many states have developed standard paternity acknowledgment forms that are presented to unwed parents for signing at the hospital along with the birth certificate. Typically, the forms explain the rights of the putative father to have blood tests to determine paternity, the presumptive effect of the acknowledgment, and its consequences, such as the obligation to pay child support. Both the mother and father must provide their addresses and sometimes their social security numbers and agree that the man signing the acknowledgment is the father. The acknowledgment usually must be notarized or witnessed and filed. If completed in the hospital, it is usually filed by the person responsible for filing the birth certificate. Generally, the state may not include an unmarried father's name on a birth certificate unless this form or other written consent by the father is provided or there is a court order establishing paternity.

he may be required to have his written acknowledgment notarized, but in others he may only have to sign Taylor's birth certificate or provide another informal acknowledgment.

What happens if Nick lives in a state that has not adopted the UPA? Some of the methods for establishing his paternity may be similar to, or even the same as, the four in the UPA. He may also have other alternatives, such as the option of filing a paternity action similar to the one Vanessa would file if she were seeking to establish Nick's paternity for child support purposes.

These legal presumptions of paternity are generally rebuttable, which means that any interested party, including the mother or the child, and in certain circumstances the father, can sue to determine the biological paternity of the presumed father. So if another man not married to Vanessa was holding himself out as Taylor's father, Nick could challenge his paternity. However, he must usually do so within a reasonable time as defined by state law. Moreover, states often impose stringent restrictions on the ability to bring a paternity suit if the mother is married to someone else at the time of conception or birth. We'll consider this complicated situation next.

The Marital Presumption

Let's change our scenario again and suppose that Vanessa is married to Ramón when she becomes involved with Nick. When she realizes she is pregnant, she confesses to Ramón and breaks off her affair with Nick. Everyone realizes that Nick is the biological father of the child she is carrying, but Vanessa and Ramón do not want Nick to have any involvement with the child. When Taylor is born, Nick would like to assume full parental rights and responsibilities. Who is Taylor's legal father?

As we've already seen, virtually all states have a marital presumption that the husband of a mother is the legal father of her child if the two were married at the time of conception or birth. In many states, this has been—and in some still is—a conclusive presumption, which means that even if Nick can prove with a 99.99 percent certainty through DNA testing that he is Taylor's biological father, the courts in these states will not even consider his petition to establish paternity, let alone order blood tests or hear evidence.

The reason for this strange rule can be understood by recalling how great a hardship it used to be for children to be considered illegitimate. Illegitimate children suffered numerous social and legal disabilities. They were not entitled to support from their fathers nor could they inherit from their fathers. Consequently, the law created a strong presumption in favor of legitimacy if a child was born during a marriage. Moreover, until recently it was very difficult to prove paternity, so this rule made considerable sense. Today our ability to ascertain paternity to a scientific certainty casts doubt on the wisdom of this rule, but many courts still consider it sound policy because it protects the marital family unit.

The marital presumption was challenged in the '80s by a man in Nick's position, referred to as Michael H., who had actually lived with his child's mother after their child Victoria was born. The mother eventually returned to her husband, and the couple refused to let Michael see Victoria. The case went all the way to the Supreme Court, and in a 1989 decision, the Court upheld the marital presumption, saying that the mother's husband, not Michael, was Victoria's legal father, even though it was undisputed that Michael was her biological father.

Although the Supreme Court thus permits states to maintain the marital presumption as conclusive, many, including those that have adopted the UPA, now make the presumption rebuttable. In some of these states, Nick would be allowed to establish his paternity, but in others, only the mother or her husband is allowed to bring an action seeking to rebut the marital presumption. Texas has gone the furthest in recognizing an unwed father's position in these cases, ruling that a man in Nick's situation has a constitutional right to establish his paternity if he has promptly demonstrated a commitment to assuming his parental responsibilities—for example, by paying child support.

If Nick lives in a state that does allow him to rebut the marital presumption, he should act quickly because some states, like California, will not consider rebuttal evidence in these circumstances after a child reaches a certain age, which in California is two. In addition, in many states, a court will order blood tests in this situation only if it finds testing to be in the child's best interests. In making this determination, the court usually will give strong weight to whether the child is already in an intact family. If the mother and her husband are united in opposing the putative father's paternity action, a court employing the best interests test commonly will refuse to order the blood tests, thus preserving the presumption that the husband is the father. By contrast, if Vanessa and Ramón divorce when Taylor is still very young, the court likely will be more solicitous of Nick's efforts to establish paternity. Courts will also be more inclined to allow the case of an unwed father like Nick to go forward if he has established a relationship with his child. Of course, even if Nick does manage to defeat the presumption in favor of Ramón,

YOUR CHILD'S NAME

Although a significant number of women now keep their own names after they marry (or reclaim them after divorce), children in this country still traditionally bear the surname of their fathers, at least when their parents have been married. Does a father have a legal right to give his child his last name? In years past, the answer to this question was generally yes when the father and mother were married. Indeed, as recently as the 1970s married women in some places were required to take their husbands' names as well. Today the law more typically provides that neither parent has a superior right to name a child. Laws requiring that a child be given her father's name on her birth certificate when her parents are married or that her name be changed to her father's when paternity is established have been successfully challenged on the grounds of unconstitutional discrimination. However, a number of states still allow the court to order a name change to match a father's when paternity is established. This is true even in some states that otherwise give an unwed mother the right to decide or amend her child's name. Other states require both parents' consent to use an unwed father's name.

the court may be cautious in deciding issues of custody and visitation in order to protect Taylor's best interests in a situation where the potential for conflict is great.

What if Nick decides that he wants nothing to do with the child Vanessa is carrying when she breaks off the affair? Can Vanessa force Nick to pay child support even though she's married to Ramón? Ironically, the answer may be yes. Some courts will not allow an unwed father in Nick's position to use the marital presumption as a *defense* against a paternity claim. They are particularly likely to take this ap-

Disputes over children's names typically reach the courts in cases of divorce or in connection with paternity proceedings involving parents who have never married, and courts take a variety of approaches to resolving the issue. When a divorced or unmarried parent petitions to change a child's name, although some courts still favor the father—recognizing a significant interest on his part in passing on his surname—most courts take a more child-centered approach; some defer to the custodial parent's wishes, either on the basis of a statute or on the theory that there will be less inconvenience and embarrassment for the child, while others apply an undefined "best interests of the child" standard or one relying on a variety of explicit factors. These may include inconvenience or confusion, the conduct of the noncustodial parent, the desire or need to maintain a connection with the noncustodial parent, the desire to have the child identify with the custodial family unit and any siblings, the length of time that the child has been known by the name, the parents' motives in seeking and opposing the change, and, if the child is old enough, his preference. These cases are very fact specific, and courts have reached different results depending on the circumstances before them, so it is difficult to predict the outcome in a particular case.

proach if the mother and husband have divorced, leaving the child without a present father.

FATHERS AND ADOPTION

To explore issues of paternity as they relate to adoption, let's alter our scenario once again. Suppose this time that after living with Nick for some time and becoming pregnant by him, Vanessa decides to break off their relationship and put their baby up for adoption. When Taylor is born, Vanessa signs a written consent and relinquishes the baby to the Garcias, who file a petition to adopt Taylor. What rights, if any, does Nick have to block the adoption and assume custody of Taylor?

Clearly, if Nick and Vanessa were married, his consent would be required before Taylor could be adopted. Since Nick is an unwed father, his rights are much less clear and vary considerably depending on the law in the state in which he and Vanessa live. Some states distinguish between an unwed father's right to *notice* of a pending adoption and his right to *consent*. In some states, certain acts will give an unwed father the right to be notified of a pending adoption of his child and the right to be heard at a hearing on whether the adoption would serve the child's best interests. For example, a number of states have established a putative father's registry. A man who puts his name on this registry is entitled to notice of any pending adoption of his child. While the procedures in each state vary, signing up on the putative father's registry can be as easy as mailing in a postcard or filling out a form at the health department or the Bureau of Vital Statistics. But enrolling in the registry does not necessarily mean that an unwed father's consent for adoption will be required. In other words, if a court finds that adoption is in a child's best interests, it may allow the adoption to go forward even if the child's unwed father appears in court and establishes himself to be a fit parent. Since courts often prefer middle-class or affluent couples to single fathers, a best interests hearing in no way guarantees an unwed father the opportunity to prevent an adoption.

By contrast, when an unwed father's *consent* is required, the only way an adoption can proceed without it is if the father is found to be unfit and his parental rights are terminated. It is important to realize, though, that the law does not require the consent of all unwed fathers, only certain ones. In most states, any man who is classified under the law as a presumed father has a right not only to be notified of a pending adoption but also to stop the adoption by withholding consent. We've already discussed the four ways that a man can establish himself as a presumed father in the eighteen states that follow the Uniform Parentage Act.

Other states give an unwed father the right to veto an adoption if he has provided financial support for his child or, in some cases, for the mother while she was pregnant. In many states, courts will recognize an unwed father's right to veto the adoption of his child if he has demonstrated a "substantial commitment" to assuming his parental responsibilities. To assess whether a father has satisfied this standard, the court will consider whether he offered to marry the mother, provided financial and emotional support during her pregnancy, and told others of his paternity. Unfortunately, there is no clear rule in these states for ascertaining when a father's efforts have been sufficient and within what period of time he must have come forward to claim his parental rights.

Two highly publicized adoption cases, the Baby Jessica and the Baby Richard cases, focused public attention on this issue. In the Baby Jessica case, the biological mother, Cara Schmidt, had lied about the identity of Jessica's father. A little more than a week after surrendering Jessica to her adoptive parents, the DeBoers, Cara changed her mind about the adoption. She also informed Dan Schmidt, the real biological father, of his paternity. Shortly thereafter, he filed a petition to establish paternity and take custody of his child. The Iowa court recognized that Dan had never relinquished his parental rights and had acted as quickly as possible to assert his paternity; therefore it concluded that he was entitled to custody of Baby Jessica. He did not get custody immediately, though, because the DeBoers appealed the ruling and, when both the Iowa Court of Appeals and the Iowa Supreme Court affirmed the lower court's ruling in Dan's favor, they attempted to relitigate the issue in Michigan. Ultimately, the DeBoers lost in Michigan as well, and the biological parents, Cara and Dan, who had married during this period, regained custody of Jessica. By that point, however, Jessica was three years old, making the return to her biological parents much more traumatic.

In the Baby Richard case, the father, Otakar, knew the mother, Daniela, was pregnant; he was living with her and planned to marry her.

But while Otakar was away in his native Czechoslovakia, Daniela was misled by a relative into thinking that he would not return, so she left him. She later told him that the child had died when, in fact, she had surrendered Baby Richard for adoption. Within a few weeks, Otakar discovered that Richard was alive and had been placed for adoption, and he went to court to obtain custody. As in the Baby Jessica case, the biological parents here reconciled and married while they pursued return of their child. Ultimately they prevailed, but only after much delay, and they have since separated. Daniela retains custody of Richard.

The tremendous publicity given to these cases and the harm suffered by the children because of the switches in custody have led to efforts to reform the law to resolve similar disputes in a way that better protects the children. The courts in two recent cases, one decided by the California Supreme Court, the other by the Florida Supreme Court, have responded harshly by requiring unwed biological fathers who seek to prevent adoption of their children to demonstrate their commitment to parenting as soon as they learn of the pregnancies. These cases have demanded that the fathers demonstrate that they consistently provided not only financial but also emotional support to the mothers during pregnancy. There appears to be little room for vacillation on the part of the father. In both of these cases, the fathers had expressed their opposition to adoption and their desire to take custody of their children before the children were even born. Nonetheless, the courts found that they had either abandoned their children or failed to demonstrate the necessary commitment to parenting because they had not provided complete and unwavering financial and emotional support for the mothers throughout their pregnancies.

If you are an unwed father who wishes to assume parental rights and responsibilities for your child, you should make your views known to the mother as soon as possible if she is considering adoption. Since the requirements for establishing legal fatherhood sufficient to veto an adoption vary significantly from one state to the next, it is very important that you protect your rights by consulting a lawyer or state adoption agency. Some states require a father to take very specific steps, such as filing a paternity action or getting his name added to the putative father's registry within a very short and strictly enforced time period. In states that require filing of a paternity action, that deadline may come within a few days after birth. Putative father's registries typically require registration no more than thirty days after birth. Failure to comply with these technical requirements can mean your consent will not be required for an adoption, and you will have no rights to your child. Courts in other states, as we've seen, will be looking to see if you have sufficiently demonstrated a commitment to parenting by evaluating your conduct toward the mother prior to birth, as well as afterward, so you should strive to provide as much support as possible and be as clear and consistent in your actions as you can.

FATHERS AND DIVORCE

Custody

As we discussed at greater length in chapter 7, most states have abolished any custody preference based on gender. As a result, in theory, men and women now have equal rights to custody. In practice, however, the vast majority of divorcing couples arrange for the mother to have primary custody and the father to have visitation. Nonetheless, some fathers do get sole custody and some do share joint custody with their ex-spouses. In contested custody cases decided by a judge, there is considerable controversy about whether fathers or mothers are at a disadvantage. Anecdotal evidence from father's rights groups suggests that judges still retain a bias in favor of mothers in custody disputes, and this may be true in cases involving infants and young children. Supported by other studies, women's groups argue that women who should be winning custody battles are losing because of sexism and a double standard that not only judges working mothers more harshly than working fathers, but overinflates any parental effort performed by men while devaluing the day-to-day caretaking handled primarily by women.

As a father, you can improve your chances of prevailing in a custody dispute, should one arise, by developing a strong relationship with your child and assuming an equal role in child care. This does not by any means guarantee that you will obtain custody since, as chapter 7 details, numerous factors play a role in that decision. But many courts weigh heavily the emotional attachment of a child to each parent and the day-to-day caretaking performed by each parent in evaluating where the best interests of the child lie. If you have played an active role in your child's upbringing and have consistently and reliably visited the child during any separation, your chances may be improved. As we've already seen, this is true whether you were ever married to your child's mother or not. Married and unmarried fathers alike have to demonstrate that placing a child in their custody will serve the child's best interests.

Stepfathers

A large percentage of divorced parents, particularly fathers, remarry, creating what are known as blended families. As chapter 7 explains, although there are some exceptions, stepparents generally have no rights to custody and visitation and do not have to pay child support. However, stepfathers' rights have been recognized in certain cases of mistaken paternity—specifically, when men have believed that they were biological fathers and they actually weren't. Let's consider a hypothetical example. Mark marries Connie, and they have one child, Timmy. When Timmy is eight, Connie and Mark divorce. During a dispute over custody, Connie reveals for the first time that Mark is not Timmy's biological father. In fact, his biological father is Dennis, a man Connie had a brief affair with during her marriage to Mark but has not seen since before Timmy was born.

In a number of cases like this, the courts have recognized the husband, Mark, as the legal father, based on various theories: the conclusive marital presumption that we discussed earlier; the doctrine of equitable parenthood, which acknowledges that Mark has functioned as a father for a substantial period of time; and the doctrine of equitable estoppel, which applies when a mother misrepresents the paternity of her child to her husband and he relies on that representation, to his detriment, in assuming the role of father. From Mark's perspective, this recognition will have both positive and negative ramifications. On the positive side, it will ensure that he can seek custody and visitation on the same terms as if he were Timmy's biological father, an arrangement that will certainly be in Timmy's best interests, as well as Mark's, since it will maintain a relationship with the only man Timmy has ever known as a father. On the other hand, designating Mark as Timmy's legal father means that Mark will remain obligated to provide child support for Timmy. Some men in Mark's position have alleged that this is unfair, but the law's primary concern is with protecting Timmy. Timmy needs support, and his biological father has never provided it for him. Under these circumstances, many courts will continue to require Mark to support Timmy, although some may allow him to challenge his paternity. Of course, if Dennis was available, a court might let Mark off the hook and order Dennis to pay support, as we saw in the section on unwed fathers' rights and responsibilities; however, this outcome is by no means certain.

What if Mark and Connie had lived together all those years but never married? Mark would not have any right to custody of Timmy, but in some states he would be allowed to seek visitation. Fathers with neither a biological tie to a child nor marriage to the child's mother generally have no legal rights or responsibilities regarding the child. However, there have been a couple of unusual cases reaching a different conclusion, both from California. In one, a man in Mark's position, who had lived for several years with a woman and believed her child was his, was able to obtain custody because the court determined that he was the boy's psychological father and that cutting off the relationship would cause harm to the child. In the other, an even stranger case, a man who claimed and initially won parental rights was never even romantically involved with the child's mother. Kevin Thomas was a close friend of Catherine Thomas and developed a strong relationship with her daughter, Courtney, so strong that he even had his last name legally changed to match hers. When Catherine revealed her plans to leave the area, Kevin sought custody and ultimately won after Catherine, unwilling to give up Courtney to Kevin, twice violated a court order and spirited Courtney out of the jurisdiction. Although the appellate court subsequently reversed the decision naming Kevin as Courtney's legal father, when the trial court reheard the case, it affirmed the award of custody to Kevin on the ground that returning custody to Catherine at that point would be detrimental to Courtney. Both these cases are highly atypical. While courts have shown some willingness to recognize psychological parenthood as a basis for affording limited parental rights, such as visitation, in certain contexts, it would be premature to view these two cases as the start of a trend. Marriage and biology are still the primary bases for recognizing paternal rights.

NONTRADITIONAL MEANS
OF BECOMING A PARENT

IN EARLIER GENERATIONS, the typical family consisted of a
mother and father married to each other and living with their biological children. Although some children were adopted or raised by single
parents, those arrangements were relatively unusual. Today the traditional
model of the family no longer dominates the demographic landscape.
Census data from 1995 reveal that only one in four U.S. households consists of a married couple with children under eighteen. As earlier chapters have shown, many children today live with single parents who are
divorced or were never married, in blended families in which parents
have remarried, or even with two parents of the same sex. In addition to
this diversity of family forms, the last few decades have witnessed a dramatic expansion in the ways people become parents. Adoption, the traditional way for people who cannot have children to become parents, has
undergone great changes and has been joined by an array of alternatives,
some made possible by advances in medical technology, such as artificial
insemination, in vitro fertilization, and surrogacy. The individuals and
couples who turn to these options face a whole set of legal issues. To understand them, let's follow the hypothetical case of Bill and Molly, a
couple who have been happily married for ten years but have been
unable to have a child. Molly has endometriosis, a disease that causes

tissue of the uterine lining to become implanted on other pelvic organs and that doctors believe will prevent her from ever conceiving a child. Nonetheless, Bill and Molly can pursue several paths to achieving their goal of having a family.

ADOPTION

Adoption is the oldest and probably most well-known alternative way of becoming a parent, and it has recently become one of the most controversial as well. The media have reported horror stories of failed adoptions—children being reclaimed by biological parents and adoptive parents unknowingly receiving children who are severely troubled. Despite the bad press, the number of families seeking to adopt still exceeds the number of available children by three to one. While adoption does entail some risks, thousands of children are successfully placed with loving adoptive parents every year.

People choose adoption for a wide range of reasons. Some married couples, like Bill and Molly, may have tried unsuccessfully to have a child, or pregnancy may pose a significant health risk for the woman. Gay couples and single men and women may not choose to have a child in the traditional way. Other couples or persons simply prefer to provide a home for a child in need.

If you are considering adopting a child, it is essential that you consult a lawyer. The sections that follow will provide you with background information and an overview of the legal issues involved, but the laws governing adoption are complex and highly technical and vary significantly from state to state. Consequently, obtaining the assistance of competent legal counsel is crucial to completing a successful adoption.

The Legal Effect of Adoption

If Bill and Molly adopt a child, they will acquire all the rights and responsibilities of parents, just as if they were the child's biological parents. At the same time, the adoption usually will sever completely any and all legal ties the child has to his or her biological parents. Reflecting the creation of this new family unit, Bill and Molly will receive a new birth certificate for the child, identifying them as the child's parents, and the court will seal the original birth records once the adoption is final. Because the adoptive family completely supplants the biological family, the decision to adopt has enormous legal, financial, and, of course, emotional and psychological consequences for everyone involved, particularly the child. For this reason, the adoption laws attempt to balance the needs and welfare of the three parties in the adoption triangle—the birth parents, the adoptive parents, and the child.

Who Can Adopt

In the past, adoption was available only to married couples of a certain age and socioeconomic status. Today many more couples have the opportunity to adopt, and all states now permit single adults to adopt as well. Although agencies still prefer married couples, approximately 10 percent of private adoptions and 20 percent of agency adoptions are by single individuals. In some places, gay individuals can adopt, although a few states expressly prohibit such adoptions (see box on page 360). Expansion of the types of people who are permitted to adopt will likely continue because of the difficulty in placing the many children with special needs, including older children, children with physical or mental disabilities, children who have been exposed to drugs during their mothers' pregnancies, and children who have experienced some significant trauma, such as abuse, neglect, or abandonment.

What factors will a court consider in approving an adoption? There remain on the books few categorical grounds for excluding an individual as an adoptive parent. However, many factors are weighed in evaluating potential adoptive parents, among them age, marital status, race, religion, and sexual orientation. There is no upper age limit on adopting, but agencies and courts generally prefer younger parents just as they do married couples.

Racial matching is one of the most controversial areas of adoption law today. In the 1980s the National Association of Black Social Workers

GAY AND LESBIAN PARENTS AND ADOPTION

Adoption agencies have begun to expand the category of people eligible to adopt so that it includes openly gay individuals, and independent adoptions also provide greater freedom for lesbians and gays seeking to become parents. Most state courts that have addressed the question of gay adoption have allowed it, and some states, like New York, prohibit public agencies from denying gays and lesbians the opportunity to adopt solely on the basis of their sexual orientation. But other states, such as New Hampshire, explicitly prohibit gays from adopting. Even in more progressive states, subtle discrimination may operate to prevent them from adopting. After allowing hundreds of adoptions involving gay parents, for example, California reinstituted a policy preferring married couples and discouraging unmarried couples, and thereby gays and lesbians, from adopting.

If you are gay and wish to adopt, presenting yourself as a single parent without mention of your sexual orientation may increase your chances of adopting in many places, but it will also increase the risk that the adoption will not be finalized. Lying about your sexual orientation constitutes fraud, which in many places could be grounds to undo even a finalized adoption and force you to relinquish your child. Pursuing an independent adoption or expressing a willingness to adopt a child with special needs can improve your chances of obtaining a child.

spearheaded a movement to block transracial adoption, fearing that such adoptions would prove harmful to the children involved. Consequently, some states passed laws and some agencies adopted policies requiring racial matching or lengthy efforts to find racially similar adoptive homes. Unfortunately, because there are many more African American children available for adoption than there are African American families seeking to adopt, this racial matching policy has left many children languishing in long-term foster care. Recognizing the damage that this delay in placement can cause, Congress in 1996 enacted legislation prohibiting discrimination based on race in foster care or adoption placement.

Religion also can be a significant factor in adoption. Some states have laws that permit religious matching when requested by a biological parent. Others give preference to adopting couples of the same religion as the birth parent. However, some courts have ruled that a judge cannot deny an adoption solely on the basis of religion.

The Adoption Process

Each state has its own laws and procedures governing adoption, and these may differ significantly from another state's. However, the main features of the adoption process are similar throughout the country.

When Can a Child Be Adopted? There are two basic ways a child can become available for adoption: 1. the birth parents can give their consent to the adoption, or 2. a court can terminate the birth parents' parental rights because they abused, neglected, or abandoned their child. In the latter case, the parents' rights are usually terminated in a proceeding separate from and prior to the adoption hearing. (See chapter 10 for a further discussion of termination of parental rights.)

The Birth Parents' Consent. If the birth parents are married, both must consent to the adoption. In the past, if the parents were unmarried, most states required only the birth mother's consent. However, in the last thirty years the role of the birth father in adoption has become much more prominent.

All states still require the birth mother's consent, which is valid only if given in writing *after* her child's birth. Some states require a waiting period of two or three days before the birth mother can validly consent to relinquish her child for adoption. State laws may also specify where and before whom the consent is to be signed. For example, in California, a state social worker generally must be present when the mother signs the consent. In New York, the relinquishing parent generally must give her consent in court.

The situation is much more complicated for unwed fathers. Most states require at a minimum that if the father's identity is known, he be officially notified that his child may be adopted. Many states today also make the father's consent a condition of the adoption if he has shown a willingness to assume his parental responsibilities. Sometimes this means that he must file certain papers with the court or put his name on a list of unwed fathers, called the putative father's registry, before his consent will be required. Many courts will consider whether he has provided financial support to the mother during pregnancy, held himself out to the world as the child's father, or done anything else that indicates a commitment to parenting. If he has failed to take a sufficient number of these steps, the court may find that he has abandoned his child, terminate his parental rights, and release the child for adoption without his consent. Unfortunately, it is often unclear when a father has satisfied this standard, so it can be difficult to predict whether or not a court will require his consent to an adoption. (For additional information regarding a birth father's rights in adoption, including a discussion of some of the well-known cases involving this issue, see chapter 11.)

If you are adopting a child, to protect yourself, you should do everything you can to obtain the birth father's consent. Of course, sometimes this will be impossible. The birth mother may be unable or unwilling to identify the father. She may even lie about his identity. Or the father's identity may be known but his whereabouts may not be. Failure to obtain the father's consent can put your adoption at risk, so you and your attorney should make every effort right from the start to identify, locate, and notify the birth father.

What if the birth mother or father changes her or his mind? Can the parent reclaim the child? The law governing revocation of consent in adoption proceedings varies widely from state to state. In some states, a birth parent's consent is irrevocable as long as it complies with the required formalities. Other states provide wide latitude for a birth parent to revoke consent. Timing can play a critical role. In some states, a birth parent can change his or her mind for ten days. In others, a birth parent may revoke consent up until the adoption decree is finalized, which may occur months after a child has been placed with an adoptive family. Once an adoption decree is finalized, it is extremely difficult to revoke consent. In general, it is harder to revoke consent in an agency adoption than in an independent adoption because of the additional procedural safeguards and counseling inherent in an agency adoption. We'll be talking about the two types of adoption momentarily.

A parent's attempted revocation of consent does not mean that she will automatically get her child back. In most states, the birth parent will have to go to court to reclaim her child. Generally, the court will not allow the birth parent to change her mind unless she can show good cause or it is in her child's best interests. Good cause can include technical problems with the consent—for example, that it was not witnessed by the appropriate person—or more substantive grounds relating to whether the birth parent acted knowingly and voluntarily in giving the consent. Was the birth mother coerced or defrauded by the agency, the adoptive parents, or the attorney involved? If she was, she may have grounds to revoke consent. Understand, though, that *good cause* and *best interests* can mean many things, and the decision to allow an adoption to go forward rests substantially in the court's discretion. In other words, the court will decide based on all the facts in the case whether to allow the birth parent to change her mind.

Agency versus Independent Adoption. In most states, Bill and Molly will have a choice of pursuing an agency adoption or an independent adoption. An agency adoption may involve a public (state- or county-run) agency or a private agency. Independent, or private, adoptions are usually arranged by an attorney, physician, clergyperson, or sometimes a family friend, but they may also be arranged directly with the birth parents. There are benefits and risks to both kinds of adoption.

What can Bill and Molly expect if they pursue an agency adoption? They will begin by filing an application with the agency and perhaps by taking a class on the adoption process offered by the agency. Agencies frequently provide educational services to prospective adoptive families. Once Bill and Molly pass the initial screening, the agency will conduct a home study—an investigation and evaluation designed to ensure the best match between a child and an adoptive family. The home study is an important means of protecting children, but it can be very intrusive and may exclude prospective parents who would provide fine homes but do not meet the agency's specific criteria. While Bill and Molly are undergoing their home study, birth parents planning to relinquish their children to the agency will be receiving counseling about their rights and options, and the birth mothers may be receiving reimbursement for certain expenses during their pregnancy.

Assuming that their home study is favorable, Bill and Molly will be notified when a suitable child becomes available. At that point, they will file a petition with the court and take custody of the child from the agency. In an agency adoption, birth parents typically give their consent and custody of their child to the agency, which subsequently transfers the child to the adoptive family. Because the birth parents have already given formal consent to the adoption by the time the adoptive parents take custody of the child, agency adoptions are considered somewhat more secure than independent adoptions.

Some time after the adoption petition has been filed, a few weeks or often months, the court will hold a hearing to determine whether the adoption is in the best interests of the child involved. In the meantime, Bill and Molly may avail themselves of postadoption services provided by the agency, and the agency will check in to see how they are doing for a report it will later present to the court. The adoption hearing will focus primarily on whether the adoptive parents can provide a suitable home for the child, since the agency has usually already obtained the consent of the birth parents or their parental rights have been terminated in a prior hearing. If the court finds in Bill and Molly's favor, as is usually the case, the adoption is granted.

The birth parents need not be present at the hearing. In fact, in the past birth parents and adoptive parents did not have any contact during the adoption process, but this is changing. For example, county adoption agencies in some states now allow birth parents to select adoptive parents from a book of biographies or videotapes prepared by the prospective parents. Nonetheless, the extent of contact between birth parents and adoptive parents remains in many places a significant distinction between agency and independent adoptions.

If Bill and Molly decide to pursue an independent adoption, how will the process differ? First, they will have to find a way to locate a child (see box on page 366). They may consider advertising for a pregnant woman who seeks to give up her child for adoption, and they may hire an attorney to assist in this process. They should be careful, however. Some states prohibit advertising in this fashion, and some forbid attorneys from serving as the go-between for prospective adoptive parents and birth mothers. Although some states permit one attorney to represent both the adoptive and the birth parents in an adoption, it is generally preferable for each to have separate counsel.

Second, independent adoptions generally do not involve formal counseling of the birth parents, although, like agency adoptions, they may provide reimbursement to the birth mother for the medical expenses of pregnancy and, depending on the state, for housing, clothing, and other financial support. A common misconception about independent adoptions is that the birth parents can receive much greater financial rewards than they can through an agency. Every state has strict laws prohibiting baby selling; consequently, many states clearly enumerate and sharply limit the expenses an adoptive family may cover in an independent adoption. Violation of these rules can put an adoption at risk.

Third, in an independent adoption, Bill and Molly will still need to submit to a home study before their adoption hearing, but it generally will be less rigorous because it is designed primarily to confirm that the birth parents' choice of the adoptive family is in the best interests of the child.

Fourth, in an independent adoption, the birth parents usually relinquish their child to the adoptive parents' custody before formally consenting to the adoption. Although riskier than the agency procedure, this practice has the benefit of allowing the adoptive parents to take the child home directly from the hospital in the case of newborns or directly from the birth parents without delay.

FOR MORE INFORMATION ON ADOPTION

If you are interested in adopting a child, you can obtain further information by contacting either of these organizations:

National Adoption Information Clearinghouse (NAIC)
10530 Rosehaven Street, Suite 400
Fairfax, VA 22030
703-246-9095

Adoptive Families of America, Inc.
2309 Como Avenue
St. Paul, MN 55108
612-645-9955 or 1-800-372-3300

If you wish to adopt a child from another country, write or phone the following organization for information and referrals:

International Concerns for Children
911 Cypress Drive
Boulder, CO 80303-2821
303-494-8333

The Internet also offers a wealth of information about adoption, including regulations from foreign countries, advice about special topics like transracial and gay adoption, and questions posed by other adoptive parents and adoptees. The National Adoption Center's web site, "Faces of Adoption: America's Waiting Children," posts photos and descriptions of children awaiting adoption throughout the country and has actually placed some children who were initially seen on the Net. Some prospective adoptive parents have begun to use the Internet to request children, as well. A word of caution, however, is in order. There is no regulation of the Internet and no screening of web sites, and some adoption agencies have complained of finding inaccurate information on the Net. Be sure to confirm any information you find there with a bona fide adoption agency or a lawyer.

TAX BREAKS AND OTHER FINANCIAL
ASSISTANCE FOR ADOPTIVE FAMILIES

Some large companies now offer financial assistance to help employees with the costs of adoption. The federal government, through a law passed in 1996, also gives eligible families who adopt a tax credit of up to five thousand dollars per child for "qualified adoption expenses," including attorney's fees, court costs, and related expenses. Families with a modified adjusted gross income greater than seventy-five thousand dollars get a smaller credit, and those with a modified adjusted gross income exceeding one hundred and fifteen thousand dollars are not eligible. The credit does not apply to illegal adoptions, surrogacy contracts, or stepparent adoptions.

Finally, in an independent adoption, as in an agency adoption, Bill and Molly will file a petition to adopt, and the court will hold a hearing. In an independent adoption, though, the hearing often serves two purposes: 1. termination of the birth parents' parental rights and 2. evaluation of whether the adoption is in the child's best interests. If the court grants the adoption petition, it will issue a final decree of adoption.

The choice between an agency and an independent adoption for Bill and Molly, as for many adoptive couples, may ultimately depend on time, money, and the kind of child the couple desires. Families wishing to adopt healthy newborns or infants, particularly white children, often have to wait years if they go through an agency and may never obtain the child they desire. On the other hand, independent adoptions are significantly more expensive, typically costing fifteen thousand to thirty thousand dollars, in contrast to agency adoptions, which run from several hundred dollars to eight thousand at religious agencies and eight thousand to twenty-five thousand dollars at nondenominational private agencies. Fortunately, some assistance is available, as discussed in the box above.

Families interested in or willing to adopt a child with special needs can often obtain one through an agency in a reasonable period of time. They may also be eligible not only for a special federal tax credit of six thousand dollars per child but also for government assistance for the cost of adopting and rearing such a child.

Anonymity, the Sealed Records Debate, and Open Adoption

In the past, most adoptions were closed adoptions, with the proceedings conducted in complete anonymity. The identities of the birth parents were not disclosed to the adoptive parents and vice versa, and once the adoption was final, all records were sealed permanently. In recent years, a movement spearheaded by adopted children and birth mothers has led to increased openness in the adoption process. Closed adoptions are still the norm, but most states now provide for disclosure of certain information, such as medical history, when an adopted child reaches the age of majority. Many states also have laws allowing access to adoption records and thereby facilitating contact between birth parents and adopted children, again when the children come of age. In most states, disclosure is made when there is mutual consent, that is, when both the birth parent and the adopted child are willing to make contact. Some of these states require the birth parent and the adopted child to sign a formal register; others use intermediaries. In the absence of mutual consent, the only way to open an adoption record is to petition the court and appear before a judge, who can order the record unsealed if the petitioner shows good cause.

An increasing number of adoptions today are described as open adoptions. The term *open adoption* covers many different arrangements and degrees of contact and information sharing between adoptive families and birth parents. In some open adoptions, contact consists of an occasional letter or holiday card keeping the birth mother apprised of her child's development and welfare. Other arrangements involve significantly more contact, such as visits with the birth mother. Open adoptions are a hotly debated topic. Some believe that they are less painful for birth mothers and ultimately better for adopted children since the children can maintain ties with their biological families and perhaps gain a more complete sense of identity. Others believe that they prolong the grieving process for birth parents and threaten the stability of adoptive homes and the security of adopted children.

If you are interested in an open adoption, you should know that some states will allow you to write an agreement permitting contact with the birth mother. However, it is unclear whether a court will enforce the agreement if you change your mind at some later date and no longer wish to allow contact. While a number of courts and a few statutes have addressed this question under varying circumstances, no consensus has emerged. Some states, like Tennessee, allow birth and adoptive parents to enter into open adoption agreements but flatly refuse to enforce them. Others will enforce visitation agreements between the surrendering biological parents and the adoptive parents if visitation is in the best interests of the child involved. This is more likely with stepparent adoptions, adoptions by other relatives, and adoptions of older children who have an established relationship with their biological parents. Moreover, some courts have found that birth parents who conditioned their consent to an adoption on continued visitation did not validly consent, and they have overturned the adoptions. Obviously, if you are considering an open adoption agreement, it is essential that you consult with a lawyer to find out whether such agreements are valid in your state and whether there are any special requirements to make them enforceable, such as filing the agreements with the court.

Wrongful Adoption
If Bill and Molly adopt a child they think is healthy and later discover that she has severe emotional or medical problems, what recourse do they have? Since human beings are not products that come with warranties, adoption agencies cannot guarantee the health of the children they place. However, adoption agencies do have a responsibility not to conceal material information about the children in their possession and can be liable for damages to adoptive parents if they fail to make necessary disclosures.

Stepparent Adoption

Although only a small percentage of children living with a stepparent are adopted, more than half the adoptions completed today are stepparent adoptions. Stepparent adoptions after a biological parent has died are among the simplest adoptions. Those involving divorced or never-married biological parents, on the other hand, can be emotionally and legally quite complicated.

Before pursuing a stepparent adoption, you should carefully weigh the implications of the decision. An adoption by a stepparent generally cuts off the rights as well as the responsibilities of the noncustodial biological parent. The noncustodial parent no longer has the right to visit her child, but she also no longer has the duty to support him. Although the custodial parent, of course, retains all of his parental rights and responsibilities, the stepparent assumes all the legal responsibilities of the noncustodial parent, including support. From the child's perspective, a stepparent adoption may grant recognition to a well-established psychological relationship and bring desired stability to the family unit. However, stripping the biological parent of her parental role may leave the child with a strong sense of loss or with guilt over divided loyalties, particularly when the child has maintained contact with the parent.

In any stepparent adoption, the custodial parent (spouse of the stepparent) obviously must consent to the adoption. If the person seeking to adopt is the stepmother, she will also need to obtain the consent of the mother or prove to the court that the mother has waived her right to consent (for reasons discussed below). If the stepfather is seeking to adopt, the need for the birth father's consent depends on a number of factors. If the father and mother were married, his consent is generally required. If the mother and father were never married, his consent may not be required unless he is considered a "presumed" father. Each state's laws define presumed fathers differently according to enumerated statutory criteria, but the definitions usually encompass any father who has established his paternity or acknowledged his child, taken the child into his home, provided support to his child, or otherwise manifested his willingness to assume his parental responsibilities and develop a relationship with his child. An unwed father who does not fall into any of the

GRANDPARENTS' RIGHTS IN STEPPARENT ADOPTIONS

Stepparent adoptions normally cut off all ties between adopted children and their biological families, including their grandparents. However, numerous cases have recognized that grandparents whose children have died have a right to seek visitation with their grandchildren, even if the grandchildren have since been adopted by a stepparent. In fact, some courts have extended this right to grandparents whose children have not died but have either relinquished their parental rights by consenting to an adoption or had their parental rights terminated by the state. But not all courts have agreed. Many have denied grandparents the right to visitation after a stepparent adoption, reasoning that the grandparents are no longer considered the legal grandparents of their biological grandchildren.

presumed father categories may still be entitled to receive notice of a pending adoption. He may also attend the hearing, but the only argument he may offer is that the adoption is not in his child's best interests.

The procedure for stepparent adoptions resembles the procedure for adoptions by strangers. The stepparent files a petition, and a hearing is held some months later. Stepparent adoptions usually do not involve an investigation by a social worker; however, diligent efforts must be made to notify and, where necessary, obtain the consent of the noncustodial parent. If the noncustodial parent gives consent, the adoption should proceed with little difficulty. If, on the other hand, the noncustodial parent contests the adoption, the stepparent will have to convince the court to waive the consent requirement, usually by showing abandonment or failure to support the child.

A parent has abandoned his child if he has consistently failed to communicate with the child for a certain period of time, usually a year (but more in some states and less in others). What constitutes "consistent" failure to communicate? Clearly, no contact for the requisite time period will suffice to abrogate the need for consent. But what if the noncustodial parent has made some minimal efforts to contact his child—for example, by sending a birthday card or a Christmas gift or dropping by for an occasional visit? For many courts, these contacts would be insufficient to protect the noncustodial parent's right to veto the adoption, but it is a matter of degree. Many states require proof that the noncustodial parent intentionally abandoned his child, and intention can be difficult to establish. Also, if the custodial parent has prevented the noncustodial parent from visiting or communicating with his child, then lack of contact usually will not be considered abandonment.

Failure to support a child is a second ground for dispensing with the need for a noncustodial parent's consent. Again, there is considerable debate over what constitutes failure to support. Generally the court can waive the consent requirement only if a noncustodial parent has failed to provide support even though she is capable of doing so. What if the noncustodial parent has provided some support but not the full amount owed? In some places, any failure to comply with a support order constitutes grounds for waving the consent requirement, but other courts view some payment as sufficient to avoid a finding of abandonment. (See chapter 10 for a further discussion of abandonment and termination of parental rights generally.)

A contested stepparent adoption can cause considerable distress for everyone involved, especially the child. You may want to explore the possibility of fashioning a compromise that can avoid costly and painful litigation. Some courts have approved stepparent adoptions that include an agreement that the noncustodial biological parent retain the right to maintain contact with the child. Also, some noncustodial parents reluctant to consent to a stepparent adoption may yield in exchange for an agreement to waive any claim to unpaid back child support.

Second-Parent Adoption—Recognizing Gay and Lesbian Parents
Closely analogous to stepparent adoptions are those by partners of gay and lesbian parents. In fact, adoption is the only way, at this point, for a gay partner to obtain full parental rights to a child related to the other

partner by birth or adoption, but it is far from the norm. To understand how second-parent adoption works, let's look at Carmen and Melissa, a lesbian couple who have been together for several years when Carmen gives birth to Evan, conceived by artificial insemination. Carmen would obviously be considered Evan's mother under the law, however, Melissa would have no legal rights or responsibilities regarding Evan. And the situation would be no different if Evan had been adopted by Carmen as an individual.

A number of courts in recent years have allowed a gay or lesbian to adopt the child of a same-sex partner without terminating that partner's parental rights. So-called second-parent adoptions recognize and preserve a child's relationship with a person who functions as a parent but would not ordinarily be recognized as such under the law. In evaluating a proposed second-parent adoption, the courts investigate whether there is already an ongoing parental relationship. So if Melissa can show that she has acted as a parent to Evan for several years and developed a parent-child relationship with him, she may be able to convince a court that it would be in Evan's best interests to allow her to adopt him— without, of course, terminating Carmen's parental rights. But you should know that some courts have denied petitions by gays and lesbians to adopt their partners' children, sometimes even in states where other courts have allowed such adoptions. Naturally, if a second-parent adoption is permitted, the petitioning parent acquires all the usual parental rights and responsibilities.

International Adoption

The shortage of healthy infants available for adoption has prompted many prospective adoptive parents to pursue children from other nations. International adoption can be difficult, time-consuming, and expensive, but it can also be very rewarding. To complete a foreign adoption, adoptive parents must meet the requirements and follow the laws of a child's home country, which may include traveling to the country and remaining there for several weeks or months before being able to bring the child home to the United States.

In addition, the adoptive family must satisfy U.S. immigration laws requiring the child to have a visa before entering the country. To obtain this visa, the adoptive parents must demonstrate that the child is orphaned and thus available for adoption. Once in the United States, most adoptive families also pursue an adoption decree from a U.S. court, and some states require them to do so. If you are considering an international adoption, you should begin by contacting one of the reputable agencies established to assist in this process (see box on page 366).

Foster Care

If Bill and Molly are interested in serving as parents temporarily, they might consider foster care. Hundreds of thousands of abused and neglected children find their way into the foster care system each year. Some children go into foster care as a result of a court order; others are voluntarily placed there by parents temporarily unable to care for them. The system depends on couples and individuals willing to provide a loving temporary home for these children. If you are interested in becoming a foster parent, you should contact your local child protection agency. Typically, you need to complete an application, undergo a screening process, and receive training. Many states require foster parents to be licensed and may limit eligibility based not only on age and income but also on sexual orientation. However, as with adoption, some states now allow gays and lesbians to become foster parents.

Foster parents do not acquire all the rights of other parents. Their rights, for the most part, are determined by the contract they sign with the state agency. The agency retains legal responsibility for a foster child and the obligation to supervise the child's placement. The agency that places a child can impose restrictions on the foster parents that would not otherwise be permitted. For example, the contract with the agency may prohibit the foster parents from striking the child, from raising the child in a certain religion, or from agreeing to major nonemergency medical procedures. The biological parents may also have a right to visit the child. However, the foster parents do have the responsibility for daily supervision and thus the right to make day-to-day decisions concerning the child. They are also entitled to receive a monthly allowance, which is generally not subject to federal income tax, to assist them in meeting their foster child's needs.

Usually, the goal of foster care is to provide temporary care until children can be reunited with their parents. For foster parents providing a "crisis home," this may be as little as a few days. Many foster parents, though, retain custody of children for years. Traditionally, foster parents have been required to agree that they will not seek to adopt a child placed in their care, and they have been instructed that the child may be removed from their home at any time. Indeed, the agency has the right to remove a child if the child is becoming *too* attached to the foster parents. While this view still prevails in some places, attitudes and policies are changing. Today many states give foster parents priority in adopting children who have been in their care, recognizing that children and foster parents form emotional attachments to each other. Foster parents may also have the right to be notified of court proceedings concerning their foster children and to intervene in those proceedings.

ASSISTED REPRODUCTION AND THE NEW REPRODUCTIVE TECHNOLOGIES

Infertile couples in previous generations were essentially limited to adoption or foster care if they wanted to become parents. But suppose that Bill and Molly feel strongly that they want a child to whom at least one of them is genetically related. What options do they have? Today the field of reproductive endocrinology has opened up new possibilities for some infertile couples.

In Vitro Fertilization

Depending on the nature and severity of Molly's endometriosis, she and Bill may be candidates for in vitro fertilization (IVF). Children born as a result of this process have been called test-tube babies because fertilization takes place outside the womb. How does the process of in vitro fertilization compare with that of natural fertilization? In natural fertilization, during each menstrual cycle a woman generally releases one mature egg into her fallopian tubes, where it may be fertilized by a man's sperm. The resulting embryo grows for a couple of days in the fallopian tubes, then travels to the uterus, where it implants and develops over the nine-month gestation period.

With in vitro fertilization, the process begins with the use of fertility drugs to stimulate a woman's ovaries, causing numerous eggs to mature. Having a large number of eggs available for fertilization greatly increases the odds that the IVF procedure will succeed. When the eggs have matured sufficiently, the physician removes them from the woman's ovaries using an outpatient surgical procedure. He then places them in a petri dish along with the husband's sperm. The sperm and eggs remain in the dish for two or three days, during which time some of the eggs may be fertilized by the sperm. When these fertilized embryos have reached a certain size, usually a small cluster of a few cells, the doctor transfers them to the woman's uterus. If one or more of the embryos implant themselves in the uterus, the woman becomes pregnant. Some couples undergo a variation on IVF, known as ZIFT, or zygote intrafallopian transfer, in which the fertilized eggs are deposited in the fallopian tube instead of the uterus, or a related procedure, GIFT—gamete intrafallopian transfer—in which the unfertilized eggs are deposited with the sperm in the fallopian tube.

IVF raises a number of important legal as well as psychological and financial issues.

Cost and Insurance. IVF is very expensive and has a relatively low success rate. One cycle of IVF averages eight thousand to ten thousand dollars, and there is only a 12 to 15 percent chance that the procedure will result in a live birth. Many couples go through several cycles costing tens of thousands of dollars. Although some insurance companies cover IVF, the extent of coverage varies widely, and many insurance companies don't cover it or any other infertility treatments at all. About a dozen states have laws requiring insurance companies to cover infertility treatments to some degree, but only some of those mandate coverage of sophisticated and costly procedures like IVF, and even in those states, the laws contain restrictions and loopholes that may allow your insurer to deny you coverage. To find out about the law in your particular state, you can contact your state insurance commissioner. If your state does not require coverage in your situation, you will need to scrutinize the terms of your policy and challenge your insurance company to provide reimbursement based on the policy.

Risks of Fertility Drugs and Multiple Births. Using IVF or fertility drugs significantly increases the likelihood of multiple births—twins, triplets, quadruplets, even quintuplets. Twenty to 25 percent of IVF parents have multiple births, while the incidence is less than 1 percent normally. Multiple births significantly increase the risk of neonatal complications, especially those associated with low birth weight. If you give birth to quintuplets that suffer from severe birth defects or other medical problems associated with multiple births, you may be able to sue your doctor if she failed to inform you of the risks before you consented to the fertility treatment. However, you will have no grounds to sue if you were adequately warned of the risks, even if a bad outcome results, unless you have evidence of other errors or carelessness on the part of your physician.

Recent studies also suggest that there may be a link between fertility drugs and an increased risk of ovarian cancer. Although the results of these studies have been disputed, you will want to discuss the risk with your fertility specialist.

Cryopreservation of Embryos. Doctors hope that more than one egg will fertilize during an in vitro cycle, but sometimes more embryos are created than can be implanted in a given cycle. If there are extra embryos, a couple will often choose to freeze them for implantation at a later date or for donation to another infertile couple. The ability to freeze embryos raises a host of legal issues.

What happens if the couple divorces before implantation? Who should get custody? In the leading case of *Davis v. Davis,* the Tennessee Supreme Court said that an ex-husband had the right to prevent his former wife from having their embryo implanted in her uterus or donated

FINDING A GOOD FERTILITY CLINIC

Pursuing parenthood through reproductive technologies like in vitro fertilization, GIFT, and ZIFT is costly both financially and emotionally. To get the most out of the available options and to maximize your chances of becoming parents, you will need to select a high-quality fertility clinic. These clinics operate virtually unregulated, so here are some suggestions to guide you:

1. Select a clinic headed by a physician who is board-certified in reproductive endocrinology. These physicians have completed fellowships in infertility treatment in addition to residencies in obstetrics and gynecology.

2. Choose a clinic that is certified under the Clinical Laboratory Improvement Amendments of 1988 (CLIA), a law that requires labs to meet certain requirements and follow certain protocols in performing complicated fertility procedures, or one accredited by the College of American Pathologists (CAP), which conducts on-site inspections and uses more rigorous criteria than CLIA.

3. Ask to see reports of success rates and scrutinize them closely. Clinics can manipulate statistics and present them in ways that are useless for comparative purposes or even misleading. In fact, the Federal Trade Commission has had to order several clinics to stop making un-

to someone else, but it is very unclear what other states will do in this situation. In 1995 a New York trial judge deciding a divorce case disagreed with the *Davis* court decision and gave custody of five frozen preembryos to the wife for implantation. However, this decision was not officially reported and therefore is of no precedential value. Only Louisiana has a law prohibiting the destruction of frozen embryos. In England, laboratory personnel destroyed thousands of frozen embryos throughout the country under a law requiring destruction after five substantiated claims regarding their success rates. You should request statistics for your age group on the particular procedure your specialist recommends and make sure that the clinic provides rates for live births, not merely pregnancies. You may also wish to contact the Society for Assisted Reproductive Technology (SART), which compiles standardized national and regional success-rate data annually. Keep in mind, though, that SART's data is provided by the clinics and not independently researched.

Society for Assisted Reproductive Technology
1209 Montgomery Highway
Birmingham, AL 35216
205-978-5000

4. Contact Resolve, a national nonprofit infertility organization, to find a support group, ask questions, locate additional resources, and get referrals in your area regarding infertility treatments as well as adoption.

Resolve
1310 Broadway
Somerville, MA 02144
617-623-0744

years unless other arrangements for the embryos were made. In this country, individual fertility clinics may have their own policies on this issue.

What if a couple dies before implantation? What should happen to their embryos? Should they be donated or destroyed? If donated, should the children who develop from the embryos be able to inherit from the biological parents' estate? A case involving this situation arose in Australia. The parents of an embryo, a California couple, were killed in a plane crash before the embryo was implanted. The Australian government decided that the embryo would be donated, and a California court ultimately ruled that the child would not inherit from the dead parents' estate.

What if a couple gets into a dispute with their doctor or fertility clinic? In one New York case, a couple sued and won after their physician destroyed their embryo instead of transferring it to another facility. Like other doctors, physicians who maintain and handle embryos resulting from fertility treatments have a legal obligation to adhere to the standard of care that prevails among their colleagues.

Artificial Insemination

What if Bill and Molly were unable to have children not because of Molly's endometriosis, but because Bill had insufficient or inadequate sperm? They might opt for artificial insemination as a way of becoming parents. Molly would be inseminated with sperm from a donor, who could be someone known to them or an anonymous donor. Through artificial insemination, in contrast to adoption, Bill and Molly could have a child genetically related to Molly, and they would both be involved from the moment of conception. When the child was born, Bill would be the father under the law, with all the usual rights and responsibilities.

The Legal Status of the Couple and the Donor. Generally, a married woman wishing to be artificially inseminated must obtain the consent of her husband in writing. In some states, the couple must file the consent with the court or with the Bureau of Vital Statistics. Elsewhere, the couple retains the consent. If the wife does not obtain this consent, the husband can later deny that he is the father and attempt to avoid his child support responsibilities. Although the wife could then attempt to prove that the husband gave his oral consent or indicated his acquiescence by his conduct, such a claim can prove difficult to establish.

The type of donor used can have serious legal consequences, so if you're considering artificial insemination, you should weigh your options carefully before proceeding. Approximately half of all artificial inseminations involve anonymous donors, and the law most clearly defines the rights and responsibilities of the individuals involved in this

ARTIFICIAL INSEMINATION FOR SINGLE WOMEN AND LESBIANS

Single women and lesbians who are artificially inseminated by a physician with sperm from an anonymous donor receive the same protection as heterosexual couples. The mother has all the legal rights and responsibilities of parenthood, while the donor has none. Single women and lesbians who choose to use a known donor or to inseminate themselves should carefully consider the consequences. When a dispute arises concerning a child conceived by artificial insemination in a way not covered by statute, the courts usually treat the parents as if they had conceived by sexual intercourse. Consequently, the donor in this situation would have the usual rights and responsibilities of fatherhood. As the text explains, agreements purporting to limit parental rights of a known donor are far from ironclad. Unless you affirmatively want the donor to play a role in your child's life, one that could ultimately lead to his assertion of parental rights, you are well-advised to use an anonymous donor and to be inseminated by a physician.

Unfortunately, not all physicians will artificially inseminate lesbians or single women. While state laws do not forbid these women from using this method of conception, some sperm banks and physicians have policies that limit provision of insemination services to married women. For example, the Repository for Germinal Choice in California, commonly referred to as the Nobel Prize sperm bank, provides services only to married women. A 1987 survey indicated that only a little more than a third of physicians who perform artificial inseminations nationwide were willing to do so for lesbians. Lesbians living in major metropolitan areas with sizable gay populations are likely to have less trouble finding a willing physician or sperm bank. Lesbians in other areas may have to travel to take advantage of this method of conceiving or may have to search out a willing donor and perform the insemination themselves. Gay and lesbian parenting support groups now in existence in communities throughout the country can be a valuable resource for locating willing physicians and donors.

situation. Many states have laws stating that anonymous donors who provide their sperm to a licensed sperm bank or physician have no parental rights or responsibilities; they cannot be obligated to pay child support, nor can they visit or seek custody of a child conceived from their sperm. From a couple's perspective, the best way to protect themselves against future claims on their child is to be artificially inseminated by a physician with semen from an anonymous donor. Likewise, a donor can best protect himself from claims that he should support a child by donating anonymously to a sperm bank or physician.

Despite these protections, many couples choose to use a donor known to them and to perform the artificial insemination themselves, without medical assistance. Avoiding the involvement of a physician can save money, since each insemination generally costs several hundred dollars. Moreover, some couples prefer a known donor for emotional and psychological reasons.

In some states, it is illegal for anyone other than a physician or someone working for a physician to perform an artificial insemination. In most, it is perfectly legal but fraught with potential problems. Using a known donor without professional intervention leaves the parties involved uncertain about their legal roles. If you choose not to use a physician, your husband will still be considered the father of the child because most states have a legal presumption that the child conceived and born during a marriage is the child of the husband, regardless of actual paternity. (See chapter 11 for further discussion of the marital presumption.) However, this presumption has come under increasing attack in recent years, and there have been cases in which sperm donors have asserted parental rights and won. There have also been cases in which sperm donors have had to pay child support.

What if Bill and Molly sign an agreement with the donor stating that Bill will be the father and that the donor will give up all his parental rights? A written agreement would certainly help to clarify the intent of the donor and the couple, but it is unclear whether it would be legally binding. In a 1994 Oregon case, a court found an agreement waiving a donor's parental rights and child support obligation, but allowing limited visitation, to be enforceable. As a general rule, though, relying on an agreement to limit a donor's involvement is extremely risky because later the donor may decide to seek parental rights or the mother (or the state) may try to obtain child support on behalf of the child. Courts are reluctant to let parents or others involved in the reproductive process decide in a contract who will have parental rights and responsibilities. Rather, the court reserves the right to ignore the contract if it would not promote the best interests of the child. In all but one case in which a known sperm donor has sought to establish paternity over the objections of a single mother, the court has sided with the donor. Moreover, one court ruled that a known donor could assert paternity even though the woman involved was inseminated by a physician if he could prove, as he claimed, that there was an agreement that he would act as the child's father. In sum, courts tend to take into account agreements that a donor will act as father; it is less clear how they view contracts to extinguish parental rights.

Information regarding an Anonymous Donor. If you decide to use an anonymous donor provided through a sperm bank or physician, the amount of information you can learn about the donor will vary depending on where you live and what the policy of the particular sperm bank or doctor is. Sperm banks operate largely unregulated in many places. In the past, anonymous sperm donors acted in complete secrecy, and sperm banks often did not keep any records so that anonymity could never be breached. Today many sperm banks keep records with basic identifying information about donors, and a number of states now mandate such record keeping, some requiring that the records be sealed and opened only by court order based on good cause. As a matter of policy, to preserve anonymity, sperm banks rarely disclose identifying information; however, they may reveal nonidentifying information, such as physical characteristics, educational background, and especially medical history. Some states actually require that sperm banks and physicians disclose any nonidentifying information that they obtain about a donor.

The danger of contracting HIV through artificial insemination has led a number of states to pass laws requiring that sperm be tested for

THE SCANDALOUS CASE OF DR. JACOBSEN

Many women over the years have been artificially inseminated with sperm from an anonymous donor without incident, but disreputable and negligent conduct has been known to occur on rare occasions. The case of Dr. Cecil Jacobsen of Fairfax, Virginia, was undoubtedly one of the most egregious. Dr. Jacobsen used his own sperm to impregnate at least seventy-five women, telling them that they were receiving semen from anonymous donors. Jacobsen was sentenced to five years in prison for defrauding his patients.

the AIDS virus and other sexually transmitted diseases. Some make it a crime to knowingly or intentionally donate HIV-infected sperm. While most states still do not require testing of sperm for genetic defects, many sperm banks do screen for them. Couples considering artificial insemination should inquire about this option, particularly if they have chosen artificial insemination to avoid passing on a known genetic disease of the husband.

Another concern about artificial insemination is the possible incestuous marriage of half siblings fathered by the same anonymous donor. Some banks address this issue by limiting the number of pregnancies that can result from one donor's semen. The American Fertility Society recommends a maximum of ten. Again, though, these practices are voluntary.

Egg Donation

Returning to our original scenario, recall that it was Molly's medical condition, endometriosis, that prevented her and Bill from conceiving a child. Let's assume that Molly and Bill have attempted in vitro fertilization several times unsuccessfully. Their fertility specialist believes the endometriosis has affected the health and availability of Molly's eggs, and he suggests that the couple try IVF using a donor egg. The donor egg would be fertilized by Bill's sperm, the resulting embryos would be implanted in Molly's uterus, and Molly would carry the baby to term.

The use of egg donors is a relatively new but growing phenomenon that raises important legal questions. Donated eggs may come from women who choose to donate them for altruistic or financial reasons or from women already attempting in vitro fertilization themselves who have extra eggs from their cycle. Either way, the donor must consent to donate her eggs. If the doctor removes or transfers eggs from one woman to another without the donor's consent, the doctor can be liable for substantial damages. In a scandal at a fertility clinic at the University of California, Irvine, former employees of the clinic alleged that eggs and embryos from participants in the IVF program were appropriated and given to other couples without the knowledge or permission of the donors. Some of these stolen eggs and embryos resulted in children, and several lawsuits have been filed. If you elect this method of conception, be sure that the clinic you use keeps careful records regarding all eggs, embryos, and sperm and that proper consent is granted for any egg you may receive.

The requirement of informed consent for egg donation on the part of all participants is clear, but egg donation raises other questions that have not been answered yet, most notably who will be considered the legal mother of a child conceived and born by this method. Logically, egg donation should be treated just as artificial insemination is: in other words, the recipient of the donated gamete should be considered the parent, and the donor should retain no parental rights. However, there are some distinctions between artificial insemination and egg donation that may warrant different treatment. To retrieve eggs for donation, the donor not only must use powerful drugs to stimulate egg production but must also undergo a risky, expensive, and invasive outpatient surgical procedure. Nonetheless, the few courts that have considered or discussed the allocation of parental rights in egg donation cases have indicated that if the recipient of the egg is the intended parent, she should be considered the legal mother.

Surrogacy

Finally, if Molly was unable to become pregnant or to carry a child to term, she and Bill might consider surrogacy—one of the most controversial alternative ways of becoming a parent. There are two basic types of surrogacy arrangements. In the first type, the more traditional of the two, the husband provides sperm to a woman other than his wife, and that woman, who is called the surrogate, conceives and bears a child for the couple. In the second type, the husband and wife undergo in vitro fertilization—the wife's egg is fertilized in a laboratory with her husband's sperm—and then the fertilized embryo is implanted in a surrogate who, as in the first type, carries the child to term and turns him over to his biological parents at birth. This second type of surrogacy is called gestational surrogacy. Variations on the two types—for example, with a gestational surrogate carrying a fetus created by sperm and egg that have both been donated—also occur.

In the landmark Baby M case (discussed in the box on p. 387), the New Jersey Supreme Court considered a traditional surrogacy arrangement and ruled that surrogacy contracts were illegal. Following New Jersey's lead, several states passed laws prohibiting either all surrogacy contracts or only those entered into for money. Other states allow surrogacy contracts that provide for payment of certain pregnancy-related expenses of the surrogate. A few states, like Virginia, have procedures for obtaining prior court approval of surrogacy contracts and defining the intended parents as the legal parents. In other states, surrogacy contracts are legal, but the courts have not decided whether they are actually enforceable. In these states, Bill and Molly would not be violating any laws if they entered into a traditional surrogacy contract; however, if they subsequently got involved in a dispute with the surrogate, they would have no guarantee of winning. A court might award custody to them based on laws dealing with custody issues generally (discussed fully in chapter 7), but they could not necessarily rely on the contract to protect their interest in the child.

In the few court cases considering gestational surrogacy, the courts have recognized the intended parents as the legal parents but, again, not

THE BABY M CASE

The highly publicized case of Baby M was the first time a court considered the legality of a traditional surrogacy contract. In the Baby M case, William Stern and his wife, Elizabeth, were unable to have children because she suffered from multiple sclerosis. The Sterns made an agreement with Mary Beth Whitehead that she would be artificially inseminated with William's sperm. If she got pregnant, she would carry the child to term, relinquish her parental rights, and turn the child over to the Sterns to raise as their own. Elizabeth Stern would then adopt the child. The Sterns agreed to pay Mary Beth ten thousand dollars, in addition to medical expenses, for her services.

Mary Beth did get pregnant, but she refused to give up her parental rights or Baby M, as required by the contract. The case went all the way to the New Jersey Supreme Court, which decided that surrogacy contracts were illegal in that state. As a result, the dispute between Mary Beth and the Sterns became simply another custody battle between two biological parents, Mary Beth and William. The court gave custody to William, but Mary Beth has regular visitation with Baby M.

based on the existence of an enforceable contract. In the landmark case *Johnson v. Calvert*, Anna Johnson had agreed to be a gestational surrogate for Mark and Crispina Calvert, but during the pregnancy she decided that she did not want to relinquish the child she was carrying. The California Supreme Court ultimately awarded custody to the Calverts, ruling that under California law, since they intended to procreate the child, they were the legal parents and Anna therefore had no parental rights. In an uncontested gestational surrogacy case, an Ohio trial court also recognized the intended parents as the child's legal parents, but it based its decision on the genetic connection between the intended parents and the child. Virginia reflects both these interests in a statute that identifies the intended parents as the legal parents if they are also the genetic parents.

While a few states, like Virginia, have statutes defining the parental rights and responsibilities of the parties to a surrogacy contract, in most places the law is in a state of flux, as it is with regard to the other reproductive technologies discussed in this section. Consequently, surrogacy arrangements, even where they are legal, entail a great deal of uncertainty and should be undertaken with full understanding of the risks involved. You will definitely want to consult a lawyer, preferably one with experience in this area, if you are considering surrogacy as a way to start your family.

APPENDIX
FINDING A LAWYER

IF YOU THINK you need a lawyer, there are several ways of finding one:

1. *Bar association referrals.* State, county, and city bar associations often have free referral services. These can be located in the phone book under "Attorney Referral Service" or "Lawyer Referral and Information Service." Be aware, though, that referral services do not typically screen the attorneys on their list, so there is no guarantee of quality.

2. *Law schools.* You may also be able to obtain a recommendation from a faculty member at a nearby law school. In addition, some law schools have clinics staffed by law students supervised by professors who are practicing lawyers. These clinics generally serve a low-income clientele and may be limited in the types of cases they handle. However, some do handle family law matters.

3. *Legal aid or legal assistance foundations.* Like law school clinics, these offices serve low-income persons in need of legal assistance, and they may specialize in certain types of cases. Even if they cannot help you or you do not qualify for their assistance, they may be able to provide a recommendation.

4. *Advertisements in the Yellow Pages or on TV.* The law permits lawyers to advertise, but no ad is an assurance of competence or quality.

5. *The Internet.* Many lawyers have web pages, and a number of organizations devoted to specialized areas of the law have sites on-line.

6. *Word-of-mouth recommendations.* A friend, relative, or coworker may have used the services of a lawyer recently with good result. Be sure to inquire, though, about the nature of the problem handled by the lawyer to ascertain whether it is comparable to yours in subject matter and complexity.

Once you have a list, how do you know which one to select? There is no way to guarantee that the lawyer you choose will be the best one for your needs, but there are several factors you should weigh:

1. *Experience.* You will want to consider how long the lawyer has been in practice and whether he has handled cases of your type before. Someone who has practiced primarily in personal injury law probably is a poor choice if you're facing a child custody battle. Most lawyers are officially generalists, able to practice in any field, but as a practical matter many tend to limit themselves to a few kinds of cases. About seventeen states certify specialists in certain fields. A few certify family law specialists. Lawyers who are certified have met requirements mandated by the state. Usually they have practiced in the field for a number of years and have passed an examination in the specialty. The American Academy of Matrimonial Lawyers also certifies family law specialists based on similar criteria.

2. *Personal qualities.* It is important to feel comfortable with your lawyer and to have confidence in her. Do you have good rapport? Is the lawyer available and responsive to your concerns? Does he return your phone calls promptly? Does she explain clearly and sufficiently her analysis of your legal problem?

3. *Cost.* Naturally cost is a limitation since you will need a lawyer you can afford, and legal fees can be quite expensive. Many lawyers charge an hourly rate, but some charge a flat fee for certain services, such as drawing up a will, and civil matters that involve money damages, such as personal injury cases, are often handled on a contingency basis—the lawyer gets paid a percentage of the damages he obtains for you. Regardless of the method a lawyer uses to charge for services, and some use a combination, the most important thing for you to remember is to discuss the fee openly with her and to put the fee agreement in writing before authorizing her to begin work on your case. Also keep in mind that you will usually be responsible for court filing fees, copy charges, process server charges, and other costs in addition to the lawyer's fee.

INDEX

Paternity (*continued*)
  marital presumption of, 344,
    346–49
  suit, 340–43
  voluntary acknowledgment of, 345
Pennsylvania, 222, 238
Percent of income method, 229
Permanency planning, 308
Physical abuse, 289–290
Physical neglect, 293–97
Planned Parenthood v. Casey, 21
Plea bargaining, 256, 258
Plyler v. Doe, 45
Polio, 132
Pornography
  dial-a-porn, 336–38
  on Internet, 335–36, 337
  movie, video, and TV, 331–34
  protecting child from exposure to,
    329–38
  See also Child pornography
PPOs. *See* Preferred provider
  organizations
Prayer, in schools, 54–55
Preconception lawsuits, 3–4
Preferred provider organizations
  (PPOs), 107, 111–12, 128, 131
Pregnancy
  prenatal care, 1–4
  rights of students, 80
  substance abuse during, 10–11, 296
  teen, 136, 137, 139
  welfare assistance during, 16–17
  workplace rights, 12–15
  See also Abortion; Fetus
Pregnancy Discrimination Act, 13
Prenatal care, 1–4
Preponderance of the evidence, 201,
  341
Presumed fathers, 343, 344, 350–51,
  370
Pretermitted heir statutes, 171

Priest, Judas, 335
Primary care physicians, 110
Private schools, 47–48
Probable cause, 249
Probate, 177–78, 180
Probation, 264–66
Product liability cases, 38–42
Property, child's right to control,
  155–56
Property guardian, 174–75
Proposition 187 (Calif.), 45
Prostitution. *See* Child prostitution
Protective custody hearing, 301, 302
Public health issues, 71–75, 132–34
Putative fathers, 340, 341
  registry, 350, 353

QMCSO. *See* Qualified medical child
  support order
Qualified medical child support order
  (QMCSO), 231–32

Race, and child custody, 190–91
Racial discrimination, 50, 75–77
Racial matching, 359–61
Reasonable mistake of age defense,
  326
Reasonable suspicion, 63–64
Record(s)
  adoption, 368
  juvenile delinquency, 270–71
  medical, 128
  school, 90–93
  sperm bank, 383
Recovered memory, 319, 320
Religion
  and adoption, 361
  and child custody, 191–92
  and refusal of medical screening,
    133
  and refusal of medical treatment, 9,
    117–20, 297